A BRITTEN SOURCE BOOK

A BRITTEN–PEARS LIBRARY PUBLICATION

A BRITTEN SOURCE BOOK

compiled by

John Evans · Philip Reed · Paul Wilson

PUBLISHED FOR THE
BRITTEN–PEARS LIBRARY ALDEBURGH
BY THE BRITTEN ESTATE LIMITED

First published in 1987
by The Britten Estate Limited for the Britten–Pears Library
The Red House, Aldeburgh, Suffolk, IP15 5PZ
Revised edition

Typeset in 10/12 Baskerville by Waveney Typesetters, Norwich
Printed in Great Britain by
Antony Rowe Limited, Chippenham, Wiltshire

All rights reserved

© 1987 The Britten–Pears Foundation

British Library Cataloguing in Publication Data
Evans, John, 1953–
A Britten source book.—Rev. ed.
1. Britten, Benjamin—Bibliography
I. Title   II. Reed, Philip, 1959–   III. Wilson, Paul, 1946–
016.78′092′4   ML134.B85
ISBN 0 9511939 2 9

This book is distributed by
St Paul's Bibliographies
West End House
1 Step Terrace
Winchester
Hampshire SO22 5BW

Dust wrapper: Head of Benjamin Britten
from a bronze by Georg Ehrlich

For Rosamund Strode

Contents

Preface and Acknowledgements — ix

A Chronology of Life and Works — 1
by John Evans

The Incidental Music: a Catalogue Raisonné — 129
by Philip Reed and John Evans

The Recorded Repertoire — 167
by Philip Reed and Paul Wilson

A Select Bibliography — 183
by Paul Wilson

Index of Britten's Works — 309

General Index — 317

The Britten–Pears Library

The Britten–Pears Library consists of the working collection of books and music assembled by Benjamin Britten and Peter Pears. It also houses a large corpus of letters, photographs, printed programmes and a sound and video archive. Its principal distinction is the unique collection of Britten's manuscripts, including those belonging to the British Library which are deposited on permanent loan.

The Library is part of the Britten–Pears Foundation, the Trustees of which are: Isador Caplan, Donald Mitchell, Marion Thorpe, Noel Periton, Colin Matthews, Hugh Cobbe.

Library committee: Hugh Cobbe, Colin Matthews, Rosamund Strode

Librarian: Paul S. Wilson

Preface and Acknowledgements

This *Source Book* seeks to place in the public domain factual detail concerning Benjamin Britten's life, public career and compositions which until now was available only in scattered form or known and knowable only to those with access to the composer's private papers and composition manuscripts.

Contact with primary sources makes it possible, for example, to enumerate for the first time an unprecedentedly detailed list of Britten's vast juvenilia in the *Chronology*. The *Catalogue Raisonné* of the composer's incidental music for the media of film, theatre and radio is the most thorough-going survey of the field incorporating recent research. The *Bibliography* (select as it is and must be) is the largest since Donald Mitchell's and Hans Keller's pioneering work of 1952. We hope that the putting together of all these data into a handy, sturdy form will please and benefit Britten students (students in the widest sense) whether they listen, play, write or teach.

In a composite volume of this kind we inevitably find ourselves greatly indebted to many persons and organisations. We are grateful to the following institutions for their patient help: The BBC (Sound Archive and Written Archive), British Film Institute, National Film Archive, National Sound Archive, the Music libraries of the Universities of Birmingham and Cambridge, the library staff of the University of East Anglia and Faber and Faber Limited. Particular thanks should be made to Jill Burrows and Penelope Sydenham.

Without the support of every member of the Britten–Pears library this book would never have reached fruition. Rosamund Strode's work, both as Benjamin Britten's assistant for the last twelve years of his life and subsequently as Keeper of Manuscripts and Archivist would justify the dedication to her of many tomes, not merely of the present volume. Anne Surfling, Pamela Wheeler and Emma Potter have also made signal contributions in their various spheres.

Paul Wilson
Aldeburgh, September 1987

BENJAMIN BRITTEN (1913–1976)
A CHRONOLOGY OF HIS LIFE AND WORKS
COMPILED BY JOHN EVANS

This chronology was begun in 1980 and was originally intended for *The Britten Companion* (Faber & Faber, 1984), but it soon outgrew its original commission and has continued to expand over the past three years. It draws on every resource of the Britten–Pears Library and Archive, from the office diaries and correspondence to Britten's manuscripts and publication assignments with Boosey & Hawkes and Faber Music. Though it is not, and could not be, entirely comprehensive (without being totally unmanageable in length) it does give a vivid impression of the extraordinary range of activities and commitments of Britten's life.

Britten's original compositions appear in the 'Works' column at the date of *completion*. Purcell realizations and folksong arrangements, which are impossible to date precisely, appear at the date of *publication*. All published works (including those published posthumously) appear in *italics*; unpublished works appear in Roman type. Certain works may appear twice in the 'First performance' column if their actual premiere was either held abroad or if the work in question was first heard in a BBC broadcast.

1913   *LIFE*

1913
22 November   Edward Benjamin Britten, born on St Cecilia's Day at 21 Kirkley Cliff Road, Lowestoft, Suffolk to Edith Rhoda, née Hockey (1874–1937), and Robert Victor Britten (1878–1934). Britten was the youngest of four children, with a brother, Robert (b. 1907) and two sisters, Barbara (b. 1902) and Beth (b. 1909)

1914
21 January   Baptised at St John's Church, Lowestoft

c. **1919**   First music lessons from his mother, a keen amateur singer and later Secretary of the Lowestoft Choral Society

23, 28 June & 5 July   Takes part in *Pageant of Dream Children* at Sparrow's Nest Theatre, Lowestoft

c. **1921**   Starts piano lessons with Miss Ethel Astle, a teacher at his first school, Southolme

1921/22

c. **1922/23**   Sits for the portrait miniature by Sarah Fanny Hockey (Britten's Aunt Queenie) which is now in the National Portrait Gallery, London

1922

1923   Enters South Lodge Preparatory School as a day boy. Starts viola lessons with Mrs Audrey Alston at Norwich

CHRONOLOGY

WORKS *FIRST PERFORMANCES*

Earliest attempts at composition

Symphony in F major/minor, for violin, cello and piano

Many early songs including *Oh, that I'd ne'er been married* (Burns) and *Beware* (Longfellow) (published posthumously in 1985)

Symphony in C, for orchestra (incomplete)

Piece in A, for violin, cello and double bass

Piece in C, for piano (incomplete)

'Here we go up in a flung festoon' (Kipling), for voice and piano

Piece in D flat, for violin and piano

Recitative: 'And seeing the Multitudes' and Aria: 'Blessed are they that mourn' (incomplete), for soprano and piano

1924   *LIFE*

1924

30 October   Attends a concert at the Norfolk and Norwich
                        Triennial Festival which includes the orchestral suite,
                        The Sea, by Frank Bridge (1879–1941), conducted by
                        the composer

1925

25 March   Begins composition of Mass in E minor
March–6 April
August–September
8–14 November

1926   Passes finals (Associated Board Grade VIII) piano
                        examination with honours
4 January
5–10 January
10–12 January

CHRONOLOGY

WORKS

FIRST PERFORMANCES

Felixtown, for piano (incomplete)

Lento con Introduczion [sic] – Allegro ma non troppo, for piano (incomplete)

Introduction, for string orchestra

Piece in C, for piano and string quartet (incomplete)

Piece in G, for strings (incomplete)

Allegro con spirito, for piano

More songs and piano music including ten Waltzes, six Scherzos, seven Fantasias, four Bourées, four Suites and four Sonatas

Presto con molto fuoco, for orchestra

Allegro molto e con brio, for orchestra (incomplete)

Allegro, for orchestra (incomplete)

Sonata in D, for violin and piano

Octett in D major, for strings

Variations on Dyke's 'How bright these glorious spirits shine', for chorus, string quintet, organ and piano

Suite No. 5 in E, for piano

Three Toccatas, for piano

Four Etudes Symphoniques, for piano

1926   *LIFE*

25–30 January

13 February

26 February   Continues composition of Mass in E minor
14 March

18 March
4 April

6 April
6–7 April

7 April

16 April

17 April
18 April
19 April
23–29 April
20–25 May
1–29 June

July

7 July
11 July
15 August
18 August–
5 September
26 September

WORKS	FIRST PERFORMANCES
Sonata (Grand) No. 8 in C minor, for piano	
Sonata in F sharp minor, for violin and viola with cello (ad lib)	
Sonata in C minor, for viola and piano	
Sonata in C sharp minor, for piano	
Sonata in G minor, for violin and piano	
First Loss, for viola and piano	
Trio in fantastic form in E minor, for violin, viola and piano	
Trio in fantastic form in C, for violin, viola and piano	
Sonate pour orgue ou pédale-pianoforte	
Sonata in A, for cello and piano	
Mazurka in F sharp minor, for piano	
Three Canons, for 2 violas and piano	
Overture No. 1 in C, for orchestra	
Rondo in C sharp minor, for piano	
Ouverture ('Never Unprepared'), for orchestra	
Mass in E minor, for soloists, chorus and orchestra	
Rondo in D, for piano	
Rondo Capriccio, for piano	
Fantasia in A, for piano	
Suite fantastique in A minor, for large orchestra and piano obbligato	
Poème No. 1 in D, for orchestra	
The Brook, for voice and violin	

1926   *LIFE*

12 November–
5 December

21 November

24 December

29 December   Begins composition of Poème No. 3 in E, for
                     orchestra.
                     Works left incomplete at the end of this year include:
                     String Quartet in B flat; a Piece in F minor; Allegro
                     Maestoso for piano and orchestra; Adagio ma non
                     troppo – Allegro quasi presto; Allegro for orchestra

1927
January

17 January–
28 February

9 February–March

12–14 February

14–19 February

5 March

March–May

June-July

15–17 July

29 July–2 August

22 August–
5 September

September   Head Boy at South Lodge

CHRONOLOGY 9

WORKS

Six Songs, for voice and piano

String Quartet in G minor

Poème No. 2 in B minor, for small orchestra

Four Nursery Rhymes (Anon.), for voice and piano

Poème No. 3 for small orchestra

Symphony in D minor, for orchestra. Arrangement of Symphony in D minor for piano duet (incomplete)

Setting of Latin texts (*Kyrie* and *Requiem*) in B minor, for chorus and orchestra

Poème No. 4 in B flat, for small orchestra

Poème No. 5 in F sharp minor, for small orchestra

Eight Rounds (Sacred), for voices

String Quartet in G

String Quartet in A minor

Cavatina in A, for string quartet

Setting of part of a scene from Shelley's *Prometheus Unbound* in B flat, for chorus, strings and piano

Chaos and Cosmos: Symphonic Poem in E, for orchestra

FIRST PERFORMANCES

1927   LIFE

27 September

29 September

October   Begins composition of Sonata No. 11 in B, for piano

27 October   Attends a concert at the Norfolk and Norwich Triennial Festival in which Frank Bridge conducts the premiere of his *Enter Spring*. Audrey Alston introduces Britten to Bridge after the concert

28 October   Goes through many of his more recent compositions with Bridge, who agrees to take him on as a private pupil. Thus begins a series of visits to Bridge's homes in London and at Friston, near Eastbourne in Sussex

November–
23 December

29 December

1928   Continues composition lessons with Bridge

25 January

February

February–6 March

28 March

11 April

16 April

16–23 April

Summer Term   Captain of cricket and Victor Ludorum at South Lodge

3 June

13 June

14 June

15–18 June

CHRONOLOGY

WORKS	FIRST PERFORMANCES

Sonata No. 10 in B flat, for piano

Rhapsodie, for piano

Three Poems, for string quartet

Sonatina, for viola and piano

Dans les Bois, for orchestra

Sonata No. 11 in B, for piano

Humoreske [sic] in C, for orchestra

Trio in G minor, for violin, viola and piano

String Quartet in F

Menuetto, for piano

Elegy, for string orchestra

The Waning Moon (Shelley), for voice and piano

Silver (de la Mare), for voice and piano (revised for *Tit for Tat* in 1968)

Piece, for piano

Dans les Bois (Gérard de Nerval), for voice (soprano) and piano

1928 LIFE

June–August

July — Leaves South Lodge under a cloud after submitting an end-of-term essay on 'Animals' in which he argued a passionate case against hunting and for pacifism

25 August

September — Enters Gresham's School, Holt, Norfolk. Starts piano lessons with Harold Samuel on Bridge's recommendation

28 September

9–13 October

31 December — Begins composition of Tit for Tat

Works left incomplete at the end of this year include two versions (Allegro moderato and Presto) of a movement for orchestra; an incomplete setting of 'Mon rêve familier' (Verlaine) – a discarded song from *Quatre Chansons Françaises*

1929 — Continues composition lessons with Frank Bridge during vacations from Gresham's

1 January–7 February

4 January

7 January–24 April

13 January

13 January–25 October
26 January–8 March
28 January–21 March

WORKS	FIRST PERFORMANCES
Quatre Chansons Françaises (Hugo and Verlaine), for soprano and orchestra (published posthumously in 1982)	
Of a' the airts (Burns), for voice and piano (revised from November 1926)	
Novelette, for string quartet	
Sonatina, for piano	
A Song of Enchantment (de la Mare), for voice and piano (revised for *Tit for Tat* in 1968)	
Oh, why did e'er my thoughts aspire (Charles Sackville), for voice and piano	
The Quartette (de la Mare), for SATB quartet	
Tit for Tat (de la Mare), for voice and piano (revised for *Tit for Tat* in 1968)	
Elizabeth Variations, for piano	
Miniature Suite, for string quartet	
Rhapsody, for string quartet	

1929   LIFE

18 February–22 March
15–19 February

21 February

26 February

22–25 March

                            Begins composition of Bagatelle for piano trio

30 March–22 April
28 April   Begins composition of *A Wealden Trio*
6 May–16 June

18 May
3 June   Begins composition of *The Birds*
4–8 September

21–31 October

27–28 October

2 November   Plays viola in chamber music recital of piano trios by Mozart (K.498) and Brahms (Op.40) at Gresham's

17 November–
24 December

1930
3 January–17 April

15 January
16 February
20 February–8 March
24 February

WORKS   FIRST PERFORMANCES

Etude, for viola

Lilian (Tennyson), for voice and piano

Witches' Song (Jonson), for voice and piano

Evening Hymn, for SATB (revised from 1923)

Two Songs (Fletcher), for SATB quartet

Rhapsody, for violin, viola and piano

The Owl (Tennyson), for voice and piano

Children of Love (Munro), for SSA

Diaphenia (Constable), for tenor and piano

Introduction and Allegro, for viola and strings

Wild Time (de la Mare), for soprano and strings

Two Pieces, for violin, viola and piano

Quartettino, for string quartet (published posthumously in 1984)

Bagatelle, for violin, viola and piano

A Poem of Hate, for piano

A Little Idyll, for piano

Everyone Sang (Sassoon), for tenor and small orchestra

1930 · LIFE

1 March	Has some of his chamber music performed at Gresham's
11 April–1 June	
30 May	
July	
8 July	
9 July–3 September	
10 July	
11 July	
25 July	
28 July–3 August	
29 July	
	Leaves Gresham's School with School Certificate
1 August	
7 August	
27 August	
10 September	
12 September	
16 September–27 December	

CHRONOLOGY

WORKS *FIRST PERFORMANCES*

Piece, for viola and piano

A Wealden Trio: The Song of the Women (Ford Madox Ford), for women's voices (revised for publication 1967)

The Birds (Belloc), for soprano and strings

May in the Greenwood (Anon.), for two voices and piano

A Hymn to the Virgin, for mixed voices

Passacaglia, for organ

Ah fly not, Pleasure, pleasant-hearted Pleasure (Wilfred S. Blunt), for two voices and piano

The Nurse's Song (Blake), for soprano, contralto and piano

Chamber Music (V) (Joyce), for soprano (or tenor) and piano

To Electra: I dare not ask a kisse (Herrick), for voice and piano

Piece for viola (published posthumously as *Elegy* in 1985)

Sextet, for flute, oboe, clarinet, bass clarinet, horn and bassoon

Sketch No. 1 'D. Layton', for string orchestra

Sketch No. 2 'EBB', for viola and strings

I saw three ships, for mixed voices (revised for publication as *The Sycamore Tree* 1967)

Three Pieces, for piano

1930 LIFE

18 September

22 September Enters the Royal College of Music, London, on an open scholarship, where he studies composition with John Ireland and piano with Arthur Benjamin. Lives first at 51 Prince's Square, Bayswater, London W2

4 October Begins composition of a Mass for four voices
5 November

23 December Begins composition of Vigil (de la Mare)

1931
5 *January*

13 January

16 January
17 January

19 January

20–21 January

22–28 January

28 January

31 January–
10 February
February–26 March

CHRONOLOGY

WORKS	FIRST PERFORMANCES
A Widow Bird Sate Mourning for Her Love (Shelley), for voice and piano	
I Saw Three Witches (de la Mare), for soprano, contralto and piano	
	I Saw Three Ships and *A Hymn to the Virgin*: Lowestoft Musical Society, St John's Church, Lowestoft
Sweet was the Song (from William Ballet's Lute Book), for women's voices	
Mass, for four voices	
Vigil (de la Mare), for bass (or contralto) and piano (revised for *Tit for Tat* in 1968)	
The Moth (de la Mare), for bass and piano	
Sport (W. H. Davies), for bass and piano	
Love me not for comely grace (Anon.), for SSAT	
To the Willow-tree, for SATB	
Autumn (de la Mare), for voice and string quartet (revised for *Tit for Tat* in 1968)	
O Lord, forsake me not, motet for double chorus	
Thy King's Birthday (Southwell and The Bible): Christmas suite for soprano, contralto and mixed chorus	

1931   *LIFE*

1 April–5 May

21 April

8 May–2 June

8–24 June

29–30 June

July   Wins Ernest Farrar Prize for composition at the RCM

                            Begins Two Psalms (130 & 150), for chorus and orchestra

12 August–
22 November

September   Moves to rooms at Burleigh House, 173 Cromwell Road, London SW5

1 December

26 December

1932

19 January

25 January–
11 February

15–20 February

4 May

WORKS	FIRST PERFORMANCES

Twelve Variations on a Theme, for piano (published posthumously in 1985)

Three Fugues, for piano

String Quartet in D major (revised and published in 1974)

Three Small Songs (Samuel Daniel, John Fletcher), for soprano and small orchestra

Two Pieces: The Moon (after Shelley), Going down hill on a bicycle (after H. C. Beeching), for violin and piano

Plymouth Town (scenario by Violet Alford), ballet for small orchestra

Variations on a French Carol (Carol of the Deanery of Saint-Ménéhould), for women's voices, violin, viola and piano

Psalm 150: Praise ye the Lord, for chorus and orchestra

Ballet on a Basque Scenario, for orchestra (incomplete)

Psalm 130: Out of the deep, for chorus and orchestra

Phantasy in F minor, for string quintet (published posthumously in 1983)

Three Two-part Songs (de la Mare), for high voices and piano

Concerto in B minor, for violin, viola and orchestra

1932   LIFE

20 May

2 June–18 July

20 June–July

22 July   Awarded the Cobbett Prize for *Phantasy in F minor*

September   Begins composition of *Phantasy*, Op. 2, and revises *Phantasy in F minor*

19 September–October

November   Begins composition of *A Boy was Born*

12 December

1933   Begins settings of children's songs for *Friday Afternoons*, composed for the boys of Clive House School, Prestatyn, where his brother Robert was headmaster

31 January

13–14 February

February–October

17 February

26 February   Composes round for Frank Bridge's birthday party at Friston

16 March   Conducts *Sinfonietta* in chamber music concert at the RCM

WORKS

Introduction and Allegro, for piano trio

Two Part-songs (Wither and Graves), for mixed voices and piano

Sinfonietta, Op. 1, for chamber orchestra

Phantasy, Op. 2, for oboe, violin, viola and cello

Alla Marcia, for string quartet (published posthumously in 1983)

Alla Quartetto Serioso: 'Go play, boy, play', for string quartet (published posthumously in 1983)

FIRST PERFORMANCES

Phantasy in F minor: student quintet, Royal College of Music, London

Three Two-part songs: Carlyle Singers conducted by Iris Lemare, Macnaghten–Lemare Concert, Ballet Club (Mercury) Theatre, London

Sinfonietta: Macnaghten–Lemare Concert, Ballet Club (Mercury) Theatre, London

Phantasy Quintet (broadcast premiere, BBC): Mangeot Ensemble with Anthony Collins

1933

4 April

May

July   Wins Ernest Farrar Prize for composition at the RCM for a second time. Moves to 559 Finchley Road, London NW3

6 August

21 November

11 December

13 December   Passes ARCM examination. Leaves the RCM
23 December   Begins composition of *Simple Symphony*

1934   Revises *The Birds* (1929), *A Hymn to the Virgin* (1930) and *The Sycamore Tree* (1930)

2 February

10 February

23 February   First meeting with Peter Pears, then a member of the BBC Singers, during rehearsals for *A Boy was Born*

WORKS	FIRST PERFORMANCES
Alla Valse (from *Alla Quartetto Serioso*), arranged for flute, oboe and piano.	
Alla Romanza (from *Alla Quartetto Serioso*), arranged for flute, oboe and piano (incomplete)	
A Boy was Born, Op. 3, for mixed voices	
	Phantasy Op.2 (broadcast premiere, BBC): Leon Goossens and the International String Quartet
	Phantasy (concert premiere): Leon Goosssens, André Mangeot, Helen Perkin and Eric Bray, The Music Society, St John's Institute, London
	Two Part-songs and three movements from *Alla Quartetto Serioso*: 'Go play, boy, play': Macnaghten–Lemare Concert, Ballet Club (Mercury) Theatre, London
Certain works now published by Boosey & Hawkes, London	
Alla Valse from *Alla Quartetto Serioso*: 'Go play, boy, play', arranged for piano	
Simple Symphony, Op. 4, for string orchestra	
	A Boy was Born (broadcast premiere, BBC): BBC Wireless Singers (A), Choirboys of St Mark's, North Audley Street conducted by Leslie Woodgate

1934   *LIFE*

6 March

14 March   Listens to broadcast of Berg's *Wozzeck* conducted by Adrian Boult, and is deeply impressed by the opera

6 April   Father dies in Lowestoft while Britten is attending International Society of Contemporary Music (ISCM) Festival at Florence where his *Phantasy* Op. 2 is performed on 5 April

9 July   Gives a piano and organ recital with the organist C. J. R. Coleman at St John's Church, Lowestoft. The programme includes Britten's own arrangements of 'Moonlight' from Bridge's suite *The Sea* and the Finale from Mozart's Symphony No. 39 in E flat, K.543

11–17 July

8–10 August

28 September

3–12 October

16 October–   Visits Europe with mother and is introduced to Erwin
29 November   Stein in Vienna

November   Begins composition of *Suite* for violin and piano in Vienna

30 November

17 December

WORKS	FIRST PERFORMANCES
	Simple Symphony: Norwich String Orchestra conducted by the composer, Stuart Hall, Norwich
Te Deum in C major, for choir and organ	
Jubilate Deo in E flat, for choir and organ (published posthumously in 1984)	
May (Anon.), for voices and piano	
Holiday Diary [Tales], Op. 5, for piano	
	Holiday Diary: Betty Humby, Wigmore Hall, London
	Three Movements from *Suite*: Henri Temianka and Betty Humby, Wigmore Hall, London.
	A Boy was Born (first concert performance): conducted by Iris Lemare, Macnaghten–Lemare Concert, Ballet Club (Mercury) Theatre, London

1935   *LIFE*

1935   Begins an active association with the GPO Film Unit, and the Group Theatre and Left Theatre companies in London

2 March

13–16 April

April–May

May–June

June

July

5 July   First meeting with W. H. Auden at Colwall, where Auden is teaching at the Downs School

August–September

September

September–October

October–November

7 November   Moves to Flat No. 2, West Cottage Road, West End Green, London NW2

13 November

19 November

25 November   Earliest negotiations with Ralph Hawkes for publishing contract

November   Begins work on Night Mail for GPO Film Unit

CHRONOLOGY

WORKS	FIRST PERFORMANCES
A Poison Tree (Blake), for baritone and piano	
Two Insect Pieces, for oboe and piano (published posthumously in 1980).	
Friday Afternoons, Op. 7, for children's voices and piano	
The King's Stamp (film)	
Coal Face (film)	
Suite, Op. 6, for violin and piano	
Telegrams, The Tocher, C.T.O. (films)	
Gas Abstract (film)	
Men Behind the Meters, Dinner Hour, Title Music III, How the Dial Works, Conquering Space, Sorting Office, The Savings Bank, The New Operator (films)	
God's Chillun (film)	
Timon of Athens (theatre), GPO Title Music I & II (films)	
	Te Deum in C major: St Michael's Singers, St Michael Cornhill
	Timon of Athens: Group Theatre, Westminster Theatre, London

1935   LIFE

4–8 December

1936
January   Revises *Alla Quartetto Serioso: 'Go play, boy, play'* as *Three Divertimenti* for string quartet (published posthumously in 1983).
                        Signs first exclusive publishing contract for a guarantee of royalties, with Ralph Hawkes of Boosey & Hawkes, London

25 February

March   Joins permanent staff of GPO Film Unit
2 March

8 March

13 March   BBC recital with Antonio Brosa (violin) includes *The Birds* and songs by Mahler with Sophie Wyss, soprano

15–16 March

April   Attends ISCM Festival at Barcelona for a performance of the *Suite*

10 May

13 May   Begins composition of *Our Hunting Fathers*
July   [Spanish Civil War begins]
23 July

CHRONOLOGY

WORKS	FIRST PERFORMANCES
Easter 1916 (theatre)	Easter 1916: Left Theatre, Islington Town Hall, London
Night Mail	
	Three Divertimenti: Stratton Quartet, Wigmore Hall, London
Peace of Britain (film)	
Russian Funeral, for brass and percussion (published posthumously in 1981)	
	Russian Funeral: directed by Alan Bush, Westminster Theatre, London
	Suite: (first complete performance, BBC) Antonio Brosa and the composer
Lullaby for a retired Colonel, for two pianos	
Stay Down Miner (theatre)	Stay Down, Miner: Left Theatre, Westminster Theatre, London
Our Hunting Fathers, Op. 8 (Auden and others), for high voice and orchestra.	
Soirées Musicales, Op. 9 (Rossini arr. Britten), for orchestra	

1936

25 September

September–October

October

September–November

November
1 November

9 November

12 November

December
12 December

15 December

31 December

1937

CHRONOLOGY

WORKS	FIRST PERFORMANCES
	Our Hunting Fathers: Sophie Wyss, London Philharmonic Orchestra, conducted by the composer, Norfolk and Norwich Triennial Festival
Calendar of the Year, Around the Village Green, Men of the Alps (films)	
The Saving of Bill Blewitt (film) The Agamemnon of Aeschylus (theatre)	
Line to the Tschierva Hut, Message from Geneva, Four Barriers (films)	
Love from a Stranger (feature film)	
	The Agamemnon of Aeschylus: Group Theatre, Westminster Theatre, London
Mother Comfort (Slater), for two voices and piano	
'Theme' for one of Four Improvised Movements for a Symphony, for organ	'Theme' for one of Four Improvised Movements for a Symphony: André Marchal, St John's, Red Lion Square, London
The Way to the Sea (film)	
Temporal Variations, for oboe and piano (published posthumously in 1980)	
	Temporal Variations: Natalie Caine and Adolph Hallis, Wigmore Hall, London
Philip's Breeches (Charles and Mary Lamb), for mixed voices	Two Ballads (*Mother Comfort* and *Underneath the Abject Willow*) Sophie Wyss and Betty Bannerman
Pacifist March (Ronald Duncan), unison song with accompaniment *Underneath the Abject Willow* (Auden), for two voices and piano. Book Bargain (film)	

1937 | *LIFE*

31 January — Mother dies at Britten's London flat

26 February

28 February

15 March

March–April

23 April

23 April

May — Close friendship with Peter Pears begins

Composes 'Now the leaves are falling fast' and 'Nocturne' (*On this Island*)

5 June — Commissioned by Boyd Neel to write a book for string orchestra for the Salzburg Festival

Selects music for Up the Garden Path, a programme of 'the world's worst words and music' devised with Auden.

13 June

21 June — Frank Bridge conducts Britten's *Sinfonietta* in a BBC broadcast from the Maida Vale Studios

21 July

August — Acquires the Old Mill, Snape, Suffolk

25 August

CHRONOLOGY

WORKS	FIRST PERFORMANCES
The Ascent of F6 (theatre)	The Ascent of F6: Group Theatre, Mercury Theatre, London
Pageant of Empire (theatre)	Pageant of Empire: Left Theatre, London
Reveille, concert study for violin and piano (published posthumously in 1983)	
King Arthur (radio)	
	King Arthur: BBC Chorus, London Symphony Orchestra conducted by Clarence Raybould
	Reveille: Antonio Brosa and Franz Reizenstein, Wigmore Hall, London
Cabaret Songs (Auden), for high voice and piano: 'Johnny' and 'Funeral Blues' (published posthumously in 1980), and 'Jam Tart'	
	Up the Garden Path: a BBC broadcast
Variations on a Theme of Frank Bridge, Op. 10, for string orchestra	
	Variations on a Theme of Frank Bridge (broadcast premiere): Boyd Neel Orchestra, directed by Boyd Neel, Hilversum, Holland

1937   *LIFE*

27 August

29 September

October   Moves from London to Peasenhall in Suffolk until the
                     renovation of the Old Mill is completed

5 October

26–27 October

19 November

25 November

5 December

12 December

1938   Begins to form regular recital partnership with Pears
January

16 January

CHRONOLOGY

WORKS	FIRST PERFORMANCES
	Variations on a Theme of Frank Bridge: Boyd Neel Orchestra directed by Boyd Neel, Mozarteum Grossersall, Salzburg Festival
The Company of Heaven (radio)	The Company of Heaven: Sophie Wyss, Peter Pears, BBC Chorus and Orchestra conducted by Trevor Harvey
On this Island, Op. 11 (Auden), for high voice and piano	
	Variations on a Theme of Frank Bridge (UK premiere): Boyd Neel Orchestra conducted by Boyd Neel, Wigmore Hall, London
To lie flat on the back (Auden) Night covers up the rigid land (Auden) The sun shines down (Auden), all for high voice and piano	
	On this Island (broadcast premiere, BBC): Sophie Wyss and the composer
Hadrian's Wall (radio)	Hadrian's Wall: Felling Male Voice Choir, Leslie Russell Quartet conducted by the composer
Out of the Picture (theatre)	Out of the Picture: Group Theatre, Westminster Theatre, London
Mont Juic, Op. 12 (with Lennox Berkeley), for orchestra	
Mony a Pickle Advance Democracy (films) Lines on the Map (radio)	
Fish in the Unruffled Lakes (Auden), for high voice and piano	

1938 *LIFE*

18 January   Attends farewell party for Auden and Isherwood who were going to China to report on the Sino–Japanese War

8 March

April   Moves into the Old Mill at Snape. Works on *Piano Concerto*. New London address with Pears – 43 Nevern Square, London SW5

13 May

5 June

June

20 June   Frederick Grinke and Britten perform *Suite* Op. 6 at ISCM Festival, London

26 July

Summer   Aaron Copland visits Britten at the Old Mill and plays through his recently completed opera, *The Second Hurricane*

5–17 August   Rehearsals of *Piano Concerto* at Queen's Hall, London

18 August

7 September   Conducts *Bridge Variations* at Queen's Hall for BBC Promenade Concerts

October

14 November

CHRONOLOGY

WORKS	FIRST PERFORMANCES
Cabaret Song (Auden), 'Tell me the truth about love' (published posthumously in 1980)	'Tell me the truth about love': Hedli Anderson and the composer, the Auden–Isherwood party at the home of the artist Julian Trevelyan, Hammersmith
Cradle Song (Blake), for two voices and piano	
The Chartists' March (radio)	The Chartists' March: section of the BBC Men's Chorus conducted by Britten
The World of the Spirit (radio)	The World of the Spirit: Sophie Wyss, Anne Wood, Emlyn Bebb, Victor Harding, BBC Chorus and Orchestra conducted by Trevor Harvey
Spain (theatre)	Spain: Binyon Puppets, Mercury Theatre, London
Piano Concerto No. 1, Op. 13	*Piano Concerto*: BBC Symphony Orchestra with the composer as soloist, conducted by Sir Henry Wood, BBC Promenade Concert, Queen's Hall, London
On the Frontier (theatre)	On the Frontier: Group Theatre, Arts Theatre, Cambridge

1938   *LIFE*

21 November

26 November   *Soirées Musicales* choreographed by Anthony Tudor for London Ballet

29 November

5 December   BBC broadcast of The Ascent of F6
16 December   Soloist in Piano Concerto conducted by Sir Adrian Boult for BBC

1939   Living with Pears at 67 Hallam Street, London W1
22 February

16 March

18 March

29 March

5 April

21 April

April–May
May   Britten and Pears sail for North America on the Cunard White Star *Ausonia*
9 May   Arrival at St Jovite, Quebec Province, Canada
11 June–16 July

WORKS	FIRST PERFORMANCES
They Walk Alone (theatre)	They Walk Alone: "Q" Theatre, London
Advance Democracy (Swingler), for chorus	
Johnson over Jordan (theatre)	Johnson over Jordan: New Theatre, London
'Being Beauteous' (Rimbaud), for soprano and string orchestra	
'Marine' (Rimbaud), for soprano and string orchestra	
Ballad of Heroes, Op. 14 (Swingler and Auden), for tenor or soprano solo, chorus and orchestra	
	Ballad of Heroes: conducted by Constant Lambert, Festival of 'Music for the People', Queen's Hall, London
	'Being Beauteous' and 'Marine' (from *Les Illuminations*) (broadcast premiere, BBC): Sophie Wyss and Birmingham Philharmonic String Orchestra conducted by Johann C. Hock
The Sword in the Stone (radio)	
	The Sword in the Stone (serialized): a section of BBC Orchestra conducted by Leslie Woodgate

1939   *LIFE*

5 July

23–29 July

2 August

5–30 August

17 August

21 August   Britten and Pears move in with Dr and Mrs William
                     Mayer and their family in Amityville, Long Island

3 September   [Second World War begins]

20 September

25 October

19 November   Recital of Purcell and Bach with Pears in Riverhead,
                     New York

10 December

1940   Working with Auden on a high school operetta, *Paul
                     Bunyan*. Continues to give recitals with Pears, and for
                     these and many subsequent recitals Britten writes
                     song-cycles, folk song arrangements and realizations
                     of songs by Purcell

WORKS	FIRST PERFORMANCES
'Aube' (discarded song from *Les Illuminations*), for soprano and string orchestra	
Young Apollo, Op. 16, for piano and strings (withdrawn; published posthumously in 1982)	
	Young Apollo: conducted by Alexander Chuhaldin with the composer as soloist, CBC, Toronto
A.M.D.G. (Gerard Manley Hopkins), for mixed chorus (withdrawn)	
	'Being Beauteous' and 'Marine' (from *Les Illuminations*) (first concert performance): Sophie Wyss and BBC Symphony Orchestra conducted by Sir Henry Wood, Promenade Concert, Queen's Hall, London
Cabaret Song (Auden) 'Calypso' (published posthumously in 1980)	
Violin Concerto, Op. 15	
Les Illuminations, Op. 18, for high voice and piano	
Canadian Carnival, Op. 19, for orchestra	
Les Sylphides (Chopin orch. Britten) *Sinfonia da Requiem*, Op. 20	

1940   *LIFE*

15 January

January–April

30 January

February–March   Seriously ill in New York with streptococcal infection
March   Begins work on the *Michelangelo Sonnets*, the first
                   song-cycle written specifically for Peter Pears
28 March

2 June

6 June

10–26 August   Trip to Owl's Head, Maine
24 August

30 October

November   Britten and Pears move into 7 Middagh Street,
                   Brooklyn Heights, the bohemian artistic commune
                   presided over by W. H. Auden

November

1941
10 January   Frank Bridge dies

WORKS	FIRST PERFORMANCES
	Piano Concerto (first American performance): composer as soloist, Illinois Symphony Orchestra conducted by Albert Goldberg, Blackstone Theatre, Chicago, Illinois
Sonatina Romantica, for piano (two movements published in 1986)	
	Les Illuminations (first complete performance): Sophie Wyss and the Boyd Neel Orchestra conducted by Boyd Neel, Aeolian Hall, London
	Violin Concerto: Antonio Brosa and the New York Philharmonic Orchestra conducted by John Barbirolli, Carnegie Hall, New York
The Dark Valley (radio)	The Dark Valley: Dame May Whitty, Columbia Theater Workshop, a CBS broadcast.
	Canadian Carnival: conducted by Clarence Raybould, a BBC Bristol broadcast
Diversions, Op. 21, for piano (left hand) and orchestra	
Seven Sonnets of Michelangelo, Op. 22, for tenor and piano	
Introduction and Rondo alla Burlesca, Op. 23 No. 1, for two pianos	
The Dynasts (radio)	The Dynasts: Columbia Theater Workshop, a CBS broadcast
Paul Bunyan (Auden), operetta	
	Introduction and Rondo alla Burlesca: Ethel Bartlett and Rae Robertson

1941   LIFE

Spring — Interest in oriental music stimulated by Colin McPhee. Appointed conductor of The Suffolk Friends of Music Orchestra, Suffolk County, Long Island

29 March

6 April

         Records McPhee's transcriptions of Balinese Ceremonial Music for two pianos, with McPhee

5 May

June

July

July–August — Britten and Pears visit Escondido, California, and stay with the piano duo Ethel Bartlett and Rae Robertson. While in California they come across E. M. Forster's article on George Crabbe in *The Listener*

21 September — Awarded Library of Congress Medal for services to chamber music

         Return to Mayer home at Amityville

October

WORKS	FIRST PERFORMANCES
	Sinfonia da Requiem: New York Philharmonic Orchestra conducted by John Barbirolli, Carnegie Hall, New York
The Rocking Horse Winner (radio)	The Rocking Horse Winner: Columbia Theater Workshop, a CBS broadcast
	Violin Concerto (UK premiere): Thomas Matthews and London Philharmonic Orchestra, conducted by Basil Cameron, Queen's Hall, London
	Paul Bunyan: Columbia University Theater Workshop, New York Schola Cantorum conducted by Hugh Ross, Brander Matthews Hall, New York
Matinées Musicales, Op. 24, for orchestra (Rossini arr. Britten)	Divertimento (*Soirées Musicales* and *Matinées Musicales*): American Ballet Company choreographed by Balanchine
String Quartet No. 1 in D, Op. 25	
Mazurka Elegiaca, Op. 23 No. 2, for two pianos	
	String Quartet No. 1: Coolidge String Quartet, Occidental College, Los Angeles
Occasional Overture, for orchestra (published posthumously in 1985 as *An American Overture*)	

1941   LIFE

27 October

28 November

Winter

1942
2 January   Attends a Boston Symphony Orchestra concert in which Serge Koussevitzky conducts the *Sinfonia da Requiem*. Tells Koussevitzky of his idea for an opera based on Crabbe's 'The Borough'

11 January   [Koussevitzky's wife Natalie dies and a Music Foundation is established in her memory]

16 January

February   Britten and Pears wait at Amityville for passage home to UK

14 March   Attends a concert at Carnegie Hall, New York, where Koussevitzky again conducts the *Sinfonia da Requiem*. The Koussevitzky Foundation offers a commission of $1000 for Britten's first opera, *Peter Grimes*

16 March   Britten and Pears sail from New York via Boston and Halifax to the UK on the MS *Axel Johnson*. During the five-week perilous voyage, Britten works on the *Hymn to St Cecilia* and *A Ceremony of Carols*, and drafts a scenario with Peter Pears for *Peter Grimes*

CHRONOLOGY

WORKS	FIRST PERFORMANCES
Scottish Ballad, Op. 26, for two pianos and orchestra	
	Scottish Ballad: Ethel Bartlett and Rae Robertson with the Cincinnati Symphony Orchestra conducted by Eugene Goossens
	Mazurka Elegiaca: Ethel Bartlett and Rae Robertson, Town Hall, New York
	Diversions: Paul Wittgenstein and the Philadelphia Orchestra conducted by Eugene Ormandy
Undated manuscripts from Britten's American years include: School Anthem: God, who created me (Henry Charles Beeching), for mixed chorus and organ Hymn: Who is this in garments gory? Underneath the abject willow (Auden) in a version for voice and piano O What is that sound? (Auden), for voice and piano What's on your mind? (Auden), for voice and piano What the wild flowers tell me (movement from Mahler's 3rd Symphony, arr. Britten)	

1942   LIFE

2 April

4 April

17 April   Arrival back in the UK. Britten and Pears register as
                  conscientious objectors and later are exempted from
                  military service by a Tribunal. The conditions for
                  exemption include the requirement that they give
                  CEMA (Council for the Encouragement of Music and
                  the Arts) and prison concerts. They live at the Old
                  Mill at Snape and at 104a Cheyne Walk, London
                  SW3, with Ursula Nettleship

                  Goes through the draft scenario for *Peter Grimes* with
                  Montagu Slater and invites him to write the libretto

20 July

22 July

27 July,
10 & 17 August

July–August

23 August

WORKS	FIRST PERFORMANCES
Cradle Song: Sleep, my darling, sleep (MacNeice), for voice and piano	
Voluntary (Chorale prelude in D minor) for organ	
Village Organist's piece (incomplete)	
Partita, for orchestra (incomplete)	
Purcell realization: The Knotting Song	
Clarinet Concerto, for Benny Goodman (incomplete)	
Hymn to St Cecilia, Op. 27 (Auden), for chorus	
Wild with Passion (Beddoes)	
If thou wilt ease thine heart (Beddoes), for voice and piano	
A Ceremony of Carols, Op. 28, for treble voices and harp	
Appointment (radio)	Appointment: RAF Orchestra conducted by Rudolf P. O'Donnell
	Sinfonia da Requiem (UK premiere): London Philharmonic Orchestra, conducted by Basil Cameron, Royal Albert Hall, London
An American in England Nos 1–3 (radio)	An American in England Nos 1–3: RAF Orchestra conducted by Rudolf P. O'Donnell
Lumberjacks of America (radio)	Lumberjacks of America: conducted by the composer
The Man Born to be King (radio)	The Man Born to be King

1942   *LIFE*

24, 31 August
7 September

20 September

20 September

23 September

24 September   Plays celesta in 'Les Six' concert at the Wigmore Hall
6–7 October   Recitals with Sophie Wyss for BBC
22 October   National Gallery recital with Pears of *Michelangelo Sonnets* and Schumann's *Dichterliebe*

7 November

20 November   Records *Michelangelo Sonnets* with Pears for HMV
22 November

5 December

21 December

1943   London address: 45a St John's Wood High Street, London NW8. Continues work on *Peter Grimes*

3 January

CHRONOLOGY

WORKS	FIRST PERFORMANCES
An American in England Nos 4–6	An American in England Nos 4–6: RAF Orchestra conducted by Rudolf P. O'Donnell
The Man Born to be King (radio)	The Man Born to be King
Britain to America, Series I: 9 (radio)	Britain to America, Series I: 9: London Symphony Orchestra conducted by Muir Mathieson
	Seven Sonnets of Michelangelo: Peter Pears and the composer, Wigmore Hall, London
Britain to America, Series II: 4 (radio)	Britain to America, Series II: 4: London Symphony Orchestra, conducted by Muir Mathieson
	Hymn to St Cecilia (broadcast premiere, BBC): BBC Singers conducted by Leslie Woodgate
	A Ceremony of Carols: Fleet Street Choir and Gwendolen Mason, conducted by T. B. Lawrence, Norwich Castle
	A Ceremony of Carols (London premiere): Fleet Street Choir and Gwendolen Mason, conducted by T. B. Lawrence, National Gallery Concerts, London
Revises *A Ceremony of Carols*	
Britain to America, Series II: 13 (radio)	Britain to America, Series II: 13: London Symphony Orchestra conducted by Muir Mathieson

1943   LIFE

21 February

March–April

25 April

28 April

May   *Prelude and Fugue* commissioned for 10th anniversary of Boyd Neel Orchestra

                          Records French Folk Songs with Sophie Wyss for Decca

2 June

5 June   Gives first performance of Tippett's *Boyhood's End* with Pears in London

23 June

5 July   Reads Mozart's letter to his wife 'And so to bed' for BBC

10 July

11 July   Recital with Pears at Wormwood Scrubs attended by Michael Tippett, who had broken the conditions of his terms of exemption as a conscientious objector and was serving a gaol sentence

17 July

21 September

CHRONOLOGY

WORKS	FIRST PERFORMANCES
The Four Freedoms No. 1: Pericles (radio)	The Four Freedoms No. 1: Pericles
Serenade, Op. 31, for tenor, horn and strings	
	Introduction and Rondo alla Burlesca and *Mazurka Elegiaca*: Clifford Curzon and the composer, Cambridge
	String Quartet No. 1 (UK premiere): Griller String Quartet, Wigmore Hall, London
Prelude and Fugue, Op. 29, for string orchestra	
Folk Songs Volume 1, British Isles (arr. Britten), for high voice and piano	
	Prelude and Fugue: Boyd Neel Orchestra, Wigmore Hall, London
	Scottish Ballad (UK premiere): Clifford Curzon and the composer, conducted by Basil Cameron, Promenade Concert, Royal Albert Hall, London
Rejoice in the Lamb, Op. 30, for soloists, chorus and organ	
	Rejoice in the Lamb: Choir of St Matthew's, Northampton

1943   LIFE

15 October

2 November   Recital with Pears of Dowland, Purcell and the
                     Michelangelo Sonnets at the City Hall, Sheffield

25–26 November

4 December

13 December

1944   Begins composition sketch of *Peter Grimes*. Continues
                     recitals and BBC broadcasts

January   Records Op. 23 two-piano pieces with Clifford
                     Curzon, and folksongs with Pears, for Decca

February

25 May   Records *Serenade* with Pears, Brain and the Boyd Neel
                     Orchestra for Decca

8–9 November

15 November
24 December

1945   Revises *Piano Concerto*
10 February

8–13 March   Four recitals with Pears in Paris
7 April   Records talk on Vienna in English, German and
                     French for BBC

CHRONOLOGY

WORKS	FIRST PERFORMANCES
	Serenade: Peter Pears, Dennis Brain and string orchestra conducted by Walter Goehr, Wigmore Hall, London
The Rescue (radio)	The Rescue: BBC Symphony Orchestra conducted by Clarence Raybould
	A Ceremony of Carols (revised version): Morriston Boys' Choir and Maria Korchinska conducted by the composer, Wigmore Hall, London
The Ballad of Little Musgrave and Lady Barnard, for male voices and piano	
	The Ballad of Little Musgrave and Lady Barnard: Richard Wood and the musicians of Oflag VIIb, Germany
Festival Te Deum, Op. 32, for chorus and organ	
Chorale	
A Poet's Christmas (radio)	*A Shepherd's Carol* and Chorale (withdrawn): A Poet's Christmas, BBC Singers conducted by Leslie Woodgate
Peter Grimes, Op. 33 (Slater), opera in three acts	

1945   LIFE

13 April	BBC broadcast of Vaughan Williams's *On Wenlock Edge* with Pears and the Zorian String Quartet
24 April	
7 May	[Germany surrenders]
31 May	Accompanies cast for a concert–introduction to *Peter Grimes* at the Wigmore Hall, London
7 June	Sadler's Wells Opera Company launches its first post-war season with the premiere of *Peter Grimes*
June	Records Folk Songs with Pears for Decca
13 June	
21 June	Recital of Purcell and Schubert with Pears at Cecil Sharp House, recorded by BBC
July	Records Vaughan Williams's *On Wenlock Edge* with Pears and the Zorian Quartet
8 July	Schumann recital with Pears, Wigmore Hall, London
11 July	Records talk on *Peter Grimes* with Pears and Joan Cross for BBC 'Music Magazine'
15 July	Broadcast of talk on *Grimes*
17 July	Broadcast of *Peter Grimes* from Sadler's Wells
July	Concert tour with Yehudi Menuhin of the German concentration camps, giving two or three short recitals a day
12 August	High fever while working on *Holy Sonnets of John Donne*
2–19 August	
15 August	

CHRONOLOGY

WORKS	FIRST PERFORMANCES
	Festival Te Deum: Choir of St Mark's, Swindon
	Peter Grimes: Peter Pears, Joan Cross, Sadler's Wells Opera Company conducted by Reginald Goodall, Sadler's Wells, London
	Four Sea Interludes from *Peter Grimes* (first concert performance): LPO, conducted by the composer
The Holy Sonnets of John Donne, Op. 35, for high voice and piano	
Epilogue: Perchance he for whom the bell tolls be so ill (discarded song from *The Holy Sonnets of John Donne*)	

1945	LIFE
11 September	Conducts *Les Illuminations* with Pears at Promenade Concert, Royal Albert Hall, London
11 October	
14 October	
20 November	Records Purcell songs with Pears for BBC
21 November	
22 November	
2 December	Recital with Maurice Gendron (cello) of Fauré and Debussy sonatas at Wigmore Hall, London
31 December	
1946	London address: 3 Oxford Square, London W2. Working on *The Rape of Lucretia* with a libretto by Ronald Duncan based on a play by André Obey
January	Records Folk Songs with Pears for Decca
21 January	
13 March	BBC broadcast of *Peter Grimes*
Winter–Spring	Recitals with Pears in Holland and Belgium
Spring	
June	European tour with Pears
14 June	
2 July	
10 July	Pre-recorded BBC talk on *Lucretia* broadcast

WORKS	FIRST PERFORMANCES
This Way to the Tomb (theatre)	This Way to the Tomb: Pilgrim Players, Mercury Theatre, London
String Quartet No. 2, Op. 36	
	String Quartet No. 2: The Zorian String Quartet, Wigmore Hall, London
	The Holy Sonnets of John Donne: Peter Pears and the composer, Wigmore Hall, London
The Instruments of the Orchestra (film)	
The Dark Tower (radio)	The Dark Tower: conducted by Walter Goehr
The Rape of Lucretia, Op. 37 (Duncan), opera in two acts	
The Queen's Epicedium (Purcell ed. Britten and Pears)	
	Piano Concerto (revised version): with Noel Mewton-Wood as soloist, conducted by the composer, Cheltenham Festival

1946　　　　　　　　　　　　　　　*LIFE*

12 July　　　　　　Glyndebourne Opera, Sussex, launches its first postwar season with Britten's *The Rape of Lucretia*

6 August　　　　　Attends American premiere of *Peter Grimes* at Koussevitzky's Tanglewood Festival, conducted by Leonard Bernstein and produced by Eric Crozier

1 September　　　BBC Northern Region broadcast recital with Pears

4 September

14 September

18 September

21 September

28 September　　Attends BBC rehearsals of *Occasional Overture*, written for launching of the BBC Third Programme

29 September

October

2 October　　　　Continental tour of *The Rape of Lucretia*. Starts work on *Albert Herring*, based on a short story by Guy de Maupassant, with librettist Eric Crozier

15 October　　　 Records talk for VIth Forms, 'The Artist and his Medium' for BBC, broadcast on 18 October

18 November　　First recital with Pears for BBC Third Programme: Schubert songs and *Michelangelo Sonnets*

29 November

CHRONOLOGY 63

WORKS	FIRST PERFORMANCES
The National Anthem (arr. Britten) for *Lucretia* orchestra	*The Rape of Lucretia*: Glyndebourne Festival Opera conducted by Ernest Ansermet, Glyndebourne, Sussex
The Eagle has Two Heads (theatre)	The Eagle has Two Heads: Lyric Theatre, Hammersmith, London
Occasional Overture (withdrawn; published posthumously in 1984)	
Prelude and Fugue on a Theme of Vittoria, for organ	
	Prelude and Fugue on a Theme of Vittoria: St Matthew's Church, Northampton
	Occasional Overture (broadcast premiere, BBC): BBC Symphony Orchestra conducted by Adrian Boult
The Duchess of Malfi (theatre)	The Duchess of Malfi: Barrymore Theater, New York
	The Young Person's Guide to the Orchestra: Liverpool Philharmonic Orchestra conducted by Malcolm Sargent, Liverpool – see p. 143
	The Instruments of the Orchestra: Crown Film Unit, Empire Theatre, Leicester Square, London

1946   *LIFE*

26 December	Recording with Pears of recital of Folksongs (arr. Britten) for BBC
31 December	
1947	Works on *Albert Herring* with Eric Crozier in Switzerland before embarking on a European tour. Revises *Lucretia*. Forms the English Opera Group with Eric Crozier and John Piper as co-Artistic Directors
24 January	British Council recital tour in Italy with Pears
1 March	Returns to England from continental tour
20 June	
	Moves with Pears from the Old Mill to Crag House, 4 Crabbe Street, Aldeburgh
August	EOG tour of *Herring* to the Holland Festival and in Europe, during which Pears proposes creating a music festival in Aldeburgh
August–December	Records *Folk Songs*, Purcell's *The Queen's Epicedium* and the *Donne Sonnets* with Pears for Decca
12 September	
27 September	Conducts EOG in Berkeley's *Stabat Mater* at BBC Concert Hall
1 November	
6 November	First performance of *Peter Grimes* at Covent Garden (Pears, Cross, Goodall)

WORKS	FIRST PERFORMANCES
Folk Songs Volume 2, France (arr. Britten), for high or medium voice and piano	
Orpheus Britannicus (Purcell ed. Britten and Pears), 7 songs for high or medium voice and piano	
Albert Herring, Op. 39 (Crozier), comic opera in three acts	
The Blessed Virgin's Expostulation (Purcell ed. Britten and Pears)	
	Albert Herring: Peter Pears and EOG conducted by the composer, Glyndebourne Opera House, Sussex
Canticle I: My beloved is mine, Op. 40 (Quarles), for high voice and piano	
	Canticle I: Peter Pears and the composer, Central Hall, London

1947	*LIFE*
9 November	Records a concert of the music of Frank Bridge with Pears and the Zorian Quartet for the BBC
24 November	Records recital of Mahler and Purcell with Pears for the BBC
26 November	Broadcast with Pears of *Canticle I* for BBC
29 November	Broadcast with Pears of seventeenth- and eighteenth-century duets and cantatas
December	Works on new realization of *The Beggar's Opera*, ballad opera by Gay and Pepusch
24 December	
25 December	
31 December	
1948	London address: 22 Melbury Road W14
January	Second British Council recital tour with Pears in Italy
	Public meeting at the Jubilee Hall, Aldeburgh, guarantees £200 for the First Aldeburgh Festival

CHRONOLOGY 67

WORKS   *FIRST PERFORMANCES*

Men of Goodwill (radio) (published posthumously in 1982)

A Charm of Lullabies, Op. 41, for mezzo-soprano and piano

Somnus the humble god that dwells in cottages and smokey cells (Denham), Come little Babe (Nicholas Breton) (discarded songs from *A Charm of Lullabies*)

Three Divine Hymns (Purcell ed. Britten and Pears)

Saul and the Witch at Endor (Purcell ed. Britten and Pears)

Men of Goodwill: London Symphony Orchestra conducted by Walter Goehr

Folk Songs Volume 3, British Isles (arr. Britten), for high or medium voice and piano

A Charm of Lullabies (broadcast premiere, BBC): Nancy Evans and Ernest Lush

The Beggar's Opera, Op. 43, ballad opera (Gay and Pepusch real. Britten)

1948   LIFE

3 January

25 March

12 April   BBC broadcast of *Albert Herring* from the Camden
                        Theatre, London

24 May

31 May

5–13 June   1st Aldeburgh Festival of Music and the Arts:
                        programme includes *St Nicolas*, *Albert Herring*, and
                        Berkeley's *Stabat Mater*

5 June

19 June–10 July   EOG tour of Holland and France
19–26 July   EOG at Cambridge Festival
24 July   *St Nicolas* at Lancing College Centenary Celebrations
6–13 September   With EOG in Birmingham
21 September   BBC broadcast of *The Beggar's Opera* from the
                        Camden Theatre, London
20–27 September   With EOG in Manchester
October   With EOG in London
17–18 December   Conducts Handel's *Messiah* with EOG at Aldeburgh
                        Parish Church

1949   Working on *The Little Sweep* and *Spring Symphony*.
                        Early discussion on libretto for *Billy Budd* with E. M.
                        Forster and Eric Crozier

21 January–   Holiday in Venice
12 February

WORKS	FIRST PERFORMANCES
	A Charm of Lullabies (first concert performance): Nancy Evans and Felix de Nobel, The Hague
Orpheus Britannicus (Purcell ed. Britten and Pears), 6 songs for high or medium voice and piano	
	The Beggar's Opera: Peter Pears, Nancy Evans and EOG conducted by Britten, Arts Theatre, Cambridge
St Nicolas, Op. 42 (Crozier), for tenor solo, chorus and orchestra, written for Lancing College	
	St Nicolas: Peter Pears, Aldeburgh Festival Choir and Chamber Orchestra conducted by Leslie Woodgate, Aldeburgh Parish Church

1949 | *LIFE*

April

16 April–21 May | Recital tour with Pears in Italy and Belgium
10–19 June | 2nd Aldeburgh Festival
14 June

23 June | Conducts *St Nicolas* with Pears as soloist at Southwark Cathedral in the presence of Queen Mary

14 July

September

29 September

13 October | Score of *A Wedding Anthem* together with a copy of *The Times* for 12 October, documents of London City Council relating to the 1951 Festival of Britain Exhibition, and a set of 1949 coins are laid beneath a foundation stone for the Royal Festival Hall

23 October–December | Recital tour with Pears of USA and Canada
31 October

WORKS	FIRST PERFORMANCES
The Little Sweep, Op. 45 (Crozier), children's opera	
	The Little Sweep, as part of *Let's Make an Opera*, an entertainment for young people by Eric Crozier: EOG conducted by Norman Del Mar, Jubilee Hall, Aldeburgh
Spring Symphony, Op. 44, for soloists, chorus and orchestra	
	Spring Symphony: Jo Vincent, Kathleen Ferrier, Peter Pears, the Dutch Radio Chorus and the Concertgebouw Orchestra conducted by Edward van Beinum, Holland Festival, Amsterdam
A Wedding Anthem (Amo Ergo Sum), Op. 46 (Duncan), for soprano, tenor, chorus and organ	
	A Wedding Anthem: conducted by the composer at the wedding of the Earl of Harewood and Miss Marion Stein, St Mark's Church, North Audley Street, London
Stratton (theatre)	Stratton: EOG Orchestra conducted by Norman Del Mar, Theatre Royal, Brighton

	LIFE
1949	
31 December	BBC recital with Pears of songs by Schubert and Wolf from the Concert Hall of Broadcasting House
1950	
2 February	Starts work on *Billy Budd* with its librettists, E. M. Forster and Eric Crozier
March	
3 March	
5 March	BBC broadcast of *Let's Make an Opera*
9 March	Attends first British performance of *Spring Symphony*
24 April	Records Schubert's *Die schöne Müllerin* with Pears for BBC
16 May	
17–25 June	3rd Aldeburgh Festival
18 June	Recital with Pears includes first performance of Aaron Copland's *Old American Songs*
20 June	
25 September	Recital with Pears and Kathleen Ferrier at Central Hall, London
29 September	Records folksongs arranged by Britten, Copland and Grainger with Pears for HMV
1951	Completes a new realized edition of Purcell's *Dido and Aeneas*
14 February	BBC recital with Pears
1 May	

CHRONOLOGY

WORKS	FIRST PERFORMANCES
Five Flower Songs, Op. 47, for chorus	
Job's Curse (Purcell ed. Britten and Pears)	
	Spring Symphony (UK premiere): Joan Cross, Anne Wood, Peter Pears, London Philharmonic Choir and Orchestra, conducted by Edward van Beinum, Royal Albert Hall, London
Lachrymae, Op. 48, for viola and piano	
	Lachrymae: William Primrose and the composer, Aldeburgh Parish Church
Six Metamorphoses after Ovid, Op. 49, for oboe	
	Dido and Aeneas (ed. Britten) Nancy Evans, Bruce Boyce and EOG conducted by Britten, Lyric Theatre, Hammersmith, London

1951 LIFE

7 May	First recital (with Pears) in Festival of Britain English Song series at Wigmore Hall: includes the first performance of Tippett's *The Heart's Assurance*
24 May	
29 May–1 June	EOG perform *Lucretia* at Wiesbaden
8–17 June	4th Aldeburgh Festival
14 June	
20–30 June	EOG season in Holland. First performance of Holst's *The Wandering Scholar* in a revised version by Britten and I. Holst
28 July	Receives Freedom of the Borough of Lowestoft
July–August	EOG at Cheltenham, Liverpool and in Belgium
23 August	Appointed to National Arts Foundation in New York
September	Short cruise with Pears and friends from Aldeburgh across the North Sea and up the Rhine to Bonn
Autumn	
1 December	

1952

January	
21 January	
March	Skiing holiday with the Harewoods in Austria
	First visit to the home of the Prince and Princess of Hesse and the Rhine at Schloss Wolfsgarten
1 March	Recital with Pears in Vienna

WORKS	FIRST PERFORMANCES
	Five Flower Songs (broadcast premiere, BBC): BBC Midlands Chorus
	Six Metamorphoses after Ovid: Joy Boughton, Thorpeness Meare
Billy Budd, Op. 50 (Forster and Crozier), opera in four acts	
	Billy Budd: Theodor Uppman, Peter Pears and soloists, chorus and orchestra of the Royal Opera House conducted by the composer, Covent Garden, London
Canticle II: Abraham and Isaac, Op. 51, for alto, tenor and piano	
	Canticle II: Kathleen Ferrier, Peter Pears and the composer, EOG Tour, Albert Hall, Nottingham

1952	*LIFE*
Spring	Starts work on opera commissioned for the coronation celebrations for HM Queen Elizabeth II with William Plomer as librettist. Imogen Holst later joins Britten as his full-time Music Assistant
May	*Billy Budd* given at Théâtre des Champs-Elysées, Paris, during Festival of Twentieth-Century Art
14–22 June	5th Aldeburgh Festival
Summer	Festival appearances at Copenhagen, Aix-en-Provence, Menton and Salzburg
October	
1953	London address: 5 Chester Gate, NW1
January	Crag House flooded in East Coast Floods
13 March	
May	Conducts EOG *Albert Herring* in Germany
1 June	Created a Companion of Honour in the Coronation Honours List
8 June	
20 June	Live recording of Variations on an Elizabethan Theme for Decca
	Morris Dance from *Gloriana*, arranged for two descant recorders
20–28 June	6th Aldeburgh Festival
2 July	Invested CH by HM Queen Elizabeth II

WORKS	FIRST PERFORMANCES
	Billy Budd (American premiere and the first Britten opera to be televised): Theodor Uppman in the title role, NBC TV, USA
Variation of 'Sellenger's Round', Variation IV from Variations on an Elizabethan Theme, for orchestra	
Gloriana, Op. 53 (Plomer), opera in three acts	
	Gloriana: Joan Cross, Peter Pears, soloists, chorus and orchestra of the Royal Opera House conducted by John Pritchard, Covent Garden, London
	Variations on an Elizabethan Theme: conducted by Britten, Aldeburgh Parish Church

1953

LIFE

September

8 October — Visits Denmark to conduct and record *A Ceremony of Carols* and *Sinfonia da Requiem* for Decca

Autumn — Starts work on *The Turn of the Screw* with a libretto by Myfanwy Piper based on the story by Henry James

November — Revival of *Peter Grimes* at Covent Garden, conducted by Reginald Goodall

Britten sits for bronze bust by Georg Ehrlich

1954 — Begins composition of *The Turn of the Screw*. Revises *Diversions* for piano (left hand) and orchestra. Article on 'Three Premieres' published in Memoir to Kathleen Ferrier

4 March

March — Records *Winter Words* and *Folk Songs* with Pears for Decca

12–20 June — 7th Aldeburgh Festival

July — Records *Michelangelo Sonnets* with Pears and *Diversions* with Julius Katchen for Decca

23 July

14 September

23 September

| WORKS | FIRST PERFORMANCES |

Winter Words, Op. 52 (Hardy), for high voice and piano
If it's ever spring again
The children and Sir Nameless
(discarded songs from *Winter Words*)

Winter Words: Peter Pears and the composer, Harewood House, Leeds Festival

Am Stram Gram (theatre)

Am Stram Gram: Toynbee Hall Theatre, London

The Turn of the Screw, Op. 54 (M. Piper), opera in two acts

The Turn of the Screw: Jennifer Vyvyan, Peter Pears, EOG conducted by the composer, Teatro La Fenice, Venice

Symphonic Suite 'Gloriana': City of Birmingham Symphony Orchestra conducted by Rudolf Schwarz, Town Hall, Birmingham

1954   *LIFE*

27 November

1955   Revises *A Boy was Born*

January   Records *The Turn of the Screw* with EOG for Decca
28 January

February   Concert tour with Pears in Belgium and Switzerland, followed by a skiing holiday with the artist Mary Potter

                          EOG tour of *The Turn of the Screw*
13–14 April   Records *St Nicolas* with Pears and the Aldeburgh Festival Chorus and Orchestra for Decca
18–26 June   8th Aldeburgh Festival
24 June

October   Records English Songs with Pears and *The Little Sweep* with EOG for Decca

20 November

November   Trip with Pears to the Far East (in the company of Prince Ludwig and Princess Margaret of Hesse and the Rhine) prefaced by recital tour of Yugoslavia (Ljubljana, Maribor, Zagreb, Belgrade), and visit to Istanbul

December   In Istanbul and Karachi

1956   Tour continues in Singapore, Indonesia, Japan, Macau, Hong Kong, Thailand, India and Ceylon

CHRONOLOGY

WORKS	FIRST PERFORMANCES
Canticle III: Still falls the rain, Op. 55 (E. Sitwell), for tenor, horn and piano	
Punch Revue: 'Old friends are best' (Plomer) (theatre) *Farfield (1928–30)*, for voice and piano	
	Canticle III: Peter Pears, Dennis Brain and the composer, Wigmore Hall, London
Alpine Suite and *Scherzo*, for recorders	
	'New Prince, New Pomp', the fourth movement of Thy King's Birthday (1931): Rosamund Strode and the Purcell Singers directed by Imogen Holst, Aldeburgh Parish Church
Hymn to St Peter, Op. 56a, for choir and organ	*Hymn to St Peter*: Choir of St Peter Mancroft, Norwich
Timpani Piece for Jimmy (Blades), for timpani and piano	

1956   *LIFE*

3 February

March   Arrival home from Far East
30 March

17 May

6 June   Holland Festival recital with Pears and Dennis Brain
15–24 June   9th Aldeburgh Festival. Imogen Holst joins Britten and Pears as an Artistic Director. Concert of Haydn and Mozart with the Aldeburgh Festival Orchestra recorded

21 June

Summer   Holiday at Schloss Tarasp, Switzerland, summer residence of the Prince and Princess of Hesse and the Rhine, where Britten works on the ballet score, *The Prince of the Pagodas*

23 September   Recital with Pears of songs by Morley, Dowland, Purcell, Schubert and Britten at Eichengalerie des Charlottenburger Schloss in Berlin

29 September

Autumn

October   Conducts EOG production of *The Turn of the Screw* in London

November   Concert tour in Germany with Pears

1957

1 January

WORKS	FIRST PERFORMANCES
Orpheus Britannicus (Purcell ed. Britten and Pears), suite of songs for high voice and orchestra	
Antiphon, Op. 56b, for choir and organ	
Prologue, Song and Epilogue (E. Sitwell), for tenor, horn and piano (to contain Canticle III)	
	Prologue, Song and Epilogue: Pears, Dennis Brain and Britten, Aldeburgh Parish Church
	Antiphon: St Michael's College, Tenbury Wells
The Prince of the Pagodas, Op. 57 (Cranko), ballet in three acts	
Malayan National Anthem for Military Band (submitted but not accepted)	
	The Prince of the Pagodas: The Royal Ballet choreographed by John Cranko, the orchestra of the Royal Opera House conducted by the composer, Covent Garden, London

1957 — LIFE

January	Records *A Boy was Born* with the Purcell Singers for Decca
February	Records *The Prince of the Pagodas* with the Covent Garden Orchestral for Decca
8 April	Elected honorary member of the American Academy of Arts and Letters and of the National Institute of Arts and Letters, New York. Records *Rejoice in the Lamb*
17 April–7 May	Holiday in Italy with Pears and the Prince and Princess of Hesse and the Rhine. Return journey to England with John and Myfanwy Piper after first Italian performance of *The Prince of the Pagodas* at La Scala, Milan
May	Arranges Courtly Dances from *Gloriana* as an orchestral suite
14–23 June	10th Aldeburgh Festival. Anniversary production of *Albert Herring*
23 June	
August	Takes EOG's *The Turn of the Screw* to the Shakespeare Festival, Stratford, Ontario, Canada
30 September	Recital of Haydn, Schubert, Wolf and Britten with Pears at Eichengalerie des Charlottenburger Schloss in Berlin
October	Conducts EOG *Screw* at the Berlin Festival
Autumn	
27 October	Begins composition of *Noye's Fludde*, a setting of the Chester Miracle Play
November	Moves from Crag House to the Red House, Aldeburgh
18 December	

CHRONOLOGY

WORKS	FIRST PERFORMANCES
The Holly and the Ivy (arr. Britten), for chorus	
	The Courtly Dances from 'Gloriana': English Chamber Orchestra conducted by the composer, Jubilee Hall, Aldeburgh
Songs from the Chinese, Op. 58, for high voice and guitar	
Noye's Fludde, Op. 59, children's opera	

1958   *LIFE*

1958   London address: 59 Marlborough Place, NW8. Co-
                   author with Imogen Holst of *The Story of Music*.
                   Revises the *Violin Concerto* and *A Boy Was Born*
                   Princess Margaret of Hesse and the Rhine opens a
                   fund to finance the Hesse Student Scheme to help
                   young people to attend the Aldeburgh Festival

13–22 June   11th Aldeburgh Festival

17 June

18 June

July   Tour of the Midlands with Pears and the Prince and
                   Princess of Hesse and the Rhine

Summer

3 September   Recital with Pears of songs by Schumann, Schubert
                   and Britten, Freemason's Hall, Edinburgh Interna-
                   tional Festival

5 September   Britten programme (*Four Sea Interludes* and *Passacag-
                   lia from Peter Grimes*, *Les Illuminations* – with Pears
                   – and *Spring Symphony*) at Usher Hall, Edinburgh
                   International Festival

14 October   Recital with Pears and Norma Procter (Purcell,
                   Schumann, Schubert, Britten) at Leeds Festival

16 October

18 October   Conducts Covent Garden Wind Ensemble in Mozart's
                   Serenade in B flat (K.361) at the Leeds Festival

14 November

WORKS	FIRST PERFORMANCES
Einladung zur Martinsgans, eight part canon for voices and piano	
	Songs from the Chinese: Peter Pears and Julian Bream, Great Glemham House, Glemham
	Noye's Fludde: Suffolk children directed by Meredith Davies, Orford Church
Nocturne, Op. 60, for tenor, seven obbligato instruments and string orchestra	
Sechs Hölderlin-Fragmente, Op. 61, for voice and piano	
	Nocturne: Peter Pears and the BBC Symphony Orchestra conducted by Rudolf Schwartz, Leeds Town Hall, Leeds Festival
	Sechs Hölderlin-Fragmente (broadcast premiere, BBC): Peter Pears and the composer

1958   LIFE

20 November

December   Records *Peter Grimes*, with Pears in the title role, for
                    Decca

1959
6–14 January   Takes part in first 'Britisch–Deutsche Musiktage' at
                    Schloss Elmau, Upper Bavaria

March

April   Records Schubert songs with Pears for Decca

May

June

19–28 June   12th Aldeburgh Festival, attended by the first Hesse
                    students

11 June   Receives Honorary Doctorate at Cambridge
22 July

Summer   Trip to Venice
Autumn   Enlargement and improvement of Jubilee Hall.
                    Property purchased for Festival Club and Exhibition
                    Gallery at Aldeburgh
September   Records *Nocturne* with Pears and LSO for Decca
October   Starts work with Pears on the libretto of *A Midsummer
                    Night's Dream* based on Shakespeare's play. Records
                    Folk Songs and Schubert's *Die schöne Müllerin* with
                    Pears for Decca
Winter   Trip to Dubrovnik with Pears and the Prince and
                    Princess of Hesse and the Rhine

WORKS	FIRST PERFORMANCES
	Sechs Hölderlin-Fragmente (first concert performance): Peter Pears and the composer, Schloss Wolfsgarten, near Darmstadt
Cantata Academica, Op. 62, for soloists, chorus and orchestra	
Fanfare for St Edmundsbury, for three trumpets	
Missa Brevis in D, Op. 63, for boys' voices and organ	
	Fanfare for St Edmundsbury: Pageant of Magna Carta, Bury St Edmunds, Suffolk
	Missa Brevis in D: Choir of Westminster Cathedral directed by George Malcolm, Westminster Cathedral, London

1960   LIFE

1960
15 April

10 May

11–26 June   13th Aldeburgh Festival
11 June

1 July

Summer   Revises *Billy Budd* from four acts to two. EOG comes
                      under the management of Covent Garden

September   Introduced to Dmitri Shostakovich and Mstislav
                      Rostropovich at the Royal Festival Hall, London.
                      Begins composition of the *Cello Sonata*

6 September

7 September

4 October
9–29 October   Trip to Greece
3 November

November   Rehearsals at BBC for broadcast of revised version of *Billy
                      Budd*. Records *Spring Symphony* for Decca

8 November   Records revised version of *Billy Budd* for BBC
13 November

WORKS	FIRST PERFORMANCES
A Midsummer Night's Dream, Op. 64, opera in three acts	
Folk Songs Volume 4, Moore's Irish Melodies (arr. Britten), for voice and piano	
	A Midsummer Night's Dream: Alfred Deller, Jennifer Vyvyan, EOG conducted by the composer, Jubilee Hall, Aldeburgh
	Cantata Academica: Agnes Giebel, Elsa Cavelti, Peter Pears, Heinz Rehfuss, Basle University Chorus, Basler Kammerorchester conducted by Paul Sacher, Basle University, Switzerland
Orpheus Britannicus (Purcell ed. Britten and Pears), 5 songs for voice and piano	
Two Divine Hymns and Alleluia (Purcell ed. Britten and Pears)	
Fanfare for SS *Oriana*	
	Fanfare for SS *Oriana*: at the launching of the vessel
	Billy Budd (broadcast premiere of revised version, BBC): conducted by the composer

	LIFE
1960	
17 November	New production of *Peter Grimes* at Covent Garden with Pears in the title role
1–11 December	Recital tour with Pears in Germany and Switzerland (Karlsruhe, Geneva, Düsseldorf, Hamburg and Hanover)
16 December	Recital with Pears and John Hahessy (alto) at Wigmore Hall, London
1961 January	Completes *Sonata in C* and works on *War Requiem*
19 January	Arranges Variation V of *A Boy was Born* as *Corpus Christi Carol* for John Hahessy
February	
14 February	
23 March	Auction at Christie's (in support of the Aldeburgh Festival) of autograph full score (pencil) of *The Young Person's Guide to the Orchestra* and the early sketches (pencil) for the *Seven Sonnets of Michelangelo*, bought by James Osborn for the Library of Yale University, USA. Sketches and MS full score of *Cantata Academica* were purchased prior to the sale by Dr and Mrs Paul Sacher (Paul Sacher Foundation, Basle)
16 March–7 April	Recitals with Pears in Canada
April	Recording sessions with Pears, John Hahessy and Barry Tuckwell of *Canticles I–III* for Decca
9 May	
24 May	
20 June	Records Schubert's *Die schöne Müllerin* with Pears for the BBC
28 June–9 July	14th Aldeburgh Festival

WORKS	FIRST PERFORMANCES
Sonata in C, Op. 65, for cello and piano	
Corpus Christi Carol, for treble solo (or unison voices) and piano	
Venite Exultemus Domino (published posthumously in 1983) and incomplete *Te Deum*, for choir and organ	
Jubilate Deo, for chorus and organ	
Folk Songs Volume 5, British Isles (arr. Britten), for voice and piano	
Fancie, for unison voices and piano	
Orpheus Britannicus (Purcell ed. Britten and Pears), 6 duets with piano	

1961   *LIFE*

7 July

July	Records the Debussy and Britten Sonatas and Schumann's 5 *Stücke im Volkston* with Mstislav Rostropovich for Decca
31 July–5 August	Conducts *Lucretia* in Dubrovnik
7 October	
8 October	
8 November	
	Records *Sechs Hölderlin-Fragmente*, with Haydn *Canzonets* and *Folk Songs* with Pears for Decca
20 December	
	Records his arrangement of *The National Anthem* with LSO and chorus for Decca
1962	Revises (with Imogen Holst) 1951 edition of Purcell's *Dido and Aeneas*
1 May	
15 May	Recital with Pears in Royal Palace, Stockholm
16 May	Conducts EOG in Purcell's *Dido and Aeneas* at the Drottningholm Court Theatre, Sweden, with Janet Baker as Dido
30 May	*War Requiem* performed for the festival of consecration of St Michael's Cathedral, Coventry

CHRONOLOGY 95

WORKS	FIRST PERFORMANCES
	Sonata in C: Mstislav Rostropovich and the composer, Jubilee Hall, Aldeburgh
The National Anthem (arr. Britten), for chorus and orchestra	*The National Anthem* (arr. Britten): Leeds Festival Chorus and Royal Liverpool Philharmonic Orchestra conducted by John Pritchard, Town Hall, Leeds Festival
	Jubilate Deo: Choir of Leeds Parish Church, Leeds
Folk Songs Volume 6, England (arr. Britten), for high voice and guitar	
War Requiem, Op. 66, for soprano, tenor and baritone solos, chorus, boys' chorus, orchestra, chamber orchestra and organ	
Psalm 150, Op. 67, for children's voices and instruments	
	War Requiem: Heather Harper, Peter Pears, Dietrich Fischer-Dieskau, Coventry Festival Chorus, boys of Holy Trinity, Leamington, and Holy Trinity, Stratford, City of Birming-

1962   *LIFE*

14–24 June   15th Aldeburgh Festival
16 June

22 October   Receives Honorary Freedom of the Borough of
                           Aldeburgh

29 December

1963   *The Ship of Rio* arranged from *Three Two-part songs*
                           (1932)
January   Records *War Requiem* for Decca
14 January–   Holiday in Greece and Tarasp with Pears and the
12 February   Prince and Princess of Hesse and the Rhine
March   British Council trip with Pears to USSR, where they
                           participate in a Festival of British Music
3 May

                           Records *Serenade* with Pears, Tuckwell and LSO and
                           The Young Person's Guide to the Orchestra with LSO for
                           Decca
25 May

2 June

20–30 June   16th Aldeburgh Festival
24 June

WORKS	FIRST PERFORMANCES
	ham Symphony Orchestra conducted by Meredith Davies, and the Melos Ensemble conducted by the composer, St Michael's Cathedral, Coventry
The Twelve Apostles (arr. Britten), for tenor, chorus and piano (published posthumously in 1981)	*The Twelve Apostles*: Peter Pears, London Boy Singers and the composer, Aldeburgh Parish Church
A Hymn of St Columba – Regis regum rectissimi, for chorus and organ	
The Ship of Rio, for voice and piano	
Symphony for Cello and Orchestra, Op. 68	
Night Piece (Notturno), for piano	
Cantata Misericordium, Op. 69, for tenor, baritone, chorus and orchestra	
	A Hymn of St Columba: The Ulster Singers conducted by Havelock Nelson, Garton, Co. Donegal, N. Ireland
	Psalm 150: Northgate (Ipswich) School Choir and Orchestra conducted by the composer, Jubilee Hall, Aldeburgh

1963   LIFE

July   Holiday in Frankfurt and Strasbourg with Pears and
                        the Prince and Princess of Hesse and the Rhine
1 September

September

October   Records Schubert's *Winterreise*, Schumann's *Dichter-
                        liebe* and songs by Ireland and Bridge with Pears for
                        Decca
11 November

22 November   50th birthday. Concert performance of *Gloriana* at
                        the Royal Festival Hall, London. BBC TV profile.
                        New production of *Peter Grimes* by Basil Coleman at
                        Sadler's Wells. Collection of 'Tributes' to Britten from
                        friends and colleagues published by Faber and Faber
                        Ltd [President J. F. Kennedy assassinated]

12 December   Conducts *War Requiem* at Royal Festival Hall. Records
                        Cantata Misericordium with Pears, Fischer-Dieskau and
                        LSO for Decca

1964
February   Trip to Venice: begins composition of *Curlew River*, a
                        parable for church performance with a libretto by
                        William Plomer

12 March   Trip to USSR

20 March   First performance of *Peter Grimes* in USSR, a concert
                        performance at the Kirov Theatre, Leningrad

Spring   Trip to Budapest: visits a children's music club and
                        hears the Jeney twins perform

2 April

                        Records *Albert Herring* with EOG for Decca

WORKS	FIRST PERFORMANCES
	Cantata Misericordium: Peter Pears, Dietrich Fischer-Dieskau, Le Motet de Genève and L'Orchestre de la Suisse Romande conducted by Ernest Ansermet, Geneva
	Notturno: Leeds International Piano Competition
Nocturnal after John Dowland, Op. 70, for guitar	
	Symphony for Cello and Orchestra: Mstislav Rostropovich and the Moscow Philharmonic Orchestra conducted by the composer, Moscow
Curlew River, Op. 71 (Plomer), parable for church performance	

1964   LIFE

10–21 June — 17th Aldeburgh Festival. Imogen Holst retires as Britten's Music Assistant and is succeeded by Rosamund Strode, who holds this post until Britten's death

12 June

13 June

18 June

July — Records *Cello Symphony* and Haydn's *Cello Concerto in C* with Rostropovich and ECO for Decca

31 July — Receives First Aspen Award at Colorado, USA

4 August — Conducts *War Requiem* at Promenade concert at the Royal Albert Hall

October — Takes EOG to Russia with *Lucretia*, *Herring* and *Screw*. Awarded Royal Philharmonic Society Gold Medal

November — Begins composition of *Suite for Cello*

December — Records *Sinfonia da Requiem* with NPO and Tippett's *Songs for Ariel* with Pears for Decca

1965

London address: 99 Offord Road, N1. Changes his publisher from Boosey & Hawkes Ltd to Faber Music Ltd. Six week tour of India and Ceylon with Pears and the Prince and Princess of Hesse and the Rhine. Begins composition of *Gemini Variations* for the Jeney twins

5 March

23 March — Awarded the Order of Merit

6 April

25 May

15–27 June — 18th Aldeburgh Festival

CHRONOLOGY 101

WORKS	FIRST PERFORMANCES
Cadenzas to Haydn's Cello Concerto in C	
	Nocturnal after John Dowland: Julian Bream, Jubilee Hall, Aldeburgh
	Curlew River: EOG, Orford Church
	Cadenzas to Haydn's Cello Concerto in C: Mstislav Rostropovich and the ECO conducted by Britten, Blythburgh Church
Suite for Cello, Op. 72	
Gemini Variations, Op. 73, quartet for two players	
Songs and Proverbs of William Blake, Op. 74, for baritone and piano	
Chacony (Purcell ed. Britten), for strings	

1965   LIFE

19 June

24 June   Edits Purcell's *When night her purple veil had softly spread*

27 June

           Records *Curlew River* with EOG for Decca

July

August   Holiday with Pears in Armenia, with Mstislav and Galina Rostropovich

23 August

28 August–   Attends Britten Festival at Yerevan, Armenia
1 September

7 October

9 October   Receives Wihuri Sibelius Prize in Helsinki

24 October

2 December

           Records *Songs and Proverbs of William Blake* with Fischer-Dieskau for Decca

1965/66   Sketches Variations for piano (incomplete) for second Leeds International Piano Competition

1966
2 February   Completes composition sketch of *The Burning Fiery Furnace*

CHRONOLOGY 103

WORKS	FIRST PERFORMANCES
	Gemini Variations: Zoltán and Gabriel Jeney, Aldeburgh Parish Church
	Songs and Proverbs of William Blake and *When night her purple veil* (Purcell ed. Britten): Dietrich Fischer-Dieskau and the composer, Jubilee Hall, Aldeburgh
	Suite for Cello: Mstislav Rostropovich, Aldeburgh Parish Church
Voices for Today, Op. 75, for chorus and organ (ad. lib.) written for 20th Anniversary of United Nations	
The Poet's Echo, Op. 76 (Pushkin), for high voice and piano	
King Herod and the Cock (arr. Britten), for voices and piano	
	Voices for Today: simultaneous triple premiere in New York, Paris and London
	The Poet's Echo: Galina Vishnevskaya and Mstislav Rostropovich, Conservatoire of Music, Moscow

1966	*LIFE*
February	Abdominal operation in London. Convalesces in Marrakesh
5 April	
	Revises *Sweet was the Song* (1931)
May	Recital tour with Pears in Austria
	Records *Voices for Today* with Cambridge University Musical Society for Decca
8–21 June	19th Aldeburgh Festival
9 June	
15 June	
July	Records *Friday Afternoons* and *Psalm 150* with Downside School Choir and Viola Tunnard (piano) for Decca
26 August	
Summer	Makes revisions to *Gloriana* for Sadler's Wells revival
September–October	Records *A Midsummer Night's Dream* with EOG for Decca
21 October	Successful revival of *Gloriana* at Sadler's Wells
	Records *Bridge Variations* and *Les Illuminations* with Pears and ECO for Decca
11 December	
Christmas	Recital tour with Pears in USSR. Christmas with Rostropovichs in Moscow
1967	Completes new realized edition of Purcell's *The Fairy Queen* with Imogen Holst

WORKS	FIRST PERFORMANCES
The Burning Fiery Furnace, Op. 77 (Plomer), parable for church performance	
Sweet was the Song the Virgin Sung, for women's voices	
	The Burning Fiery Furnace: EOG, Orford Church
	Sweet was the Song the Virgin Sung: Purcell Singers directed by Imogen Holst, Aldeburgh Parish Church
	Cadenzas to Mozart's Piano Concerto in E flat (K.482): Sviatoslav Richter
The Golden Vanity, Op. 78 (Graham), vaudeville for boys and piano	
Hankin Booby, for wind and drums	
The Fairy Queen (Purcell ed. Britten and I. Holst), masque for soloists, chorus and orchestra in a shortened version for concert performance by Peter Pears	

1967 LIFE

3 February	Completes composition sketch of *The Building of the House*
1 March	
16 March	
19 April	
May	Records *The Burning Fiery Furnace* with EOG for Decca
2–25 June	20th Aldeburgh Festival. HM Queen Elizabeth II, accompanied by the Duke of Edinburgh, attends the first concert in the Festival (which is recorded by Decca) and opens The Maltings Concert Hall at Snape
3 June	
25 June	
17 August	
September–October	Takes EOG to Expo '67 at Montreal where they perform *Curlew River* and *The Burning Fiery Furnace*. Recital tour with Pears to Montreal, New York, Mexico, Peru, Chile, Argentina, Uruguay and Brazil
November	Revises *I saw Three Ships* (1930) as *The Sycamore Tree*. Receives BBC commission for a television opera. Revises *The Wealden Trio* (1929). Records the *Donne Sonnets* and Holst's *Humbert Wolfe Songs* with Pears for Decca
December	Records *Billy Budd* for Decca
1968	Trip to Venice: works on *The Prodigal Son*
	Completion of *The Prodigal Son* delayed owing to illness on return from Venice

WORKS	FIRST PERFORMANCES
	Hankin Booby: ECO conducted by the composer, at the opening of the Queen Elizabeth Hall, London
The Building of the House, Op. 79, for orchestra and optional chorus	
The Oxen, for women's voices and piano	
	The Building of the House: ECO and Chorus of East Anglian Choirs conducted by the composer, The Maltings, Snape
	The Golden Vanity: Vienna Boys' Choir, The Maltings, Snape
	The Fairy Queen (Purcell ed. Britten and I. Holst): EOG conducted by Britten, The Maltings, Snape
Second Suite for Cello, Op. 80	
The Sycamore Tree, for chorus. *A Wealden Trio*, for women's voices	

1968   *LIFE*

22 April	
Spring	Starts work on scenario of *Owen Wingrave* with a libretto by Myfanwy Piper, based on the story by Henry James
25 May	Receives Sonning Prize at concert in his honour in Copenhagen
	Records *Simple Symphony* and Mozart's *Serenata notturna* (K.239) and Symphony No. 40 in G minor (K.550) for Decca
8–30 June	21st Aldeburgh Festival. Philip Ledger becomes an Artistic Director
10 June	
17 June	
19 June	
July	Records Sonatas by Schubert and Bridge with Rostropovich for Decca
Summer	Revises settings of Walter de la Mare (1928–31)
August–September	Participates with Pears in the Edinburgh International Festival which features the music of Schubert and Britten, including a performance on 1 September of *War Requiem* with Vishnevskaya, Pears and Fischer-Dieskau conducted by Giulini and Britten
10 November	
December	Records 'Salute to Percy Grainger', Schubert songs with Pears, Bach's *Brandenburg Concertos*, and music for strings by Purcell, Elgar, Delius and Bridge for Decca

WORKS	FIRST PERFORMANCES
The Prodigal Son, Op. 81 (Plomer), parable for church performance	
	The Prodigal Son: EOG, Orford Church
	Second Suite for Cello: Mstislav Rostropovich, The Maltings, Snape
	The Sycamore Tree and *A Wealden Trio*: Ambrosian Singers directed by Philip Ledger, Aldeburgh Parish Church
Tit for Tat (de la Mare), for voice and piano	
Children's Crusade (Kinderkreuzzug), Op. 82, ballad for children's voices and orchestra	

1968	*LIFE*
22 December	Conducts Bach concert at St Andrew's, Holborn
1969	
6–13 January	Recitals with Pears at Schloss Elmau for tenth anniversary season of 'Britisch–Deutsche Musiktage'
	Edits *Five Spiritual Songs (Geistliche Lieder)* of J. S. Bach
February	Conducts BBC Television production of *Peter Grimes*, with Pears in the title role, at The Maltings
18 March	
Spring	Revises piano waltzes (1923–5)
6 April	Conducts chamber orchestra in *War Requiem* at Royal Albert Hall, with Giulini
	Begins composition of *Owen Wingrave*
19 May	
May	Records *The Prodigal Son* with EOG for Decca
7–29 June	22nd Aldeburgh Festival. Colin Graham becomes an Artistic Director. The Maltings Concert Hall burns down on the first night of the festival
10 June	Conducts Mozart's *Idomeneo* at Blythburgh Church
18 June	
23 June	
24 June	
Summer	

CHRONOLOGY

WORKS

Five Spiritual Songs (Geistlich Lieder) (Bach ed. Britten with English translation by Pears), for high voice and piano

Suite for Harp, Op. 83

Five Walztes (Waltzes), for piano

Who are these children?, Op. 84 (Soutar), for tenor and piano

FIRST PERFORMANCES

Children's Crusade: Wandsworth School Choir and Orchestra directed by Russell Burgess, St Paul's Cathedral, London

Five Spiritual Songs (Geistliche Lieder) (Bach ed. Britten): Peter Pears and Britten, Blythburgh Church

Tit for Tat: John Shirley-Quirk and the composer, Jubilee Hall, Aldeburgh

Suite for Harp, Osian Ellis, Jubilee Hall, Aldeburgh

1969   *LIFE*

August

6 September	Conducts EOG *Idomeneo* at Queen Elizabeth Hall
September	Conducts *The Rape of Lucretia* at Sadler's Wells with Janet Baker as Lucretia
October	Recital tour with Pears of New York and Boston in aid of the rebuilding of The Maltings. Records *The Golden Vanity* and *Children's Crusade* with Wandsworth School Choir for Decca
2 November	BBC TV broadcast of *Peter Grimes*
10 December	Conducts Mozart/Britten concert at Royal Festival Hall
19 December	Conducts Bach's *Christmas Oratorio* at Southwark Cathedral. Due to Musician's Union dispute over Philip Ledger (harpsichord), ECO called out on strike; Britten conducts with organ and harpsichord only
1970	London address: 8 Halliford Street, N1. Purchases Chapel House, Horham, Suffolk
February	Completes composition sketch of *Owen Wingrave*
Spring	Takes EOG to Australia. Recital tour with Pears of Australia and New Zealand
10 May	Conducts EOG production of *Idomeneo* for BBC TV
14 May	Formation of Aldeburgh Festival–Snape Maltings Foundation announced
16 May	Takes part in Acoustics Test Concert in rebuilt Maltings
June	
5–28 June	23rd Aldeburgh Festival, HM Queen Elizabeth II and the Duke of Edinburgh attend the opening concert in the rebuilt Maltings. Festival includes *Idomeneo* conducted by Britten and a recital of Schubert's last songs with Pears, and on 14 June Britten conducts the first performance outside the USSR of Shostakovich's *Symphony No. 14*, which is dedicated to him

WORKS	FIRST PERFORMANCES
Dawtie's Devotion, Tradition, The Gully (discarded songs from *Who are these children?*)	
A Fanfare for D.W. [David Webster]	

1970   *LIFE*

30 June

July — Records *The Rape of Lucretia* with EOG, the *Violin Concerto* with Lubotsky and Mozart's 'Prague' Symphony (K.504) with ECO for Decca

August

September — Records Purcell's *The Fairy Queen* with EOG for Decca

10–17 October — Holiday with Pears and the Princess of Hesse and the Rhine in Iceland

15 November — Pre-recorded recital with Pears of Schubert's *Winterreise* on BBC TV (recorded Sept. 9–11)

22–30 November — Conducts BBC TV production of *Owen Wingrave*, filmed at The Maltings

December — Records *Owen Wingrave* with EOG and *Piano Concerto* with Richter and ECO for Decca

13 December — Conducts for 'An Evening of Music' at the Royal Opera House in aid of Snape Maltings, in the presence of HM Queen Elizabeth the Queen Mother, Patron of the Aldeburgh Festival

1971
January

12–22 January

30 January–10 February — Working holiday with Pears and John and Myfanwy Piper on *Death in Venice* in South of France

February — Records Mozart's Symphony No. 29 (K.201) with ECO for Decca

23 February — Begins composition of *Third Suite for Cello*

3 March

7 March

WORKS	FIRST PERFORMANCES
	A Fanfare for D.W. [David Webster]: Royal Opera House, Covent Garden, London
Owen Wingrave, Op. 85 (M. Piper), opera for television	
A New Year Carol, for SSA and piano (from *Friday Afternoons*)	
Canticle IV: Journey of the Magi, Op. 86 (T. S. Eliot), for countertenor, tenor, baritone and piano	
Third Suite for Cello, Op. 87	
	Songs from *Who are these children?*: Peter Pears and the composer, New Hall, Department of Music, University College, Cardiff Festival

1971	*LIFE*
April	Records Bach's *St John Passion* for Decca
9 April	Conducts a performance of the *St John Passion* at The Maltings
14–24 April	Takes part, with Pears, in a festival of British music in Leningrad and Moscow
18 April	Broadcast of BBC TV production of EOG *The Burning Fiery Furnace* directed by the composer
4 May	
9 May	
16 May	
4–27 June	24th Aldeburgh Festival
9 June	Conducts Elgar's *The Dream of Gerontius* with Pears and the Mozart *Requiem* at The Maltings
13 June	
26 June	
July	Records *The Dream of Gerontius* for Decca
September	Conducts *The Fairy Queen* in a Promenade Concert at the Royal Albert Hall. Records Symphonies by Mozart and Schubert with ECO for Decca
October	Trip to Venice with Pears and John and Myfanwy Piper. Starts work on *Death in Venice* with a libretto by Myfanwy Piper, based on the novella by Thomas Mann
November	

WORKS	FIRST PERFORMANCES
	Who are these children? (first complete performance): Peter Pears and the composer, National Gallery of Scotland, Edinburgh
God Save the Queen (arr. Britten), for orchestra	
	Owen Wingrave (broadcast premiere, BBC2): EOG and ECO conducted by the composer
	God Save the Queen (arr. Britten): ECO conducted by Britten, The Maltings, Snape
	Canticle IV: James Bowman, Peter Pears, John Shirley-Quirk and the composer, The Maltings, Snape
Alleluia! For Alec's 80th Birthday (for Alec Robertson)	

1972   LIFE

1972
Spring   Visits Schloss Wolfsgarten and continues work on *Death in Venice*

2–19 June   25th Aldeburgh Festival

11 June   Conducts Schumann's *Scenes from Goethe's 'Faust'* at The Maltings

June–July   Holiday with Pears and the Princess of Hesse and the Rhine in the Shetlands

3–12 September   Records Schumann's *Scenes from Goethe's 'Faust'* for Decca, the last occasion Britten conducted

22 September   Last Britten–Pears recital at The Maltings includes *Winter Words*. This formed part of the first of the master-class courses at The Maltings from which developed the Britten–Pears School for Advanced Musical Studies

November   Records *Canticle IV*, *Tit for Tat*, *Who are these children?*, and songs by Purcell and Schubert, with Pears, Bowman and Shirley-Quirk, for Decca. Supervises recording of second 'Salute to Percy Grainger' for Decca conducted by Steuart Bedford

17 December   Completes composition of *Death in Venice* (ending revised on 24 December)

1973
7–11 January   Gives last public recitals with Pears at Schloss Elmau, West Germany, including *Winterreise* and Schumann's *Sechs Gedichte*, Op. 90

March   Visits Wolfsgarten

7 May   Open heart surgery at National Heart Hospital, London, which leaves him an invalid

CHRONOLOGY 119

WORKS   *FIRST PERFORMANCES*

Death in Venice, Op. 88 (M. Piper),
opera in two acts

1973 LIFE

10 May

15 June–2 July | 26th Aldeburgh Festival, Britten convalescing at Horham and unable to attend

16 June

27 August | Makes minor revisions to *Death in Venice*
12 September | Sees *Death in Venice* for the first time in a special private performance at The Maltings
2–12 October | Trip with Pears to Wales
18 October | Attends London premiere of *Death in Venice* at Covent Garden

October | Holiday with Donald and Kathleen Mitchell at Barcombe Mills, Sussex
22 November | 60th Birthday
25 November | Day of celebration in the press and on radio and television

1974 | Revises *Death in Venice* and *String Quartet in D major* (1931). Rita Thomson, his nurse, joins staff at the Red House

Easter | Attends Decca recording of *Death in Venice* at The Maltings

7–24 June | 27th Aldeburgh Festival. Steuart Bedford becomes an Artistic Director

23 June

July

WORKS	FIRST PERFORMANCES
	Owen Wingrave (stage premiere): EOG, ECO conducted by Steuart Bedford, Royal Opera House, Covent Garden
	Death in Venice: Peter Pears, John Shirley-Quirk, EOG, ECO conducted by Steuart Bedford, The Maltings, Snape
	Death in Venice (London premiere): Peter Pears, John Shirley-Quirk, EOG, ECO conducted by Steuart Bedford, Royal Opera House, Covent Garden
String Quartet in D major (1931)	
	Excerpts from *Paul Bunyan* (European premiere): Heather Harper, Janet Baker, Peter Pears, John Shirley-Quirk with Steuart Bedford (piano), The Maltings, Snape
Canticle V: The Death of Saint Narcissus, Op. 89 (T. S. Eliot), for tenor and harp	

1974   LIFE

Summer	Holiday with Donald and Kathleen Mitchell at Barcombe Mills, Sussex. Works on revision of *Paul Bunyan*
October	Visits Schloss Wolfsgarten and begins composition of *Suite on English Folk Tunes*
16 November	
	Awarded the Ravel Prize
December	Begins composition of *Sacred and Profane*
21 December	

1975

January	Revises *Paul Bunyan* (1941)
15 January	
21 March	*A Birthday Hansel*, written at the request of HM The Queen for the 75th birthday of HM Queen Elizabeth The Queen Mother
May	Holiday with Pears on the Oxford Canal
6–23 June	28th Aldeburgh Festival
7 June	
13 June	
7 July	Attends revival of *Death in Venice* at Covent Garden
9 July	Attends new production of *Peter Grimes* at Covent Garden, with Jon Vickers as Grimes, conducted by Colin Davis.
12 August	
14 September	

CHRONOLOGY

WORKS	FIRST PERFORMANCES
Suite on English Folk Tunes, Op. 90, 'A time there was . . .', for orchestra	
	Third Suite for Cello: Mstislav Rostropovich, The Maltings, Snape (postponed from June 1972)
Sacred and Profane, Op. 91, for unaccompanied voices	
	Canticle V: Peter Pears and Osian Ellis, Schloss Elmau, Upper Bavaria
A Birthday Hansel, Op. 92 (Burns), for high voice and harp	
	String Quartet in D major: Gabrieli String Quartet, The Maltings, Snape
	Suite on English Folk Tunes: ECO conducted by Steuart Bedford, The Maltings, Snape
Phaedra, Op. 93, dramatic cantata for mezzo-soprano and small orchestra	
	Sacred and Profane: Wilbye Consort directed by Peter Pears, The Maltings, Snape

	· LIFE
1975	
October	Begins composition of *String Quartet No. 3*
November	Final visit to Venice where he completes the *String Quartet No. 3*
1974/76	
1976	Orchestrates *Lachrymae*
5 January	
1 February	
February	
19 March	
2 May	
4–20 June	29th Aldeburgh Festival
4 June	
12 June	Created a Life Peer, Baron Britten of Aldeburgh in the County of Suffolk, in the Birthday Honours List
16 June	
July	Last holiday with Pears to Bergen, Norway. Begins composition of Cantata on Edith Sitwell's 'Praise we great men'
19 August	

CHRONOLOGY

WORKS **FIRST PERFORMANCES**

String Quartet No. 3, Op. 94

Considers texts for a Christmas Sequence and a Sea symphony

Tema – 'Sacher', for solo cello

Paul Bunyan (broadcast premiere): BBC Northern Singers and Symphony Orchestra conducted by Steuart Bedford (recorded April, 1975)

Lachrymae, Op. 48a, for viola and string orchestra

A Birthday Hansel: Peter Pears and Osian Ellis, New Hall, Music Department, University College, Cardiff

Tema – 'Sacher': Mstislav Rostropovich, Tonhalle, Zürich

Paul Bunyan (revised version, stage premiere): English Music Theatre (successor to EOG) conducted by Steuart Bedford, The Maltings, Snape

Phaedra: Janet Baker and ECO conducted by Steuart Bedford, The Maltings, Snape

Welcome Ode, Op. 95, for young people's chorus and orchestra, written for Suffolk schoolchildren to perform in 1977 (Silver Jubilee Year)

1976   *LIFE*

Summer

28–29 September   Works on the *String Quartet No. 3* with the Amadeus Quartet in the Library at the Red House

October–November Continues work on Sitwell Cantata but becoming considerably weaker

late November

4 December   Dies at his home in Aldeburgh

7 December   Funeral Service and Burial at Aldeburgh Parish Church

19 December

WORKS	FIRST PERFORMANCES
Eight Folk Song Arrangements (arr. Britten), for voice and harp (or piano)	
	Oh, that I'd ne'er been married (broadcast premiere, Thames TV): Pears and Roger Vignoles
	String Quartet No. 3: Amadeus String Quartet, The Maltings, Snape

BENJAMIN BRITTEN
THE INCIDENTAL MUSIC:
A CATALOGUE RAISONNÉ
BY PHILIP REED AND JOHN EVANS

CATALOGUE RAISONNÉ

This catalogue of Benjamin Britten's incidental music is divided into three chronological lists under the genres of Film (p. 131), Theatre (p. 144) and Radio (p. 154). The title of each work is given together with the date of composition of Britten's score. The catalogue's format owes something to Eric Walter White's important article 'Britten in the Theatre: a provisional catalogue' (*Tempo*, 107, 1973). Indeed, a debt of gratitude must be paid to the late Mr White for his pioneering work on Britten's incidental music (see 'Bibliography of Benjamin Britten's Incidental Music', in *Benjamin Britten: a commentary on his music from a group of specialists*; edited by Donald Mitchell and Hans Keller. London, Rockliffe, 1952). It is now thirty-five years since Mr White's original catalogue was first published and further research – particularly since the opening of the Britten–Pears Library – has brought to light many previously unknown or simply forgotten incidental music scores. While no catalogue of this kind can ever claim with absolute certainty to be complete, every effort has been made to approach that ideal.

Unless otherwise stated, all Britten's manuscripts listed in this catalogue are preserved in the Britten–Pears Library, Aldeburgh. Those manuscripts belonging to the British Library are on permanent loan to the Britten–Pears Library.

BIBLIOGRAPHICAL ABBREVIATIONS

BA   Mitchell, Donald, *Britten and Auden in the Thirties: the year 1936*. London, Faber and Faber, 1981.
EA   *The English Auden – poems, essays and dramatic writings 1927–1939*; edited by Edward Mendelson. London, Faber and Faber, 1977.
LM   Coulton, Barbara, *Louis MacNeice in the BBC*. London, Faber and Faber, 1980.
PL   Mitchell, Donald, and Evans, John, *Benjamin Britten, 1913–76: Pictures from a Life*. London, Faber and Faber, 1978.

GENERAL ABBREVIATIONS

A	alto	pf	piano
acd	accordion	pic	piccolo
B	bass (voice)	S	soprano
b	bass	sax	saxophone
Bar	baritone	sd	side drum
bcl	bass clarinet	str	strings
bd	bass drum	str qt	string quartet
bl	block	str qnt	string quintet
bn	bassoon	sus cym	suspended cymbal
ca	cor anglais	T	tenor (voice)
cast	castanets	t	tenor
cel	celesta	tamb	tambourine
cl	clarinet	td	tenor drum
cor	cornet	timp	timpani
cym	cymbals	tpt	trumpet
db	double bass	trbn	trombone
dbn	double bassoon	trgl	triangle
euph	euphonium	uke	ukelele
glock	glockenspiel	v(v)	voice(s)
hn	horn	va	viola
hpd	harpsichord	vc	violoncello
Mez	mezzo-soprano	vib	vibraphone
ob	oboe	vn	violin
org	organ	xyl	xylophone
perc	percussion		

MUSIC FOR FILM

The King's Stamp April–May 1935
GPO Film Unit/EMPO[1]
Director: William Coldstream

The first work undertaken by Britten for the GPO Film Unit. The film documented the preparation of the King George V Silver Jubilee stamp and featured the stamp's designer, Barnett Friedmann.

---

[1] 'EMPO' was the purely fictitious name invented by John Grierson and used by him at the GPO as the brand name for experimental material. *The King's Stamp* probably merits the 'EMPO' label by virtue of the use of the Dufay colour process during a number of sequences.

MSS: Composition sketch (pencil), an early version scored for 2 pianos
Composition sketch (pencil)
Full score, autograph (ink, pencil)
Instrumental parts, autograph (ink)
Scoring: fl (doubling pic), cl (B flat, A), perc (trgl, sus cym, cym, bl, sd, bd), 2 pf

A fairly extensive score including some characteristic 'machine' music to accompany the sequence at the stamp printing works. Some music written for this film was redubbed for use in other GPO films, including *Men of the Alps* and *Mony a Pickle* (below pp. 140 and 143).

Coal Face   May–June 1935
GPO Film Unit/EMPO
Producer: John Grierson   Director and script: Alberto Cavalcanti
Verse: W. H. Auden, Montagu Slater

One of the most famous of the GPO Film Unit's experimental documentaries, an informative account of the coal industry in Britain.

MSS: Composition sketch (pencil)
Full score, autograph (ink)
Chorus part, non-autograph (ink)
Scoring: commentator, whistler, chorus (SATB); perc (tamb, sus cym, sd, bd), pf

The most extended musical sequence in the film, culminating in the first Britten setting of an Auden text, occurs after the shift has ended and the miners are returning to the surface. This sequence begins with the whirling sound of the pit wheel (a continuous roll with side-drum sticks on suspended cymbal) and the low texture of male voices underground. The piano moves slowly from its lower regions to its highest register as the men rise to the surface. At this point female voices take over with Britten's setting of the Auden lyric 'O lurcher-loving collier'.[2]

A later sequence (concerning the distribution and costs of produce and transport) is scored for commentator and an enlarged experimental percussion orchestra in which Britten used the reversed sound-track of a cymbal struck with a hard beater to achieve the 'whoosh' effect of a train. The resourceful percussion score is laid out as follows:

  1   side drum, block, triangle, cymbal, bass drum, gong

---

[2] See *EA*, p. 290.

CATALOGUE RAISONNÉ   133

2   chains, 2 coconut shells, large drill, cup in bucket of water, sandpaper
3   sandpaper, trip gear, notched wood & wooden stick, sheet of metal & wooden mallet
4   wooden whistle, small cart on sandy asbestos, small drill, rewinder, hooter, chains.

In addition to the composer's music manuscripts, a number of typed sheets of text material with several additional pages of handwritten notes, including quotations of passages from Pope, Keats and Shelley, have survived.

Telegrams July 1935
GPO Film Unit

MSS: Composition sketch (pencil)
        Instrumental parts, non-autograph (ink)
Scoring: boys' vv; fl, ob, cl(A), 2 perc (glock, xyl, trgl, sus cym, sd), pf

It has proved impossible to match this music to a known GPO Film. Although it was originally believed to belong to the GPO animated film *H.P.O.* (Heavenly Post Office) – sometimes also known as *6d. Telegram* – the credits of *H.P.O.* attribute the music to Brian Easdale. For reasons unknown Britten's score was not used. *H.P.O.* was not released until 1938.

The Tocher[3] July 1935
GPO Film Unit
Producer: Alberto Cavalcanti   Animator: Lotte Reiniger

Described as a 'film ballet', this silhouette film advertised the virtues of the Post Office Savings Bank.

MSS: Composition sketch (pencil)
        Full score entitled 'Rossini-Suite', autograph (ink)
        Instrumental parts, autograph and non-autograph (ink, pencil)
Scoring: boys' vv; fl (doubling pic), ob, cl (B flat, A), 2 perc (glock, xyl, trgl, tamb, sus cym, bl, cast, sd, bd), pf

This score consists of arrangements of music by Rossini; Britten later re-orchestrated some of this music for *Soirées Musicales*, Op. 9 and *Matinées Musicales*, Op. 24. The third movement of the film score – 'Passo

---

[3] *Tocher* (Scots): marriage portion or dowry.

a sei' from *Gugliemo Tell* – also appears in two later films, *Calendar of the Year* and *Men of the Alps* (below p. 139 and p. 140).

C.T.O. – The Story of the Central Telegraph Office   July 1935
GPO Film Unit
Producer: Stuart Legg

The history and development of the Central Telegraph Office in London.

MSS: Composition sketch (pencil)
          Full score, autograph (ink)
Scoring: fl, ob, cl (B flat), 2 perc (xyl, sd), pf

Britten's score consists of title and end title music only.

Gas Abstract   August–September 1935
? British Commercial Gas Association/Gas, Light & Coke Co.

MSS: Composition sketch (pencil)
          Full score, autograph (ink)
Scoring: fl, cl (B flat), bn, perc (trgl, tamb, sus cym, sd, bd), pf

It has been impossible to match this music to a film. The manuscript indicates that it may once have been called 'Coal Abstract'.

God's Chillun   September–November 1935
GPO Film Unit
Script: W. H. Auden   Editors: Max Anderson, Gordon Hales and Rona Morrison

During the autumn of 1935 Britten, Auden and William Coldstream worked together on a documentary provisionally entitled 'Negroes'. This ambitious project appears to have been abandoned for financial reasons in early November 1935. The idea was revived in a much revised form two years later; not released at the time, it deals with the slave trade in the West Indies.

MSS: Full score entitled 'Negroes', autograph (ink)
Scoring: commentator, S, T, B, chorus (TB); ob (doubling ca, tamb), 2 perc (tamb, sus cym, 3 tam, sd, td, bd), harp, pf (doubling bd)

There is a link between this project and the Auden–Isherwood play *The Ascent of F6*, for which Britten provided incidental music in 1937 (see below pp. 146–7). A page of text belonging to the 'Negroes' project comprises four stanzas written in Britten's hand, beginning 'Acts of injustice done'. These words, though not set in the score, are spoken at the end of the film, as indicated by the following pencil note which appears after the final page of score: 'Acts of injustice done? 1st & last verses'.[4] These same stanzas reappear in a different context at the end of *The Ascent of F6*, in a section for which Britten did provide music.[5]

Men Behind the Meters September 1935
British Commercial Gas Association
Director: Arthur Elton

The training of gas fitters, and the development and testing of domestic gas appliances.

MSS: Composition sketch, fragment (pencil)
  Full score, autograph (ink)
  Discarded page of full score, autograph (ink)
Scoring: fl, ob, cl (B flat, A), perc (glock, trgl, sus cym, bl, sd, bd), pf, vn, vc

Although this film is quite lengthy, Britten had to provide music for only two sequences in addition to the usual title and end title, including an arrangement of the song 'I dreamt that I dwelt in marble halls' from *The Bohemian Girl* by Michael Balfe.

Dinner Hour September 1935
British Commercial Gas Association
Producer: Arthur Elton Director: Edgar Anstey

A promotional film, released in 1936, illustrating the manufacture of gas and its use by a large bakery, a West End restaurant, a hospital kitchen and a staff canteen.

MSS: Composition sketch (pencil)
  Full score, autograph (ink)
Scoring: fl, cl (A), perc (trgl, sd), pf, vn, vc

The score consists of title and end title music only.

---

[4] For an extract of the 'Negroes' script, including these four stanzas, see *EA*, pp. 292–3.
[5] See W. H. Auden and Christopher Isherwood, *The Ascent of F6*. London, Faber and Faber, 1972, p. 96.

Title Music III September 1935
British Commercial Gas Association

MSS: Full score, autograph (ink)
Scoring: fl (doubling pic), cl (B flat), perc (sus cym, bd), pf, vn, vc

It has been impossible to match this music to a known documentary film. Britten's diary entries for September 1935 and the manuscript itself indicate that it was written for another BCGA film, commissioned at the same time as *Men Behind the Meters* and *Dinner Hour*.

These 'gas film' manuscripts were originally placed in the order:
– I dreamt that I dwelt in marble halls, *Men Behind the Meters*
– Title Music I, *Men Behind the Meters*
– Title Music II, *Dinner Hour*
– Title Music III [no subtitle],
possibly the sequence in which they were recorded.

How the Dial Works September 1935
GPO Film Unit
Producers: Ralph Elton and Rona Morrison

A short film explaining the principles behind the automatic telephone exchange, released in 1937.

MSS: Full score, autograph (ink)
Scoring: fl, ob, cl (B flat), 2 perc (glock, trgl, sus cym, bl, sd, bd), pf

The score consists of title and end title music only; the end title was apparently not used in the film.

Conquering Space – The Story of Modern Communications
GPO Film Unit September 1935
Producer: Stuart Legg

A brief history of transport and communications with special emphasis on the Post Office's services.

MSS: Full score, autograph (ink)
Scoring: fl, ob, cl (B flat, A), bn, perc (tamb, sus cym, bl, sd, bd), pf

The music for this film (three sequences in all) included music from two differently named manuscripts – 'Modern Post Office Methods' and 'Methods of Communication'. From a total of five sequences, two are not used in this film: 'Modern P.O. Methods: Radio mast sequence' and

'Methods of Communication: Title and End Title'. Possibly they were found to be unsuitable and discarded, and were later incorporated into another film.

Sorting Office September 1935
GPO Film Unit
Director: Harry Watt

Originally a silent film. Britten provided music for a projected sound version of this film which, for reasons unknown, was never made. The music may have been transferred to another film, as yet unidentified.

MSS: Full score, autograph (ink)
Scoring: fl, ob, cl (B flat), bn, perc (sd), pf

The score consists of title and end title music only.

The Savings Bank September 1935
GPO Film Unit
Producer: Stuart Legg

A short film illustrating the workings of the Post Office Savings Bank.

MSS: Full score, autograph (ink)
Scoring: fl, ob, cl (A), bn, perc (sd), pf

The manuscript bears an additional pencil title: 'Banking for 1,000,000s'. The score consists of title and end title music only.

The New Operator September 1935
Empire Marketing Board Film Unit[6]/GPO Film Unit
Producer: John Grierson   Director: Stuart Legg

A silent film with this title was made by the Empire Marketing Board Film Unit for the Post Office in 1932–3. As with *Sorting Office*, Britten provided music for a projected sound version which was not made.

MSS: Full score, autograph (ink)
Discarded page of full score, autograph (ink), now forming the outer cover of the full score of 'Negroes' (*God's Chillun*, see above p. 134)
Scoring: fl, ob, cl (B flat), bn, perc (trgl), pf

The score consists of title and end title music only.

---

[6] The Empire Marketing Board Film Unit (EMB) was the immediate forerunner of the GPO Film Unit, and like its successor was administered by John Grierson.

Night Mail
GPO Film Unit

November 1935–January 1936

Producer: John Grierson   Directors: Harry Watt and Basil Wright
Script: John Grierson, Harry Watt and Basil Wright
Verse: W. H. Auden   Sound supervision: Alberto Cavalcanti

The special postal express train collecting, sorting and delivering mail as it travels overnight from London to Glasgow. One of the most celebrated documentary films of the 1930s.

MSS: Composition sketch (pencil)
Full score, autograph (ink)
Discarded page of full score, autograph (ink), all British Library Additional MS No. 60621

Scoring: commentator, fl, ob, bn, tpt (C), perc (sus cym, sandpaper, sd, bd, wind machine), harp, str qt (vn, va, vc, db)

Britten employs an experimental percussion orchestra (as he did in *Coal Face*, see above p. 132) to portray the steam engine:

I   Steam (compressed air)
II Sandpaper on slate
III Rail (small trolley)
IV Booms (clank)
V   { Aluminium on Drill
      Motor Moy [hand-cranked, chain-operated camera]
VI { Hammer on Conduit
             Boom
      Siren
VII Coal falling down shaft

The end sequence comprises Britten's setting of Auden's specially written verse, 'This is the night mail crossing the border'.[7]

GPO Title Music 1 and 2

November 1935

MSS: Full score, autograph (ink)
Scoring: fl, ob, bn, tpt (C), perc (trgl, sus cym, sd, bd), harp, str qt (vn, va, vc, db)

It has been impossible to match either of these scores to known documentary films. Both open with the same trumpet fanfare that

---

[7] See *EA*, pp. 290–2. The first page of Britten's manuscript of this end sequence is reproduced in *PL*, plate 94.

features prominently in *Night Mail*. The title musics may possibly be preliminary essays for *Night Mail*.

Calendar of the Year March, September–October 1936
GPO Film Unit
Producer: Alberto Cavalcanti   Director: Evelyn Spice

A film about the role played by Post Office communications throughout the year. It was released in 1937, although Britten's diaries reveal that he was first approached for music as early as November 1935. W. H. Auden makes a brief appearance as Father Christmas.

MSS: Instrumental parts, autograph (ink, pencil)
vn for winter, spring and autumn sequences;
fl, vn, va, vc, harp for docks sequence
Scoring: fl, cl, tpt, trbn, perc, harp, str qnt (2 vn, va, vc, db)[8]

Apart from Britten's original music, the score also includes a small number of self-borrowings, one of them from the Rossini arrangements made for *The Tocher* (see above p. 133). Towards the end of *Calendar of the Year* there is a sequence of Christmas music performed by voices to the accompaniment of a Salvation Army band with organ.

Peace of Britain March 1936
Strand Films
Producer: Paul Rotha

A short anti-war propaganda film made under the Strand label for Freenat Films, the League of Nations Film Unit.

MSS: Full score, autograph (ink)
Scoring: fl, cl (B flat), tpt (B flat), perc (sus cym, sd, bd), pf, str qnt (2 vn, va, vc, db)

Around the Village Green April, September–October 1936
Travel and Industrial Development Association
Producers and directors: Marion Grierson and Evelyn Spice

MSS: Instrumental parts entitled 'Irish Reel' (title music), non-autograph (ink)
Scoring: 2 fl, (II doubling pic), ob, cl (B flat), tpt (B flat), trbn, timp, harp, str

---

[8] Scoring deduced from Britten's diary, other film scores recorded during the same session and the film soundtrack.

This is one of Britten's finest film scores, incorporating a riotous medley of folksongs and traditional tunes arranged for large orchestra, including a version of Shield's 'The Ploughboy'.

Men of the Alps September–October 1936
GPO Film Unit/Pro Telephon, Zürich
Producer: Harry Watt   Director: Alberto Cavalcanti

A study of Swiss geography and history.

MSS: Full score entitled 'Swiss Telephone',[9] autograph (ink)
Scoring: fl (doubling pic), cl (B flat), tpt (C), perc (trgl, tamb, sus cym, bd), harp, str qnt (2 vn, va, vc, db)

Men of the Alps comprises original music by Britten, Rossini arranged by Walter Leigh and Britten (including a reappearance of part of Britten's 1935 'Rossini-Suite' composed for *The Tocher*, above p. 133) and a sequence of the 'machine music' from *The King's Stamp* (above, pp. 131–2). In his original music Britten incorporates Swiss folksong.

Line to the Tschierva Hut September–November 1936
GPO Film Unit/Pro Telephon, Zürich
Producer: John Grierson   Director and script: Alberto Cavalcanti

The laying of the telephone line to the Tschierva mountain hut above Pontresina, Switzerland. Released in 1937.

MSS: Full score entitled 'Swiss Telephone', autograph (ink, pencil)
Scoring: fl (doubling pic), cl (B flat), tpt (C), perc (trgl, tamb, sus cym, bd) harp, str qnt (2 vn, va, vc, db)

Message from Geneva ?September–November 1936
GPO Film Unit/Pro Telephon, Zürich
Director and script: Alberto Cavalcanti

The importance of the landline linking the BBC in London with Geneva, the centre of international affairs. Released in 1937.

MSS: Missing
Scoring: Unknown

---

[9] 'Swiss Telephone' would seem to be the source manuscript for at least two films: *Men of the Alps* and *Line to the Tschierva Hut*. Two other films made by the GPO under the same contract with Pro Telephon, Zürich – *Message to Geneva* and *Four Barriers* – have music which has been attributed to Britten.

Four Barriers ?September–November 1936
GPO Film Unit/Pro Telephon, Zürich
Producer: Harry Watt

An account of Swiss economics illustrating how the Swiss overcame the four barriers of mountains, lack of raw materials, and political and economic nationalism. Released in 1937. Music by Britten and John Foulds.

MSS: Missing
Scoring: Unknown

The Saving of Bill Blewitt October 1936
GPO Film Unit
Producers: John Grierson and Alberto Cavalcanti
Director and script: Alberto Cavalcanti

A new direction in the development of the documentary: the story or anecdotal film. Shot in the Cornish fishing village of Mousehole with a cast consisting mainly of local people. Released in 1937.

MSS: Missing
Scoring: fl, cl, tpt, trbn, perc, harp, str qnt (2 vn, va, vc, db)[10]

In addition to the title and end title music, there is a brief sequence featuring a solo tuba.

Love from a Stranger November 1936
Trafalgar Films
Producer: Max Schach   Director: Rowland V. Lee
Screenplay: Frances Marion   Musical director: Boyd Neel

Britten's only feature film score. The film (with Ann Harding and Basil Rathbone) was based upon Frank Vosper's stage play of the short story *Philomel Cottage* by Agatha Christie. It received its gala premiere in London on 7 January 1937.

MSS: Composition sketch (pencil)
Scoring: 2 fl, 2 ob, 2 cl, alto sax (E flat), bn, 2 tpt, 2 trbn, perc (xyl, sus cym, cym, bd, tam), harp, str

---

[10] Scoring deduced from Britten's diary, other film scores recorded during the same session and the film soundtrack.

Apart from Britten's original music, the film included music from Grieg's *Peer Gynt Suite No. 1*, 'In the Hall of the Mountain King', and dance music by Phil Green and his band. Britten's music includes a long waltz-like movement using the seductive sounds of the solo saxophone.

The Way to the Sea December 1936
Strand Films for Southern Railways
Producer: Paul Rotha   Director: John B. Holmes
Verse: W. H. Auden

An historical representation of Portsmouth and the London–Portsmouth road is followed by a journey on the electrified London–Portsmouth railway line. Released in 1937.

MSS: Composition sketch (pencil)
         Full score, autograph and non-autograph (ink, pencil)
         Instrumental parts, autograph (ink, pencil)
Scoring: commentator; fl (doubling pic), ob (doubling ca), cl (B flat, A), alto sax (E flat), tpt (C), t trbn, perc (xyl, trgl, sus cym, cym, foot cym, sd, td, bd, wind machine), harp, pf

The most impressive feature of this score is the extended final sequence comprising Auden's specially written verse commentary beginning 'The line waits'.[11] There is also a series of pastiche numbers to accompany the historical sequence.

Book Bargain ?1937
GPO Film Unit
Director: Norman McLaren

The manufacture of the London Telephone Directory. Released in 1937.

MSS: Missing (except those originally belonging to *The King's Stamp*, see above pp. 131–2)
Scoring: pic, cl (A), perc (sd), 2 pf

Apart from the brief extract from sequence G of Britten's first film score (probably redubbed without his knowledge), there are three other musical sequences in the film.

[11] See *BA*, pp. 90–3.

Mony a Pickle ?1938
GPO Film Unit
Producers and directors: Alberto Cavalcanti and Richard Massingham

Like so many GPO productions, this film advocates thrift through the use of the Post Office Savings Bank. Released in 1938, music by Britten, John Foulds and Victor Yates.

MSS: Missing (except those originally belonging to *The King's Stamp*, see above pp. 131–2)
Scoring: fl (doubling pic), cl (B flat, A), perc (sd), 2 pf

This composite score includes sequences C and G from Britten's first film score (instrumentation as above) and a waltz sequence, probably not by Britten, scored for full orchestra.[12]

Advance Democracy 1938
Realistic Film Unit
Director and script: Ralph Bond

This socialist film was made for the four London Co-operative Societies. It centres around a London docker who begins to take a more active interest in his union after listening to a radio broadcast on the Co-operative movement. Released in October 1938.

MSS: Composition sketch (pencil)
Scoring: chorus (SATB); perc (?cym, sd, bd)[13]

The most notable feature of the score is the end title music, a medley of various left-wing songs including *The Internationale* and *The Red Flag*. The music written for this film is not identical to the motet *Advance Democracy* (words by Randall Swingler) written by Britten in the autumn of 1938.

The Instruments of the Orchestra 1945
Crown Film Unit
Producer: Alexander Shaw   Director: Muir Mathieson
Script: Montagu Slater

Better known as *The Young Person's Guide to the Orchestra* (and subtitled 'Variations and Fugue on a Theme of Henry Purcell'),[14] this film was

---

[12] Scoring deduced from the film soundtrack.
[13] Scoring deduced from the composition sketch and film soundtrack.
[14] The concert version of the film score with a script by Eric Crozier.

produced for the Ministry of Education and was first screened on 29 November 1946 at the Empire Theatre, Leicester Square, London. The music was performed by the London Symphony Orchestra conducted by Malcolm Sargent.

MSS: Full score, autograph (ink), Yale University, Beinecke Library, Osborn Music MS 509[15]

Scoring: pic, 2 fl, 2 ob, 2 cl (B flat, A), 2 bn, 4 hn (F), 2 tpt (C), 2 t trbn, b trbn, tuba, timp, 3 perc (xyl, trgl, tamb, cast, bl, whip, cym, sd, bd, gong), harp, str

MUSIC FOR THEATRE

Timon of Athens October–November 1935
Group Theatre
Author: William Shakespeare   Producer: Nugent Monck
Designer: Robert Medley   Choreographer: Rupert Doone
Musical director: Herbert Murrill
First performance: 19 November 1935, Westminster Theatre, London

Britten's introduction to the Group Theatre.

MSS: Composition sketch (pencil)
Full score, autograph (ink, pencil)
Piano rehearsal score of the pavane, autograph (ink)
Piano rehearsal score of a discarded pavane, autograph (ink)
Scoring: 2 ob (doubling ca), perc (glock, xyl, trgl, drums), hpd

The music includes the customary fanfares (scored for oboes) and a ballet for Doone[16] in the first banquet scene.[17] The most notable sequences are the unaccompanied cor anglais solo that precedes the death of Timon (closely foreshadowing the music of Lucretia's final entrance and suicide in *The Rape of Lucretia*) and the final funeral march coloured by the same plangent sonority.

[15] Microfilm in the Britten–Pears Library, Aldeburgh.
[16] Rupert Doone, the Group Theatre's principal producer, had been a *premier danseur* with Diaghilev's Ballets Russes.
[17] A production photograph of this scene is reproduced in *PL*, plate 99.

Easter 1916 December 1935
Left Theatre and the North London Area Committee of the Amalgamated Engineering Union
Author: Montagu Slater   Producer: André van Gyseghem
Musical director: Charles Kahn
First performance: 4 December 1935, Islington Town Hall, London
(private performance)

Britten's first collaboration with the poet and playwright Montagu Slater, who later wrote the libretto for *Peter Grimes*. *Easter 1916* was a documentary play – described by Slater as 'a chronicle, and as true to history as I could make it'[18] – beginning with the 1913 tram strike in Dublin and ending with the fighting of Easter week in 1916. Music by Britten and Albert Arlen.

MSS: Missing
Scoring: male and female vv; perc (drums, gong), acd[19]

Stay Down Miner May 1936
Left Theatre
Author: Montagu Slater   Producer: Wilfred Walter
Musical director: Charles Kahn
First performance: 10 May 1936, Westminster Theatre, London

MSS: Composition sketch (pencil)
         Full score, autograph (ink, pencil)
         Instrumental parts, autograph and non-autograph (ink, pencil)
Scoring: T or Bar, chorus (TB); cl (B flat), perc (tamb, sus cym, sandpaper, metronome, sd, td, bd), vn, vc

The score inevitably includes a good deal of 'pump' and 'pit' music. The pit music is imaginative in its exploitation of an ostinato of a metronome ticking at $\mathord{\downarrow} = 60$, taken up by various overlapping permutations of percussion instruments. There is also an atmospheric chorus entitled 'Wind Song', a setting for tenor (or baritone) and male chorus of Slater's 'These foothills which we speak of as mountains',[20] and a distortion of *Cwm Rhondda* (the Welsh hymn tune composed by John Hughes in 1907) scored for clarinet, percussion, violin and cello.

---

[18] From the Author's Note in the programme of the original production.
[19] Scoring deduced from the original programme and the published text of *Easter 1916*, London, Lawrence and Wishart, 1936.
[20] The first page of Britten's full score of 'Wind Song' is reproduced in *PL*, plate 91.

The Agamemnon October 1936
Group Theatre
Author: Aeschylus, translated Louis MacNeice
Producer and choreographer: Rupert Doone
Designer: Robert Medley[21]   Musical director: Brian Easdale
First performance: 1 November 1936, Westminster Theatre, London

MSS: Composition sketch used as a full score (pencil)
Full score of Ballet Music [I], autograph and non-autograph (ink, pencil)
Full score of Ballet Music II, autograph and non-autograph (ink, pencil)
Scoring: chorus (SATB); 2 fl, ca, cl (B flat), perc (sus cym, bl, sd, bd)

The score includes a number of fanfares, a chorus ('But Honest Dealing is clear'), a Robing Ceremony (cf. the church parables) and ballet music. In the programme for the original production Britten acknowledges the assistance of Alfred Nieman in the adaptation of the choral music, and the general assistance of Grace Williams, who studied composition at the Royal College of Music at the same time as Britten and may have acted as copyist on this occasion.

The Ascent of F6 February 1937
Group Theatre
Authors: W. H. Auden and Christopher Isherwood
Producer: Rupert Doone   Designer: Robert Medley
Musical director: Brian Easdale
First performance: 26 February 1937, Mercury Theatre, London

Britten's first music-theatre collaboration with Auden and Isherwood. The original cast included the cabaret singer Hedli Anderson (who later married Louis MacNeice), for whom Britten wrote his *Cabaret Songs*. *F6* proved to be the most successful Group Theatre production: it transferred to the Little Theatre in April 1937 and was revived at the Old Vic two years later.

MSS: Composition sketch (pencil)
Full score, autograph and non-autograph (ink), British Library Additional MS No. 60622

---

[21] Some of these designs are reproduced in *PL*, plate 98.

	Full score, discarded pages, autograph and non-autograph (ink, pencil)
	Chorus scores, non-autograph (ink), photocopies
Scoring:	female v, 2 male vv, chorus (SATB); perc (glock, trgl, tamb, sus cym, bl, sd, td, bd) uke, 2 pf

This is a fairly substantial score with an instrumental overture and an introduction to Act II, a variety of entractes, choruses and solo songs and a particularly brilliant cabaret jazz song for vocal trio, percussion and 2 pianos. 'Funeral Blues' ('Stop all the clocks')[22] from the final scene was later arranged by Britten with a revised text from Auden for solo voice and piano as one of the *Cabaret Songs*.[23] The play was much revised during its initial run,[24] hence the discarded pages from the full score which include a second song for Gunn, a melodrama ('Let the eye of the traveller consider this country and weep') and an alternative ending with the chorus 'Honour – service – Duty – sacrifice – England – OSTNIA'. Yet another possible ending is suggested by a note in Britten's hand on the back page of the full score of the Mother's Song ('Still the dark forest'): 'No. 44 Matthew O Lord, who dares to smite me [sic]'. This is written in red crayon beside the text of the last two stanzas of the play (beginning 'Free now from indignation'), the first of which is also written in the composer's hand. It is interesting to note that Auden's text for those stanzas fits perfectly the metre of the chorale from Bach's *St. Matthew Passion*.

Pageant of Empire February 1937
Left Theatre
Author: Montagu Slater   Musical director: Charles Kahn
First performance: 28 February 1937, Collins' Music Hall, London

A satirical revue displaying Slater's left-wing humour at its most savage. Britten completed his incidental music for the *Pageant* on 26 February, the day of the first performance of *The Ascent of F6*.

MSS:	Composition sketch (pencil) and additional composition sketch page located with *The Ascent of F6*, full score, discarded pages
	Full score, discarded pages, autograph (ink)

---

[22] The first page of Britten's full score of 'Funeral Blues' is reproduced in *PL*, plate 103.
[23] Published posthumously as *Four Cabaret Songs*, London, Faber Music, 1980.
[24] For detailed accounts of the writing and revisions of *F6*, see Christopher Isherwood, *Christopher and his kind*. London, Eyre Methuen, 1977, pp. 180–201; and Brian Finney, *Christopher Isherwood: a critical biography*. London, Faber and Faber, 1979, pp. 162–6.

Scoring: male and female vv, chorus (male vv); cl (B flat), alto sax (E flat), tpt (B flat), perc (sd, drums), pf, vn, vc, db

Britten recorded in his diary on 20 February 1937: 'In morning I work at music for the Left Review [sic] – Montagu Slater's very amusing & provoking *Pageant of Empire*. I finish sketching three or four little Music Hall songs.' 'Music Hall songs' is an accurate reflection of the popular idiom of this score, which is made up of a series of eight short, witty instrumental and vocal numbers.[25]

Out of the Picture December 1937
Group Theatre
Author: Louis MacNeice   Producer: Rupert Doone
Designers: Robert Medley and Geoffrey W. Monk
Musical director: Brian Easdale
First performance: 5 December 1937, Westminster Theatre, London

MSS: Full score, autograph and non-autograph (ink, pencil)
Chorus scores, non-autograph (ink)
Vocal and Instrumental parts, non-autograph (ink)
Scoring: male v, S, chorus (SATB); tpt (C, B flat), perc (trgl, sus cym, bl, sd, bd, gong), pf (2 & 4 hands)

In comparison with the previous scores, *Out of the Picture* is distinguished by the quality of its vocal and choral writing. In addition to fanfares, marches, a waltz and a ballet, there are two songs for Portright, four choruses, a song for the Announcer and a final chorus with soprano solo, 'Sleep and Wake'. The soloist for the original production was the soprano Sophie Wyss, for whom Britten composed *Our Hunting Fathers* Op. 8 (1936), *On This Island* Op. 11 (1937) and *Les Illuminations* Op. 18 (1939).

Spain June 1938
Binyon Puppets – Puppet Show 1938
Author: Montagu Slater   Designer: Helen Binyon
Puppeteers: Helen and Margaret Binyon
Musical director: Frank Kennard
First performance: 22 June 1938, Mercury Theatre, London

---

[25] A verse from the final chorus, referred to by Britten in his diary as 'Blimps' Parade', is quoted in *BA*, p. 99.

Montagu Slater contributed three short plays to the programme: *Spain*[26] with music by Britten, and *Seven Ages of Man* and *The Station Master* with scores by Lennox Berkeley.

MSS: Missing
Scoring: male and female vv; cl, vn (doubling dulcitone), pf[27]

On the Frontier October 1938
Group Theatre
Authors: W. H. Auden and Christopher Isherwood
Producer: Rupert Doone   Designer: Robert Medley
Musical director: Brian Easdale
First performance: 14 November 1938, Arts Theatre, Cambridge

The distinguished cast included Peter Pears as the Ostnian Announcer, a Worker, a Dancer, a Westland Soldier and a Journalist. The composer played the piano for the original production. *On the Frontier* received a single Sunday night performance at the Globe Theatre, London, in February 1939. Auden and Isherwood dedicated the play to Britten with the following verse:

> The drums tap out sensational bulletins;
> Frantic the efforts of the violins
> To drown the song behind the guarded hill:
> The dancers do not listen; but they will.

MSS: Composition sketch (pencil, violet crayon)
Full score, autograph (ink, pencil)
Full score, discarded pages, autograph (ink, pencil)
Fair copy of Soldiers' duet ('Ben was a four foot seven Wop'), autograph (ink)
Piano rehearsal score, autograph (ink)
Instrumental parts, autograph and non-autograph (ink)
Scoring: male v, chorus (SSMezTBarB); 2 tpt (C), perc (sus cym, sd, td, bd), acd, pf (2 & 4 hands)

Like that for *Out of the Picture*, this score makes large demands on the chorus who are given two substantial numbers: a blues ('The clock on the wall gives an electric tick') and a waltz before the curtain of Act II scene 2 ('The papers say there'll be war before long'). The contrapuntal combination of the Westland and Ostnian National Anthems (sung by

---

[26] The published text is entitled *Old Spain*. *Old Spain* and *Seven Ages of Man* are included in Montagu Slater, *Peter Grimes and other poems*. London, John Lane, The Bodley Head, 1946.
[27] Scoring deduced from the original programme.

the London Labour Choral Union and recorded by Decca for the original production) is adumbrated by the trumpet fanfares of the overture.

They Walk Alone 1938
Author: Max Catto   Producer: Bertold Viertel
Designer: Herman Herrey
First performance: 21 November 1938, "Q" Theatre, London

Britten's first venture into West End commercial theatre.

MSS: Composition sketch (pencil)
Scoring: org

A melodramatic tale of suspense, suspicion and murder in which Britten's mainly fragmentary organ music announces each fresh corpse. The production was very successful, transferring from the "Q" Theatre to the Shaftesbury Theatre in January 1939 and then to the Comedy Theatre in May.

Johnson over Jordan 1939
Author: J. B. Priestley   Producer: Basil Dean
Designer: Edward Carrick   Costumes and Masks: Elizabeth Haffenden
Choreographer: Antony Tudor   Musical director: Ernest Irving
First performance: 22 February 1939, New Theatre,[28] London

The most substantial and ambitious incidental music score that Britten composed in the 1930s. Following its initial run it was transferred to the Saville Theatre in a revised version in March 1939. Subsequently there were three radio productions in the composer's life-time: Act III only, broadcast on 11 August 1940; an adaptation by Frank Hauser, broadcast on 23 July 1951; and a version made by Raymond Raikes, broadcast on 23 March 1955. In 1985 a new radio production of *Johnson over Jordan* was mounted which sought to reinstate all of Britten's original music.

MSS: Composition sketch (ink, pencil)
       Full score, autograph and non-autograph (ink, pencil)[29]
       Piano rehearsal score, autograph (ink)
       Vocal and Instrumental parts, autograph and non-autograph (ink)
Scoring: S; fl (doubling pic), ob (doubling ca), 2 cl (E flat, B flat, A), bcl (doubling alto sax), bn, 2 tpt (C, B flat, A), trbn, perc (glock, xyl, sus cym, bl, sd, td, bd, timp, gong), pf, str

[28] Now the Albery Theatre.
[29] In private ownership, on loan to the Britten-Pears Library, Aldeburgh.

In addition to Britten's original score, a jazz orchestration of his music for the night-club scene, entitled 'The Spider and the Fly', was recorded by Geraldo's Orchestra and played from a disc in the original production. This was scored for 3 clarinets (B flat), bass clarinet, 3 trumpets (B flat), 2 trombones, percussion (side drum, timpani, gong), piano, guitar, violin and double bass. The score also includes arrangements by Ernest Irving of Brahms, Handel, Humperdinck, Liszt, Mozart, Schubert and traditional tunes, and 'Valse Bleue' by Alfred Margis.

This Way to the Tomb 1945
Pilgrim Players
Author: Ronald Duncan   Producer: E. Martin Browne
Musical director: Arthur Oldham
First performance: 11 October 1945, Mercury Theatre, London

MSS: Composition sketch (pencil)
Full score, non-autograph (ink)
Scoring: S, A, T, B, chorus (SATB); perc (sus cym, sd, bd), pf (4 hands)

Duncan's play was written in the form of masque and anti-masque. The music of the masque is in three parts with an *a capella* chorus ('Deus in adjutorium meum'),[30] a soprano solo and 'St Anthony's Meditation' for soloists and chorus. The anti-masque, by contrast, has a chant, litany, two marches for piano duet and percussion, and a 'Quasi Boogie' for solo trio, piano duet and percussion.

The Eagle Has Two Heads 1946
Company of Four
Author: Jean Cocteau, translated Ronald Duncan
Producer: Murray MacDonald
First Performance: 4 September 1946, Lyric Theatre, Hammersmith

Produced only two months after the première at Glyndebourne of another Britten–Duncan collaboration: the chamber opera *The Rape of Lucretia*.

---

[30] This setting of Psalm 70, 'Haste thee, O God, to deliver me', was published by Boosey and Hawkes in 1983.

MSS: Composition sketch (pencil)
Full score, autograph (ink)
Scoring: 4 cor (B flat), 3 tpt (B flat), 2 t trbn, b trbn, euph, E flat bass, perc (cym, sd)

Britten composed a fanfare for brass and percussion which was recorded for the original production by the Band of the Household Cavalry.

The Duchess of Malfi 1946
Author: John Webster, adapted by W. H. Auden
Producer: George Rylands
Scenery: Harry Bennett   Costumes: Miles White
First performance: 20 September 1946, Metropolitan Theatre, Providence, Rhode Island

An adaptation of Webster's play was begun by Bertolt Brecht and H. R. Hays in the spring of 1943. W. H. Auden joined this collaboration in December of that year following which Hays withdrew. During the next two years work progressed, with Brecht and Auden producing several versions. The appointment of George Rylands as director in August 1946 brought about a return, at Rylands' insistence, to the original Webster text with some minor appendages by Auden alone; Brecht subsequently withdrew his name from the production.[31] Following a short provincial tour the production, which featured Elisabeth Bergner as Giovanna, opened on 15 October 1946 at the Ethel Barrymore Theatre, New York.

MSS: Missing
Scoring: Unknown

It is believed that it was Brecht's suggestion that Britten adapt material from his setting of the Lyke Wake Dirge from the *Serenade* for tenor, horn and strings. According to the original programmes Britten's music was arranged by Ignatz Strasfogel.

Stratton 1949
Author: Ronald Duncan   Producer: John Fernald
Designer: Reece Pemberton
First performance: 31 October 1949, Theatre Royal, Brighton

MSS: Missing
Scoring: Unknown

---

[31] For a full account of this production see James K. Lyon, *Bertolt Brecht in America*. New Jersey, Princeton University Press, 1980, pp. 141–150.

The music for this play was recorded by the English Opera Group Orchestra conducted by Norman Del Mar in 1949. According to Ronald Duncan in *Working with Britten*, only six copies of the disc were pressed, four of them being used in the theatre production; a copy is now in the possession of the Ronald Duncan Literary Foundation.

Am Stram Gram 1954
Author: André Roussin   Producer: Victor Azavia
First performance: 4 March 1954, Tonybee Hall Theatre, London

MSS: Composition sketch (pencil)
          Fair copy, autograph (ink)[32]
Scoring: male and female vv; pf

A setting of the lyric 'Am stram gram, c'est moi, c'est toi, c'est nous, c'est vous'.

The Punch Revue 1955
Compiler: Ronald Duncan   Authors of Britten's contribution: W. H. Auden, William Plomer   Producer: Vida Hope
First performance: 28 September 1955, Duke of York's Theatre, London

MSS: Composition sketch (pencil)
Scoring: female v; pf

Britten contributed three items to the revue: 'Tell me the truth about love', one of the Auden *Cabaret Songs* composed in 1938; 'Old friends are best' (1955), a specially written setting for voice and piano of a text by William Plomer; and a Waltz for piano based upon 'Old friends are best'.

---

[32] In private ownership. For a reduced facsimile of the composer's manuscript see Eric Walter White, 'Britten in the theatre: a provisional catalogue', *Tempo*, 107, December 1973, p. 9.

MUSIC FOR RADIO

King Arthur March–April 1937
BBC, London
Author: D. Geoffrey Bridson   Producer: Val Gielgud
First broadcast: 23 April 1937; BBC Chorus, London Symphony Orchestra, Clarence Raybould (conductor)

A dramatization of the King Arthur legend. The first of Britten's scores for the BBC. In scale, content and forces employed these tend to be more substantial than the scores written for theatre or film.

MSS: Composition sketch (pencil)
Full score, autograph and non-autograph (ink, pencil)
Chorus score, non-autograph (ink)
Instrumental parts, autograph and non-autograph (ink, pencil)

Scoring: chorus (SATB); 3 fl (III doubling pic), 2 ob, 2 cl (B flat, A), cl (E flat, B flat), 2 bn (II doubling dbn), 4 hn (F), 3 tpt (C), 2 t trbn, b trbn, tuba, timp, 2 perc (glock, trgl, cym, sus cym, sd, td, bd), harp, str

This is a very considerable score with much motivic interrelation between the movements. An orchestral scherzo (No. XIVA)[33] was later used for the 'Dance of Death' in *Ballad of Heroes*, Op. 14 (1939), and other material from the score was used in the revised Impromptu (1945) of the Piano Concerto, Op. 13 (1938).

The Company of Heaven August–September 1937
BBC, London
Compiler: R. Ellis Roberts   Producer: Robin Whitworth
First broadcast: 29 September 1937; Felix Aylmer, Leo Genn, Robert Speaight (readers), Sophie Wyss (soprano), Peter Pears (tenor), BBC Chorus and Orchestra, Trevor Harvey (conductor)

MSS: Composition sketch (pencil)
Full score, autograph (ink)
Short score of solo soprano part, autograph (ink)[34]
Chorus scores, non-autograph (ink, pencil)
Chorus parts, non-autograph (ink, pencil)

Scoring: S, T, chorus (SATB); timp, org, str

---

[33] The first page of Britten's full score of this scherzo is reproduced in *PL*, plate 104.
[34] In the Library of Northwestern University, Illinois, USA.

The score is cyclic, with an orchestral introduction entitled 'Chaos' concealing and finally yielding a quotation of the hymn tune 'Ye watchers and ye holy ones', which (in a setting for soloists, chorus and orchestra) forms the finale of the work. No. IV is another hymn set for the same forces ('Christ the fair glory') which Britten later arranged for tenor, cello and piano for a wartime recital with Peter Pears. But perhaps the most fascinating element of the work is the setting for tenor and strings of Emily Brontë's 'A thousand gleaming fires' from 'A Day Dream'; composed with the certain knowledge that it was to be performed by Pears, it is possibly the very first song Britten wrote for him.

Hadrian's Wall November 1937
BBC, Newcastle upon Tyne
Author: W. H. Auden   Producer: John Pudney
First broadcast: 25 November 1937; Felling Male Voice Choir, Leslie Russell Quartet, Benjamin Britten (conductor)

MSS: Missing
Scoring: male v, chorus ([SA]TB), perc, str qt[35]

It seems likely, from the evidence of the composer's annotated typescript which has survived (and now preserved at the Britten–Pears Library), that the score contained about fifteen numbers, including a choral setting of Purcell's 'Fairest Isle' and a song setting of Auden's 'Roman Wall Blues' ('Over the heather the wet wind blows').[36]

Lines on the Map January 1938
1. Communication by Land   2. Communication by Sea
3. Communication by Wireless   4. Communication by Air
BBC, London
Authors: 1. Stephen Potter   2. James Miller
         3. D. F. Aitken and E. J. Alway   4. Stephen Potter
Producers: John Pudney and Leslie Stokes
First broadcast: 1. 27 January 1938   2. 25 February 1938
                 3. 25 March 1938   4. 22 April 1938

A series of programmes concerning national and international communications.

---

[35] Scoring deduced from Britten's annotated typescript.
[36] See *EA*, pp. 389–90.

MSS: Composition sketch (pencil)
Scoring: 2 tpt, 2 t trbn, perc (sus cym, sd, bd)

Britten's score comprises a sarabande and a march with trio.

The Chartists' March April–May 1938
BBC, London
Author: J. H. Miller   Producer: John Pudney
First broadcast: 13 May 1938; section of BBC Men's Chorus, Benjamin Britten (conductor)

MSS: Missing
Scoring: chorus (TB), perc[37]

The World of the Spirit April–May 1938
BBC, London
Compiler: R. Ellis Roberts   Producer: Robin Whitworth
First broadcast: 5 June 1938; Felix Aylmer, Leo Genn, Robert Speaight (readers), Sophie Wyss (soprano), Anne Wood (contralto), Emlyn Bebb (tenor), Victor Harding (bass), BBC Singers and Orchestra, Trevor Harvey (conductor)

A second special feature devised by Ellis Roberts for which Britten composed a large-scale choral and orchestral score (see also *The Company of Heaven*, p. 154). A Whitsun programme of words and music.

MSS: Composition sketch (pencil)
Full score, autograph (ink)[38]
Vocal and Instrumental parts, autograph and non-autograph (ink)
Scoring: S, A, T, B, chorus (SATB); 2 fl (II doubling pic), 2 ob, 2 cl (B flat, A), 2 bn, 4 hn (F), 2 tpt (C), 2 t trbn, b trbn, tuba, timp, perc (tamb, cym, sus cym, sd, bd, gong), harp, org, str

In correspondence with the BBC Britten refers to *The World of the Spirit* as an 'Oratorio', which in effect it is. This is a considerably more substantial score than *The Company of Heaven*, yet makes frequent chamber-musical demands on its heavy forces. The choral movements tend to use full orchestra, the solo movements being scored for a variety of small ensembles: No. 4 ('This is my commandment') for tenor, vocal

---

[37] Scoring deduced from correspondence between Britten and the BBC.
[38] A page from the composer's full score is reproduced in *PL*, plate 93.

octet (SSAATTBB), horn, two violins and viola, and No. 8 ('O Knowing, glorious spirit!'), an obbligato aria for soprano, flute, violin and harp. The 'Oratorio' is framed by an overture and a final chorus based on the plainsong tune 'Veni Creator Spiritus', with a coda for soprano and orchestra ('O Comforter, that name is thine').

The Sword in the Stone April–May 1939
BBC, London
Adapter: Marianne Helweg, from the novel *The Sword in the Stone* by T. H. White
Producer: John Cheatle
First broadcast: series of six programmes, 11 June–16 July 1939; BBC Singers (male voices), section of BBC Orchestra, Leslie Woodgate (conductor)

The last work Britten completed before leaving for North America in May 1939.

MSS: Composition sketch, fragmentary (pencil)
Full score, autograph (ink)[39]
Instrumental parts, non-autograph (ink), photostat copies
Scoring: female v, male vv, chorus (TB); fl (doubling pic), cl (B flat), bn, tpt (C), t trbn, perc (glock, trgl, cym (foot), sus cym, bl, sd, td, bd, gong), harp

The score comprises fifteen numbers. The orchestral introduction contains a busy trumpet fanfare which symbolizes the sword, and it is taken up by the piccolo and clarinet for the first of the 'Boys' Tunes', 'Wart'. Merlyn has a learned contrapuntal movement, and the Witch, Madame Mim, a characteristic 'Dance of Death'. The score also includes a touching lullaby, amusing quotations of 'Forty Years On' and the Eton Boating Song in the jousting scene, and bird calls from Beethoven's *Pastoral Symphony*, Wagner's *Siegfried*, Strauss's *Le bourgeois gentilhomme*, Liza Lehmann's *Bird Songs* and Delius's *On hearing the first cuckoo in spring* in the movement entitled 'Bird Music'.

For many years the manuscript was thought to be lost. When it was rediscovered in 1952, a new radio production was mounted by Francis Dillon complete with Britten's music conducted by Walter Goehr; it was broadcast in one long episode on 26 March 1952. A third adaptation was presented on 26 December 1981, produced by Graham Gould and conducted by Steuart Bedford.

[39] In private ownership; a microfilm is in the Britten–Pears Library, Aldeburgh.

The Dark Valley 1940
CBS (Columbia Workshop), New York
Author: W. H. Auden   Producer: Brewster Morgan
First broadcast: 2 June 1940; Bernard Herrmann (conductor)

A monologue written specially for Dame May Whitty.

MSS: Composition sketch (pencil) (some located with the discarded composition sketch pages of *Sinfonia da Requiem*, Op. 20)
Vocal and Instrumental parts, non-autograph (ink)
Scoring: female v; fl, ca, cl (B flat), tpt, perc (bells)

Britten's score includes a fanfare, a chime of bells, two unaccompanied songs, and title and end title music scored for flute, cor anglais and clarinet.

The Dynasts 1940
CBS (Columbia Workshop), New York
Author: Thomas Hardy
First broadcast: late 1940

MSS: Missing
Scoring: brass, perc, str

Virtually nothing is known about this radio adaptation of Hardy's Napoleonic epic. The only clue to the nature of Britten's score lies in a brief review entitled 'Over the Air' by Charles Mills, which appeared in *Modern Music*, 18/2, January–February 1941, p. 232: 'Two workshop dramas presented by CBS contained incidental music especially commissioned by the network for these programs.[40] The score of the first, Thomas Hardy's *Dynasts*, was by Benjamin Britten. Largely a military affair of brass and percussion, it was appropriate enough, only there was too much of it. As background, the music seemed over-prominent and to lack subtlety of timing, though there was an exception in the string mood accompanying the verbal soliloquy of Napoleon.'

The Rocking-Horse Winner 1941
CBS (Columbia Workshop), New York
Authors: W. H. Auden and James Stern, from the short story *The Rocking-Horse Winner* by D. H. Lawrence   Producer: Guy della Cioppa
First broadcast: 6 April 1941; Bernard Herrmann (conductor)

[40] The other was Virgil Thomson's setting of Euripides' *Trojan Women*.

MSS: Missing
Scoring: male vv; fl, cl, perc (sus cym), harp[41]
Britten's score comprises eight items, including title and end-title music for flute, clarinet and harp.

Appointment 1942
BBC, London
Author and producer: Norman Corwin
First broadcast: 20 July 1942

A half-hour drama set in an internment camp in France.

MSS: Full score, autograph (ink)
Instrumental parts, non-autograph (ink)
Scoring: 2 fl (II doubling pic), 2 ob (II doubling ca), 2 cl (B flat, A), 2 bn, 2 hn (F), 2 tpt (B flat), 2 t trbn, b trbn, timp (doubling trgl), perc (bells, sus cym, sd, gong), harp, str

An American in England No 1: London by Clipper 1942
CBS, New York/BBC, London
Author: Norman Corwin   Producer: Edward R. Murrow
First broadcast: 27 July 1942; RAF Orchestra, Rudolf P. O'Donnell (conductor)

An American in England comprised a series of six dramas. Produced from England for live transmission in the United States, it was designed to inform an American audience about conditions in wartime Britain. The series was also broadcast on the various Forces' Networks in the UK, Canada and Australia.

MSS: Full score, autograph (pencil)
Instrumental parts, non-autograph (ink)
Scoring: 3 fl (III doubling pic), 2 ob, ca, 2 cl (B flat, A), bcl, 2 bn, dbn, 4 hn (F), cor (A), 3 tpt (B flat), 2 t trbn, b trbn, tuba, timp, 3 perc (tamb, cym, sus cym, sd, td, bd, small gong or large cym, gong, timp), pf, harp, str

An American in England No 2: London to Dover 1942
CBS, New York/BBC, London
Author: Norman Corwin   Producer: Edward R. Murrow
First broadcast: 10 August 1942; RAF Orchestra, Rudolf P. O'Donnell (conductor)

---

[41] Scoring deduced from a soundtrack of the original broadcast in the Britten–Pears Library.

MSS: Full score, autograph (pencil)
Instrumental parts, non-autograph (ink)
Scoring: pic, 2 fl, 2 ob, 2 cl (B flat), 2 bn, 4 hn (F), 2 tpt (B flat), 2 t trbn, b trbn, euph, timp (doubling small gong), 2 perc (glock, tamb, sus cym, cym, 2 bl, sd, td, bd, small gong, large gong), harp, str

An American in England No 3: Ration Island 1942
CBS, New York/BBC, London
Author: Norman Corwin   Producer: Edward R. Murrow
First broadcast: 17 August 1942; RAF Orchestra, Rudolf P. O'Donnell (conductor)

MSS: Full score, autograph (ink, pencil)
Instrumental parts, autograph and non-autograph (ink, pencil)
Scoring: 2 fl (II doubling pic), 2 ob (II doubling ca), 2 cl (B flat), 2 bn, 4 hn (F), 2 tpt (B flat), 4 trbn, tuba, timp, 2 perc (trgl, tamb, sus cym, cym, bl, sd, td, bd, gong, timp), pf, harp, str

The Man Born To Be King No 10: The Princes of this World 1942
BBC, London
Author: Dorothy L. Sayers   Producer: Val Gielgud
First broadcast: 23 August 1942

Britten set songs for two episodes in this long and famous series: a four-line stanza ('Bring me garlands, bring me wine') for the tenth episode; and Mary Magdalen's Song ('Soldier, soldier, why will you roam?') for the eleventh episode.

MSS: Vocal score, non-autograph (ink)[42]
Scoring: male vv; pf[43]

Lumberjacks of America July–August 1942
BBC, London/New York
Author: Ranald MacDougall   Producer: Charles A. Schenk, Jnr
First broadcast: 24 August 1942; Benjamin Britten (conductor)

A survey of the American timber industry.

---

[42] In the Marion E. Wade Collection, Wheaton College, Wheaton, Illinois, USA.
[43] The piano accompaniment is not to be heard on the BBC Sound Archive recording of the original production; presumably it was intended for rehearsal purposes only.

MSS: Full score entitled 'Timber', autograph (pencil)
           Instrumental parts, non-autograph (ink)
Scoring: fl, cl (B flat), bn, 2 tpt (C), t trbn, perc (trgl, sus cym, bl, sd, bd, gong, timp), pf, harp, db

An American in England No 4: Women of Britain   1942
CBS, New York/BBC, London
Author: Norman Corwin   Producer: Edward R. Murrow
First broadcast: 24 August 1942; RAF Orchestra, Rudolf P. O'Donnell (conductor)

MSS: Full score, autograph (pencil)
           Instrumental parts, autograph and non-autograph (ink, pencil)
Scoring: 2 fl (II doubling pic), 2 ob (II doubling ca), 2 cl (B flat, A), 2 bn, dbn, 4 hn (F), 2 tpt (B flat), 3 t trbn, b trbn, timp (doubling trgl), 2 perc (xyl, vib, tamb, sus cym, 2 bl, whip, sd, td, bd, gong), harp, str

An American in England No 5: The Yanks Are Here   1942
CBS, New York/BBC, London
Author: Norman Corwin   Producer: Edward R. Murrow
First broadcast: 31 August 1942; RAF Orchestra, Rudolf P. O'Donnell (conductor)

MSS: Full score, autograph (pencil)
           Instrumental parts, autograph and non-autograph (ink, pencil)
Scoring: 2 fl, 2 ob, 2 cl (B flat, A), 2 bn, dbn, 4 hn (F), 2 tpt (C), 2 t trbn, b trbn, tuba, timp, 2 perc (xyl, trgl, tamb, sus cym, cym, bl, sd, bd), pf, harp, str

An American in England No 6: The Anglo-American Angle   1942
CBS, New York/BBC, London
Author: Norman Corwin   Producer: Edward R. Murrow
First broadcast: 7 September 1942; RAF Orchestra, Rudolf P. O'Donnell (conductor)

MSS: Full score, autograph (ink)
           Instrumental parts, non-autograph (ink)
Scoring: fl, ob, 2 cl (B flat, A), 2 bn, 2 hn (F), 2 tpt (C), t trbn, b trbn, timp, perc (xyl, vib, trgl, sus cym, sd, bd), harp, 3 vn, 2 va, 2 vc, db

The Man Born To Be King No 11: King of Sorrows   September 1942
BBC, London
Author: Dorothy L. Sayers   Producer: Val Gielgud
First broadcast: 20 September 1942

MSS: Fair copy, autograph (ink, pencil)
Scoring: female v, male chorus; pf

Britain to America, Series I No 9: Britain Through American Eyes
BBC, London for NBC, New York   1942
Author: Louis MacNeice   Producer: Lawrence Gilliam
First broadcast: 20 September 1942; London Symphony Orchestra,
          Muir Mathieson (conductor)

Two series of thirteen and nine half-hour programmes about Britain and the British, made at the request of NBC, New York. Described in the *Radio Times* as a 'Special BBC feature series broadcast weekly in the BBC North American Service, and rebroadcast in the United States by the NBC'. Series I ran from 14 August to 9 October 1942, and Series II from 17 October 1942 until 9 January 1943.

MSS: Full score, autograph (ink, pencil)
          Instrumental parts, non-autograph (ink)
Scoring: 2 fl (II doubling pic), 2 ob, 2 cl (B flat), 2 bn, 2 hn (F), 2 tpt
          (B flat), 2 t trbn, timp, perc (xyl, tamb, sus cym, sd, td, bd,
          gong), harp, str (vn, va, vc, db)

Britain To America, Series II No 4: Where Do I Come In?   1942
BBC, London for NBC, New York
Author: Louis MacNeice   Producer: Lawrence Gilliam
First broadcast: 7 November 1942; London Symphony Orchestra, Muir
          Mathieson (conductor)

MSS: Full score, autograph (pencil)
Scoring: fl (doubling pic), ob (doubling ca), 2 cl (B flat), bn, 2 hn (F),
          2 tpt (B flat), t trbn, b trbn, timp (doubling sus cym), 2 perc
          (xyl, tamb, sus cym, cym, small bl, sd, td, bd, gong), harp, str
          (vn, va, vc, db)

Britain to America, Series II No 13: Where Do We Go From Here?
BBC, London for NBC, New York   1942
Author: Louis MacNeice   Producer: Lawrence Gilliam
First broadcast: 3 January 1943; London Symphony Orchestra, Muir
          Mathieson (conductor)

MSS: Full score, autograph (ink, pencil)
Vocal and Instrumental parts, autograph and non-autograph (ink)
Scoring: A; fl (doubling pic), ob, 2 cl (B flat, A), alto sax (E flat), bn, 2 hn (F), 2 tpt (B flat), t trbn, b trbn, timp, perc (xyl, sus cym, cym, sd, bd, gong), harp, str (vn, va, vc, db)

The Four Freedoms No 1: Pericles 1943
BBC, London
Author and producer: Louis MacNeice
First broadcast: 21 February 1943

A series of six short feature programmes. Britten composed music for the first programme in the series – Pericles – and MacNeice is said to have asked him for music 'of a rather special nature, being an impression of early Greek music'.[44]

MSS: Missing
Scoring: Unknown

The Rescue 1943
BBC, London
Author: Edward Sackville-West   Producer: John Burrell
First broadcast: 25 & 26 November 1943; BBC Symphony Orchestra, Clarence Raybould (conductor)

An epic drama in two parts based upon Homer's *Odyssey*. Following the first production there have been subsequent new productions in 1948, 1951, 1956, 1962 and 1973.

MSS: Composition sketch subsequently used as a rehearsal score, autograph and non-autograph (pencil)
Full score, autograph (pencil)
Scoring: S, Mez, T, B; 2 fl (II doubling pic), 2 ob, 2 cl (B flat, A; II doubling bcl), alto sax (E flat) 2 bn, 4 hn (F), tpt (D), 2 tpt (B flat), 2 t trbn, b trbn, tuba, timp (doubling tamb), 2 perc (cel, xyl, tamb, sus cym, cym, whip, large bl, sd, bd, small gong, large gong, timp), pf, harp, str

A considerable score of about eighty items – some very brief, some more extended – including functional background music, interludes and songs. Much of the success of Britten's score depends on the use of an intricate *Leitmotiv* technique, characterizing each of the chief protagonists in turn.

[44] Quoted in *LM*, p. 62.

A Poet's Christmas 1944
BBC, London
Authors: W. H. Auden, Frances Cornford, Cecil Day Lewis, John Heath-Stubbs, Laurie Lee, Louis MacNeice, Henry Reed, Ann Ridler, Vita Sackville-West, Edith Sitwell
Producer: Edward Sackville-West
First broadcast: 24 December 1944; BBC Singers, Leslie Woodgate (conductor)

A programme of words and music for Christmas.

MSS: Composition sketch (pencil)
Full score, autograph (ink)
Scoring: chorus (SSAATTBB)

Britten composed two choral settings of texts by W. H. Auden for this programme. Both texts were taken from Auden's draft text of *For the Time Being: A Christmas Oratorio*, an abortive Britten–Auden project from the war years: 'A Shepherd's Carol' ('O lift your little pinkie')[45] and 'Chorale (after an old French Carol)'.[46] Other music in the programme included new settings by Lennox Berkeley of Frances Cornford's 'There was neither grass nor corn' and by Michael Tippett of Edith Sitwell's 'The Weeping Babe'.

The Dark Tower 1946
BBC, London
Author and producer: Louis MacNeice
First broadcast: 21 January 1946; Walter Goehr (conductor)

Britten worked closely with MacNeice in the preparation of the incidental music score for this radio play.[47] MacNeice dedicated the published text to Britten.

MSS: Composition sketch (pencil)
Full score, autograph and non-autograph (pencil), British Library Additional MS No. 60623
Scoring: tpt (C), perc (E flat bell, trgl, tamb, sus cym, sd, bd, gong, timp), str

---

[45] First published in 1962 by Novello & Co., it received its first concert performance on 17 October 1962 at Holy Trinity Church, London, SW7.
[46] Unpublished, though a BBC copyist's score appeared in facsimile in *The Score*, 28, January 1961, pp. 47–51.
[47] For an account of the Britten-MacNeice collaboration on *The Dark Tower*, see *LM*, pp. 79–82.

This score prominently features a motto-like trumpet fanfare, forever summoning Browning's 'Childe Roland' to the Dark Tower. Perhaps the most interesting section is the 'Forest music', with exotic bird calls for solo string quartet over muted trills, and glissandi for muted tutti strings as in *A Midsummer Night's Dream*.[48]

Men of Goodwill: The Reunion of Christmas[49] 1947
BBC, London
Compilers and producers: Lawrence Gilliam and Leonard Cottrell
First broadcast: 25 December 1947; London Symphony Orchestra, Walter Goehr (conductor)

Described by the BBC as 'a Christmas journey across the world', this programme brought together goodwill messages from around the globe and immediately preceded the King's Christmas Day Message to the Empire.

MSS: Composition sketch (pencil)
  Full score, autograph (pencil)
Scoring: pic, 2 fl, 2 ob, 2 cl (B flat, A), 2 bn, 4 hn (F), 2 tpt (C), 2 t trbn, b trbn, tuba, timp, 2 perc (xyl, cym, sus cym, sd, td, bd), harp, str

Britten's score for this programme is a set of short orchestral variations on the carol 'God rest ye merry, Gentlemen'. A fugal finale, marked 'new last section' in Britten's full score, was for some reason not used in the original broadcast.

---

[48] A page from the composer's full score of the 'Forest Music', together with the appropriate page from the BBC script are reproduced in *PL*, plates 210–11.
[49] Published as *Men of Goodwill – Variations on a Christmas Carol for orchestra*. London, Faber Music, 1982.

BENJAMIN BRITTEN
THE RECORDED REPERTOIRE
COMPILED BY PHILIP REED AND PAUL WILSON

THE RECORDED REPERTOIRE

Note: The following list of Britten's recorded repertoire comprises all commercially issued recordings. It falls into four sections: I Britten as conductor; II Britten as pianist; III Britten as viola-player; IV Britten as speaker. The dates given are dates of first publication rather than recording. All records are 33⅓ rpm except where stated and where both stereophonic and monophonic recordings were made the stereo version only is indicated. Record company codes may be elucidated by reference to the alphabetical index which appears quarterly in the *Gramophone Classical Catalogue*.

I AS CONDUCTOR

BACH	Brandenburg Concertos 1–6 ECO/Britten (1969) SET 410–1
BACH	St. John Passion Pears/Howell/Harper/Hodgson/Tear/Shirley-Quirk/ Wandsworth School Boys' Choir/ECO/Britten (1972) SET 531–33
BRIDGE	Sir Roger de Covereley ECO/Britten (1969) SXL 6405
BRITTEN	Albert Herring Fisher/Peters/Noble/Brannigan/E. Evans/Cantelo/Ward/ Wilson/Rex/Pears/Amit/Pashley/Terry/ECO/Britten (1964) SET 274–6
BRITTEN	Billy Budd Glossop/Pears/Langdon/Shirley-Quirk/Drake/Kelly/ Dempsey/D. Bowman/Brannigan/Tear/R. Bowman/ Bryn-Jones/Garrett/Lumsden/Rogers/Luxon/Coleby/ Newby/Read/Bush/Boys from Wandsworth School/ Ambrosian Opera Chorus/LSO/Britten (1968) SET 379–81
BRITTEN	A Boy Was Born Purcell Singers/Hartnett/Boys' voices of EOG/Choir of All Saints, Margaret Street/Britten (1958) LXT 5416
BRITTEN	The Burning Fiery Furnace Pears/Drake/Shirley-Quirk/Tear/Dean/Leeming/ Adeney/Sanders/Brenner/Aronowitz/Marjoram/Ellis/ Blades/Ledger/Tunnard/Britten (1967) SET 356
BRITTEN	Cantata Misericordium Pears/Fischer-Dieskau/London Symphony Chorus/ LSO/Britten (1965) SXL 6175

BRITTEN	A Ceremony of Carols Copenhagen Boys' Choir/Simon/Britten (1954) LW 5070
BRITTEN	Children's Crusade Wandsworth School Boys' Choir/Burgess/Britten (1970) SET 445
BRITTEN	Curlew River Pears/Shirley-Quirk/Blackburn/Drake/Webb/Adeney/ Sanders/Aronowitz/S. Knussen/Ellis/Blades/Ledger/ Tunnard/Britten (1966) SET 301
BRITTEN	Diversions Katchen/LSO/Britten (1955) LXT 2981
BRITTEN	Friday Afternoons (1–3, 5–12) Downside School Choir, Purley/Tunnard/Britten (1967) SXL 6264
BRITTEN	Gloriana – Fanfare ECO/Britten (1972) 5BB 119–20
BRITTEN	Les Illuminations Pears/ECO/Britten (1967) SXL 6316
BRITTEN	The Little Sweep (Let's make an opera) Hemmings/Vyvyan/N. Thomas/Cantelo/Ingram/ M. Baker/Fairhurst/Soskin/L. Vaughan/Anthony/Pears/ Choir of Alleyn's School/EOG Orchestra/Britten (1956) LXT 5163
BRITTEN	A Midsummer Night's Dream A. Deller/Harwood/Terry/Dakin/Pryer/Wodehouse/ G. Clark/Alder/Shirley-Quirk/Watts/Pears/Hemsley/ Veasey/Harper/Brannigan/Lumsden/Macdonald/Kelly/ Tear/Raggett/Downside School Choir, Purley/ Emmanuel School Choir/LSO/S. Bedford/Britten (1967) SET 338–40
BRITTEN	Nocturne Pears/LSO/Britten (1960) SXL 2189
BRITTEN	Our Hunting Fathers Pears/LSO/Britten (1981) REGL 417
BRITTEN	Owen Wingrave Luxon/J. Baker/Shirley-Quirk/Harper/Pears/Fisher/ Vyvyan/Douglas/Wandsworth School Boys' Choir/ECO/ Britten (1971) SET 501–2
BRITTEN	Peter Grimes Pears/C. Watson/Pease/Kelly/Brannigan/Elms/ J. Watson/Studholme/Kells/Nilsson/Lanigan/G. Evans/ Norman/ROH Chorus/ROH Orchestra/Britten (1959) SXL 2150–2

BRITTEN	Piano Concerto Richter/ECO/Britten (1971) SXL 6512
BRITTEN	Prelude and Fugue for 18-part string orchestra ECO/Britten (1977) SXL 6847
BRITTEN	The Prince of the Pagodas ROH Orchestra/Britten (1957) LXT 5336–7
BRITTEN	The Prodigal Son Pears/Shirley-Quirk/Drake/Tear/Adeney/P. Jones/ Sanders/Aronowitz/Marjoram/Ellis/Blades/Ledger/ Tunnard/Britten (1970) SET 438
BRITTEN	Psalm 150 Boys of Downside School, Purley/Tunnard/Britten (1967) SXL 6264
BRITTEN	The Rape of Lucretia Pears/Harper/Shirley-Quirk/Drake/Luxon/J. Baker/ Bainbridge/Hill/ECO/Britten (1971) SET 492–3
BRITTEN	The Rape of Lucretia (excerpts) Pears/Cross/Kraus/Donlevy/Brannigan/Ferrier/ Ritchie/Pollak/EOG Orchestra/Britten (1981) IGI 369
BRITTEN	Rejoice in the Lamb Hartnett/Steele/Todd/Francke/Purcell Singers/ Malcolm/Britten (1958) LXT 5416
BRITTEN	Saint Nicolas Pears/Hemmings/Aldeburgh Festival Chorus/ Aldeburgh Festival Orchestra/Britten (1955) LXT 5060
BRITTEN	Serenade Pears/Brain/Boyd Neel Orchestra/Britten (1945) AK1151–3 (78 rpm)
BRITTEN	Serenade Pears/Tuckwell/LSO/Britten (1964) SXL 6110
BRITTEN	Simple Symphony ECO/Britten (1969) SXL 6405
BRITTEN	Sinfonia da Requiem Danish SO/Britten (1955) LXT 2981
BRITTEN	Sinfonia da Requiem New Philharmonia Orchestra/Britten (1965) SXL 6175
BRITTEN	Sinfonia da Requiem German South-west Radio Symphony Orchestra/ Britten (1978) 0629 029
BRITTEN	Spring Symphony Vyvyan/Procter/Pears/ROH Chorus/ROH Orchestra (1961) SXL 2264
BRITTEN	Symphony for Cello and Orchestra Rostropovich/ECO/Britten (1964) SXL 6138

BRITTEN	The Turn of the Screw Pears/Vyvyan/Hemmings/Dyer/Cross/Mandikian/EOG Orchestra/Britten (1955) LXT 5038–9
BRITTEN	Variations on a Theme of Frank Bridge ECO/Britten (1967) SXL 6316
BRITTEN	Violin Concerto Lubotsky/ECO/Britten (1971) SXL 6512
BRITTEN	War Requiem Vishnevskaya/Pears/Fischer-Dieskau/Bach Choir/London Symphony Chorus/Highgate School Choir/Preston/Melos Ensemble/LSO/Britten (1963) SET 252–3
BRITTEN	The Young Person's Guide to the Orchestra LSO/Britten (1964) SXL 6110
DELIUS	Two Aquarelles ECO/Britten (1969) SXL 6405
ELGAR	The Dream of Gerontius Pears/Minton/Shirley-Quirk/King's College Choir, Cambridge/London Symphony Chorus/LSO/Britten (1972) SET 525–6
ELGAR	Introduction and Allegro for Strings ECO/Britten (1969) SXL 6405
FOLKSONG	
arr. Grainger	Bold William Taylor Shirley-Quirk/ECO/Britten (1969) SXL 6410
arr. Grainger	The 'Duke of Marlborough' Fanfare ECO/Britten (1969) SXL 6410
arr. Grainger	I'm seventeen come Sunday Ambrosian Singers/ECO/Britten (1969) SXL 6410
arr. Grainger	Lisbon ECO/Britten (1969) SXL 6410
arr. Grainger	Lord Maxwell's Goodnight Pears/ECO/Britten (1969) SXL 6410
arr. Grainger	The Lost Lady Found Ambrosian Singers/ECO/Britten (1969) SXL 6410
arr. Grainger	My Robin is to the Green Wood gone ECO/Britten (1969) SXL 6410
arr. Grainger	Shallow Brown Shirley-Quirk/ECO/Britten (1969) SXL 6410
arr. Grainger	Shepherd's Hey ECO/Britten (1969) SXL 6410
arr. Grainger	There was a pig went out to dig Ambrosian Singers/Britten (1969) SXL 6410
arr. Grainger	Willow Willow Pears/ECO/Britten (1969) SXL 6410

HANDEL	Ode for St. Cecilia's Day – The trumpet's loud clangour; But bright Cecilia Pears/Chorus of East Anglian Choirs/ECO/Britten (1972) 5BB 119–20
HAYDN	Cello Concerto in C major Rostropovich/ECO/Britten (1964) SXL 6138
HAYDN	Symphony No. 45 'Farewell' Aldeburgh Festival Orchestra/Britten (1957) LXT 5312
HAYDN	Symphony No. 55 'Schoolmaster' Aldeburgh Festival Orchestra/Britten (1957) LXT 5312
MOZART	Piano Concerto in A, K.414 Aldeburgh Festival Orchestra/Britten (directed from the keyboard) (1957) LW 5294
MOZART	Piano Concerto in D minor, K.466 Curzon/ECO/Britten (1982) SXL 7007
MOZART	Piano Concerto in B flat, K.595 Richter/ECO/Britten (1979) Baton 1009
MOZART	Piano Concerto in B flat, K.595 Curzon/ECO/Britten (1982) SXL 7007
MOZART	Serenata Notturna, K.239 ECO/Britten (1968) SXL 6372
MOZART	Symphony No. 25 ECO/Britten (1978) SXL 6879
MOZART	Symphony No. 29 ECO/Britten (1978) SXL 6879
MOZART	Symphony No. 38 'Prague' ECO/Britten (1972) SXL 6539
MOZART	Symphony No. 40 ECO/Britten (1968) SXL 6372
THE NATIONAL ANTHEM arr. Britten	London Symphony Chorus/LSO/Britten (1962) SEC 5119
THE NATIONAL ANTHEM arr. Britten	Chorus of East Anglian Choirs/ECO/Britten (1972) 5BB 199–20
PURCELL ed. Britten	Chacony in G minor, Z.730 ECO/Britten (1969) SXL 6405
PURCELL ed. Britten and I. Holst	The Fairy Queen Vyvyan/J. Bowman/Brett/Pears/Wells/Partridge/Shirley-Quirk/Brannigan/Burrowes/Hodgson/Ambrosian Opera Chorus/ECO/Britten (1972) SET 499–500
SCHUBERT	Symphony No. 8 'Unfinished' ECO/Britten (1972) SXL 6539

SCHUMANN	Cello Concerto Rostropovich/LSO/Britten (1982) RR 500
SCHUMANN	Scenes from Goethe's 'Faust' Fischer-Dieskau/Harwood/Shirley-Quirk/Pears/Vyvyan/ Palmer/Dickinson/Stevens/Lloyd/Hodgson/Aldeburgh Festival Singers/Wandsworth School Choir/ECO/ Britten (1973) SET 567–8
VARIATIONS ON AN ELIZABETHAN THEME	by Oldham, Tippett, Berkeley, Britten, Searle and Walton Aldeburgh Festival Orchestra/Britten (1952) LXT 2798

II AS PIANIST

BEETHOVEN	Quintet in E flat for piano and wind, op. 16 Dennis Brain Wind Quintet/Britten (1979) IGI 370
BERKELEY, L.	How love came in Pears/Britten (1956) LW 5241
BRIDGE	Cello Sonata Rostropovich/Britten (1970) SXL 6426
BRIDGE	Go not, happy day Pears/Britten (1956) LW 5241
BRIDGE	Goldenhair Pears/Britten (1964) ZRG 5418
BRIDGE	Journey's end Pears/Britten (1964) ZRG 5418
BRIDGE	Love went a-riding Pears/Britten (1956) LW 5241
BRIDGE	So perverse Pears/Britten (1964) ZRG 5418
BRIDGE	'Tis but a week Pears/Britten (1964) ZRG 5418
BRIDGE	When you are old Pears/Britten (1964) ZRG 5418
BRITTEN	The Birds Hahessy/Britten (1961) ZFA 18
BRITTEN	Canticle I Pears/Britten (1962) ZRG 5277
BRITTEN	Canticle II Hahessy/Pears/Britten (1962) ZRG 5277
BRITTEN	Canticle III Pears/Tuckwell/Britten (1962) ZRG 5277
BRITTEN	Canticle IV J. Bowman/Pears/Shirley-Quirk/Britten (1973) SXL 6608

RECORDED REPERTOIRE

BRITTEN	A Charm of Lullabies
	Watts/Britten (1981) REGL 417
BRITTEN	Corpus Christi Carol
	Hahessy/Britten (1961) ZFA 18
BRITTEN	Friday Afternoons (3,5,6,8,11)
	Hahessy/M. Berkeley/Britten (1961) ZFA 18
BRITTEN	The Golden Vanity
	Wandsworth School Boys' Choir/Britten/Burgess (1970) SET 445
BRITTEN	The Holy Sonnets of John Donne
	Pears/Britten (1949) DB 6689–91 (78 rpm)
BRITTEN	The Holy Sonnets of John Donne
	Pears/Britten (1969) SXL 6391
BRITTEN	Introduction and Rondo alla Burlesca
	Curzon/Britten (1945) K1117 (78 rpm)
BRITTEN	Mazurka Elegiaca
	Curzon/Britten (1945) K 1118 (78 rpm)
BRITTEN	On this Island
	Pears/Britten (1981) REGL 417
BRITTEN	On this Island – Let the florid music praise!
	Pears/Britten (1956) LW 5241
BRITTEN	Sechs Hölderlin-Fragmente
	Pears/Britten (1963) SWL 8507
BRITTEN	Seven Sonnets of Michelangelo
	Pears/Britten (1942) B 9302 & C 3312 (78 rpm)
BRITTEN	Seven Sonnets of Michelangelo
	Pears/Britten (1956) LXT 5095
BRITTEN	Sonata in C for cello and piano
	Rostropovich/Britten (1962) SXL 2298
BRITTEN	Songs and Proverbs of William Blake
	Fischer-Dieskau/Britten (1969) SXL 6391
BRITTEN	Tit For Tat
	Shirley-Quirk/Britten (1973) SXL 6608
BRITTEN	Who are these children?
	Pears/Britten (1973) SXL 6608
BRITTEN	Winter Words
	Pears/Britten (1956) LXT 5095
BRITTEN	Winter Words
	Pears/Britten (1980) AF 001
BUTTERWORTH	A Shropshire Lad – Is my team ploughing?
	Pears/Britten (1956) LW 5241
DEBUSSY	Cello Sonata
	Rostropovich/Britten (1962) SXL 2298
DIBDIN	Tom Bowling
arr. Britten	Pears/Britten (1961) CEP 711

FOLKSONG
arr. Britten	The ash grove Pears/Britten (1944) R 10009 (78 rpm)
arr. Britten	The ash grove Pears/Britten (1955) LW 5122
arr. Britten	The ash grove Pears/Britten (1962) SXL 6007
arr. Britten	Avenging and bright Pears/Britten (1962) SXL 6007
arr. Britten	La belle est au jardin d'amour Wyss/Britten (1944) M 568 (78 rpm)
arr. Britten	La belle est au jardin d'amour Pears/Britten (1962) SXL 6007
arr. Copland	The Boatmen's dance Pears/Britten (1951) DA 7038–9 (78 rpm)
arr. Britten	The Bonny Earl o' Moray Pears/Britten (1945) M 594 (78 rpm)
arr. Britten	The Bonny Earl o' Moray Pears/Britten (1954) LW 5122
arr. Britten	The Bonny Earl o' Moray Pears/Britten (1962) SXL 6007
arr. Britten	The brisk young widow Pears/Britten (1954) LW 5122
arr. Britten	The brisk young widow Pears/Britten (1962) SXL 6007
arr. Britten	Ca' the yowes Pears/Britten (1962) SXL 6007
arr. Britten	Come you not from Newcastle? Pears/Britten (1947) DA 1873 (78 rpm)
arr. Britten	Come you not from Newcastle? Pears/Britten (1962) SXL 6007
arr. Copland	The Dodger Pears/Britten (1951) DA 7038–9 (78 rpm)
arr. Britten	Early one morning Pears/Britten (1962) SXL 6007
arr. Britten	The foggy, foggy dew Pears/Britten (1947) DA 1873 (78 rpm)
arr. Britten	The foggy, foggy dew Pears/Britten (1961) CEP 711
arr. Britten	The foggy, foggy dew Pears/Britten (1980) AF 001
arr. Britten	Heigh-ho! Heigh-hi! Pears/Britten (1945) M 594 (78 rpm)
arr. Britten	How sweet the answer Pears/Britten (1962) SXL 6007

RECORDED REPERTOIRE

arr. Copland	I bought me a cat Pears/Britten (1951) DA 7038–9 (78 rpm)
arr. Grainger	The jolly sailor song Pears/Britten (1980) RLS 748
arr. Britten	The last rose of summer Pears/Britten (1962) SXL 6007
arr. Grainger	Let's dance gay in Green Meadow Tunnard/Britten (1969) SXL 6410
arr. Britten	The Lincolnshire poacher Pears/Britten (1961) CEP 711
arr. Britten	Little Sir William Pears/Britten (1944) M 555 (78 rpm)
arr. Britten	Little Sir William Pears/Britten (1955) LW 5122
arr. Copland	Long time ago Pears/Britten (1951) DA 7038–9 (78 rpm)
arr. Britten	The Miller of Dee Pears/Britten (1955) LW 5122
arr. Britten	The Miller of Dee Pears/Britten (1962) SXL 6007
arr. Britten	The Miller of Dee Pears/Britten (1980) AF 001
arr. Britten	The Minstrel Boy Pears/Britten (1962) SXL 6007
arr. Britten	O Waly, Waly Pears/Britten (1950) DA 2032 (78 rpm)
arr. Britten	O Waly, Waly Pears/Britten (1962) SXL 6007
arr. Britten	Oft in the stilly night Pears/Britten (1962) SXL 6007
arr. Britten	Oliver Cromwell Pears/Britten (1944) M 555 (78 rpm)
arr. Britten	Oliver Cromwell Pears/Britten (1954) LW 5122
arr. Grainger	The Pretty Maid Milkin' her Cow Pears/Britten (1969) SXL 6410
arr. Britten	Le roi s'en va-t'en chasse Wyss/Britten (1944) M 568 (78 rpm)
arr. Britten	Le roi s'en va-t'en chasse Pears/Britten (1962) SXL 6007
arr. Britten	Le roi s'en va-t'en chasse (sung in English) Pears/Britten (1980) RLS 748
arr. Britten	The Salley Gardens Pears/Britten (1944) M 555 (78 rpm)

arr. Britten	The Salley Gardens Pears/Britten (1955) LW 5122
arr. Britten	Sally in our alley Pears/Britten (1962) CEP 711
arr. Copland	Simple gifts Pears/Britten (1951) DA 7038–9 (78 rpm)
arr. Grainger	Six dukes went a-fishin' Pears/Britten (1953) DA 2032 (78 rpm)
arr. Grainger	The Sprig of Thyme Pears/Britten (1969) SXL 6410
arr. Britten	Sweet Polly Oliver Pears/Britten (1946) M678 (78 rpm)
arr. Britten	Sweet Polly Oliver Pears/Britten (1955) LW 5122
arr. Britten	Sweet Polly Oliver Pears/Britten (1962) SXL 6007
arr. Britten	There's none to soothe Pears/Britten (1946) M 678 (78 rpm)
arr. Britten	There's none to soothe Pears/Britten (1955) LW 5122
HAYDN	Six Canzonets Pears/Britten (1963) SWL 8507
HOLST, G.	Twelve Songs Pears/Britten (1968) ZRG 512
HOLST, G.	Twelve Songs – Persephone Pears/Britten (1956) LW 5241
IRELAND	Friendship in misfortune Pears/Britten (1964) ZRG 5418
IRELAND	I have twelve oxen Pears/Britten (1956) LW 5241
IRELAND	The Land of lost content Pears/Britten (1964) ZRG 5418
IRELAND	Love and friendship Pears/Britten (1964) ZRG 5418
IRELAND	The One Hope Pears/Britten (1964) ZRG 5418
MOERAN	In youth is pleasure Pears/Britten (1956) LW 5241
MOZART	Sonata in C Major, K.521 Richter/Britten (1978) 2RR–2145–2
THE MUSIC OF BALI transcribed by McPhee	Pemŭngah Rébong Gambangan Lagŭ Délĕm Tabŭ Telŭ McPhee/Britten (1941) Schirmer 513–4 (78 rpm)

OLDHAM	Three Chinese Lyrics Pears/Britten (1956) LW 5241
PURCELL real. Britten	The Queen's Epicedium Pears/Britten (1948) DB 6763 (78 rpm)
PURCELL real. Britten	Sweeter than roses J. Bowman/Britten (1973) SXL 6608
SCHUBERT	Abendbilder Pears/Britten (1981) REGL 410
SCHUBERT	Abendstern Pears/Britten (1975) SXL 6722
SCHUBERT	Am See Pears/Britten (1944) 1009 (78 rpm. USA only)
SCHUBERT	An die Entfernte Pears/Britten (1975) SXL 6722
SCHUBERT	An die Laute Pears/Britten (1961) SEC 5084
SCHUBERT	Andantino varié in B minor, D.823/2 Richter/Britten (1980) 2RR 2121–1
SCHUBERT	Arpeggione Sonata Rostropovich/Britten (1970) SXL 6426
SCHUBERT	Atys Pears/Britten (1975) SXL 6722
SCHUBERT	Auf dem Wasser zu singen Pears/Britten (1975) SXL 6722
SCHUBERT	Auf der Bruck Pears/Britten (1952) DB 21423 (78 rpm)
SCHUBERT	Auflösung Pears/Britten (1975) SXL 6722
SCHUBERT	Der blinde Knabe Pears/Britten (1981) REGL 410
SCHUBERT	Das war ich Pears/Britten (1981) REGL 410
SCHUBERT	Du bist die Ruh Pears/Britten (1960) BR 3066
SCHUBERT	Eight variations on an original theme in A flat, D.813 Richter/Britten (1980) 2RR 2121–1
SCHUBERT	Der Einsame Pears/Britten (1961) SEC 5084
SCHUBERT	Der Einsame Pears/Britten (1975) SXL 6722
SCHUBERT	Fantasie in F minor, D.940 Richter/Britten (1980) 2RR 2121–2
SCHUBERT	Geheimes Pears/Britten (1961) SEC 5084

Schubert	Der Geistertanz
	Pears/Britten (1975) SXL 6722
Schubert	Gesang des Harfners
	Pears/Britten (1960) BR 3066
Schubert	Die Götter Griechenlands
	Pears/Britten (1981) REGL 410
Schubert	Grand Duo in C major, D.812
	Richter/Britten (1980) 2RR 2121
Schubert	Ihr Grab
	Pears/Britten (1981) REGL 410
Schubert	Im Frühling
	Pears/Britten (1952) DB 21423 (78 rpm)
Schubert	Im Frühling
	Pears/Britten (1975) SXL 6722
Schubert	Lachen und Weinen
	Pears/Britten (1975) SXL 6722
Schubert	Das Lied im Grünen
	Pears/Britten (1981) REGL 410
Schubert	Der Musensohn
	Pears/Britten (1969) BR 3066
Schubert	Nacht und Träume
	Pears/Britten (1975) SXL 6722
Schubert	Nachtstück
	Pears/Britten (1975) SXL 6722
Schubert	Die schöne Müllerin
	Pears/Britten (1960) SXL 2200
Schubert	Schwanengesang-Das Fischermädchen
	Pears/Britten (1975) SXL 6722
Schubert	Schwanengesang – Die Stadt
	Pears/Britten (1961) SEC 5084
Schubert	Schwanengesang – Die Taubenpost
	Pears/Britten (1961) SEC 5084
Schubert	Sprache der Liebe
	Pears/Britten (1975) SXL 6722
Schubert	Der Winterabend
	Pears/Britten (1981) REGL 410
Schubert	Die Winterreise
	Pears/Britten (1965) SET 270–1
Schumann	Dichterliebe
	Pears/Britten (1965) SET 270–1
Schumann	Fünf Stücke im Volkston
	Rostropovich/Britten (1962) SXL 2298
Shield arr. Britten	The Plough Boy
	Pears/Britten (1947) DA 1873 (78 rpm)

SHIELD arr. Britten	The Plough Boy Pears/Britten (1962) SXL 6007
SHIELD arr. Britten	The Plough Boy Pears/Britten (1980) AF 001
TIPPETT	Songs for Ariel Pears/Britten (1965) ZRG 5439
VAUGHAN WILLIAMS	On Wenlock Edge Pears/Zorian Quartet/Britten (1948) AM 585–7 78 rpm)
WARLOCK	Yarmouth Fair Pears/Britten (1956) LW 5241
WOLF	An einer Aeolsharfe Pears/Britten (1980) AF 001
WOLF	Beherzigung Pears/Britten (1981) REGL 410
WOLF	Bei einer Trauung Pears/Britten (1980) AF 001
WOLF	Bei einer Trauung Pears/Britten (1981) REGL 410
WOLF	Denk'es, o Seele! Pears/Britten (1980) AF 001
WOLF	Die den Gott gebarst Pears/Britten (1981) REGL 410
WOLF	Frühling übers Jahr Pears/Britten (1981) REGL 410
WOLF	Führ' mich, Kind Pears/Britten (1981) REGL 410
WOLF	Ganymed Pears/Britten (1981) REGL 410
WOLF	Der Gärtner Pears/Britten (1981) REGL 410
WOLF	Heimweh Pears/Britten (1980) AF 001
WOLF	Im Frühling Pears/Britten (1980) AF 001
WOLF	Jägerlied Pears/Britten (1980) AF 001
WOLF	Lied eines Verliebten Pears/Britten (1980) AF 001
WOLF	Sankt Nepomuks Vorabend Pears/Britten (1981) REGL 410
WOLF	Schlafendes Jesuskind Pears/Britten (1981) REGL 410
WOLF	Der Scholar Pears/Britten (1981) REGL 410

WOLF	Spottlied
	Pears/Britten (1981) REGL 410
WOLF	Wenn ich dein gedenke
	Pears/Britten (1981) REGL 410
WOLF	Wie sollt' ich heiter bleiben?
	Pears/Britten (1981) REGL 410

III AS VIOLA PLAYER

PURCELL	Fantasia upon one note, Z.745
	Zorian Quartet/Britten (1946) C3539 (78 rpm)

IV AS SPEAKER

KATHLEEN FERRIER THE SINGER AND THE PERSON (1979) REGL 368
1. Benjamin Britten describes the first time he heard Kathleen Ferrier singing in *Messiah*.
2. Gerald Moore and Benjamin Britten talk about Kathleen Ferrier's singing of folksongs.
3. Benjamin Britten recalls Kathleen Ferrier's singing the role of Lucretia in *The Rape of Lucretia*.
4. Benjamin Britten sums up the qualities of Kathleen Ferrier's voice.
5. Benjamin Britten talks of Kathleen Ferrier's singing of his *Canticle II Abraham and Isaac*.

BENJAMIN BRITTEN
A SELECT BIBLIOGRAPHY
COMPILED BY PAUL WILSON

This bibliography is an attempt to present writings and broadcasts relating to Benjamin Britten from the earliest years to the present date. It includes Britten's own prose writings under the heading BRITTEN. All articles, theses, books, record sleeve notes and broadcasts are collected under the relevant headings of Britten's works if they are mainly or wholly concerned with those works. The category GENERAL is necessarily large and the reader is recommended constantly to consult it alongside the more specific categories. Following the *New Grove*, items are listed in chronological order. Reprints are as a general rule *not* included and programme notes fairly lightly treated in view of the exigencies of space. The abbreviations AFPB relate to Aldeburgh Festival Programme Books, a rich source for Britten studies. I have abbreviated the title of the pioneering work in the field of both Britten studies in general and bibliography in particular as MITCHELL/KELLER 1952; its proper citation is: BENJAMIN BRITTEN: a commentary on his works from a group of specialists; edited by Donald Mitchell and Hans Keller. London, Rockcliff, 1952. Reprinted: Westport, Greenwood Press, 1972.

BIBLIOGRAPHY

A.M.D.G.
STRODE, R. *'A.M.D.G.'* (1939) AFPB 1984

ALBERT HERRING
HAWKES, R. *'Albert Herring' Tempo* 3 (March 1947)
CROZIER, E. 'Foreword to *Albert Herring' Tempo* 4 (Summer 1947)
KELLER, H. 'Glyndebourne Preface' *Sound* (June 1947)
SHAWE-TAYLOR, D. 'Britten's comic opera' *Listener* (June 12 1947)
HUSSEY, D. 'New Britten opera in world premiere' *New York Times* (June 21 1947)
STUART, C. 'Maupassant reversed' *Observer* (June 21 1947)
'Albert Herring – Britten's new comic opera' *The Times* (June 21 1947)
HUSSEY, D. 'Soft Roes on Toast' *Listener* (June 26 1947)
COOPER, M. 'On the Air' *Spectator* (June 27 1947)
SHAWE-TAYLOR, D. *New Statesman* (June 28 1947)
NEWMAN, E. 'Mr Britten and *Albert Herring* – I' *Sunday Times* (June 29 1947)
MCNAUGHT, W. 'Opera at Glyndebourne' *Musical Times* (July 1947)
GODDARD, S. 'Benjamin Britten writes a comic opera' *Picture Post* (July 5 1947)
NEWMAN, E. *'Albert Herring'* – II *Sunday Times* (July 6 1947)
KLEIN, J. W. 'Albert Herring' *Musical Opinion* (August 1947)
STEIN, E. 'Form in opera: *Albert Herring* examined' *Tempo* 5 (Autumn 1947)
MENGELBERG, K. 'De Opera *Albert Herring* von Benjamin Britten' *Mens en Melodie* (September 1947)
'Notes of the day' *Monthly Musical Record* 77 (September 1947)
CARDUS, N. *'Albert Herring' Manchester Guardian* (October 10 1947)
KELLER, H. 'The Rape of Lucretia. Albert Herring'. London, Boosey & Hawkes, 1947
WILLIAMS, S. 'Opera in London' *Penguin Music Magazine* 5 (February 1948)
POOT, M. 'La Création de *Albert Herring' Nation Belge* (June 2 1948)
MICHEL, A. *'Albert Herring* et *Peter Grimes' Le Phare* (June 3 1948)
CROZIER, E. *'Albert Herring'* AFPB 1948
HAREWOOD, Earl of *'Albert Herring'* AFPB 1949
SABIN, R. 'A masterly comedy of the first rank?' *Musical America* 69 (September 1949)
SMITH, C. 'An adroit example of mere artifice?' *Musical America* 69 (September 1949)

MITCHELL, D. 'The Cheltenham Festival – Britten Operas'
Manchester Guardian (July 14 1950)
BOLLERT, W. '*Albert Herring* in Berlin' *Musica* 4 (December 1950)
'*Albert Herring* (Hanover)' *Opera* 2 (May 1951)
MITCHELL, D. 'The Lyric, Hammersmith: Britten Season' *Music Survey* 3
No. 4 (June 1951)
DEL MAR, N. '*Albert Herring*' MITCHELL/KELLER 1952
HINTON, J. 'Workshop gives *Albert Herring* New York Premiere'
Musical America 22 (June 1952)
GATHORNE-HARDY, R. '*Albert Herring*' AFPB 1953
'New York College of Music gives *Albert Herring*' *Musical America* 77 (June 1956)
'Hipp – Hipp – Hurra für *Albert Herring*' *Musica* 11 (May 1957)
SARGEANT, W. 'Heavy Hands' *New Yorker* 33 (May 11 1957)
GISHFORD, A. '*Albert Herring*' AFPB 1957
'Brittens *Albert Herring* auf dem Thespiskarren' *Melos* 27 (December 1960)
BAPTISTA, J.A. 'Circulo de Cultura Musical' *Arte Musicale* 29 No. 15 (1961)
LANGE, N. 'Akzente in Musikleben' *Musica* 15 (March 1961)
SZENDREY, J. 'Britten opera in Budapest' *Opera* 12 (March 1961)
'Covent Garden' *Music Review* 23 No. 3 (1962)
'Stürmischer Erfolg für *Albert Herring*' (reprinted from *Neue Tagespost*)
Orchester 10 (April 1962)
CROSS, J. 'Recollections of a Dowager Lady Billows' AFPB 1962
BARKER, F. G. 'Soused "Herring"' *Music and Musicians* 10 (August 1962)
'Aldeburgh' *Opera* 13 (Autumn 1962)
LARNER, G. 'Albert from Aldeburgh' *Records and Recording* 8 No. 1
(October 1964)
GOODWIN, N. 'Records' *Music and Musicians* 13 (December 1964)
London's '*Albert Herring*' *American Record Guide* 31 (July 1964)
LAWRENCE, R. 'Caviare from Opera Workshops' *Hi-Fi/Musical America*
15 (August 1965)
'Summer Festivals (Edinburgh)' *Opera* 16 (November 1965)
POSPISIL, V. '*Albert Herring* potreti the jedne sezone' *Hudebni Rozhledy* 19
No. 16 (1966)
HONOLKA, K. '*Albert Herring* in veränderter Instrumentation' *Musica* 20
No. 2 (1966)
POSPISIL, V. 'Dvakrat *Albert Herring*' *Hudebni Rozhledy* 19 No. 6 (1966)
ABRASHEV, B. '*Albert Khering* (Sofia)' *Bulgarska Muzika* 17 (February 1966)
HONOLKA, K. 'Ulm' *Opera* 17 (February 1966)
GREENE, P. 'Los Angeles' *Opera News* 30 (March 12 1966)

NARI, P. 'Création en France d'un Opéra de Benjamin Britten' *Musique (Chaix)* 146 (May 1966)
ECKSTEIN, P. 'Prague' *Opera News* 30 (May 1966)
ECKSTEIN, P. 'Prague' *Opera* 17 (July 1966)
GOODWIN, N. 'Well-Pickled Herring (Hamburg's First Production)' *Music and Musicians* 14 (August 1966)
GREBE, K. 'Hamburg' *Opera* 17 (August 1966)
JURIK, M. '*Albert Herring* v Bratislave' *Hudebni Rozhledy* 20 No. 2 (1967)
'Objavenie interpretov' *Sovetskaya Vetskaya Hudebni* 11 No. 9 (1967)
CHRIST, R. B. 'Basle' *Opera* 18 (May 1967)
HONOLKA, K. 'In guter Laune komponiert' *Opern Welt* 6 (June 1967)
TUMPFF, G. A. 'Schwetzingen: Festspiele in Carl Theodors Sommerresidenz' *Neue Zeitschrift für Musik* 128 (July–August 1967)
'*Albert Herring* i Fjensynsteatret' *Norsk Musikerblad* 56 (December 1967)
SNYDER, R. D. 'The use of the comic idea in selected works of contemporary opera' Ph.D Indiana University (1968)
ZIJLSRA, M. '*Albert Herring* van Benjamin Britten – voorstelling door de Opera Studio' *Mens en Mel* 23 (January 1968)
KANSKI, J. 'Poland' *Opera* 19 (September 1968)
'*Albert Herring* v Olomouci' *Hudebni Rozhledy* 22 No. 6 (1969)
KRAUSE, E. 'Mixtur aus Komik und Tragik' *Opern Welt* 1 (January 1969)
LIMMERT, E. 'Hannover' *Neue Zeitschrift für Musik* 130 (July–August 1969)
HOMMEL, F. 'Impressionen vom Karl-Marx-Platz' *Opern Welt* 10 (October 1969)
'Albert Herring de Britten' *Schweizerische Musikzeitung* 110 No. 4 (1970)
BARKER, F. G. 'Guildford: Fresh Herring' *Music and Musicians* 19 (September 1970)
BLYTH, A. 'South of the Thames' *Opera* 21 (September 1970)
FORBES, E. 'Wexford Delights' *Opera* 22 (January 1971)
MARTIN, G. 'King of the May' *Opera News* 36 (September 1971)
SMITH, P. J. 'New York' *Hi-Fi/Musical America* 21 (December 1971)
TURRO, R. 'Opera de Camara del Teatro Colón' *Buenos Aires Musicale* 27 No. 436 (1972)
LOHMUELLER, H. 'Da Monaco di Daviera' *Nuova Rivista Musicale Italiana* 6 No. 1 (1972)
SCHMIDT-GARRE, H. 'München: Brittens *Albert Herring* – ein Publikumserfolg' *Neue Zeitschrift fur Musik* 133 (March 1972)
SCHMIDT, D. N. 'München: Drollige Spasse' *Opern Welt* 3 (March 1972)
DANLER, K. R. 'München: Henzes 6. Sinfonie – *Albert Herring* von Benjamin Britten' *Orchester* 20 (April 1972)

KANSKI, J. 'Albert Herring we Wroclawiu' Ruch Muzyczny 17 No. 4 (1973)
LOPPERT, M. 'At Snape' Opera 25 (October 1974)
TAYLOR, P. 'The English Opera Group at the Sadler's Wells Theatre' Musical Opinion 98 (December 1974)
GOODWIN, N. 'Albert Herring; English Opera Group at Sadler's Wells' Opera 25 (December 1974)
'Chautauqua' Opera Canada 16 No. 3 (1975)
ZOTTOS, Ian 'Albert Herring tou Benjamin Britten' Mousikologia (Spring 1975)
REGITZ, H. 'Erfreulicher Ersatz – Brittens Albert Herring in Stuttgart' Opern Welt No. 5 (May 1975)
FELDMAN, M. A. 'Saint Paul' Opera News 40 (August 1975)
STEIN, E. Albert Herring The Britten Companion: edited by Christopher Palmer. London, Faber (1984)
AN ALBERT HERRING ANTHOLOGY; compiled by Eric Crozier, Donald Mitchell, Philip Reed and Rosamund Strode and edited by Donald Mitchell. Glyndebourne Festival Programme Book 1985
CROZIER, E. Letters to Nancy Evans. Glyndebourne Festivl Opera Programme Book, 1985.
CROSS, J. 'Albert Herring: The Early Performances' AFPB 1986
CROZIER, E. 'Albert Herring' AFPB 1986
CROZIER, E. 'Albert the Good' AFPB 1986
MITCHELL, D. 'The serious comedy of Albert Herring' Opera Quarterly 4 No. 3 (Autumn 1986)
LAW, J. E. 'Daring to Eat a Peach: Literary Allusion in Albert Herring' Opera Quarterly (Spring 1987)

THE ALDEBURGH FESTIVAL
KELLER, H. 'A Britten Festival' Everybody's (June 5 1948)
CROZIER, E. 'The Origin of the Aldeburgh Festival' AFPB 1948
HAREWOOD, Earl of 'The Aldeburgh Festival' AFPB 1948
FORSTER, E. M. 'Looking back on the first Aldeburgh Festival' AFPB 1949
MAYER, T. 'Aldeburgh Festival Focuses on various works by Britten' Musical America 70 (July 1950)
MITCHELL, D. 'Aldeburgh, England' Opera News 15 No. 1 (October 1950)
KOLODIN, I. 'More Festival, and Tea in Surrey' Saturday Review 34 (June 23 1951)
'Aldeburgh Festival reflects Britten's musical personality' Musical America 71 (July 19 1951)
'The Aldeburgh Festival' Musical Times 93 (August 1952)
CRANBOOK, Lady PEARS, P. and BRITTEN, B. Foreword AFPB 1955

CADBURY-BROWN, H. T. 'Notes on an opera house for Aldeburgh' AFPB 1957
OSBORNE, C. 'Britten's Festival' *New York Times* 113 (July 5 1964)
GOODWIN, N. 'Commentary from Aldeburgh' *Music and Musicians* 12 (August 1964)
SUGDEN, D. 'Snape Concert Hall' *The Arup Journal* (June 1967)
SUGDEN, D. 'The Maltings' AFPB 1967
WOCKER, K. H. 'Protest gegen die Routine (Aldeburgh)' *Opern Welt* 9 (September 1967)
'Aldeburgh Festival Issue' *East Anglian Magazine* 28 (June 1969)
GREENFIELD, E. 'Maltings will rise again for Aldeburgh 1970' *Guardian* (June 9 1969)
GREENFIELD, E. 'Aldeburgh – the phoenix festival' *Guardian* (June 10 1969)
'Aldeburgh Festival continues' *The Times* (June 11 1969)
DAY-LEWIS, S. 'Festival arises from the ashes' *Daily Telegraph* (May 14 1970)
BROCKMAN, H. A. N. 'New Aldeburgh concert hall out of the ashes' *Financial Times* (May 15 1970)
DAVIES, M. 'After the Flames. Aldeburgh's Dream takes shape' *Illustrated London News* 256 (June 1970)
HEINITZ, T. 'Ein Benjamin Britten Festival (Aldeburgh)' *Stereophonie* 9 (August 1970)
ALDEBURGH ANTHOLOGY; edited by Ronald Blythe. Aldeburgh, Snape Maltings Foundation in association with Faber Music (1972)
CROZIER, E. 'The origin of the Aldeburgh Festival' *Aldeburgh Anthology* ed. R. Blythe, Snape Maltings Foundation in association with Faber Music (1972)
FORSTER, E. M. 'Looking back on the first Aldeburgh Festival' *Aldeburgh Anthology* ed. R. Blythe, Aldeburgh, Snape Maltings Foundation in association with Faber Music (1972)
REISS, S. 'How the Festival developed' *Aldeburgh Anthology* ed. R. Blythe, Snape Maltings Foundation in association with Faber Music (1972)
BEHREND, G. 'Early Days in Aldeburgh: recollections of a railway enthusiast' AFPB 1972
GISHFORD, A. Sleeve note for Decca 5BB119–20 (1972)
HOLST, I. 'Recollections of Times Past' AFPB 1978
STRODE, R. First performances at the Aldeburgh Festival AFPB 1982
STIMPSON, M. 'The Aldeburgh Festival' *European Gay Review* 1 (1986)

ALLA MARCIA
EVANS, J. *'Alla Marcia* (1933)' AFPB 1983
MITCHELL, D. and EVANS, J. Sleeve note for Unicorn-Kanchana DLP 9020 (1983)

ALLA QUARTETTO SERIOSO
'Young composers' concert' *Daily Telegraph* (December 12 1933)

ALPINE SUITE
'Alpine Suite, for Recorder Trio' *Musical Opinion* 79 (June 1956)
'Alpine Suite, for Recorder Trio' *Music and Letters* 37 (October 1956)
'Alpine Suite' AFPB 1960
NOBLE, J. 'The Recorder in Twentieth Century Music' *The Recorder and Music Magazine* 1 (February 1965)

AN AMERICAN OVERTURE
MITCHELL, D. *'An American Overture* (1941)' AFPB 1984
MITCHELL, D. Sleeve note for EMI EL2702631 (1986)

ANTIPHON
'Antiphon; for SATB, with optional soloists' *English Church Music* 27 (February 1957)
'Antiphon' Op. 56B AFPB 1965

BALLAD OF HEROES
(Review of first performance) *Times* (April 6 1939)
(Review of first performance) *Observer* (April 9 1939)
'London Concerts FMP=x' *Musical Times* (May 1939)
Tempo 4 (O.S.) (July 1939)
STUCKENSCHMIDT, H. H. 'Bekenntnismusik ausserhalb der Kirche' *Schweizriesche Musikzeitung* 108 No. 6 (1968)
BRITTEN, B. *Ballad of Heroes* Op. 14 AFPB 1973
COLEMAN, T. 'Voices' *Music and Musicians* 21 (August 1973)

BALLAD OF LITTLE MUSGRAVE AND LADY BARNARD
Tempo 7 (O.S.) (June 1944)
'Music in prison camp: Festival behind barbed wire' *Times* (March 2 1945)
'The Ballad of Little Musgrave and Lady Barnard for TBB and piano *Music and Letters* 34 (April 1953)
BRITTEN, B. *'The Ballad of Little Musgrave and Lady Barnard'* AFPB 1969
JOSEPHSON, D. *'The Ballad of Little Musgrave and Lady Barnard'* AFPB 1974
STRODE, R. *'The Ballad of Little Musgrave and Lady Barnard'* AFPB 1979

THE BEGGAR'S OPERA
PAAP, W. *'The Beggar's Opera'* *Mens en Melodie* 3 No. 8 (1948)

DENT, E. J. 'The Beggar's Opera' *The Listener* (September 16 1948)
BLOM, E. 'Beggar's Opera' *Birmingham Post* (September 20 1948)
HUSSEY, D. 'Broadcast music' *Listener* (September 30 1948)
KELLER, H. 'Britten's *The Beggar's Opera*' *The Listener* (October 14 1948)
KELLER, H. 'Britten's *Beggar's Opera*' *Tempo* 10 (Winter 1948–1949)
MELLERS, W. H. '*The Beggar's Opera* (review of vocal score)' *Music Survey* 2 No. 1 (1949)
KELLER, H. 'New Music in the Old Year *Music Parade* 1 No. 10 (1949)
'*The Beggar's Opera*: a Ballad opera in a new musical version' *Music Survey* 2 No. 1 (1949)
'*The Beggar's Opera*, in a new musical version realised from the original airs' *Monthly Musical Record* 79 (October 1949)
KELLER, H. 'Benjamin Britten's *Beggar's Opera*' *Schweizerische Musikzeitung* 1 (January 1950)
PRAWY, M. 'Beggars in Vienna' *Opera News* 14 (January 16 1950)
'*Beggar's Opera*' *Music Review* 11 (February 1950)
BONDY, F. '*Die Bettleroper* nach Britten und nach Brecht' *Die Weltwoche* (February 24 1950)
SABIN, R. 'Juilliard School presents Britten's *Beggar's Opera*' *Musical America* 70 (April 1950)
CRAIG, M. '*Beggar's Opera* produced by Juilliard' *Musical Courier* 141 (April 15 1950)
SCHRANN, F. '*Die Bettleroper* und ihre Wandlungen' *Musica* 4 (May–June 1950)
WHITE, E. W. '*The Beggar's Opera*' AFPB 1950
MITCHELL, D. 'The Cheltenham Festival – Britten Opera' *Manchester Guardian* (July 14 1950)
MITCHELL, D. 'Opera Notes; Aldeburgh, England' *Opera News* 15 (October 1950)
RODENANN, A. '*Die Bettler-Oper* Renoviert' *Melos* 18 (March 1951)
'*The Beggar's Opera* (Hamburg)' *Opera* 2 (May 1951)
'Round and About the Folk Songs and *The Beggar's Opera*' *Disc* 5 (Autumn 1951)
LINDLAR, H. 'Brittens *Bettler-Oper*' *Musica* 10 (July–August 1956)
LAWRIE, J. H. '*The Beggar's Opera*' AFPB 1963
LUTTWITZ, H. 'von Wuppertal; Benjamin Brittens *Bettleroper* nach Gay und Pepusch' *Neue Zeitschrift für Musik* 132 (March 1971)
SCHREIBER, U. 'Wuppertal Parodie des Hausstils' *Opern Welt* 3 (March 1971)
LUTTWITZ, H. 'von Wuppertal; Benjamin Brittens *Bettleroper* nach Gay und Pepusch' *Orchester* 19 (April 1971)

BOEHM, H. 'Jubiläums – Finale; *Die Bettleroper* in Dresden-Radebeul' *Musik und Gesellschaft* 31 (October 1971)
REMENYI-GYENES, I. 'Hungary' *Opera Canada* 16 No. 1 (1975)
SADIE, S. 'Britten; *The Beggar's Opera*' *Musical Times* 122 (1981)
HYTNER, N. *'The Beggar's Opera'* AFPB 1982
KELLER, H. *'The Beggar's Opera' The Britten Companion:* edited by Christopher Palmer. London, Faber (1984)

BILLY BUDD

CROZIER, E. 'An Opera Team sets to work' *Picture Post* (October 15 1949)
STEIN, E. 'The music of *Billy Budd*' *Opera* 3 (April 1950)
CROZIER, E. 'Writing a Britten opera' *Music Parade* 2 No. 6 (1951)
'*Billy Budd*' *Tempo* 21 (Autumn 1951)
'*Billy Budd:* A Synopsis' *Tempo* 21 (Autumn 1951)
COLEMAN, B. and PIPER, J. '*Billy Budd* on the stage; an early discussion between producer and designer' *Tempo* 21 (Autumn 1951)
WHITE, E. W. '*Billy Budd*' *Listener* (November 22 1951)
CROZIER, E. 'The Strange Story of *Billy Budd*' *Radio Times* (November 23 1951)
VAN DELDEN, L. 'Benjamin Brittens Opera *Billy Budd*' *Mens en Mel* 6 (December 1951)
SHAWE-TAYLOR, D. *'Billy Budd* – I' *New Statesman* (December 1 1951)
BLOM, E. 'Britten's *Billy Budd*' *Observer* (December 2 1951)
CAPELL, R. '*Billy Budd* at Covent Garden' *Daily Telegraph* (December 3 1951)
MITCHELL, D. 'Britten's Latest Opera Opens at Covent Garden' *Eastern Daily Press* (December 3 1951)
HOPE-WALLACE, P. 'Britten's *Billy Budd*' *Manchester Guardian* (December 3 1951)
'Britten's new opera: *Billy Budd* at Covent Garden' *Times* (December 3 1951)
CAPELL, R. '*Billy Budd* Questions' *Daily Telegraph* (December 7 1951)
'*Billy Budd:* the interval of the second' *Times* (December 7 1951)
SHAWE-TAYLOR, D. '*Billy Budd* – II' *New Statesman* (December 8 1951)
MASON, C. 'Opera' *Spectator* (December 8 1951)
WILLIAMS, S. 'Premiere of Britten's *Billy Budd* London' *New York Times* 101 (December 9 1951)
NEWMAN, E. '*Billy Budd*' *Sunday Times* (December 9 1951)
'*Billy Budd* First performance' *Newsweek* 38 (December 10 1951)
'Britten's Seventh' *Times* 58 (December 10 1951)
MITCHELL, D. '*Billy Budd*' *Tribune* (December 14 1951)

CARDUS, N. 'Let's Make an Opera' *Manchester Guardian* (December 15 1951)
NOTCUTT, A. '*Billy Budd* Bows at Covent Garden' *Musical Courier* 144 (December 15 1951)
CROZIER, E. 'How *Billy Budd* Became an Opera' *London Calling* (December 20 1951)
HOPE-WALLACE, P. '*Billy Budd*' *Picture Post* (December 22 1951)
HEINITZ, T. 'The Other Side (imported recordings)' *Saturday Review* 34 (December 29 1951)
'Lord Harewood discusses Britten's new opera *Billy Budd*' *Opera News* 16 (December 31 1951)
TREWIN, J. C. 'World Reviews' *World Theatre II* No. 1(1951/2)
STEIN, E. '*Billy Budd*' MITCHELL-KELLER 1952
CAMPBELL, C. 'Second thoughts on *Billy Budd*' *Adam* 20 Nos. 224-6 (1952)
CROZIER, E. 'Writing an Opera' *Adam* 20 Nos. 224-6 (1952)
WHITE, E. W. '*Billy Budd*' *Adelphi* 28 no. 2 (1952)
KNYVETT, G. 'Benjamin Brittens anden store opera' *Danks Musik* 27 (1952)
HOLST, I. 'Benjamin Britten's *Billy Budd*' *Foyer* 2 (1952)
GODMAN, S. 'Aus dem Musikleben' *Musica* 1 (1952)
SMITH, L. G. '*Donald of the burthens* and *Billy Budd*' *Music Parade* 2 No. 10 (1952)
'*Billy Budd*, Opera en quatre actes; synopsis' *Revue Musicale* 213 (1952)
GODDARD, S. 'London Letter' *Chesterian* 26 (January 1952)
LITTLEFIELD, J. '*Billy Budd*' *Counterpoint* 17 (January 1952)
RUTZ, H. '*Billy Budd*' *Melos* 19 (January 1952)
CAPELL, R. 'Opera and Concerts' *Monthly Musical Record* 82 (January 1952)
GODMAN, S. '*Billy Budd*, die neue Britten-Oper' *Musica* 6 (January 1952)
LOCKSPEISER, E. '*Billy Budd* has Premiere' *Musical America* 72 (January 1952)
'*Billy Budd:* First Performance' *Musical Opinion* 75 (January 1952)
'*Billy Budd*' *Musical Times* 93 (January 1952)
MCNAUGHT, W. 'Britten's *Billy Budd*' *Musical Times* (January 1952)
DEAN, W., GODDARD, S. and GOLDBECK, F. 'First Impressions' *Opera* 3 (January 1952)
'*Billy Budd*' *Opera* 3 (January 1952)
MASON, C. 'Lettera da Londra' *Rassegna Musicale* 22 (January 1952)
GOLDBECK, F. 'A propos du nouvel Opéra de Benjamin Britten' *Revue Musicale* 210 (January 1952)
GATTI, G. 'Entusiasmus come per Puccini' *Tempo* (January 1952)

FITZGERALD, D. and P. M. '*Billy Budd* – The Novel by Herman Melville' *World Review* (January 1952)

STUART, C. '1. The novel by Melville, 2. The score by Britten' *World Review* (January 1952)

HUSSEY, D. 'Britten's new opera *Billy Budd*' *Britain Today* (February 1952)

FOSS, H. '*Billy Budd*' *Canon* 5 (February 1952)

MANN, W. 'Britten's *Billy Budd*' *London Musical Events* 7 No. 2 (February 1952)

'*Billy Budd*' *Music Review* 13 (February 1952)

MITCHELL, D. 'More Off than On *Billy Budd*' *Music Survey* 4 No. 2 (February 1952)

HOWES, E. '*Billy Budd*' *R.C.M. Magazine* 48 (February 1952)

FOSS, H. 'Hubert Foss Looks Back' *Canon* 5 No. 8 (March 1952)

KLEIN, J. W. 'Britten's advance to Mastery' *Musical Opinion* 75 (March 1952)

MASON, C. '*Billy Budd* Comes to Manchester' *Manchester Guardian* (March 15 1952)

RODEMANN, A. 'Olle Kamellen im neuen Gewande' *Melos* 19 (April 1952)

PORTER, A. '*Billy Budd*' *Music and Letters* 33 No. 2 (April 1952)

RODEMANN, A. '*Billy Budd* oder die "Schicksalstragödie"' *Musikleben* 5 (April 1952)

STEIN, E. 'The Music of *Billy Budd*' *Opera* 3 (April 1952)

'Wiesbaden' *Opera* 3 (May 1952)

MILNER, A. and GELLHORN, P. '*Billy Budd*' *Score* 6 (May 1952)

COOPER, M. 'Music' *Spectator* (May 2 1952)

'*Billy Budd* Piano reduction by E. Stein' *Musical Opinion* 75 (June 1952)

GRANIER, M. L. 'Théâtres Lyriques: *Falstaff* – *Billy Budd* (review of 1st Paris performance)' *Journal Musical Français* (June 5 1952)

MCNAUGHT, W. 'Britten's *Billy Budd*' *Musical Times* (July 1952)

DEAN, W. and others '*Billy Budd*; the story with comments on the opera' *Opera* (July 1952)

MASON, R. 'Herman Melville and *Billy Budd*' *Tempo* No. 21 (Autumn 1952)

DOWNES, O. 'Power of TV; *Billy Budd* gains new stature on television' *New York Times* 101 (October 26 1952)

EYER, R. 'American premiere of *Billy Budd* launches NBC–TV Opera Season' *Musical America* 72 (November 1952)

'Britten's *Billy Budd* has its US bow on NBC–TV' *Musical Courier* 146 (November 1952)

RAYNOR, H. 'Britten, Stravinsky and the Future of Opera' *Musical Opinion* 76 (November 1952)

'Britten's *Billy Budd* on NBC–TV' *Saturday Review* 35 (November 1952)

HINTON, J. '*Billy Budd* on television in USA' *Musical Times* 93 (December 1952)
EATON, Q. '*Billy Budd* Takes the Air' *High Fidelity* 2 (January–February 1953)
'America (Television version)' *Opera* 4 (February 1953)
ADLER, P. H. 'Eight years with Opera on Television' *Opera* 8 (December 1957)
HOLST, I. *Billy Budd*' *Foyer* No. 2 (1958)
'*Billy Budd* Revised (Third Programme Broadcast)' *Tempo* 55–56 (Autumn–Winter 1960)
DEAN, W. '*Billy Budd*; BBC Third Programme' *Opera* 12 (February 1961)
POPE-HENNESSY, J. 'A Note on Melville's *Billy Budd*' *About the House* 1 No. 5 (1963)
MITCHELL, D. 'Britten's Revisionary Practice; Practical and Creative' *Tempo* 66–7 (Autumn–Winter 1963)
'Covent Garden' *Music Review* 25 No. 3 (1964)
KLEIN, J. W. 'A New Version of *Billy Budd*' *Musical Opinion* 87 (January 1964)
'An opera about good and evil' *Times* (January 10 1964)
GRIER, C. '*Billy Budd* revised' *Listener* 71 (January 16 1964)
MELLERS, W. 'Vere' *New Statesman* 67 (January 17 1964)
'*Billy Budd* at the Royal Opera House: the new and revised version *Illustrated London News* 244 (January 18 1964)
NOBLE, J. 'Greater than *Grimes*' *Music and Musicians* 12 (February 1964)
CHAPMAN, E. '*Budd*'s Return' *Musical Events* 19 (February 1964)
'Covent Garden Opera' *Musical Opinion* 87 (February 1964)
TRACEY, E. '*Billy Budd*' *Musical Times* 105 (March 1964)
'*Billy Budd*; Covent Garden' *Opera* 15 (March 1964)
HENDERSON, R. L. '*Budd* and *Gloriana* Reconsidered' *Tempo* 68 (Spring 1964)
WEISSMANN, J. S. 'Puccini, Mozart e Britten sulle scene londinesi' *Musica d'Oggi* 8 No. 6 (1965)
BARKER, F. G. 'Man or Superman?' *Music and Musicians* 13 (June 1965)
'*Billy Budd*; Covent Garden' *Opera* 16 (June 1965)
WEAVER, W. 'Florence' *Opera* 16 (Autumn 1965)
HEINEMANN, R. 'Musik unserer Zeit' *Musica* 20 No. 3 (1966)
FREEMAN, J. W. '*Billy Budd* Returns' *Opera News* 30 (January 1966)
SARGEANT, W. 'Musical Events' *New Yorker* 41 (January 15 1966)
MOVSHON, T. 'Concert opera – Donizetti and Britten' *Hi-Fi/Musical America* 16 (March 1966)
MOVSHON, G. 'New York Opera' *Hi-Fi/Musical America* 17 (March 1966)
EIMERT, H. 'Brittens umgearbeiteter *Billy Budd* in der Kolner Oper' *Melos* 33 (March 1966)

VON LUTTWITZ, H. 'Köln: das Seeannsgarn von *Billy Budd' Neue Zeitschrift für Musik* 127 (March 1966)
ARDOIN, J. 'New York' *Opera* 17 (March 1966)
KOEGLER, H. 'Cologne' *Oper* 17 (April 1966)
VON LUTTWITZ, H. 'Das Seeannsgarn von *Billy Budd*; Versuch mit Benjamin Brittens Oper *Orchester* 14 (April 1966)
WALSH, S. 'BBC 2 Budd on the small screen' *Music and Musicians* 15 (February 1967)
PAYNE, A. '*Billy Budd* on BBC 2' *Tempo* 80 (Spring 1967)
KLEIN, J. W. 'Opera on Television' *Musical Opinion* 90 (April 1967)
CULSHAW, J. 'Three for the Road (recording)' *Gramophone* 45 (March 1968)
GREENFIELD, E. 'Culshaw, Britten, and *Billy Budd*' *Hi-Fi/Musical America* 18 (March 1968)
HOWARD, P. 'Bellipotent versis Indomitable: a genealogy of *Billy Budd*' *Musical Times* 109 (July 1968)
CHAPMAN, E. 'Revival of *Billy Budd*' *Musical Events* 23 (September 1968)
'Covent Garden Opera' *Musical Opinion* 91 (September 1968)
'*Billy Budd:* Covent Garden' *Opera* 19 (September 1968)
WARRACK, J. Sleeve note for Decca SET 379–81 (1968)
LARNER, G. 'Britten's *Billy Budd*' *Records and Recording* 11 (September 1968)
HAMILTON, D. 'Britten's *Billy Budd* – Fine Moments do not an Opera Make (recording)' *Hi-Fi/Musical America* 18 (December 1968)
WEINSTOCK, H. '*Billy Budd* Foretopman (recording)' *Saturday Review* 51 (December 14 1968)
'Benjamin Britten's Moving and Dramatic *Billy Budd* (recording)' *Stereo Review* 22 (January 1969)
RIZZO, F. 'The Return of *Billy Budd*' *Opera News* 35 (October 1970)
FREEMAN, J. W. 'Chicago' *Opera News* 35 (December 19 and 26 1970)
DETTMER, R. 'Chicago' *Opera* 22 (February 1971)
HEYWORTH, P. 'Dalla Gran Bretagna (Welsh National Opera)' *Nuova Rivista Musicale Italiana* 6 No. 4 (1972)
'Hamburg: Benjamin Brittens *Billy Budd*' *Oper und Konzert* 10 No. 7 (1972)
'Hamburg: Benjamin Brittens *Billy Budd*' *Oper und Konzert* 10 No. 11 (1972)
CHAPMAN, E. 'Aspects of *Billy Budd*' *Musical Events* 27 (February 1972)
GREENHALGH, J. 'Covent Garden' *Music and Musicians* 20 (March 1972)
FABIAN, I. 'Erworbenes und Erlerntes' *Opern Welt* No. 6 (June 1972)
KELLER, H. 'Why this piece is about *Billy Budd*' *Listener* 88 (September 28 1972)
BOYD, M. 'Wales' *Musical Times* 113 (November 1972)

MILNES, R. *'Billy Budd*; New Theatre Cardiff' *Opera* 23 (November 1972)
WAGNER, K. *'Billy Budd* in Hamburg' *Tempo* 103 (December 1972)
WEBSTER, E. 'Cardiff' *Music and Musicians* 21 (January 1973)
GOULD, S. 'Bologna/Reggio Emilia' *Opera News* 38 (June 1974)
WHITTALL, A. 'A War and a Wedding: two modern British Operas' *Music and Letters* 55 No. 3 (July 1974)
SUTCLIFFE, J. H. 'Hamburg' *Opera* 26 (May 1975)
ALIER, R. 'Barcelona' *Opera* 26 (June 1975)
CHISSELL, J. 'Aria: Billy in the Darbies from *Billy Budd*' Op. 50 AFPB 1975
BRETT, P. 'Salutation at Sea: Britten's *Billy Budd*' *San Francisco Opera Magazine* (1978)
KAPLAN, A. 'From the Beginning' *San Francisco Opera Magazine* (1978)
VON BUCHAU, S. 'Understanding Captain Vere' *San Francisco Opera Magazine* (1978)
EATON, Q. 'Billy's Bow' *Opera News* 43 No. 19 (March 31 1979)
MITCHELL, D. 'A *Billy Budd* Notebook' *Opera News* 43 No. 19 (March 31 1979)
BRADLEY, N. 'The Non-clinical test of a clinical theory: *Billy Budd*, novel and libretto.' *International Review of Psycho-Analysis* 7 (1980)
FISCHER-WILLIAMS, B. 'Men O'War' *Opera News* 44 No. 20 (April 19 1980)
WADSWORTH, S. 'The Go-Between' *Opera News* 44 No. 20 (April 19 1980)
SCHMIDGALL, G. 'Epitaph for Innocence' *Opera News* 44 No. 20 (April 19 1980)
BRETT, P. 'Salvation at sea' *The Britten Companion*; edited by Christopher Palmer. London, Faber (1984)
CROZIER, E. 'The Writing of *Billy Budd*' *Opera Quarterly* 4 No. 3 (Autumn 1986)

A BIRTHDAY HANSEL

G. P. 'Burns set by Britten' *Daily Telegraph* (March 20 1976)
STUART, C. 'A Birthday premiere' *Western Mail* (March 20 1976)
LOPPERT, M. *'A Birthday Hansel' Financial Times* (March 22 1976)
'Magical Touch from Britten' *South Wales Echo* (March 22 1976)
WALSH, S. 'King of soap opera' *Observer* (March 28 1976)
MITCHELL, D. Sleeve note for Decca SXL 6788 (1976)

A BOY WAS BORN

ANDERSON, W. R. 'Wireless Notes' *Musical Times* (February 1936)
FOX STRANGWAYS, A. H. 'Christmas' *Music Observed* ed. Steuart Wilson Methuen (1936)

MAINE, B. 'Benjamin Britten's *A Boy Was Born* is performed by the BBC in London' *Musical America* (January 25 1938)
'Choral Variations: *A Boy Was Born*' AFPB 1960
MILLINGTON, B. 'Iris Lemare' *Musical Times* 123 (1982)

BRIDGE, FRANK
BRITTEN, B. Bridge: *Quintet for Piano, Two Violins, and Violoncello* AFPB 1951
BRITTEN, B. Bridge: *Quartet No. 3* AFPB 1955
BRITTEN, B. Bridge: *Piano Trio* (1929) AFPB 1963
BRITTEN, B. Bridge: *Trio (Rhapsody)* for two violins and viola AFPB 1965
BRITTEN, B. 'Early influences: a tribute to Frank Bridge 1879–1941' *Composer* 19 (Spring 1966)
PEARS, P. Three pieces for strings AFPB 1974
PEARS, P. Two songs for mezzo soprano and orchestra AFPB 1974
BRITTEN, B. Bridge: *Sextet in E flat major* AFPB 1976
OLIVER, D. Frank Bridge: a memory AFPB 1979

BRITTEN, BENJAMIN
BRITTEN, B. 'Soviet opera at B.B.C.: Shostakovitch's "Lady Macbeth"' *World Film News* 1 No. 1 (1936)
BRITTEN, B. '"As You Like It" Walton's music' *World Film News* 1 No. 7 (1936)
BRITTEN, B. 'Programme note on the *Piano Concerto*'. Promenade Concert Thursday 18 August 1938
BRITTEN, B. 'An English composer sees America' *Tempo* 1 No. 2 (American edition) (April 1940)
BRITTEN, B. 'England and the folk-art problem' *Modern Music* 8 (January/February 1941)
BRITTEN, B. 'Au revoir to the U.S.A.' *Modern Music* 9 (January/February 1942)
BRITTEN, B. 'On behalf of Gustav Mahler' *Tempo* 2 No. 2 (American edition) (February 1942)
BRITTEN, B. 'How a musical work originates' *Listener* (July 30 1942)
BRITTEN, B. 'How to become a composer' *Listener* (November 7 1942)
BRITTEN, B. 'Interview' *Tempo* 1 (February 1944)
BRITTEN, B. '250th Anniversary of the death of Henry Purcell (Nov. 21st 1695–Nov. 21st 1945): homage by Benjamin Britten and Michael Tippett'. London, Boosey & Hawkes, 1945
BRITTEN, B. Introduction to BENJAMIN BRITTEN: Peter Grimes; essays by Benjamin Britten and others. London, Governors of Sadler's Wells Foundation, 1946
BRITTEN, B. 'Profile: Benjamin Britten' *Observer* (October 27 1946)

BRITTEN, B. 'Film Music' Huntley, J. *British Film Music London*, Shelton Robinson (1947)

BRITTEN, B. Bridge: *Phantasy Quartet in F sharp minor* AFPB 1948

BRITTEN, B. Foreword to THE RAPE OF LUCRETIA: a symposium by Benjamin Britten and others. London, Bodley Head, 1948

BRITTEN, B. Bach: *Cantatas* 156 and 161 AFPB 1949

BRITTEN, B. Haydn: *Quartet in C major* Op. 33 No. 3 AFPB 1949

BRITTEN, B. Pergolesi: *Concertino No. 6 in B flat for strings and continuo (organ)* AFPB 1949

BRITTEN, B. Piano works by Frédéric Chopin (1810–1849) and Gabriel Fauré (1845–1924) AFPB 1949

BRITTEN, B. 'A new Centre for Music' *Chelsea Week* (1949)

BRITTEN, B. Introduction to NEEL, B. The Story of an Orchestra. London, Vox Mundi, 1950

BRITTEN, B. A note on the *Spring Symphony*. Music Survey 2 (Spring 1950)

BRITTEN, B. Introduction to White, E. W. *The Rise of English Opera*. London, Lehmann (1951)

BRITTEN, B. 'Verdi: a symposium' *Opera* (February 1951)

BRITTEN, B. 'Bridge: *Quintet for Piano, Two Violins, Viola and Violoncello*' AFPB 1951

BRITTEN, B. 'Mozart Concert' AFPB 1951

BRITTEN, B. 'Verdi: *Quartet in E minor*' AFPB 1951

BRITTEN, B. 'A conversation' *Tempo* 5 (August 1951)

BRITTEN, B. 'Address on being made an honorary freeman of Lowestoft' *Tempo* 21 (Autumn 1951)

BRITTEN, B. 'Contribution to Obituary: Arnold Schoenberg' *Music Survey* 4 No. 1 (October 1951)

BRITTEN, B. 'A composer in our times' *Adam* 20 (1952)

BRITTEN, B. 'Variations on a critical theme' *Opera* 3 No. 3 (March 1952)

BRITTEN, B. 'The Marriage of Figaro' *Opera* 3 No. 5 (May 1952)

BRITTEN, B. *Lachrymae*' AFPB 1952

BRITTEN, B. Contribution to KATHLEEN FERRIER: a memoir; edited by Neville Cardus. London, Hammish Hamilton, 1954

BRITTEN, B. Letter to the editor regarding a review of the recording of *Serenade for tenor, horn and strings*. *Tempo* 34 (Winter 1954–55)

BRITTEN, B. 'Bridge: *Quartet* No. 3' AFPB 1955

CRANBROOK, *Lady*, PEARS, P. and BRITTEN, B. Foreword to AFPB 1955

BRITTEN, B. Sleeve note for Decca LW 5163 (1955)

BRITTEN, B. and HOLST, I. The Story of Music. London, Rathbone Books, 1958

BRITTEN, B. 'Dennis Brain (1921–1957)' *Tempo* 46 (Winter 1958)
BRITTEN, B. 'Ireland: *The Land of Lost Content*' AFPB 1959
BRITTEN, B. 'On realizing the Continuo in Purcell's Songs'. HENRY PURCELL 1659–1595: essays on his music; edited by Imogen Holst. London, O.U.P., 1959
BRITTEN, B. 'Paul Beck 1895–1958' AFPB 1959
BRITTEN, B. 'On Writing English opera' *Opera* 12 (January 1961)
BRITTEN, B. Foreword to STEIN, E. *Form and Performance* London, Faber, 1962
BRITTEN, B. Foreword to HOLST, I. *An ABC of Music* London, O.U.P., 1963
BRITTEN, B. SCHAFER, M. British composers in interview London, Faber, 1963
BRITTEN, B. 'An Interview' *The London Magazine* 3 (October 1963)
BRITTEN, B. 'Speech on receiving Honorary degree at Hull University 1962' *The London Magazine* 3 (October 1963)
BRITTEN, B. 'Britten looking back' *Daily Telegraph* (November 17 1963)
BRITTEN, B. *'Curlew River'* AFPB 1964
BRITTEN, B. 'Francis Poulenc 1899–1963' AFPB 1964
BRITTEN, B. 'On Receiving the first Aspen Award'. London, Faber Music in association with Faber & Faber, 1964. 2nd impression 1978
BRITTEN, B. 'On Winning the First Aspen Award' *Saturday Review* (August 22 1964)
BRITTEN, B. 'Benjamin Britten: Musician of the Year (Interview with John Warrack)' *Musical America* 84 (December 1964)
BRITTEN, B. Contribution to MICHAEL TIPPETT: a symposium on his 60th Birthday; edited by Ian Kemp. London, Faber, 1965
BRITTEN, B. Bridge: *Trio (Rhapsody) for two violins and viola* AFPB 1965
BRITTEN, B. 'A Composer in Russia' *Daily Telegraph* (October 24 1965)
BRITTEN, B. Contribution to ZOLTAN KODALY: Mein Weg zur Musik. Zürich, Die Arche, 1966
BRITTEN, B. Sleeve note for Decca SET 301 (1966)
BRITTEN, B. 'Early influences: a tribute to Frank Bridge 1879–1941' *Composer* 19 (Spring 1966)
BRITTEN, B. 'Gemini Variations' *Faber Music News* (Autumn 1966)
BRITTEN, B. 'Benjamin Britten talks to Edmund Tracey' *Sadler's Wells Magazine* (Autumn 1966)
BRITTEN, B. 'Sir Arthur Bliss at 75' *Performing Right* 45 (October 1966)
BRITTEN, B. 'Statement on Shostakovich's Music' *Dmitri Shostakovich*. Moscow: Sovetskii Kompozitor (1967)
'Contemporary Composers on Contemporary Music (Schwartz, E. and Childs, B. eds.) New York: Holt, Rinehart & Winston (1967)

BRITTEN, B. 'Communicator, an interview with England's best-known composer' *Opera News* 31 No. 16 (1967)

BRITTEN, B. 'Interview with E. Forbes' *Opera News* 31 No. 16 (February 11 1967)

BRITTEN, B. *'The Golden Vanity'* AFPB 1967

BRITTEN, B. 'Overture (with chorus) "*The Building of the House*" Op. 79' AFPB 1967

BRITTEN, B. 'Aldeburgh and the Future (Interview with H. Rosenthal)' *Opera* 18 (Autumn 1967)

BRITTEN, B. 'An interview with R. Mercer' *Opera Canada* 9 No. 4 (December 1967)

BRITTEN, B. Message for The Royal College of Music New Building and Development Fund Appeal. London, R.C.M., 1968

BRITTEN, B. and HOLST, I. 'The Wonderful World of Music'. London, MacDonald, 1968

BRITTEN, B. 'Some notes on Forster and music' *Aspects of E. M. Forster:* essays and recollections written for his ninetieth birthday (January 1 1969) London, Arnold (1969)

BRITTEN, B. 'No Ivory Tower: Benjamin Britten talks to *Opera News*' *Opera News* 33 No. 23 (April 1969)

BRITTEN, B. *'The Ballad of Little Musgrave and Lady Barnard; The Golden Vanity; Children's Crusade'* AFPB 1969

BRITTEN, B. *'Overture (with chorus) "The Building of the House"'* AFPB 1969

BRITTEN, B. 'Mendelssohn: *String Quintet No. 11 in A major*' AFPB 1969

BRITTEN, B. *'Suite in C for harp solo* Op. 83' AFPB 1969

BRITTEN, B. *'Tit for Tat'* AFPB 1969

BRITTEN, B. Aaron Copland: Seventieth Birthday Tribute AFPB 1970

BRITTEN, B. 'Artist's Choice: Cecil Aronowitz' AFPB 1970

BRITTEN, B. 'Schubert: *Symphony No. 8 in B minor* D.759 (Unfinished)' AFPB 1970

BRITTEN, B. 'Three scenes from *Gloriana*' AFPB 1970

BRITTEN, B. Foreword to BLADES, J. Percussion instruments and their History. London, Faber, 1970

BRITTEN, B. and HOLST, I. Introduction to vocal score of *The Fairy Queen* (Purcell arr. Britten and I. Holst). London, Faber Music, 1970

BRITTEN, B. Foreword to NORDHOFF, P. and ROBBINS, C. Therapy in Music for Handicapped Children. London, Gollancz, 1971

BRITTEN, B. Message and drawing of fishes in MILLIGAN, S. and HOBBS, J. Milligans's Ark. Walton on Thames, M & J Hobbs, 1971

BRITTEN, B. 'Mozart: *Requiem* K.626' AFPB 1971

BRITTEN, B. 'Orchestral concert' AFPB 1971

BRITTEN, B. *'Piano Concerto in D* Op. 13' AFPB 1971
BRITTEN, B. Introduction to GRAND OPERA; edited by Anthony Gishford. London, Weidenfeld & Nicolson, 1972
BRITTEN, B. 'Mozart: *Adagio and Fugue in C minor* K.546' AFPB 1972
BRITTEN, B. 'Schubert: *Sonata in A minor* D.821 *"The Arpeggione";* Schumann: *Fünf Stücke im Volkston;* Debussy: Sonata in D minor for cello and piano' AFPB 1972
BRITTEN, B. and PEARS, P. 'Schumann: *Scenes from Goethe's "Faust"'* AFPB 1972
BRITTEN, B. *'Third Suite for Cello* Op. 87' AFPB 1972
BRITTEN, B. *'Ballad of Heroes* Op. 14' AFPB 1973
BRITTEN, B. 'Purcell: *Chacony in G minor*' AFPB 1973
BRITTEN, B. 'Mozart: *Quintet in C major* K.515; Shostakovich: *Quartet No. 13 in B flat minor* Op. 138; Schubert: *Quartet in D minor* D.810 *("Death and the Maiden")*' AFPB 1973
BRITTEN, B. 'Moeran: *Nocturne* for baritone, chorus and orchestra' AFPB 1973
BRITTEN, B., PEARS, P. and HOLST, I. *'Dido and Aeneas'* AFPB 1974
BRITTEN, B. *'String Quartet in D major'* AFPB 1975
BRITTEN, B. *'Suite on English Folk Tunes: "A Time there was"* Op. 90' AFPB 1975
BRITTEN, B. 'Beethoven: *Piano Trio in B flat "The Archduke"* Op. 97' AFPB 1976
BRITTEN, B. 'Bridge: *Sextet in E flat major*' AFPB 1976
BRITTEN, B. *'Phaedra* Op. 94' AFPB 1976
BRITTEN, B. 'Schumann: *Andante and Variations in F major* Op. 46' AFPB 1976
BRITTEN, B. *'Third suite for Cello* Op. 87' AFPB 1976
BRITTEN, B. Letters to Anthony Gishford on Mahler, Stravinsky and Shostakovich *Tempo* 120 (1977)
BRITTEN, B. 'Britten on Oedipus Rex and Lady Macbeth (introduced by Donald Mitchell)' *Tempo* 120 (March 1977)
BRITTEN, B. *'Curlew River'* AFPB 1979
BRITTEN, B. *'Sonata in C* Op. 65 for cello and piano' AFPB 1979
BOYD, M. 'Benjamin Britten and Grace Williams: chronicle of a friendship' (letters) Welsh Music Vol. 6 No. 6 (1980)
BRITTEN, Baron cr. 1976 (Life peer) of Aldeburgh, Suffolk. Who Was Who 1971–1980. London Adam & Charles Black 1981
BRITTEN, B. 'Mozart: *Sinfonia concertante in E flat* (K.Anh.9)' AFPB 1982
BRITTEN, B. 'Mapreading: Benjamin Britten in conversation with Donald Mitchell' *The Britten Companion:* edited by Christopher Palmer. London, Faber (1984)
BRITTEN, B. 'The composer's *Dream*' *The Britten Companion:* edited by Christopher Palmer. London, Faber (1984)

BRITTEN, B. *'Fanfare for St Edmundsbury* (1959)' AFPB 1984
BRITTEN, B. 'Schubert: *Quintet in A* (D.667) *(The Trout)*' AFPB 1984
BRITTEN, B. 'Schubert: *Quintet in C* (D.956)' AFPB 1984
BRITTEN, B. *'Spring Symphony* Op. 44' AFPB 1986

BRITTEN–PEARS SCHOOL FOR ADVANCED MUSICAL STUDIES
ALDOUS, T. 'Music schools in harmony' *Illustrated London News* 268 (July 1980)

THE BUILDING OF THE HOUSE
PORTER, A. 'Aldeburgh' *Musical Times* 108 (July 1967)
BRITTEN, B. 'Overture (with chorus) "*The Building of the House*" Op. 79' AFPB 1967
GOODWIN, N. 'Vaudeville for the Vienna Boys' *Music and Musicians* 15 (August 1967)
GREENFIELD, E. 'Britten and the Aldeburgh Miracle' *Hi-Fi/Musical America* 17 (September 1967)
WOCKER, K. H. 'Britische Musikfeste' *Neue Zeitschrift für Musik* 128 (September 1967)
FLEMING, S. 'Powell Hall: Old "House", New Sound' *Hi-Fi/Musical America* 18 (April 1968)

THE BURNING FIERY FURNACE
PLOMER, W. *'The Burning Fiery Furnace'* AFPB 1966
STADLEN, P. 'Britten uses system entirely his own.' *Daily Telegraph* (June 10 1966)
'Britten parable of Nebuchadnezzar' *Times* (June 10 1966)
SHAWE-TAYLOR, D. 'Britten's *Burning Fiery Furnace*' *Sunday Times* (June 12 1966)
EVANS, P. 'Britten's new church opera' *Listener* 75 (June 16 1966)
WARRACK, J. *'The Burning Fiery Furnace'* *Tempo* 78 (Autumn 1966)
'The Burning Fiery Furnace: some drawings by Angela Conner of the English Opera Group's Production' *About the House* 2 No. 4 (1966)
EVANS, P. 'England' *Musical Quarterly* 52 No. 4 (1966)
PAAP, W. 'Muziektonale tijdens het Holland Festival' *Mens en Mel* 21 (June 1966)
SENIOR, E. 'Fruits of Rest' *Music and Musicians* 14 (June 1966)
PANTER-DOWNES, M. 'Letter from London' *New Yorker* 42 (July 23 1966)
NOBLE, J. 'Aldeburgh Festival' *Musical Times* 107 (August 1966)
GOODWIN, N. 'Britten in Babylon' *Music and Musicians* 14 (August 1966)
'Aldeburgh' *Opera* 17 Autumn 1966
WARRACK, J. 'First Performances' *Tempo* 78 (Autumn 1966)

GREENFIELD, E. 'Festivals in England' *Hi-Fi/Musical America* 16 (September 1966)
'Britten's second parable at City Festival' *Musical Events* 21 (September 1966)
MONTAGU, G. 'Festival of the City of London' *Musical Opinion* 89 (September 1966)
HOLLANDER, H. 'Aldeburgh and Cheltenham' *Neue Zeitschrift für Musik* 127 (September 1966)
KULLBERG, B. L. 'Das Holland Festival 1966' *Neue Zeitschrift für Musik* 127 (September 1966)
CONNER, A. 'Aldeburgh' *Opera News* 31 (September 1966)
CROSS, A. 'Liverpool' *Musical Times* 108 (January 1967)
LARNER, G. 'Furnace in the Cathedral' *Music and Musicians* 15 (January 1967)
'Britten's Fiery Furnace Makes a Glorious Noise (recording techniques)' *Hi-Fi/Musical America* 17 (September 1967)
DAVIS, P. G. 'Caramoor Report. *The Burning Fiery Furnace*' *Hi-Fi/Musical America* 17 (September 1967)
FRENCH, P. 'The London Concert Scene' *Musical Opinion* 90 (September 1967)
'Catonah, N.Y.' *Opera News* 32 (September 1967)
BREUER, R. 'Caramoor, N.Y.: June 17–July 9' *Opera* 18 (November 1967)
WOEHELER, W. 'Kammermusiktage mit wenig Kammermusik (Braunschweig)' *Musica* 23 No. 1 (1969)
VERNON, T. 'A Medieval *Burning Fiery Furnace*' *Opera Journal* 2 No. 2 (1969)
LIMMERT, E. 'Benjamin Britten bei den Tagen neuer Kammermusik in Braunschweig' *Melos* 36 (January 1969)
JACOBS, H. 'Festliche Tage neuer Kammermusik in Braunschweig' *Orchester* 17 (January 1969)
BUNTING, J. 'Letters to the Editor: *The Burning Fiery Furnace*' *Musical Times* 110 (June 1969)
JACOBSON, R. and KERNER, L. 'New York' *Opera News* 38 (February 1974)
SMEDLEY, B. R. 'Contemporary sacred chamber opera: a medieval form in the twentieth century' *M.D. George Peabody College for Teachers* (1977)
FLOR, G. J. 'The Alto Trombone' *Woodwind, Brass and Percussion* 21 (1982)

CADENZAS TO HAYDN'S CELLO CONCERTO IN C (Hoboken VIIb.i)
HOLST, I. and STRODE, R. 'Haydn: *Cello Concerto in C major* Hob.VIIb.i' AFPB 1976

CALENDAR OF THE YEAR
REED, P. 'Calendar of the Year' AFPB 1983

CANADIAN CARNIVAL
TEMPO 1 (American series) No. 1 (March 1940)
TEMPO 5 (O.S.) (August 1941)
SADIE, S. 'The Proms' *Musical Events* 17 (September 1962)
MITCHELL, D. Sleeve note for EMI ASD 4177 (1982)

CANTATA ACADEMICA
'New Britten Work to be conducted by Paul Sacher' *Schweizerische Musik* 4 (December 1959)
BRADSHAW, S. 'Britten's *Cantata Academica*' *Tempo* 53–4 (Spring–Summer 1960)
MURY, A. 'Schweiz: Neue Musik zum Universitatsjubiläum' *Musica* 14 (September 1960)
EHINGER, H. 'Für die fünfhundertjährige Universität komponiert' *Neue Zeitschrift für Musik* 121 (September 1960)
REICH, W. '500th Birthday' *Musical America* 80 (December 1960)
SADIE, S. 'Britten's *Cantata Academica*' *Musical Events* 16 (January 1961)
KEATING, R. 'Cambridge' *Musical Times* 102 (January 1961)
MYERS, R. H. 'British Music' *Canon* 14 (January–February 1961)
KEATING, R. 'Britten's *Cantata Academica*' *Musical Times* 102 (March 1961)
'London Symphony Orchestra' *Musical Opinion* 84 (April 1961)
WIDDER, R. 'Cleveland' *Music Magazine* 163 (December 1961)
'La *Cantata academica* de Benjamin Britten' *Le Courier* (April 11 1962)
WALTER, F. 'Oeuvres de Britten' *Journal de Geneve* (April 12 1962)
'*Cantata Academica* de Benjamin Britten' *La Suisse* (April 12 1962)
'First Recordings of Unfamiliar Britten' *American Record Guide* 28 (May 1962)
BRADSHAW, S. '*Cantata Academica*' AFPB 1962
MAACK, R. and YOUNG, P. M. 'Report from Germany' *American Choral Review* 14 No. 4 (1972)

CANTATA MISERICORDIUM
EHINGER, H. 'Für das Rote Kreuz komponiert' *Neue Zeitschrift für Musik* 124 No. 12 (1963)
SCHULE, B. 'Zeitgenössische Musik im Dienst des Roten Kreuzes' *Schweizerische Musikzeitung* 3 No. 5 (1963)
MITCHELL, D. 'A memorable cantata by Britten' *Daily Telegraph* (September 2 1963)
MITCHELL, D. 'A Birthday Card in Music' *Daily Telegraph* (September 13 1963)
ROSEBERRY, E. 'Britten's *Cantata Misericordium* and Psalm 150' *Tempo* 66–67 (Autumn–Winter 1963)

THOMPSON, K. L. 'Radio in Retrospect' *Musical Opinion* 87 (October 1963)
CHAPMAN, E. 'The Proms Concluded' *Music Events* 18 (October 1963)
CAIRNS, D. 'First Performances' *Musical Times* 101 (November 1963)
PAYNE, A. 'Britten and the Proms' *Music and Musicians* 12 (November 1963)
'Britten's new cantata celebrates richness.' *Times* (November 13 1963)
'Cantata Misericordium' AFPB 1965
BLYTH, A. 'Britten's Parable' *Music and Musicians* 14 (July 1966)
WILLIAMS, P. *'Cantata Misericordium* Op. 69' Edinburgh Festival Programme (23 August 1968)
WEBSTER, E. M. *'The Three Choirs; the Function of a Festival'* *Musical Opinion* 92 (October 1968)
CALDWELL, J. 'Oxford' *Musical Times* 110 (January 1969)
CREHAN, J. H. 'Britten and the Good Samaritan' *The Catholic Herald* (March 18 1977)
EVANS, J. *'Cantata Misericordium* Op. 69' AFPB 1983

CANTICLES
BROWN, D. 'Britten's Three Canticles' *Music Review* 21 (1960)
'Britten's Canticles; a masterly evocation (recording)' *American Record Guide* 29 (January 1963)

CANTICLE I
'Performance of Britten's *Canticle* and *Violin Concerto*' *Times* (November 3 1947)
PEARS, P. *'Canticle* (Op. 40)' AFPB 1948
Francis Quarles *'Canticle I'* *Music Review* 11 No. 4 (November 1950)
REDLICH, H. F. 'New English Song (review of *Canticle I*)' *Music Review* 11 No. 4 (November 1950)
Francis Quarles *'Canticle I'* *Monthly Musical Record* 80 (December 1950)
Francis Quarles *'Canticle I'* *Music and Letters* 32 (April 1951)
EVANS, J. Sleeve note for Hyperion A66209 (1986)
REED, P. *'Canticle I: My Beloved is Mine* Op. 40' AFPB 1987

CANTICLE II
MASON, C. 'English Opera Group: Britten's New York' *Manchester Guardian* (January 26 1952)
'Benjamin Britten' *Canon* 5 (March 1952)
'Abraham and Isaac, Op. 51; first performance' *Musical Times* 93 (March 1952)
Canticle II Op. 51 *'Abraham and Isaac'* AFPB 1952
PORTER, A. 'Benjamin Britten's *Canticle II'* *London Music* 8 (June 1953)
'Abraham and Isaac; Canticle II' *Musical Opinion* 76 (June 1953)

'Abraham and Isaac; Canticle II' Music and Letters 34 (October 1953)
'Abraham and Isaac, Canticle II, Op. 51, for alto, tenor and piano' Notes (11 March 1954)
'Canticle II, Abraham and Isaac, Op. 51, for alto, tenor and piano' Music Review 16 (August 1955)
WALTER, F. 'Vu et entendu Spoleto' Musique (Chaix) (October 1965)
SENIOR, E. 'For Home Town' Music and Musicians 16 (September 1967)
STRODE, R. 'Canticle II: Abraham and Isaac Op. 51' AFPB 1979

CANTICLE III

MITCHELL, D. 'Some First Performances' Musical Times 96 (March 1955)
'Canticle III' AFPB 1955
R.B. The Heart of the Matter AFPB 1956
'Canticle III Still Falls the Rain: for tenor, horn and piano' Chesterian 31 (August 1956)
'Canticle III Still Falls the Rain: for tenor, horn and piano' Musical Opinion 80 (October 1956)
'Canticle III Still Falls the Rain: for tenor, horn and piano, Op. 55' Music and Letters 38 (January 1957)
SADIE, S. 'New, New, New' Music and Musicians 10 (July 1962)
STRODE, R. 'Canticle III: Still falls the Rain Op. 55' AFPB 1984
EVANS, J. Sleeve note for EMI 27 0653 1 (1987)

CANTICLE IV

'First Performances and Commissions' Composer 40 (Summer 1971)
MANN, W. 'Britten's novelty' Times (June 25 1971)
PORTER, A. 'Britten's new canticle' Financial Times (June 28 1971)
GREENFIELD, E. and COLE, H. 'Aldeburgh' Musical Times 112 (August 1971)
'Uraufführungen' Neue Zeitschrift für Musik 132 (August 1971)
GOODWIN, N. 'Aldeburgh Festival' Music and Musicians 20 (October 1971)
MITCHELL, D. Sleeve note for Decca SXL 6608 (1972)
'Central Presbyterian Church' Music Journal 31 (March 1973)
KERNER, L. 'New York' Opera News 37 (March 1973)
JACOBSON, A. S. 'Analysis of Journey of the Magi' M.Mus. King's College, University of London (1980)
JACOBSON, A. S. 'Analysis of Journey of the Magi, Benjamin Britten' RMA Research Chronicle 16 (1980)

CANTICLE V

STADLEN, P. 'Deep significance of Britten's Canticle' Daily Telegraph (June 17 1975)

MANN, W. 'A cycle song baptized' *Times* (June 17 1975)
LOPPERT, M. 'Plomer celebration' *Financial Times* (June 18 1975)
SHAWE-TAYLOR 'On Britten's home ground' *Sunday Times* (June 22 1975)
'Aldeburgh' *Musical Times* 116 (August 1975)
'Aldeburgh' *Music and Musicians* 23 (August 1975)
GREENFIELD, E. 'Glyndebourne, Aldeburgh and Covent Garden' *Hi-Fi/Musical America* 25 (October 1975)
PORTER, A. 'Musical Events: Ladies' Night' *New Yorker* 51 (November 1975)
MITCHELL, D. Sleeve note for Decca SXL 6788 (1976)

CELLO MUSIC
LOW, D. G. 'The solo cello music of Felix Mendelssohn; the cello sonatas of Boni, Scipriani, and Vandini; the solo cello chamber music of Benjamin Britten *D.M. Northwestern University* (1973)
LLOYD-WEBBER, J. 'The Cello music of Benjamin Britten' *Strad* 86 (September 1975)

CELLO SONATA
'Sonata in C Op. 65 for cello and piano' AFPB 1961
'Britten at Aldeburgh' *Music Review* 22 No. 3 (1961)
EVANS, P. 'Britten's *Cello Sonata*' *Tempo* 58 (Summer 1961)
GOODWIN, N. 'Great Britain' *Musical Courier* 163 (August 1961)
'Aldeburgh' *Musical Times* 102 (August 1961)
'Sonata in C for Cello and Piano' *Musical Times* 103 (March 1962)
SIGMON, C. 'Chamber Music in New York' *Musical America* 83 (February 1963)
'Mstislav Rostropovich' *Musical America* 83 (December 1963)
FELIX, V. 'Anglicka hudba neni jen Britten' *Hudebni Rozhledy* 17 No. 3 (1964)
WILLIAMS, P. 'Sonata in C major for cello and piano Op. 65' Edinburgh Festival Programme (3 September 1968)
BRITTEN, B. 'Sonata in C Op. 65 for cello and piano' AFPB 1979

CELLO SUITES
TRIMBLE, L. 'Two Monumental Suites for Unaccompanied Cello (Rostropovich recording)' *Stereo Review* 25 (October 1970)

CELLO SUITE NO. 1
'Suite for cello solo' AFPB 1965
COOPER, M. 'Rostropovich soloist in new Britten suite' *Daily Telegraph* (June 28 1965)
MANN, W. 'Aldeburgh' *Musical Times* 106 (August 1965)

GOODWIN, N. 'Suffolk Constellation' *Music and Musicians* 13 (August 1965)
WALSH, S. 'Three New Britten Works' *Tempo* 74 (Autumn 1965)
GREENFIELD, E. 'Bumper Britten Crop' *Hi-Fi/Musical America* 15 (September 1965)
AFFELDER, P. 'Mstislav Rostropovich' *Hi-Fi/Musical America* 16 (March 1966)
WILLIAMS, P. *'Suite No. 1 for cello* Op. 72' Edinburgh Festival Programme (28 August 1968)
HOLLOWAY, S. C. 'Benjamin Britten, *Suite for cello*, Op. 72: a commentary' MM, *University of Texas/Austin* (1982) Available from Sarah Boling, 4800 N. Stanton, 129, El Paso, Texas, 79902, USA

CELLO SUITE NO. 2

CRICHTON, R. 'Concerts at the Maltings' *Musical Times* 109 (August 1968)
GOODWIN, N. 'Punch and Prodigal' *Music and Musicians* 16 (August 1968)
WILLIAMS, P. *'Suite No. 2 for cello* Op. 80' Edinburgh Festival Programme Book (30 August 1968)
GREENFIELD, E. 'The Flowering of Festivals' *Hi-Fi/Musical America* 18 (September 1968)
JACOBSON, R. 'Weekend with Rostropovich' *Saturday Review* 52 (May 1969)
'Editorial Notes' *Strad* 80 (June 1969)
LOWE, S. 'Mstislav Rostropovich, cello' *Hi-Fi/Musical America* 19 (July 1969)

CELLO SUITE NO. 3

BRITTEN, B. *'Third Suite for Cello* Op. 87' AFPB 1972
'First Performances' *World Music* 14 No. 2 (1972) [but see p. 123]
WALSH, S. 'Britten's latest' *Observer* (December 19 1974)
ORR, B. 'First Performances and Commissions of British Music' *Composer* 54 (Spring 1975)
KOLODIN, I. 'Rostropovich in Exile – Penny Dreadful, Pound Foolish Salome' *Saturday Review* 2 (April 1975)
BRITTEN, B. *'Third Suite for Cello* Op. 87' AFPB 1976
TIEMEYER, H. C. 'An analysis of *Third Suite for cello* Op. 87 by Benjamin Britten' DMA *Catholic University of America* (1977)
LLOYD WEBBER, J. 'Britten's *Third Cello Suite*' *Strad* 91 (March 1981)

CELLO SYMPHONY

EVANS, P. 'Britten's *Cello Symphony*' *Tempo* 66–67 (Autumn–Winter 1963)
'Symphony in D Op. 68' AFPB 1964
WARRACK, J. 'Britten's *Cello Symphony*' *Musical Times* 105 (June 1964)
'Britten *Cello Symphony* a masterpiece' *Times* (June 19 1964)

OSBORNE, C. 'Britten's Festival' *Musical Times* 113 (July 5 1964)
EVANS, P. Sleeve note for Decca SXL 6138 (1964)
GOODWIN, N. 'Commentaries on Aldeburgh' *Music and Musicians* 12 (August 1964)
VLASOV, V. 'Mstislav Rostropovich' *Sovetskaya Muzyka* 28 (August 1964)
NOBLE, J. 'Britten's *Cello Symphony* and *Curlew River*' *Musical Times* 105 (September 1964)
'Editorial Notes' *Strad* 75 (September 1964)
STUCKENSCHMIDT, H. H. 'Igor Strawinsky bei den Berliner Festwochen' *Mels* 31 (November 1964)
LARNER, G. 'Elusive Britten' *Records and Recording* 8 No. 3 (December 1964)
HENDERSON, R. 'Britten's *Cello Symphony*' *Tempo* 70 (Autumn 1964)
FLANAGAN, W. 'A Forceful New Work by Benjamin Britten (recordings)' *Hi-Fi/Review* 14 (March 1965)
DIETHER, J. 'Britten's New *Cello Symphony* (recording)' *American Record Guide* 31 (July 1965)
'Boston Symphony' (October 22 1965)
'*Symphony for Cello and Orchestra* Op. 68' *Buffalo Philharmonic Orchestra Programme Notes* (December 5 1965)
CANTIENI, R. 'Mstislav Rostropovich violoncelliste; réflexions en marge d'un récent concert a l'OSR' *Schweizerische Musikzeitung* 106 No. 4 (1966)
FLEMING, S. 'The Rostropovich Whirlwind' *Hi-Fi/Musical America* 17 (May 1967)
'New Works: New York' *Music Journal* 25 (May 1967)
'*Cello Symphony*' *Pittsburg Symphony* (May 26 1967)
MITCHELL, D. '*Symphony for Cello and Orchestra* Op. 68' AFPB 1970
DALE, S. S. 'Contemporary cello concerti. No. 6: Benjamin Britten' *Strad* 83 (March 1973)
EVANS, J. Sleeve note for Chandos ABTD 1126 (1985)

A CEREMONY OF CAROLS

Tempo 2 (American series) No. 3 (September 1942)
Tempo 8 (O.S.) (September 1944)
'"Noels" de B. Britten' *Disques* 63, 64 (March–April 1954)
VAN REETH, M. 'Een muzikaal schouwspel rond het aerstgebeuren enkle lessen voor de advents – en kersttijd voor lager en hoger secundair' *Adem* 10 No. 4 (1974)

A CHARM OF LULLABIES

'*A Charm of Lullabies*' *Music Review* 10 (May 1949)

POSTON, E. 'A Charm of Lullabies' AFPB 1949
'A Charm of Lullabies, for mezzo-soprano and piano, Op. 41' Music Survey 2 (Spring 1950)
HAMBURGER, P. 'Review' Music Survey 2 No. 4 (Spring 1950)
MITCHELL, D. Sleeve note for BBC Artium REGL 417 (1981)
EVANS, N. 'A Charm of Lullabies Op. 41' AFPB 1987

CHILDREN'S CRUSADE
ROCKER, K. H. 'Britten vertönt Brecht' Musica 23 No. 4 (1969)
KELLER, H. 'Britten's latest' Music and Musicians 17 (May 1969)
HEYWORTH, P. 'Brecht for the children' Observer (May 25 1969)
BRITTEN, B. 'Children's Crusade' AFPB 1969
GILL, D. 'Music in London' Musical Times 110 (July 1969)
GREENFIELD, E. 'London/Brighton' Hi-Fi/Musical America 19 (August 1969)
CRANKSHAW, G. 'Britten for Boys' Music and Musicians 18 (October 1969)
MITCHELL, D. Sleeve note for Decca SET 445 (1970)
'Central Presbyterian Church' Music Journal 31 (March 1973)
KERNER, L. 'New York' Opera News 37 (March 1973)
DERHEN, A. 'Musica Sacra: Britten' Hi-Fi/Musical America 23 (April 1973)
'Children's Crusade. Illustrations by S. Nolan' Musical Times 115 (February 1974)
JOSEPHSON, D. 'Children's Crusade' AFPB 1974
'Kinderkreuzzug' Tempo 112 (March 1975)
MITCHELL, D. 'Children's Crusade' The Britten Companion: edited by Christopher Palmer. London, Faber (1984)

CHORAL MUSIC
'Choral Music – by Benjamin Britten (includes list of works)' Choir Guide 4 (September 1951)
HANSLER, G. E. 'Stylistic characteristics and trends in choral music of five twentieth century British composers: a study of the choral works of Benjamin Britten, Gerald Finzi, Constant Lambert, Michael Tippett and William Walton' Ph.D. New York University (1957)
STONE, K. 'Reviews of Records (Elizabethan Singers)' Musical Quarterly 51 No. 4 (1965)
DAWNEY, M. 'Some Notes on Britten's Church Music' Tempo 82 (August 1967)
DUNDORE, M. M. '1. The Choral Music of Benjamin Britten. 2. The Russian Grand Opera Company in the Pacific North West 1921. 3. Documentation for choral concert given on June 10 1969.' D.M.A. University of Washington (1969)
HINES, R. S. 'Benjamin Britten b. 1913 – (a Review of his Choral Compositions)' Choral Journal 11 No. 6 (1971)

ENGLAND, G. A. 'A Study to provide self-administering improvement in conducting specific rhythmic problems in two choral works of Benjamin Britten' *E.D. University of Northern Colorado* (1972)

NICHOLAS, M. 'The choral music of Benjamin Britten' *English Church Music* (1977)

SCHIAVONE, S. 'Britten's choral music' *M.A. University of Wales (Aberystwyth) in progress* (1983)

CHORALE

Tempo (O.S.) (December 1944)

'*Chorale* (after an old French Carol) Music only' *Score* 48 (January 1961)

CHURCH MUSIC

WYTON, A. 'Benjamin Britten and Church Music Today' *Music Clubs* 39 (1960)

HALSEY, L. 'Britten's church music' *Musical Times* 103 (October 1962)

DAWNEY, M. 'Some notes on Britten's church music' *Tempo* 82 (Autumn 1967)

CHURCH PARABLES

'Britten's parables compared' *Times* (July 15 1966)

MANN, W. 'Britten's Three Church Parables' *Times* (July 26 1968)

WEITZMAN, R. 'Benjamin Britten and the three Church Parables' *London Magazine* 8 (November 1968)

KROLZIG, G. 'Benjamin Brittens Kirchenopern' 20 (May–June 1969)

McCREDIE, A. 'Adelaide' *Opera* 21 (June 1970)

MITCHELL, D. 'Britten's Church Parables'. ALDEBURGH ANTHOLOGY; edited by Ronald Blythe. Aldeburgh, Snape Maltings Foundation in association with Faber Music Ltd, 1972

EVANS, J. 'The musical language of the Church Parables' AFPB 1979

HOLLOWAY, R. 'The Church Parables II; Limits and renewals' *The Britten Companion:* edited by Christopher Palmer. London, Faber (1984)

MITCHELL, D. 'The Church Parables I; Ritual and restraint' *The Britten Companion:* edited by Christopher Palmer. London, Faber (1984)

COAL FACE

MANVELL, R. 'Film. Revised edition.' Harmondsworth (Middlesex) Pelican Books (1946)

MITCHELL, D. and BURROWS, J. 'Britten's Theatre Music' AFPB 1980

REED, P. 'Coal Face' AFPB 1983

CURLEW RIVER

LITTLEFIELD, J. 'La Parabola de Britten' *Buenos Aires Musicales* 19 No. 315 (1964)
WEISSMANN, A. S. 'L'ultimo Britten duro scoglio per la critica' *Musica d'Oggio* 7 No. 6 (1964)
MACIEJEWSKI, B. M. 'Lit z Londynu' *Ruch Muzyczny* 8 No. 19 (1964)
BRITTEN, B. *'Curlew River'* AFPB 1964
'East meets West in New Britten Music Drama' *Times* (June 15 1964)
KELLER, H. 'Britten's new opera: *Curlew River*' *Spectator* (June 19 1964)
COOPER, M. 'England' *Musical America* 84 (July 1964)
MELLERS, W. 'Britten's Yea play' *New Statesman* (July 3 1964)
OSBORNE, C. 'Britten's Festival' *New York Times* 113 (July 5 1964)
KLINGER, A. 'Ein Gleichnis zur Aufführung in der Kirche von Benjamin Britten' *Melos* 31 (July–August 1964)
VERMEULEN, E. 'Höhepunkt des Holland–Festivals: *Curlew River* von Britten' *Melos* 31 (August 1964)
GOODWIN, N. 'Commentary from Aldeburgh' *Music and Musicians* 12 (August 1964)
'Non-opera and Noh opera' *Opera* 15 (August 1964)
HEINITZ, T. 'The Other Side' *Saturday Review* 47 (August 1964)
WARRACK, J. 'Britten's *Curlew River*' *Tempo* 70 (Autumn 1964)
APRAHAMIAN, F. 'Notes from our Correspondents' *Hi-Fi* 14 (September 1964)
CHAPMAN, E. 'City of London Festival' *Musical Events* 19 (September 1964)
MONTAGU, G. 'City of London Festival' *Musical Opinion* 87 (September 1964)
NOBLE, J. 'Britten's *Cello Symphony* and *Curlew River*' *Musical Times* 105 (September 1964)
GOLEA, A. 'Les Festivals' *Musique* 127 (October 1964)
WARNKE, F. J. 'Birthdays in Holland' *Opera News* 29 (October 1964)
NEWLIN, D. 'Britten's Latest Works' *Pan Pipes* 57 No. 3 (1965)
MITCHELL, D. Sleeve note for Decca SET 301 (1966)
EVANS, P. 'England' *Musical Quarterly* 52 No. 4 (1966)
LARNER, G. 'Britten's Noh Opera' *Records and Recording* 9 No. 4 (January 1966)
GOODWIN, N. 'Oriental Britten (recording)' *Music and Musicians* 14 (April 1966)
SENIOR, E. 'Prize for Belgium (Television film of the English Opera Group's performance)' *Music and Musicians* 14 (May 1966)
FRANKENSTEIN, A. 'Britten's *Curlew River* – Burnished Bronze Solemnity (Recording)' *Hi-Fi/Musical America* 16 (June 1966)

DIETHER, J. 'A Parable by Britten: *Curlew River*' *American Record Guide* 32 (July 1966)
OSBORNE, C. L. 'At Caramoor' *Hi-Fi/Musical America* 16 (September 1966)
'New Works' *Music Journal* 24 (September 1966)
WARD, H. 'Opera/Concert Talk' *Music Journal* 24 (September 1966)
'Catonah, N. Y.' *Opera News* 31 (September 1966)
FLANAGAN, W. 'Benjamin Britten's Extraordinary *Curlew River*' *Hi Fi Review* 17 (October 1966)
LIMMERT, E. 'Braunschweig: Britten auf dem Spuren des No-Spiels' *Melos* 33 (December 1966)
EATON, Q. 'New York' *Opera News* 32 (December 30 1967)
'*Curlew River* (Calvary Episcopal Church, New York City)' *Music (Ago)* 2 (January 1968)
GOLEA, A. 'Vu et entendu' *Journal de Musique Francais* 169 (May 1968)
LAADE, W. 'Benjamin Brittens Mysterienspiel *Curlew River* und die japanischen Vorbilder' *Musikbildung* 1 (December 1969)
JACOBS, A. 'The Californian Experience' *Opera* 20 (July 1969)
SHERLOCK, K. '*Curlew River*' AFPB 1970
MOVSHON, G. 'Caramoor's Dido and Aeneas' *Hi-Fi/Musical America* 21 (October 1971)
'Ulm' *Oper Und Konzert* 12 No. 2 (1974)
JACOBSON, R. and KERNER, L. 'New York' *Opera News* 38 (February 1974)
SCHMIDT, D. N. 'Unbekannter Britten; Möwenfluss in Ulm' *Opern Welt* 2 (February 1974)
WELSH, C. N. 'The Vienna Chamber Opera' *Opera* 26 (Autumn 1975)
JAMES, R. 'Britten's Curlew River' *Current Musicology* 26 (1978)
BRITTEN, B. '*Curlew River*' AFPB 1979
HODGINS, J. 'Orientalism in Benjamin Britten's *Curlew River*' M.A. University of British Columbia (1981)
MAYER, M. 'A structural and stylistic analysis of the Benjamin Britten *Curlew River*' Ed.D Columbia University Teachers College (1983)

THE DARK TOWER
Tempo 14 (O.S.) (March 1946)

DEATH IN VENICE
NURSE, K. 'Britten writing *Death in Venice* opera' *Daily Telegraph* (December 7 1971)
BLADES, J. 'Making percussion instruments for Benjamin Britten' *Listener* (June 15 1972)

'Opera: English Opera Group' *About the House* 4 No. 2 (1973)
REED, T. J. *'Death in Venice'* (Study of the Thomas Mann novel, with pictures of Britten opera) *About the House* 4 No. 3 (1973)
SCHIFFER, B. 'Thomas Manns Aschenbach lernt durch Britten singen' *Melos* 40 No. 6 (1973)
WOCKER, K. H. 'Brittens Oper *Tod in Venedig*' *Musica* 27 No. 5 (1973)
'Urauffuhrüngen' *Musikhandel* 24 No. 4 (1973)
SCHREIBER, W. 'Britten – Oper an originalen Schauplatz' *Neue Musik Zeitung* 22 No. 6 (1973)
HOLLANDER, H. 'Aldeburgh: *Der Tod in Venedig* Uraufführung von Benjamin Brittens neuer Oper' *Neue Zeitschrift für Musik* 134 No. 8 (1973)
'Uraufführungen' *Neue Zeitschrift für Musik* 134 No. 4 (1973)
RINALDI 'Britten a Venezia' *Rassegna Musicale Curci* 26 No. 3 (1973)
SCHMIDGALL, G. 'A New Britten Opera *Death in Venice*' *Opera Canada* 14 No. 4 (1973)
LINDBERG, H. 'Venice' *Opera Canada* 14 No. 4 (1973)
MESSINIS, M. 'Opinioni' *Nuova Rivista Musicale Italiana* 7 No. 2 (1973)
'First Performances' *World Music* 15 No. 2 (1973)
HEYWORTH, P. 'Da Londra' *Nuova Rivista Musicale Italiana* 7 Nos. 3–4 (1973)
NOBLE, J. 'Britten's *Death in Venice*' *Listener* 89 (January 21 1973)
ORR, B. 'First Performances and Commissions' *Composer* 47 (Spring 1973)
REED, T. J. 'Thomas Mann's Death in Venice' *AFPB* 1973
PIPER, M. *'Death in Venice'* *AFPB* 1973
EVANS, P. 'Britten's *Death in Venice*' *Opera* 24 (June 1973)
MANN, W. 'Something old, something new from Britten' *Times* (June 18 1973)
NOBLE, J. 'Britten's *Death in Venice*' *Listener* (June 21 1973)
HEYWORTH, P. 'Road to the abyss' *Observer* (June 24 1973)
SHAWE-TAYLOR, D. 'Britten's Venetian triumph' *Sunday Times* (June 24 1973)
LAMBERT, J. W. 'New Benjamin Britten Opera Premieres; *Death in Venice* at Aldeburgh Festival' *Christian Science Monitor* 65 (July 19 1973)
KOLODIN, I. 'Britain's Bayreuth and the Marshalltown Maecenas' *World* 2 (July 31 1973)
GOODWIN, N. *'Death in Venice* (Aldeburgh)' *Music and Musicians* 21 (August 1973)
DEAN, W. 'Aldeburgh' *Musical Times* 114 (August 1973)
BLYTH, A. 'Aldeburgh Festival: *Death in Venice*' *Opera* 24 (August 1973)
'Aldeburgh' *Opera News* 38 (August 1973)
TRILLING, O. 'Wir haben Viscontis Film nicht gesehen: Gespräch mit Myfanwy Piper' *Opern Welt* 8 (August 1973)

WOCKER, K. H. *Der Tod in Venedig:* Brittens neue Opera in Aldeburgh uraufgeführt' *Opern Welt* 8 (August 1973)
'Opera News' *Arts Reporting Service* 3 (August 20 1973)
FOSTER, W. 'Mann and a woman' *Scotsman* (August 20 1973)
GREENFIELD, E. 'Britten's *Death in Venice.* Owen Wingrave staged' *Hi-Fi/Musical America* 23 (September 1973)
MORTE A VENEZIA Programme Book of La Fenice September 1973
LOSSMAN, H. 'Edinburgh: Schottische Salzburg' *Bühne* 181 (October 1973)
PLEASANTS, H. 'A plethora of Modern Operas' *Stereo Review* 31 (October 1973)
SCHRIEBER, W. 'Venedig: Brittens *Tod in Venedig*' *Orchester* 21 (November 1973)
LINDBERG, H. 'A New Britten Opera: *Death in Venice*' *Opera Canada* 14 No. 4 (Winter 1973)
EECKELS, G. 'Brussels' *Music and Musicians* 22 (December 1973)
GOODWIN, N. and REYNOLDS, M. '*Death in Venice* (Covent Garden)' *Music and Musicians* 22 (December 1973)
HOWARD, P. '*Death in Venice* (Covent Garden)' *Musical Times* 114 (December 1973)
ROSENTHAL, H. '*Death in Venice*; English Opera Group' *Opera* 24 (December 1973)
BRITTEN'S *Death in Venice* (radio feature) New York Radio 1974
MITCHELL, D. Sleeve note for Decca SET 581–3 (1974)
'*Death in Venice*; Covent Garden' *Music Review* 35 No. 1 (1974)
SCHWINGER, W. 'Brittens *Tod in Venedig* (Berlin)' *Musica* 28 No. 6 (1974)
FREEMAN, J. W. 'Da New York' *Nuova Rivista Musicale Italiana* 8 No. 4 (1974)
BURDE, W. 'Blasser Tod – Brittens Thomas–Mann–Oper in deutscher Erstaufführung' *Neue Zeitschrift für Musik* 135 No. 11 (1974)
'Snape (Suffolk): Summer at The Maltings' *Oper Und Konzert* 12 No. 1 (1974)
METDEPENNINGHEN, E. 'Brüssel' *Oper und Konzert* 12 No. 2 (1974)
BREUER, R. 'New York' *Oper und Konzert* 12 No. 12 (1974)
'New York' *Opera Canada* 15 No. 4 (1974)
McCANN, J. 'Brussels' *Opera* 23 (January 1974)
GREENFIELD, E. 'London: a church transformed; Schoenberg and Penderecki' *Hi-Fi/Musical America* 24 (June 1974)
DICKINSON, A. E. 'Britten's New Opera' *Musical Quarterly* 60 No. 3 (July 1974)
KERNER, L. 'Looking to Venice a preview of Britten's new opera' *Opera News* 39 No. 4 (October 1974)

'Ageing man, pretty boy; operatic *Death in Venice* a thin show' *Variety* 276 (October 1974)
HOELTERHOFF, M. 'A man perplexed in a plagued year' *Wall Street Journal* 54 (October 1974)
LOSSMAN, H. 'Berlin' *Bühne* 194 (November 1974)
FABIAN, I. 'Aschenbachs dreistündiger Monolog – Deutsche Erstaufführung von Brittens *Tod in Venedig* in der Deutschen Oper Berlin' *Opern Welt* 11 (November 1974)
GREENHALGH, M. *'Death in Venice' Records and Recordings* 18 (November 1974)
KOLODIN, I. 'Britten's *Death in Venice* live and recorded' *Saturday Review/World* 2 (November 1974)
'Graz: Britten – Premiere' *Bühne* 195 (December 1974)
'München: Brittens Thomas–Mann–Oper der *Tod in Venedig*' *Melos* 1 No. 3 (1975)
'The Met' *Music Journal* 32 (December 1974)
'*Death in Venice*. (Whole issue)' *Opera News* 39 (December 1974)
BRUNNER, G. 'Wieder attraktiv – zwei Premieren in Graz' *Opern Welt* 12 (December 1974)
JACOBSON, R. 'New York' *Opera News* 39 (December 1974)
SUTCLIFFE, J. H. 'West Berlin' *Opera News* 39 (December 1974)
FISCHER-WILLIAMS, B. 'Britten's Grenadiers: interviews with Graham, Bedford, Shirley-Quirk' *Opera News* 39 No. 7 (December 14 1974)
MAREK, G. R. 'Mann and Music' *Opera News* 39 No. 7 (December 14 1974)
WHITE, E. W. 'The Voyage to Venice: a guide to Britten's newest opera' *Opera News* 39 No. 7 (December 14 1974)
KOEGLER, H. 'Brittens der *Tod in Venedig* (Düsseldorf)' *Musica* 29 No. 1 (1975)
'Kassel' *Oper Und Konzert* 13 No. 2 (1975)
'München' *Oper und Konzert* 13 No. 4 (1975)
JACOBY, J. B. 'Germany: Berlin' *Opera Canada* 16 No. 1 (1975)
LUDICKE, H. 'In West Berlin: Britten Oper Tod in Venedig' *Musik und Gesellschaft* 25 (January 1975)
'San Francisco' *Opera Canada* 16 No. 3 (1975)
WELSH, C. N. 'Graz: Holn as Aschenbach' *Opera* 26 (January 1975)
KOEGLER, H. 'In Düsseldorf' *Opern Welt* No. 1 (January 1975)
OPPENS, K. '*Tod in Venedig* – an der New Yorker Met.' *Opern Welt* 1 (January 1975)
'West Berlin' *Opera* 26 (January and November 1975)
DETTMER, R. C. 'Benjamin Britten's *Death in Venice* (recording)' *Stereo Review* 24 (January 1975)

DAVIES, P. G. '*Death in Venice:* The Triumph of Chaos (London label original cast recording)' *Hi-Fi/Musical America* 25 (February 1975)

MOOR, P. 'A Footnote to *Death in Venice* (comparison of Luschino Visconti's version of Thomas Mann novella)' *Hi-Fi/Musical America* 25 (February 1975)

MOVSHON, G. 'The Metropolitan Opera' *Hi-Fi/Musical America* 25 (February 1975)

HARRIS, D. 'New York' *Music and Musicians* 23 (February 1975)

KOEGLER, H. 'Düsseldorf: *Death in Venice* vindicated' *Opera* 26 (February 1975)

'Düsseldorf' *Opera News* 39 (February 1975)

WEBER, H. 'Zwei Reisen in den Tod – Brittens Thomas–Mann–Oper in Dusseldorf und Kassel (reprinted from *Frankfurter Allgemeine Zeitung* December 6 1974)' *Orchester* 23 (February 1975)

ROREM, N. 'Britten's Venice' *The New Republic* 172/6 (8 Feb 1975)

MOVSHON, G. 'Two New Met. Productions' *Opera* 26 (March 1975)

'München: Brittens musiktheatrialischer Subjektivismus' *Orchester* 25 (April 1975)

SUTCLIFFE, J. H. 'A Scott in Germany' *Opera* 26 (May 1975)

DANNENBERG, P. 'Zweimal Britten – der *Tod in Venedig* in München unk Kiel' *Opern Welt* 5 (May 1975)

KREMER, L. '*Death in Venice*' AFPB 1975

PEARS, P. The New York *Death in Venice* AFPB 1975

BENESCH, G. 'Bern: Brittens *Tod in Venedig*' *Bühne* 201 (June 1975)

'San Francisco' *Opera News* 39 (June 1975)

'San Francisco' *Opera* 26 (July 1975)

FRANKENSTEIN, A. '*Death in Venice:* New Dimensions of Absurdity?' *Hi-Fi/Musical America* 25 (August 1975)

'Düsseldorf' *Music and Musicians* 23 (August 1975)

ROSENTHAL, H. '*Death in Venice*; English Opera Group at Covent Garden' *Opera* 26 (August 1975)

TAYLOR, P. 'Opera and Ballet in London' *Musical Opinion* 98 (September 1975)

DANNENBERG, P. 'Zum Thomas–Mann–Jahr–Brittens *Tod in Venedig* in Lübeck' *Opern Welt* 9 (September 1975)

GREENFIELD, E. 'Glyndebourne, Aldeburgh and Covent Garden' *Hi-Fi/Musical America* 25 (October 1975)

'Two more Deaths in Venice (Kiel and Munich)' *Opera* 26 (November 1975)

MILLIMAN, J. A. 'Benjamin Britten's symbolic treatment of sleep, dream and death as manifest in his opera *Death in Venice*' Ph.D *University of Southern California* (1977)

LINDENBERG, V. 'Special features of dramaturgy in Benjamin Britten *Death in Venice*' *Latysskaja Muzyka* 13 (1978)
PORTER, A. *'Death in Venice'* in PORTER, A. *Music of Three Seasons* Farrar Straus and Giroux (1978)
SPRATLING, H. 'How Britten's last opera was conceived' *Classical Music* (April 1 1978)
KERNER, L. *'Death in Venice'* AFPB 1978
PORTER, A. 'The last opera: *Death in Venice*'. THE OPERAS OF BENJAMIN BRITTEN; ed. D. Herbert. London, Hamish Hamilton, 1979
ZIETSCH, H. 'Mit Bravour dem Labyrinth entgangen' *Darmstadter Echo* (February 4 1980)
MACAULAY, A. 'A new clarity' (Royal Ballet)' *Dancing Times* 72 (1982)
'The Thomas Mann Archives in Zürich (Exhibition of the Roseman Drawings of Britten's *Death in Venice*)' *Opera* 33 (1982)
MITCHELL, D. *'Death in Venice:* the dark side of perfection' *The Britten Companion;* edited by Christopher Palmer. London, Faber (1984)
PALMER, C. 'Towards a genealogy of *Death in Venice*' *The Britten Companion:* edited by Christopher Palmer. London, Faber (1984)
BEDFORD, S. 'Suite from the opera *"Death in Venice"* Op. 88' AFPB 1984
FREDMAN, M. *'Death in Venice' Performance* (June 1984)
EVANS, J. 'Benjamin Britten *Death in Venice:* perspectives on an opera' *Ph.D University of Wales* (1984)
EVANS, J. 'Britten's Venice Workshop 1. The Sketch Book' *Soundings* 12 (Winter 1984–85)
BEDFORD, S. Sleeve note for *Death in Venice Suite* Chandos ABTD 1126 (1985)
BEDFORD, S. The Struggle with the Word. PETER PEARS: a Tribute on His 75th Birthday; edited by Marion Thorpe. London, Faber in association with the Britten Estate, 1985 (A Britten–Pears Library Publication)
EVANS, J. 'On the Recititative of *Death in Venice*'. PETER PEARS: a Tribute on His 75th Birthday; edited by Marion Thorpe. London, Faber in association with the Britten Estate, 1985 (A Britten–Pears Library Publication).
EVANS, J. 'Britten's Venice Workshop 2: the composition and revision' *Soundings* 13 (Summer 1985)
EVANS, J. *'Death in Venice:* the Apollonian/Dionysian conflict' *Opera Quarterly* 3 No. 3 (Autumn 1986)
BENJAMIN BRITTEN: Death in Venice; compiled and edited by Donald Mitchell. Cambridge, C.U.P., 1987 (Cambridge Opera Handbook)
BRITTEN AND THE WRITING OF *DEATH IN VENICE* (C. Matthews) BBC Radio 3 1987
COOKE, M. 'Britten and the gamelan: Balinese influences in *Death in Venice*'. BENJAMIN BRITTEN: Death in Venice; compiled and edited by Donald

Mitchell. Cambridge, C.U.P., 1987 (Cambridge Opera Handbook)
EVANS, J. 'Twelve-note structures and tonal polarity'. BENJAMIN BRITTEN: Death in Venice; compiled and edited by Donald Mitchell. Cambridge, C.U.P., 1987 (Cambridge Opera Handbook)
EVANS, P. 'Synopsis: the story, the music not excluded'. BENJAMIN BRITTEN: Death in Venice; compiled and edited by Donald Mitchell. Cambridge, C.U.P., 1987 (Cambridge Opera Handbook)
GRAHAM, C. 'The first production'. BENJAMIN BRITTEN: Death in Venice; compiled and edited by Donald Mitchell. Cambridge, C.U.P., 1987 (Cambridge Opera Handbook)
GREENFIELD, E. Review of first performance. Guardian 18 Junee 1973. Reprinted in BENJAMIN BRITTEN: Death in Venice; compiled and edited by Donald Mitchell. Cambridge, C.U.P., 1987 (Cambridge Opera Handbook)
HEYWORTH, P. Review of first performance. Observer 24 June 1973. Reprinted in BENJAMIN BRITTEN: Death in Venice; compiled and edited by Donald Mitchell. Cambridge, C.U.P., 1987 (Cambridge Opera Handbook)
'I was Thomas Mann's Tadzio'. BENJAMIN BRITTEN: Death in Venice; compiled and edited by Donald Mitchell. Cambridge, C.U.P., 1987 (Cambridge Opera Handbook)
MATTHEWS, C. 'The Venice Sketchbook'. BENJAMIN BRITTEN: Death in Venice; compiled and edited by Donald Mitchell. Cambridge, C.U.P., 1987 (Cambridge Opera Handbook)
MATTHEWS, D. *'Death in Venice* and the *Third String Quartet'* BENJAMIN BRITTEN: Death in Venice; compiled and edited by Donald Mitchell. Cambridge, C.U.P., 1987 (Cambridge Opera Handbook)
MITCHELL, D. 'An introduction in the shape of a memoir'. BENJAMIN BRITTEN: Death in Venice; compiled and edited by Donald Mitchell. Cambridge, C.U.P., 1987 (Cambridge Opera Handbook)
NORTHCOTT, B. Review of first performance. The New Statesman 22 June 1973. Reprinted (with afterthought) in BENJAMIN BRITTEN: Death in Venice 1987 (Cambridge Opera Handbook)
PALMER, C. 'Britten's Venice orchestra'. BENJAMIN BRITTEN: Death in Venice; compiled and edited by Donald Mitchell. Cambridge, C.U.P., 1987 (Cambridge Opera Handbook)
PIPER, M. 'The libretto'. BENJAMIN BRITTEN: Death in Venice; compiled and edited by Donald Mitchell. Cambridge, C.U.P., 1987 (Cambridge Opera Handbook)
REED, P. 'Aschenbach becomes Mahler: Thomas Mann as film'. BENJAMIN BRITTEN: Death in Venice; compiled and edited by Donald Mitchell. Cambridge, C.U.P., 1987 (Cambridge Opera Handbook)
REED, T. J. 'Mann and his novella: *Death in Venice*'. BENJAMIN BRITTEN: Death in Venice; compiled and edited by Donald Mitchell. Cambridge, C.U.P., 1987 (Cambridge Opera Handbook)

ROREM, N. 'Britten's Venice'. BENJAMIN BRITTEN: Death in Venice; compiled and edited by Donald Mitchell. Cambridge, C.U.P., 1987 (Cambridge Opera Handbook)

ROSEBERRY, E. 'Tonal ambiguity in *Death in Venice:* a symbolic view'. BENJAMIN BRITTEN: Death in Venice; compiled and edited by Donald Mitchell. Cambridge, C.U.P., 1987 (Cambridge Opera Handbook)

SHAWE-TAYLOR, D. Review of first performance. Sunday Times 24 June 1973. Reprinted in BENJAMIN BRITTEN: Death in Venice 1987 (Cambridge Opera Handbook)

STRODE, R. 'A *Death in Venice* chronicle'. BENJAMIN BRITTEN: Death in Venice; compiled and edited by Donald Mitchell. Cambridge, C.U.P., 1987 (Cambridge Opera Handbook)

DEUS IN ADJUTORIUM MEUM

STRODE, R. *'Deus in adjutorium meum'* AFPB 1983

DIDO AND AENEAS

PEARS, P. *'Dido and Aeneas'* AFPB 1951

SMITH, C. 'European Musical Events observed by American critic (*Dido and Aeneas* first performance)' *Musical America* 71 (June 1951)

MALCOLM, G. 'Dido and Aeneas' MITCHELL/KELLER 1952

BRITTEN, B., PEARS, P. and HOLST, I. 'Dido and Aeneas' AFPB 1974

HOLST, I. Sleeve note for Decca SET 615 (1978)

LAURIE, M. 'Review of Bedford recordings of *Dido and Aeneas*, criticizing Britten edition of score' *Musical Times* 119 (December 1978)

DIVERSIONS

Tempo 1 (American series) No. 3 (September 1940)

Tempo 1 (American series) No. 4 (January 1941)

'*Diversions on a theme for piano (left hand) and orchestra*, Op. 21. First performance.' *Monthly Musical Record* 80 (December 1950)

'*Diversions for piano (left hand) and orchestra*' *Musical Opinion* 78 (May 1955)

'*Diversions, Op. 21, for piano (left hand) and orchestra*, arranged for two pianos' *Musical Courier* 154 (September 1956)

'*Diversions for Piano and Orchestra*' Rochester Philharmonic Orchestra Programme Notes (October 17 1968)

ELEGY

STRODE, R. and MATTHEWS, C. *'Elegy* (1930) for viola' AFPB 1984

EVANS, J. Sleeve note for EMI EX 0502 5 (1986)

THE ENGLISH OPERA GROUP
KELLER, H. 'The English Opera Group' *Music Parade* 1 No. 7 (1948)
'Comment (The English Opera Group)' *Opera* 2 (May 1951)
MANN, W. 'English Opera Group Season' *Opera* 2 (July 1951)
'The English Opera Group' *About the House* 1 No. 8 (1964)
GROSHEVA, Y. 'The English Opera Group toured Russia: "Realistic Traditions"' *Musical Events* 19 (December 1964)
HOWARD, M. 'The English Opera Group; 21st Aldeburgh Festival' *About the House* 2 No. 11 (1968)

THE FAIRY QUEEN
'*The Fairy Queen*' AFPB 1967
PEARS, P. and HOLST, I. *The Fairy Queen*, Henry Purcell (1659–95) AFPB 1969
BRITTEN, B. and I. HOLST eds. *The Fairy Queen*, H. Purcell. Version for concert performance by P. Pears. (London, Faber, 1970) *Music Review* 32 No. 4 (1971)
LANG, P. H. 'The Dramatic Genius of Henry Purcell – the Problematical *Fairy Queen*: gloriously salvaged by Britten (recording)' *Hi-Fi/Musical America* 23 (July 1973)
GRAHAM, C. '*The Fairy Queen*' AFPB 1977
HOLST, I. Sleeve note for Decca SET 615 (1978)

FANFARE FOR ST EDMUNDSBURY
BRITTEN, B. '*Fanfare for St Edmundsbury* (1936)' AFPB 1984

FARFIELD (1928–30)
BRITTEN, B. 'Farfield 1928–30 (score)' *Grasshopper* (1955) [Farfield was Britten's House at Gresham's School]

FESTIVAL TE DEUM
Tempo 1 No. 9 (December 1944)
NETTEL, R. 'Britten's *Festival Te Deum*' *Musical Times* (July 1945)
ENGLAND, G. A. 'Critique: a study to provide self administering improvement in conducting specific rhythmic problems in two choral works of Benjamin Britten (University of North Colorado E. D.) 1972' *Council for Research in Music Education Bulletin* 38 (Summer 1974)

FILM MUSIC
KELLER, H. 'Film Music' *Music Survey* 2 (Spring 1950)
WRIGHT, B. 'Britten and documentary' *Musical Times* 104 (November 1963)

THIEL, W. 'Bausteine zu einer Asthetik der Dokumentarfilm-musik' *Dokument und Kunst* (1977)

FIVE FLOWER SONGS
'*Five Flower Songs* for mixed chorus' *Music and Letters* 32 (October 1951)
'*Five Flower Songs* for mixed chorus' *Music Survey* 4 (October 1951)
'*Five Flower Songs*, settings for mixed chorus, SATB, A Cappella' *Musical America* 25 (June 1955)
'To Daffodils and The Succession of the Four Sweet Months' *Notes* 12 (September 1955)

FOLKSONGS
VAUGHAN WILLIAMS, R. 'Folk Song Arrangements Vol. 1 (British Isles) Review' *Journal of the English Folk Dance and Song Society* 4 No. 4 (1943)
ROSEBERRY, E. 'Britten's Purcell Realisations and Folksong Arrangements' *Tempo* 57 (Spring 1961)
'Folksong Arrangements, Volumes 5, 6' *Musical Times* 103 (March 1962)
WARBURTON, A. O. 'Set work for O Level, GCE' *Music Teacher and Piano Student* 49 (April 1970)
GREENFIELD, E. 'Aldeburgh' *Guardian* (June 18 1976)
MATTHEWS, C. Sleeve note for EMI RLS 748 (1980)
MATTHEWS, C. Sleeve note for EMI ASD 4397 (1983)
EVANS, J. Sleeve note for Hyperion A66209 (1986)
EVANS, J. Sleeve note for EMI EL 2706541 (1987)

FOR A SONG
EVANS, J. Sleeve note for EMI 27 0653 1 (1987)

GEMINI VARIATIONS
'Benjamin Britten writes for Hungarian twins' *New Hungary* (May 1965)
BRITTEN, B. '*Gemini Variations* Op. 73' AFPB 1965
GOODWIN, N. 'Suffolk Constellation' *Music and Musicians* 13 (August 1965)
SADIE, S. 'Aldeburgh' *Musical Times* 106 (August 1965)
GREENFIELD, E. 'Bumper Britten Crop' *Hi-Fi/Musical America* 15 (September 1965)
WALSH, S. 'Three New Britten Works' *Tempo* 74 (Autumn 1965)

GENERAL
'Benjamin Britten' *Daily Telegraph* (December 16 1933)
FRANK, A. 'New Orchestral Works' *The Listener* (January 6 1937)
EVANS, E. 'Contemporary British Composers' *The Listener* (April 21 1937)

BOYS, H. 'Younger English Composers' *Monthly Musical Record* (October 1938)
WHITE, E. W. 'A musician of the people' *Life and Letters* (April 1939)
'Composer would knock out Fascists by mighty song' *Toronto Daily Star* (June 21 1939)
MACLEAN, R. 'Famous Young Composer Gives Easy Way to Learn How to Appreciate Music' *The Evening Telegraph* (June 22 1939)
ROBINSON, J. 'Atuning Art to its Times to the Left' *The Globe and Mail* (June 28 1939)
KING, W. 'Music and Musicians' *New York Sun* (April 27 1940)
COCKSHOTT, G. 'English composer goes West' *Musical Times* (August 1941)
EVANS, E. 'New Britten scores' *Tempo* 5 (O.S.) (August 1941)
COCKSHOTT, G. 'English composer goes West' *Musical Times* (September 1941)
WESTRUP, J. A. 'The virtuosity of Benjamin Britten' *Listener* (July 16 1942)
McNAUGHT, W. 'Broadcast Music – Mainly about Britten' *Listener* (July 30 1942)
'Return to England' *Tempo Am.* No. 3 (September 1942)
BLOM, E. 'Benjamin Britten' *Birmingham Post* (May 17 1943)
MANNING, R. 'Benjamin Britten' *Monthly Musical Record* 73 No. 847 (June 1943)
GLOCK, W. 'Music' *Observer* (June 24 1943)
MASON, C. 'Britten: Another View' *Monthly Musical Record* 73 No. 849 (September 1943)
SACKVILLE-WEST, E. 'Music: Some aspects of the contemporary problem' *Horizon* 10 Nos 54, 55, 56 (June, July, August 1944)
ESCHER, R. 'Benjamin Britten' *De Groene* (May 4 1946)
WOOD, R. W. 'Concerning Sprechgesang' *Tempo* 2 (December 1946)
MURRILL, H. 'Purcell Britten – A challenge' *Music Lover* (April 1947)
NEWMAN, E. 'Strauss, Britten and Gounod' *Sunday Times* (October 19 1947)
DOUGLAS, P. 'Benjamin Britten: another Purcell' *Town and Country* (December 1947)
GODDARD, S. 'Benjamin Britten' *Disc* 1 (Winter 1947)
KELLER, H. 'Britten and Mozart: A Challenge in the form of Variations on an Unfamiliar Theme' *Music and Letters* 29 No. 1 (January 1948)
'The Composer of *Peter Grimes*' *Opera News* 12 No. 21 (March 8 1948)
MELLERS, W. H. 'Stylization in Contemporary British Music' *Horizon* 17 No. 101 (May 1948)
MASON, C. 'Britten' *Musical Times* (March–May 1948)
KELLER, H. 'A Britten Festival' *Everybody's* (June 5 1948)

FORSTER, E. M. 'Looking back on the Aldeburgh Festival' *The Listener* (June 24 1948)

HUSSEY, D. 'Broadcast Music' *The Listener* (September 30 1948)

MILA, M. 'Posizione di Britten nella musica inglese' *Rassagna Musicale* (October 1948)

MANNING, R. 'From Holst to Britten: a study of modern choral music.' *London, Workers' Music Association* (1949)

GODDARD, S. 'Instrumental Composer' *The Listener* (July 7 1949)

KLEIN, J. W. 'Britten and English opera' *Musical Opinion* (July 1949)

KELLER, H. 'Benjamin Britten and the Young' *The Listener* (September 29 1949)

HUSSEY, D. 'New works by Britten' *Britain Today* (October 1949)

KELLER, H. 'Profile – Benjamin Britten' *Crescendo* 23 (October 1949)

CROZIER, E. 'An Opera Team Sets to Work' *Picture Post* (October 1949)

'Peter Pears, Benjamin Britten arrive for tour' *Musical Courier* 140 (November 1 1949)

'Benjamin Britten, composer – pianist' *Musical America* 69 (November 15 1949)

'Peter Pears, Benjamin Britten' *Musical Courier* 140 (November 15 1949)

GOLDBERG, A. 'Britten is Guest Conductor with Los Angeles Orchestra' *Musical America* 69 (December 4 and 15 1949)

'Living British Composers' *Hinrichsen* 6 (1949–50)

COWAN, J. L. 'The problem of modern Opera' *Music* (1950)

'Britten in Los Angeles' *International Musician* 48 (January 1950)

LAING, J. 'Bouquets for Britten' *Opera* 15 (January 1950)

DUNCAN, R. 'A Sketch of Benjamin Britten' *World Review* (January 1950)

STEIN, E. 'Benjamin Britten's operas' *Opera* 1 (February 1950)

HARMAN, C. 'Thoughts on writing an opera; an interview with Benjamin Britten' *Boston Symphony Concert Bulletin* 15 (February 10 1950)

MILA, M. 'Musica per il consumatore' *La Fiera Litteraria* (February 28 1950)

CROZIER, E. 'Correspondence' *Music Survey* 2 No. 4 (Spring 1950)

KELLER, H. 'Resistances to Britten's music: their psychology' *Music Survey* 2 (Spring 1950)

REDLICH, H. 'The Significance of Britten's Operatic Style' *Music Survey* 2 (Spring 1950)

STUART, C. 'Britten "The Eclectic"' *Music Survey* 2 (Spring 1950)

DUNCAN, R. 'A sketch of Benjamin Britten' *World Review* (July 1950)

OTTOWAY, D. H. 'Serge Prokofiev and Benjamin Britten' *Musical Opinion* (July 1950)

KELLER, H. 'Britten and Mozart' (Unauthorized and partly wrong translation of *Britten and Mozart*: A Challenge in the Form of Variations on an Unfamiliar Theme, Music and Letters 29 No. 1 January 1948) *Oesterreichische Musikzeitschrift* 5 nos. 7/8 (July/August 1950)
'Britten's Operas' *Strad* 61 (October 1950)
MONTAGU, G. 'Benjamin Britten' *Musical Europe* 1 (Autumn 1950)
ROSENWALD, H. 'Contemporary Music' *Music News* 42 (December 1950)
HAMBURGER, P. 'Mainly about Britten' *Music Survey* 3 No. 2 (December 1950)
KELLER, H. 'Musical self-contempt in Britain (elaboration of Resistances to Britten's Music: Their Psychology, Music Survey 2 no. 4 Spring 1950)' *Paper To Social Psychology Section of British Psychological Society* (November 4 1950)
'Caricature by Byrom' *Music Parade* 2 No. 6 (1951)
HAMBURGER, P. 'Mainly about Britten' *Music Survey* 3 No. 2 (1951)
'Peter Pears' *London Music* 6 (January 1951)
SKULSKY, A. 'Gustav Mahler (His influence on contemporary composers)' *Musical America* 71 (February 1951)
'British Personalities' *Canon* 4 (March 1951)
ANDREWS, A. 'The Arbiter of Aldeburgh' *Public Opinion* 4858 (March 2 1951)
REES, C. B. 'Benjamin Britten' *London Musical Events* 6 No. 4 (April 1951)
REES, C. B. 'Impressions' *London Music* 6 (May 1951)
'Britten's chamber operas' *Opera* (May 1951)
HIND, J. 'Un estudio de la opera de Benjamin Britten' *Platea* 7 and 8 (July–August 1951)
KELLER, H. 'Festatmosphärische Störungen (Britten and Aldeburgh Festival)' *Salzburger Nachrichten* (August 29 1951)
MITCHELL, D. 'Britten on Records' *Disk* 5 (Autumn 1951)
MITCHELL, D. 'The Young Person's Composer' *Making Music* 17 (Autumn 1951)
'Comment ("The Sleeping Children": An Inquest)' *Opera* 2 (September 1951)
OTTAWAY, B. H. 'A Note on Britten' *Monthly Musical Record* 81 No. 930 (October 1951)
FRANK, A. 'Contemporary Portraits (includes discussion of works)' *Music Teacher* 30 (December 1951)
MITCHELL, D. 'The Brilliance of Mr. Britten' *Disk* 4 (Winter 1951)
VAN DER LINDEN, A. 'A Short History in Pictures of opera in the 20th century' *World Theatre* (1951/2)
AURIC, G. 'The Piano Music:I It's place in Britten's development' MITCHELL/KELLER 1952

BENJAMIN BRITTEN: a Commentary on his works from a group of specialists; edited by Donald Mitchell and Hans Keller. London, Rockliff, 1952. Reprinted: Westport, Greenwood Press, 1972
BERKELEY, L. 'The Light Music' MITCHELL/KELLER 1952
CHISSELL, J. 'The Concertos' MITCHELL/KELLER 1952
DICKINSON, A. E. F. 'The Piano Music: II Critical survey' MITCHELL/KELLER 1952
HAMBURGER, P. 'The Chamber Music' MITCHELL/KELLER 1952
HAMBURGER, P. 'The Pianist' MITCHELL/KELLER 1952
HAREWOOD, Earl of 'The Man' MITCHELL/KELLER 1952
HOLST, I. 'Britten and the Young' MITCHELL/KELLER 1952
KELLER, H. 'The Musical Character' MITCHELL/KELLER 1952
MANN, W. 'The Incidental Music' MITCHELL/KELLER 1952
MITCHELL, D. 'The Musical Atmosphere' MITCHELL/KELLER 1952
NEEL, B. 'The String Orchestra' MITCHELL/KELLER 1952
PEARS, P. 'The Vocal Music' MITCHELL/KELLER 1952
SHAWE-TAYLOR, D. Discography MITCHELL/KELLER 1952
STEIN, E. 'The Symphonies' MITCHELL/KELLER 1952
WHITE, E. W. Bibliography of Benjamin Britten's incidental music MITCHELL/KELLER 1952
'Music Lover's Diary' *Music Parade* 5 (1952)
LOCKHART, L. B. 'The Story of Gresham's' *East Anglian Magazine* 21 (February 1952)
KNYVETT, G. 'Benjamin Britten' *Dansk Muskitidsskrift* (February 27 1952)
KLEIN, J. W. 'Britten's advance to mastery' *Musical Opinion* (March 1952)
MELLERS, W. 'Recent Trends in British Music' *Music Quarterly* 38 No. 2 (April 1952)
SHAFFER, P. 'Benjamin Britten' *Panorama* 6 (Spring 1952)
REES, C. B. 'Musical Roundabout (Benjamin Britten's attack on critics)' *Music Teacher* 31 (May 1952)
SCHONBERG, H. C. 'Facing the Music (Britten does not like facing the critics)' *Musical Courier* 145 (May 1952)
MITCHELL, D. 'The later Development of Benjamin Britten (includes discussion of works)' *Chesterian* 27 (July and October 1952)
'The Aldeburgh Festival' *Musical Times* 93 (August 1952)
'On the Front Cover' *Musical America* 72 (September 1952)
TAYLOR, R. 'The place of Britten in contemporary music' *Cambridge Journal* (October 1952)
RAYNOR, H. 'Britten, Stravinsky and the Future of Opera' *Musical Opinion* 76 (October 1952)

CROZIER, E. 'He puts England on the Opera Map' *New York Times* 101 (October 26 1952)

MYERS, R. H. 'L'école anglaise' *Revue Musicale* 212 (1952)

STEIN, E. 'Britten seen against his English Background' *Orpheus in New Guises* London, Rockliff (1953)

'Mr. Britten's admirers (review of Mitchell/Keller)' *World Review* (1953)

SHAWE-TAYLOR, D. 'Britten Considered' *New Statesman* (January 3 1953)

TRANCHELL, P. 'Britten and Brittenites (review of Mitchell/Keller)' *Music and Letters* (April 1953)

DEAN, W. 'Review of Mitchell/Keller' *Musical Times* (April 1953)

GODMAN, S. 'Britten's first publication' *Monthly Musical Record* 83 (July–August 1953)

RAYNOR, H. 'The Battle of Britten' *Musical Opinion* 76 (July 1953)

MASON, C. 'Sweet Reason' *Opera* 4 (December 1953)

GODDARD, S. 'London Letter' *Chesterian* 28 (January 1954)

LINDLAR, H. 'Britten Britannicus: Aspekte der englischen Musik' *Musica* 8 (December 1954)

MASON, C. 'Operatic Highroad, Symphonic Rut' *Saturday Review* 38 (May 1955)

LINDLAR, H. 'Orpheus Britannicus; Pears–Britten auf Deutschland–Tournee' *Musikleben* 8 (July–August 1955)

HESSE, *Prince Ludwig of Hesse and the Rhine* Ausflug Ost. Darmstadt, Roether, 1956

KLEIN, J. W. 'A Decade of English Opera' *Musical Opinion* 79 (January 1956)

WRIGHT, A. 'Britten's Miniatures and Magnums' *Opera News* 20 (February 1956)

CARPENTER, R. 'William Baines and Britten: some affinities' *Musical Times* 97 (April 1956)

MASON, C. 'Modern Music on the Gramophone' *Music and Letters* 37 (July 1956)

YZERDRAAT, B. 'Begegnung mit Sudostasien; zu Benjamin Brittens Besuch auf Bali' *Musica* 10 (July–August 1956)

'Menuhin and Britten exchange Festival performances' *Musical Courier* 156 (August 1956)

RAYNOR, H. 'Influence and Achievement; some thoughts on 20th century English Song' *Chesterian* 30 (Winter 1956)

HAUSLER, J. 'Britten am Pult des Sudwest-funkorchesters' *Melos* 24 (January 1957)

GONNE, A. and PIRIE, P. J. 'Correspondence: formality in Music.' *Music Review* 18 (February 1957)

PARMENTER, R. 'Menuhin and Britten agree to play in each other's home town' *New York Times* 106 (March 17 1957)

'Birthday Honours' *London Music* 12 (August 1957)

SCHWEIZER, G. 'Britten; Die in Schatten leben' *Musica* 12 (April 1958)

STUCKENSCHMIDT, H. H. 'Britten und die Wiener Schule in Berlin' *Melos* 25 (June 1958)

KLEIN, J. W. 'Is Britten a One-Opera Composer?' *Musical Opinion* 81 (July 1958)

BROWN, D. 'Stimulus and Form in Britten's Work' *Music and Letters* 39 (July 1958)

LINDLAR, H. 'From Purcell to Britten Von Purcell zu Britten; Geburt und Wiedergeburt der Oper in England' *Musica* 12 (July–August 1958)

BLON, E. 'Zwischen Vierzig und Fünfzig' *Musica* 12 (July–August 1958)

MAYHEAD, R. 'The cult of Benjamin Britten (review of Mitchell/Keller)' *Scrutiny* 19 No. 3 (1959)

WHITE, E. W. 'Benjamin Britten' *Canon* 12 (January 1959)

JAROCINSKI, S. 'Benjamin Britten' (includes discussion of works) *Slovenska Hudba* 3 (February 1959)

REID, C. 'Back to Britain with Britten' *Hi-Fi* 9 (December 1959)

SEEBOHM, C. Conscripts to an age: British expatriates 1939–1945: Unpublished typescript [1960]

HEADINGTON, C. 'Britten's Music and its Significance Today' *Chesterian* 34 202 (1960)

KLEIN, J. W. 'The enigma of Britten' *Musical Times* (1960)

NOBLE, J. 'Music in London' *Canon* 13 (January 1960)

MELLERS, W. 'Benjamin Britten and English Opera' *Listener* 63 (January 21 1960)

NOBLE, J. 'Britten–Pears Recital at the Wigmore Hall' *Musical Events* 15 (March 1960)

RUTLAND, H. 'I.C.A. Concert' *Musical Times* 101 (March 1960)

KLEIN, J. W. 'The Enigma of Britten' *Musical Times* 101 (October 1960)

WILCZEK, J. 'Rozmowa z Benjaminen Brittenen' *Ruch Muzyczny* 5 No. 22 (1961)

'Britten at Aldeburgh' *Music Review* 22 No. 3 (1961)

WEBER, J. 'Wykonawcy Festiwalu' *Ruch Muzyczny* 5 No. 21 (1961)

'Covent Garden Opera' *Musical Opinion* 84 (January 1961)

'Covent Garden' *Opera* 12 (January 1961)

SADIE, S. 'Britten and Pears at Wigmore Hall' *Musical Events* 16 (February 1961)

'Macnaghten Concerts' *Musical Opinion* 84 (February 1961)

MANN, W. 'London Music' *Musical Times* 102 (February 1961)
SZENDREY, J. 'Britten opera in Budapest' *Opera* 12 (March 1961)
EMERY, W. 'Bach versus the Bible' *Musical Times* 102 (April 1961)
SARTORI, C. 'Sutherland and Britten at Milan' *Opera* 12 (July 1961)
TIERNEY, N. 'Dazzling Liverpool Messiah' *Music and Musicians* 10 (February 1962)
WOOD, H. 'Britten's latest scores' *Musical Times* 103 (March 1962)
FLUCK, A. 'Benjamin Britten and Schools' *Music in Education* 26 (May 1962)
WHITTALL, A. N. 'Benjamin Britten' *Music Review* 23 No. 4 (1962)
NOBLE, J. 'Aldeburgh' *Musical Times* 103 (August 1962)
MITCHELL, D. 'Edinburgh' *Opera* 13 (Autumn 1962)
GRAF, M. 'Yugoslavia' *Music and Musicians* 11 (September 1962)
FAULKNER, M. 'Dubrovnik; Britain's Britten with Peer, Pears' *Music Magazine* 164 (September 1962)
'Absentees' *Music and Musicians* 11 (October 1962)
HEINITZ, T. 'Late Verdi' *Music and Musicians* 11 (November 1962)
GOODWIN, N. 'The Unfamiliar Britten' *Records and Recording* 6 No. 3 (December 1962)
JOHNSTON, D. 'Bach and the Bible' *R.M.A.* 90 (1963–64)
BERKELEY, L. 'Britten's Characters' *About the House* 1 No. 5 (1963)
BERKELEY, L. 'A Tribute to Benjamin Britten on his Sixtieth Birthday' *Composer* 12 (1963)
POSPISIL, V. 'Padesat met Benjamin Brittena' *Hudebni Rozhledy* 16 No. 20 (1963)
CROZIER, E. 'Writing an Opera' *Music and Education* 26 (No. 299 (1963)
VON HEIJNE, I. 'Slagrutemannens lov – sprippa tankar kring jubilaren Britten' *Musikrevy* 18 No. 7–8 (1963)
PLEIJEL, B. 'Benjamin Britten paa skiva' *Musikrevy* 18 No. 7–8 (1963)
SCHAFER, M. 'British composers in interview' Faber (1963)
'Britten and After' *Music and Musicians* (January 1963)
'Goethe Prize for Benjamin Britten' *Canon* 16 (February 1963)
'Britten–Pears: Recommended without Qualifications' (Folksongs arranged by Benjamin Britten sung by Peter Pears – recording) *American Record Guide* 29 (March 1963)
GOODWIN, N. 'Britten in Britain' *Music and Musicians* 11 (May 1963)
CRUFT, J. 'British Music in Moscow and Leningrad' *Music Events* 18 (May 1963)
'Britten rasskazyvaet' *Sovetskaya Muzyka* 27 (June 1963)
NEST'EV, I. 'Moskichi aplodiruyut' *Sovetskya Muzyka* 27 (June 1963)

ROZHDESTVENSKAYA, N. 'Neobyknovennyy duet' *Sovetskaya Muzyka* 27 (June 1963)
'BBC Invitation Concerts' *Strad* 74 (June 1963)
PAYNE, A. 'Britten's "Spring"' *Music and Musicians* 11 (July 1963)
ANDREWES, J. 'The Composer as a Young Person's Guide (Music for Children)' *Tempo* 66–67 (Autumn–Winter 1963)
'Britten at Fifty' *Tempo* 66–67 (Autumn–Winter 1963)
KELLER, H. 'The World Around Britten' *Tempo* 66–67 (Autumn–Winter 1963)
TIPPETT, M. 'Benjamin Britten: a birthday tribute' *Composer* 12 (Autumn 1963)
REES, C. B. 'The Genius of Britten' *Music Events* 18 (September 1963)
COLEMAN, B. 'Producing the opera' *The London Magazine* 3 (October 1963)
DEL MAR, N. 'The Orchestral music' *The London Magazine* 3 (October 1963)
OSBORNE, C. 'Britten on Discs' *The London Magazine* 3 (October 1963)
PLOMER, W. 'Let's Crab an Opera' *The London Magazine* 3 (October 1963)
TIPPETT, M. 'Starting to know Britten' *The London Magazine* 3 (October 1963)
CURZON, C. 'Twenty Years Ago'. TRIBUTE TO BENJAMIN BRITTEN on his Fiftieth Birthday; edited by Anthony Gishford. London, Faber, 1963
COPLAND, A. 'A visit to Snape'. TRIBUTE TO BENJAMIN BRITTEN on his Fiftieth Birthday; edited by Anthony Gishford. London, Faber, 1963
GIULINI, C. M. Excerpt from a letter to the Editor. TRIBUTE TO BENJAMIN BRITTEN on his Fiftieth Birthday; edited by Anthony Gishford. London, Faber, 1963
POULENC, F. 'Hommage à Benjamin Britten'. TRIBUTE TO BENJAMIN BRITTEN on his Fiftieth Birthday; edited by Anthony Gishford. London, Faber, 1963
ROSTROPOVICH, M. 'Dear Ben...' TRIBUTE TO BENJAMIN BRITTEN on his Fiftieth Birthday; edited by Anthony Gishford. London, Faber, 1963
TRIBUTE TO BENJAMIN BRITTEN on his Fiftieth Birthday; edited by Anthony Gishford. London, Faber, 1963
BRITTEN AT FIFTY (TV Documentary) BBC TV 1963
'Britten on the Stage (includes list of Operas and Premiere Data)' *Music and Musicians* 12 (November 1963)
'Peter Pears' *Music and Musicians* 12 (November 1963)
BARKER, M. G. 'Britten on Record' *Music and Musicians* 12 (November 1963)
GOODWIN, N. 'A Viewpoint on Britten' *Music and Musicians* 12 (November 1963)
KELLER, H. 'How great is Britten? or Why I am Right' *Music and Musicians* 12 (November 1963)

SCHAFER, M. 'Britten in Interview (reprinted from British Composers in Interview)' *Music and Musicians* 12 (November 1963)
HEINITZ, T. 'Birthday for Britten' *Saturday Review* 46 (November 1963)
REID, C. 'Britten at 50 – a Protean composer' *New York Times Magazine* (November 17 1963)
SHAWE-TAYLOR, D. 'A "King Lear" in prospect' *Sunday Times* (November 17 1963)
MASON, C. 'Benjamin Britten at 50' *Guardian* (November 21 1963)
'Composer who reconciles opposites' *Times* (November 22 1963)
JACOBSON, D. 'Dowland's 400th' *Music and Musicians* 12 (December 1963)
PAYNE, A. 'Birthday Reflections' *Music and Musicians* 12 (December 1963)
'Benjamin Britten' *Musik und Gesellschaft* 13 (December 1963)
SCHAFER, M. 'Kompozitor rasskazyvaet' *Sovetskaya Muzyka* 27 (December 1963)
TAURAGIS, A. 'Vydayushchiysya master sovrenennosti' *Sovetskaya Muzyka* 27 (December 1963)
CAIRNS, D. 'Britten and Tippett' *Spectator* (December 6 1963)
DREW, D. 'Tributaries' *New Statesman* 66 (December 17 1963)
BAJER, J. and POSPISIL, V. 'Britten a Pears zpivali, hrali a hovorili' *Hudebni Rozhledy* 17 No. 10 (1964)
BERGFORS, P. G. 'Benjamin Brittens senaste (Holland Festival)' *Muzykrevy* 19 No. 6 (1964)
MASON, E. 'After Fifty' *Music and Musicians* 12 (January 1964)
BRITTEN, B. 'Britten Looking Back (reprinted from London *Daily Telegraph* 22 November 1963)' *Musical America* 84 (February 1964)
SORIA, D. J. 'Artist Life (Dishes made in Honour of Britten's Sixtieth Birthday)' *Hi-Fi/Musical America* 24 (March 1964)
BRITTEN, B. 'O moem velikon sootechestvellike' *Sovetskaya Muzyka* 28 (April 1964)
FOWLES. J. 'The Heart of Britten' *Show* 4 (May 1964)
'U nas v gostyakh B. Britten' *Sovetskaya Muzyka* 28 (May 1964)
EVANS, P. 'Britten since the *War Requiem*' *Listener* 71 (May 28 1964)
COOPER, M. 'England' *Musical America* 84 (July 1964)
'Benjamin Britten ends Thirty Year link with Boosey & Hawkes' *Variety* 235 (July 8 1964)
JACOBSON, B. 'Delight in NW5' *Music and Musicians* 12 (August 1964)
GREENS, T. 'High Honour for a Shy Genius' *Life* 57 (August 7 1964)
BRITTEN, B. 'On Winning the First Aspen Award' *Saturday Review* 47 (August 22 1964)

CAMPBELL, C. 'Music and poetry: with some notes on Benjamin Britten's setting of words' *Critical Quarterly* (Autumn 1964)

'Benjamin Britten Honoured by Aspen Institute' *Music Leader* 96 (September 1964)

YOUNG, A. 'Colorado/Bundle for Britten (Aspen Award)' *Musical America* 84 (September 1964)

HIGGINS, R. 'Britten's elusive ideal' *New Society* 8 (October 1964)

ENTELIS, L. 'Britten's Leningrad success (translated from Leningradskya Pravda)' *Opera* 15 (November 1964)

BRITTEN, B. 'The Artist and Society' *Records and Recording* 8 No. 2 (November 1964)

MITCHELL, D. 'The Operas of Britten' *Musical America* 84 (December 1964)

CARDUS, N. 'Britten's humanity' *Guardian* (December 3 1964)

'Opera and other music Britten would like to write' *Times* (December 14 1964)

ROSTROPOVICH, M. 'Till Benjamin Britten' *Nutida Musik* 9 Nos. 5–6 (1965–6)

BRITTEN, B. 'Pisi pro lidi' *Hudebni Rozhledy* 18 No. 4 (1965)

'Brittenotes' *Pan Pipes* 57 No. 3 (1965)

BREWSTER, R. G. 'The Relationship between Poetry and Music in original solo works of Benjamin Britten' *Ph.D University of Washington* (1965)

GOODWIN, N. 'Aspen Aspects' *Music and Musicians* 13 (January 1965)

KLEIN, J. W. 'The Supreme Challenge of Lear' *Musical Opinion* 88 (January 1965)

PIERS, P. 'Put'pevtsa' *Sovetskaya Muzyka* 29 (February 1965)

GREENFIELD, E. 'Notes from our Correspondents' *Hi-Fi/Musical America* 15 (March 1965)

'Govorit Bendzhamin Britten' *Sovetskaya Muzyka* 29 (March 1965)

LEONT'EVA, O. 'Novye perspekcivy' *Sovetskaya Muzyka* 29 (March 1965)

CARDUS, N. 'Britten and his critics' *Guardian* 10 (April 1965)

STRODE, R. 'Benjamin Britten and the recorder' *The Recorder and Music Magazine* 1 (May 1965)

BRITTEN, B. 'Der Komponist und das Wort' *Oesterreichische Musikzeitung* 20 (May–June 1965)

OSBORNE, C. L. 'Peter Pears and Julian Bream: in a word, musicality' (recording) *Hi-Fi/Musical America* 15 (June 1965)

CARVELL, P. 'Festival-on-Sea' *Tatler* 265 No. 3329 (June 16 1965)

'Mr. Britten and the Loud Speaker' *Hi-Fi/Musical America* 15 (July 1965)

'English Lute Music in extraordinary performances; lutenist Julian Bream, tenor Peter Pears are ideal interpreters (recording)' *Hi-Fi Review* 15 (October 1965)

OGANESYAN, E. 'Dni Brittena the Armenii' *Sovetskaya Muzika* 29 (December 1965)
VON HEIJNE, I. 'Analys utan facit; naagra Notiser till en Britten-Konsert' *Nutida Musik* 9 Nos 5–6 (1965–6)
HURD, M. 'Benjamin Britten'. London, Novello, 1966 (Biographies of Great Musicians)
YOUNG, P. 'Britten'. London, Benn, 1966
MENERTH, E. F. 'Singing in Style: Modern' *Music Education Journal* 53 No. 4 (1966)
CROZIER, E. 'Composer and Librettist' *Composer* 18 (January 1966)
KLEIN, J. W. 'Lear, a challenge to Opera' *Music and Musicians* 14 (February 1966)
'Benjamin Britten' *San Francisco Symphony* (March 1966)
NOBLE, J. 'Britten's Babylon' *New Statesman* 71 (June 17 1966)
REID, C. 'Great Britten' *Spectator* (July 8 1966)
Senior, E. 'Wheel of Fortune' *Music and Musicians* 14 (August 1966)
HOPKINS, B. 'Selling Britten short?' *Music and Musicians* 15 (September 1966)
BRITTEN AND HIS FESTIVAL (TV Documentary) ITV 1967
LEDESMA, O. 'Recital Britten – Pears' *Buenos Aires Musicale* 22 No. 372 (1967)
WOOLRIDGE, D. 'Some Performance Problems in Contemporary Music' *Tempo* 79 (1966–67)
KODALY, Z. 'Utan a Zenehez. A konyv haron eloszava. Prefaces by Benjamin Britten, Ernest Ansermet and Yehudi Menuhin' *Magyar Zene* 8 No. 2 (1967)
'Recital de Peter Pears y Benjamin Britten' *Revista Musicale Chile* 21 No. 102 (1967)
MELLERS, W. 'Caliban reborn; renewal in Twentieth Century Music' *World Perspectives* 36 (1967)
'Spotlight on Britten (Opera being presented in the United States)' *Opera News* 31 (January 1967)
CRANKSHAW, G. 'Britten Conducts Bach' *Music and Musicians* 15 (February 1967)
'Britten Country (photographs of Aldeburgh by Tony Ray-Jones)' *Opera News* 31 (February 1967)
DUNCAN, R. 'The Problems of the Librettist – is Opera emotionally immature?' *Composer* 23 (Spring 1967)
DOUGLAS, J. R. 'The Composer and his music on record' *Library Journal* 92 (March 1967)
ZHIVOV, L. 'Prazdnik muzyka' *Sovetskaya Muzyka* 31 (March 1967)
WHITTALL, A. 'A new starting point?' *Opera* 18 (April 1967)
CHAPMAN, E. 'Pears Returns to Sadler's Wells' *Musical Events* 22 (June 1967)

'Pears und Britten – Liederabend in der Kolnishchen Oper' *Musik und Gesellschaft* 17 (June 1967)

'*Peter Grimes*; Sadler's Wells' *Opera* 18 (June 1967)

KOLODIN, I. 'Britten and Aldeburgh' *Saturday Review* 50 (July 29 1967)

BALZER, J. 'Readers' Letters: Britten's Operas in Denmark' *Opera* 18 (August 1967)

'And Peter Pears Writes' *Opera* 18 (Autumn 1967)

CROSS, J. 'Twenty years on' *Opera* 18 (Autumn 1967)

HAREWOOD, Countess of 'Opera in Aldeburgh' *Opera* 18 (Autumn 1967)

HOLST, I. 'A role for everyone' *Opera* 18 (Autumn 1967)

EVANS, P. 'Sonata structures in early Britten' *Tempo* 82 (Autumn 1967)

PAYNE, A. 'No Broad Span' *Music and Musicians* 15 (September 1967)

BLYTH, A. 'Gala Re-opening' *Music and Musicians* 16 (November 1967)

FORBES, E. 'Communicator – an Interview with England's Best Known Composer' *Opera News* 31 (November 1967)

'Britten and Pears' *Audio Record Review* (December 1967)

GELATT, R. 'Peter Pears, Benjamin Britten Recital' *Hi-Fi/Musical America* 17 (December 1967)

SEIFERT, W. 'Expo – 67 als Musikfest betrachtet' *Neue Zeitschrift für Musik* 128 (December 1967)

YOUNG, P. 'Report from England' *American Choral Review* 10 No. 2 (1968)

COLDING-JORGENSEN, G. 'Britten – Moderne Operakomponist?' *Danks Musiktadsskrift* 43 No. 4 (1968)

WOOD, H. 'En filosof, der ikke taler kinesisk (translated from the *Musical Times*)' *Dansk Musiktidsskrift* 43 No. 4 (1968)

SCHWINGER, E. 'Britten und Pears: Berlin' *Musica* 22 No. 2 (1968)

CHIUSANO, M. 'Grace Rainey Rogers auditorium' *Music and Artists* 1 No. 2 (1968)

PIRIE, P. J. and SHARP, G. N. 'Edinburgh 1968' *Music Review* 29 No. 4 (1968)

CRICHTON, R. 'Choral' *Musical Times* 109 (February 1968)

ORR, B. 'Awards and Appointments' *Composer* 27 (Spring 1968)

MASON, E. 'Britten's Prize (Sonning Prize for Music)' *Music and Musicians* 16 (April 1968)

DUNCAN, R. 'Working with Britten' *Times* 8 (June 1968)

'Early Britten – by Britten and Pears (recording)' *Hi/Fi/Musical America* 18 (July 1968)

BRADBURY, E. 'Edinburgh' *Musical Times* 108 (October 1968)

SEIFERT, W. 'Schubert und Britten an Firth of Forth' *Neue Zeitschrift für Musik* 129 (October 1968)

WHITWELL, D. 'Twentieth Century English Composers – their music for Winds' *Instrument* 23 (November 1968)

GISHFORD, A. 'Der Aussenseiter von Aldeburgh' *Melos* 35 (November 1968)

WILSON, C. 'Diamand's Third Year' *Music and Musicians* 17 (November 1968)

HOWARD, P. 'The Operas of Benjamin Britten: an introduction'. London, Barrie & Rockliff, 1969

EVANS, P. Sleeve note for Decca SXL 6391 (1969)

VOELCKERS, J. 'Britisch-deutsche Musiktage' *Musica* 23 No. 2 (1969)

RHOADS, M. R. S. 'Influences of Japanese Hogaku manifest in selected compositions by Peter Mennin and Benjamin Britten' *Ph.D Michigan State University* (1969)

GABBARD, J. H. 'Benjamin Britten: his music, the man, and his times *Ed. D. University of Northern Colorado* (1969)

HOUGHLAND, L. G. 'Unity in the solo song cycles of Benjamin Britten' *M.A. University of North Carolina at Chapel Hill* (1969)

LITTEN, J. D. 'Three song cycles of Benjamin Britten' *Ed. D Columbia University* (1969)

SADIE, S. 'Music in London' *Musical Times* 110 (February 1969)

CRANKSHAW, G. 'Sweeping Passion' *Music and Musicians* 17 (May 1969)

HOLST, I. 'Purcell made Practicable' *Music and Musicians* 17 (June 1969)

CRANKSHAW, G. 'A home for English music' *Records and Recording* 12 No. 9 (June 1969)

'Benjamin Britten et Peter Pears' *Journal de Musique Francais* 182–3 (July–August 1969)

HEINITZ, T. 'The Other Side' *Saturday Review* 62 (July 1969)

FLANAGAN, W. 'Benjamin Britten; the Composer conducts' (recording of Mozart *Symphony no. 40* and *Serenata Notturna*) *Stereo Review* 23 (September 1969)

SEELNANN-EGGEBERT, G. 'Luzerner Musikfest auf neuen Wegen' *Neue Zeitschrift fur Musik* 130 (November 1969)

PEYSER, J. 'Composers talk too much' *New York Times* (November 16 1969)

MOVSHON, G. 'Peter Pears, Benjamin Britten' *Hi-Fi/Musical America* 20 (January 1970)

NORTHCOTT, B. 'Composers of the Sixties' *Music and Musicians* 18 (January 1970)

STEVENS, D. 'New York' *Musical Times* 111 (January 1970)

BOEHN, H. 'Meissen' *Musik und Gesellschaft* 20 (January 1970)

RIZZO, F. 'A Youthful Air' *Opera News* 34 (January 1970)

LOVELAND, K. 'Britons in the Cantons' *Music and Musicians* 18 (February 1970)

GARVIE, P. 'Darkly Bright: Britten's Moral Imagination' *Canadian Music Book* 1 (Spring–Summer 1970)

HEINITZ, T. 'On the Winds of the North Sea (Britten and the Borough)' *Saturday Review* 53 (March 1970)

BLYTH, A. 'Benjamin Britten' *Gramophone* 48 (June 1970)

'Sänger und Persönlichkeit dazu' *Opern Welt* 6 (June 1970)

GREEN, T. 'Benjamin Britten's World of Music' *Reader's Digest* 96 No. 598 (June 1970)

LARNER, G. 'Guide to Britten' *Records and Recording* 13 No. 9 (June 1970)

LUCAS, J. 'At the court of Benjamin Britten' *Observer* (June 7 1970)

GREENFIELD, E. 'The Master Singer of the Maltings' *Guardian* (June 22 1970)

UNWIN, R. 'The World of Benjamin Britten: a Young Person's Guide to his Music (recordings)' *Melody Maker* 45 (July 1970)

TUGGLE, R. A. 'Aldeburgh/Edinburgh' *Opera News* 35 (September 1970)

HANDEL, D. 'Britten's use of the Passacaglia' *Tempo* 94 (Autumn 1970)

HOPKINS, G. W. 'Record Guide' *Tempo* 94 (Autumn 1970)

MARTIN, G. 'Benjamin Britten: Twenty-five years of Opera' *Yale Review* 60 (October 1970)

CRANKSHAW, G. 'Britten Conducts Purcell' *Music and Musicians* 19 (November 1970)

HIGBEE, D. 'J. S. Bach's Music for Recorder on records – the Brandenburg Concerto, BWV 1046–1051 (an up-dating)' *American Recorder* 21 No. 1 (1971)

SIMONS, H. R. 'The use of the chorus in the Operas of Benjamin Britten' *D.M. Indiana University* (1971)

KEOHANE, S. 'The Operas of Benjamin Britten: Peter Grimes to Gloriana' *B.Mus University of Manchester* (1971)

WHITTALL, A. 'Tonality in Britten's Song Cycles with Piano' *Tempo* 96 (Spring 1971)

COOPER, M. 'The drama of opera' *Daily Telegraph* (May 22 1971)

OSBORNE, R. 'Britten: The compassionate genius' *Records and Recording* 14 (June 1971)

HARRIS, N. 'In terms of world eminence he must take his place alongside Shostakovich' *Guardian* (June 7 1971)

SHCHEDRIN, R. 'Novaya vstrecha' *Sovetskaya Muzyka* 35 (August 1971)

WYTON, A. 'What's Happening in Church Music today?' *Journal of Church Music* 13 (October 1971)

CRICHTON, R. 'Summer Song (South Bank)' *Musical Times* 112 (October 1971)

DICKINSON, A. E. F. 'Renaissance opera' *Music Review* 32 (November 1971)

STEDMAN, J. W. and MCELORY, G. 'Britten's Britons' *Opera News* 36 (November 1971)

ROUTH, F. 'Benjamin Britten' *Contemporary British Music* London, Macdonald, (1972)

ALDEBURGH ANTHOLOGY: edited by Ronald Blythe. Aldeburgh, Snape Maltings Foundation in association with Faber Music Ltd, 1972

CROZIER, E. 'Writing an opera' *Aldeburgh Anthology* ed. R. Blythe, Snape Maltings Foundation in association with Faber Music Ltd, (1972)

MITCHELL, D. 'Britten's Church Parables' *Aldeburgh Anthology* ed. R. Blythe, Snape Maltings Foundation in association with Faber Music Ltd, (1972)

MITCHELL, D. 'Double portrait: some personal recollections' *Aldeburgh Anthology* Ed. R. Blythe Snape Maltings Foundation in association with Faber Music (1972)

'Brittenoba Zebracka Opera v Usti' *Hudebni Rozhledy* 25 No. 3 (1972)

SCHLOTEL, B. 'Benjamin Britten's Music for Young People' *Music Teacher and Piano Student* 51 (June 1972)

CRICHTON, R. 'Aldeburgh' *Musical Times* 113 (August 1972)

STOCKBRIDGE, J. 'Benjamin Britten and his music' *Religion and Life (BBC Radio)* (Autumn 1972)

KENDALL, A. 'Benjamin Britten'. London, Macmillan, 1973

HARDWICK, P. 'The influence of Old English Music on four contemporary English Composers' *CAUSM Journal* 3 No. 1 (1973)

SCHMIDGALL, G. 'Britten's Aldeburgh: an appreciation' *Opera Canada* 14 No. 3 (1973)

POTTER, K. 'Cardiff' *Music and Musicians* 21 (May 1973)

KOVNATSKAYA, L. 'O novom angliyskom muzyka-l'nom vozrozhdenii' *Sovetska Muzyka* 37 (July 1973)

DEAN, W. 'Aldeburgh' *Musical Times* 114 (August 1973)

BLISS, A. and others 'Benjamin Britten's Sixtieth Birthday' *Tempo* 106 (Septembr 1973)

EVANS, P. 'Britten's 4th creative decade' *Tempo* 106 (September 1973)

KELLER, H. 'Benjamin Britten and the role of suffering' *Frontier* (Winter 1973)

GOODWIN, N. 'Three score' *Music and Musicians* 22 (November 1973)

KOVNATSKAYA, L. 'Vydayushchiysya master – k60 – letiyu B. Brittena' *Sovetskaya Muzyka* 37 (November 1973)

SCHAEFER, H. 'Der Gemeinschaft dienen – zum 60.' Geburtstag Benjamin Britten *Musik und Gesellschaft* 23 (November 1973)

SHAFFER, P. 'What we owe Britten' *Sunday Times* (November 18 1973)

COLE, H. 'Britten is 60 today' *Guardian* (November 22 1973)

KELLER, H. 'Britten and Reger' *Listener* 90 (November 22 1973)

COLE, H. 'The age of Britten' *Guardian* (December 1 1973)

YOUNGMAN, A. 'Benjamin Britten, O.M., C.H. A sixtieth birthday greeting' *RCM Magazine* 69 No. 3 (Christmas 1973)

KOVNATSKAYA, L. 'Benjamin Britten (in Russian)'. Moscow, All-Union Publishing House, 1974

NORTHCOTT, B. 'Since Grimes: a concise survey of the British musical stage' *Musical News* 4 No. 2 (1974)

'Benjamin Britten, 60' *Musikhandel* 25 (1974)

KERN, H. 'Genf' *Oper und Konzert* 12 No. 1 (1974)

'Benjamin Britten: a Royal Crown Derby Service (designs representing operas and musical quotations on set of plates and bowls)' *Pan Pipes* 67 No. 1 (1974)

SCOTT, P. 'Britten's use of the Passacaglia' *B.A. Thesis University of Sydney* (1974)

SPENCE, K. 'Television (Britten's Sixtieth Birthday programme by the BBC)' *Musical Times* 115 (January 1974)

'Editorial Notes (Sixtieth Birthday Celebration by London Symphony Orchestra)' *Strad* 84 (January 1974)

WHITE, E. W. 'Britten in the Theatre – a provisional catalogue: Letters to the Editor' *Tempo* 107 (March 1974)

DAVIS, P. G. 'Schumann's echt-Goethe Faust (Benjamin Britten recording)' *Hi-Fi/Musical America* 24 (August 1974)

HOELTERHOFF, M. 'A Man Perplexed in a plague year (Benjamin Britten's Death in Venice)' *Wall Street Journal* 54 (October 1974)

JENKINS, S. 'Peter Pears bows at the Met.' *New York Post* (November 2 1974)

DANIELS, R. D. 'American Friends – Peter Pears and Benjamin Britten found a warm welcome when they first came to these shores' *Opera News* 39 No. 7 (December 14 1974)

BLYTH, A. 'Britten returns to composing' *Times* (December 30 1974)

BENJAMIN BRITTEN (Radio Documentary) CBC 1975

'Prazsti synfonikove' *Hudebni Rozhledy* 28 (No. 7 1975)

NORTHCOTT, B. 'Opening up: British Concert Music since the war' *Music News* 5 No. 3 (1975)

WYATT, T. 'Our President' *Recorder and Music* 5 No. 1 (1975)

MOVSHON, G. 'The Metropolitan Opera' *Hi-Fi/Musical America* 26 (February 1975)

HARRIS, D. 'New York' *Music and Musicians* 23 (February 1975)

MOVSHON, G. 'Two new Met. productions' *Opera* 26 (March 1975)

GOODWIN, N. 'Aldeburgh' *Music and Musicians* 23 (August 1975)

PORTER, A. 'Musical Events: Ladies' Night' *New Yorker* 51 (November 1975)

'Prize for Benjamin Britten (Ravel Foundation)' *Music Teacher and Piano Student* 54 (December 1975)

BRITTEN AND THE VOICE (Musical Triangles Series) (TV Documentary) Tyne Tees Television, 1976

HÜRLIMANN, M. Landatio auf Benjamin Britten. Munich, Callway, 1976
POUNCY, S. L. 'The variation concept in the works of Benjamin Britten' *M.A. University of Wales (Bangor)* (1976)
CRICK, R. 'Britten as conductor and performer: a discography' *British Music Yearbook* (1976)
'Musician of the Year: Benjamin Britten' *British Music Yearbook* (1976)
CULSHAW, J. 'Recording with Benjamin Britten' *British Music Yearbook* (1976)
ROWE, H. H. 'Nytt korverk av Benjamin Britten pabegynt; Os' *Bergen Tidende* (July 3 1976)
HEYWORTH, P. 'Putting our music on the map' *Observer* (December 5 1976)
SHAWE-TAYLOR, D. 'Britten: the purity of vision' *Sunday Times* (December 5 1976)
COOPER, M. 'The Brilliance of Britten' *Daily Telegraph* (December 6 1976)
CRICHTON, R. 'Benjamin Britten' *Financial Times* (December 1976)
GREENFIELD, E. 'Inspired genius oblivious to musical fashion' *Guardian* (December 6 1976)
'A Dedicated life (leader)' *Times* (December 6 1976)
'Lord Britten: a major contribution to English music (obituary)' *Times* (December 6 1976)
JOHNSTON, C. and FURZE, S. 'Suffolk sings a simple farewell as Benjamin Britten is buried' *East Anglian Daily Times* (December 8 1976)
WILSON, D. 'Addition to obituary' *Times* (December 9 1976)
SAMS, E. 'Benjamin Britten 1913–1976' *New Statesman* (December 10 1976)
'The Britten Era' *The Economist* 261 (December 11 1976)
TIPPETT, M. 'Benjamin Britten' *Listener* 96 (December 16 1976)
BENJAMIN BRITTEN: Obituary Tribute BBC TV 1976
SCHREINER, U. 'Pathos und Liberalität. Zum Tod des Komponisten Benjamin Britten' *Hi-Fi-Stereophonie* 16 (1977)
KRELLMAN, H. 'Death of Benjamin Britten' *Musica* 31 (1977)
SADIE, S. 'Obituary of Benjamin Britten' *Musical Times* 118 (1977)
HEINSHEI, H. 'Born in exile' *Opera News* 42 (1977)
MATTHEWS, C. 'Britten's Indian Summer' *Soundings* 6 (1977)
MITCHELL, D. 'Britten on Oedipus Rex and Lady Macbeth' *Tempo* 120 (1977)
ROSTROPOVICH, M. 'Aldeburgh Deutsch' *The Listener* (January 6 1977)
WHITE, E. W. 'Benjamin Britten 1913–1976' *Records and Recordings* (January 7 1977)
KELLER, H. 'Death of a genius' *Spectator* (January 15 1977)
CULSHAW, J. 'Ben: a tribute to Benjamin Britten' *Gramophone* (February 1977)

PATON, J. G. 'In Memoriam: Benjamin Britten (1913–1976)' *NATS Bulletin* (February 1977)
GRAHAM, C. 'Working with Britten' *Opera* 28 (February 1977)
MITCHELL, D. 'Britten's "dramatic" legacy' *Opera* 28 (February 1977)
SOLTI, G. 'A conductor remembers' *Opera* 28 (February 1977)
RAMEY, P. 'Benjamin Britten: November 22 1913–December 4 1976' *Opera News* 41 No. 13 (February 5 1977)
THOMAS, W. 'Britten as humanist: a redefinition' *Composer* 60 (Spring 1977)
TIPPETT, M. 'Benjamin Britten: a tribute' *Intermezzo* (March 1977)
HOLST, I. 'Working for Benjamin Britten' *Musical Times* 118 (March 1977)
'Benjamin Britten: tributes and memories' *Tempo* 120 (March 1977)
MITCHELL, D. 'Benjamin Britten: Three letters to Anthony Gishford' *Tempo* 120 (March 1977)
HUNT, R. 'Droga tworcza Benjamin Brittena (I)' *Ruch Muzyczny* 21 No. 8 (April 10 1977)
HUNT, R. 'Droga Tworcza Benjamin Brittena (II(' *Ruch Muzyczny* 21 No. 9 (April 24 1977)
'Lord Britten leaves £100,000 for fund' *Times* (September 6 1977)
FAITH, N. 'Tax tangle of Britten's estate' *Sunday Times* (September 11 1977)
NURSE, K. 'Britten scores may be accepted' *Daily Telegraph* (September 13 1977)
MITCHELL, D. 'Britten's Chamber Music' Benson & Hedges Music Festival Programme Sept–Oct 1977
WIDDICOMBE, G. 'Three Friends' *Observer* (November 27 1977)
WADSWORTH, S. 'Irish Heather' *Opera News* 42 No. 7 (December 10 1977)
PEARS, P. 'The Fugue Interview by Eric Friesen' *Fugue* 3 No. 4 (1978)
MEYER, E. H. 'Benjamin Britten zum Gedenken' *Handel Jahrbuch* 24 (1978)
SUTCLIFF, J. H. 'Der Komponist Benjamin Britten: Versuch einer Würdigung I' *Oper Heute: en Almanach der Musikbuhne* (1978)
BERKELEY, L. 'Berkeley at 75: Peter Dickinson talks to Sir Lennox Berkeley to mark his 75th birthday' *Musical Times* 119 (May 1978)
ROSTROPOVICH, M. 'Bonds of friendship' *Music Magazine* (August 1978)
BUTT, J. 'Lord Britten: some recollections' *East Anglian Daily Times* (December 5 1978)
EVANS, J. 'The illustrated Britten' *Classical Music* (December 9 1978)
EVANS, P. 'The Music of Benjamin Britten'. London, Dent, 1979
BAKER, J. 'Working with Britten'. THE OPERAS OF BENJAMIN BRITTEN; edited by David Herbert. London, Hamish Hamilton, 1979
COLEMAN, B. 'Staging first productions 2'. THE OPERAS OF BENJAMIN BRITTEN; edited by David Herbert. London, Hamish Hamilton, 1979

CROZIER, E. 'Staging first performances 1'. THE OPERAS OF BENJAMIN BRITTEN; edited by David Herbert. London, Hamish Hamilton, 1979
GRAHAM, C. 'Staging first productions 3'. THE OPERAS OF BENJAMIN BRITTEN; edited by David Herbert. London, Hamish Hamilton, 1979
KELLER, H. 'Introduction: operatic music and Britten'. THE OPERAS OF BENJAMIN BRITTEN; edited by David Herbert. London, Hamish Hamilton, 1979
THE OPERAS OF BENJAMIN BRITTEN; edited by David Herbert. London, Hamish Hamilton, 1979
PIPER, M. 'Writing for Britten'. THE OPERAS OF BENJAMIN BRITTEN; edited by David Herbert. London, Hamish Hamilton, 1979
PIPER, J. 'Designing for Britten'. THE OPERAS OF BENJAMIN BRITTEN; edited by David Herbert. London, Hamish Hamilton, 1979
JENNINGS, J. W. 'The influence of W. H. Auden on Benjamin Britten' *Ph.D University of Illinois* (1979)
WEITZMAN, R. 'Suffolk Music' *London Magazine* 18 (February 1979)
KELLER, H. and MITCHELL, D. 'Britten in Retrospect' (discussion) BBC Radio 3 (31 March 1979)
GRAHAM, C. 'The Britten opera that is and might have been' *Yorkshire Post* (May 22 1979)
PORTER, P. 'Review of *Benjamin Britten; Pictures from a Life 1913–1976*' Tempo 128 (1979)
TUCHOWSKI, A. 'Artystyczne credo Benjamin Brittena' *Ruch Muzyczny* 19 (September 1979)
BRENTON, N. 'The Sound of Britten' *Set to Music* 4 No. 1 (September/October 1979)
WARD, C. 'The Great Britten industry' *New Society* (November 29 1979)
WHITTALL, A. 'The Study of Britten: Triadic Harmony and Tonal Structure' *Proceedings of the RMA* 106 (1979–80)
A TIME THERE WAS (TV Documentary) London Weekend Television 1980
EVANS, P. 'Britten (Edward) Benjamin'. The New Grove Dictionary of Music and Musicians edited by Stanley Sadie. London, Macmillan, 1980
BENJAMIN BRITTEN 1913–1976: PICTURES FROM A LIFE; a pictorial biography compiled by Donald Mitchell with the assistance of John Evans. London, Faber, 1980
BENJAMIN BRITTEN: 'The Early Years' compiled by Donald Mitchell (Radio Documentary) BBC Radio 3 1980
HOLST, I. 'Britten'. 3rd ed. London, Faber, 1980 (The Great Composers)
SANDERSON, G. 'The dramatic role of percussion in selected operas of Benjamin Britten' *M. Mus University of Alberta* (1980)
MITCHELL, D. 'Britten and Auden in the 30's' *TLS* (February 15 1980)

NORTHCOTT, B. 'The search for simplicity' *TLS* (February 15 1980)
WIDDICOMBE, G. 'The Good Companions' *Observer* (March 30 1980)
ANDREWES, J. A Composer and his Publisher. Benjamin Britten and Ralph Hawkes AFPB 1980
FORBES, E. 'Interview with Graham Johnson, mentioning influence of Benjamin Britten' *Music and Musicians* 7 (July 1980)
BOYD, M. 'Benjamin Britten and Grace Williams: Chronicle of a Friendship' *Welsh Music* 6 No. 6 (Winter 1980–81)
BENJAMIN BRITTEN London, Caradoc's Music information Folios [1981]
DUNCAN, R. 'Working with Britten: a personal memoir'. Welcombe, The Rebel Press, 1981
MITCHELL, D. 'Britten and Auden in the Thirties: The Year 1936'. London, Faber, 1981
BRITTEN, GRAINGER AND THE CEREMONY OF INNOCENCE (Radio Documentary) BBC Radio 3 1981
HEADINGTON, C. Britten. London, Eyre Methuen, 1981 (The Composer as Contemporary)
KENNEDY, M. Britten. London, Dent 1981 (The Master Musicians Series)
THE MUSIC OF BENJAMIN BRITTEN. (Radio Documentary – 13 programmes) CBC 1981
REMEMBERING BRITTEN; edited by Alan Blyth. London, Hutchinson, 1981
ROSENTHAL, H. 'Working with Britten: a personal memoir (review of Ronald Duncan's book)' *Opera* 31 (1981)
TIERNEY, N. 'Britten and Auden in the 30's The year 1936 (Review of Donald Mitchell's book)' *Powys Review* 3 (1981)
SHAW, C. 'Remembering Britten (Review of Alan Blyth's book)' *Tempo* 139 (1981)
LARKIN, P. 'Words for music, perhaps (Review of Britten and Auden in the 30's)' *TLS* (February 27 1981)
KEATES, J. 'Nest of stifled lovebirds (Review of Britten and Auden in the 30's)' *Spectator* (March 7 1981)
WILSON, R. G. 'Elements of textual and musical structure and interpretation in the song cycles of Benjamin Britten' *B. Mus University of Aberdeen* (1981–82)
WHITTALL, A. 'The Music of Britten and Tippett: studies in themes and technique'. Cambridge C.U.P., 1982
BACH, J. 'The music of Benjamin Britten (Review of Peter Evans' book)' *Musical Quarterly* 68 (1982)
THE ALDEBURGH STORY (Tape/slide presentation) Aldeburgh Foundation 1983
ORR, B. 'Some reflections on the operas of Benjamin Britten'. PETER GRIMES/GLORIANA Benjamin Britten. London, John Calder, 1983 (English National Opera/The Royal Opera Guide 24)

PORTER, P. 'Benjamin Britten's librettos'. PETER GRIMES/GLORIANA Benjamin Britten. London, John Calder, 1983 (English National Opera/The Royal Opera Guide 24)

SCHMIDELL, G. 'Benjamin Britten für Sie porträtiert'. Leipzig, Deutscher Verlag für Musik, 1983

WHITE, E. W. 'Benjamin Britten: his life and operas'. Revised edition prepared by John Evans. London, Faber & Faber in association with Boosey & Hawkes, 1983

FLYNN, W. 'Britten the progressive' *Music Review* 44 (1983)

MARK, C. M. 'Simplicity in early Britten' *Tempo* 147 (1983)

STADLEN, P. 'Britten between the lines' *Daily Telegraph* (July 2 1983)

THE BRITTEN COMPANION; edited by Christopher Palmer. London, Faber, 1984

CULSHAW, J. ' "Ben" – a tribute to Benjamin Britten' *The Britten Companion:* edited by Christopher Palmer. London, Faber (1984)

EVANS, J. 'The Concertos' *The Britten Companion:* edited by Christopher Palmer. London, Faber (1984)

HOLST, I. 'Working for Benjamin Britten I' *The Britten Companion:* edited by Christopher Palmer. London, Faber (1984)

JOHNSON, G. 'Voice and piano' *The Britten Companion:* Edited by Christopher Palmer, London, Faber (1984)

MATTHEWS, D. 'The String Quartets and some other chamber works' *The Britten Companion:* edited by Christopher Palmer, London, Faber (1984)

MILNER, A. 'The choral music' *The Britten Companion:* edited by Christopher Palmer, London, Faber (1984)

MITCHELL, D. 'The Chamber music: an introduction' *The Britten Companion:* edited by Christopher Palmer, London, Faber (1984)

MITCHELL, D. 'What do we know about Britten now?' *The Britten Companion:* edited by Christopher Palmer, London, Faber (1984)

PALMER, C. 'Chaos and cosmos in Peter Grimes' *The Britten Companion:* edited by Christopher Palmer, London, Faber (1984)

PALMER, C. 'Embalmer of the midnight: the orchestral song-cycles' *The Britten Companion:* edited by Christopher Palmer, London, Faber (1984)

PALMER, C. 'The Ceremony of innocence' *The Britten Companion:* edited by Christopher Palmer, London, Faber (1984)

PALMER, C. 'The orchestral works: Britten as instrumentalist' *The Britten Companion:* edited by Christopher Palmer, London, Faber (1984)

PORTER, P. 'Composer and poet' *The Britten Companion:* edited by Christopher Palmer, London, Faber (1984)

ROSEBERRY, E. 'The solo chamber music' *The Britten Companion:* edited by Christopher Palmer, London, Faber (1984)

STRODE, R. 'Working for Benjamin Britten II' *The Britten Companion:* edited by Christopher Palmer, London, Faber (1984)

MITCHELL, D. 'Outline model for a biography of Benjamin Britten (1913–1976) *Festschrift Albi Rosenthal* Ed. R. Elvers, Tutzing, Schneider (1984)

KETUKAENCHAN, S. 'The oriental influence on Benjamin Britten' *M.A. University of York* (1984)

PIPER, M. 'Set to Music; notes on working with Britten and Hoddinott'. Welsh Music Vol. 7 No. 7 (Summer 1984)

THE COLLABORATION (Auden and Britten) (Radio Documentary) BBC Radio 3 1985

YOUNG APOLLO (TV Documentary) BBC TV 1985

COOKE, M. 'Britten and Bali: a study in stylistic synthesis' *M.Phil University of Cambridge* (1985)

ELLIOTT, G. 'Benjamin Britten: the things spiritual' *Ph.D University of Wales* (1985)

LAW, J. K. 'Linking the Past with the Present: a conversation with Nancy Evans and Eric Crozier' *Opera Quarterly* 3 No. 1 (Spring 1985)

SLOAN, I. and S. *Opera Quarterly* 3 No. 2 (Summer 1985)

RAMEY, P. 'Benjamin Britten' *Ovation* 6 No. 6 (July 1985)

BRITTEN: composer of string quartets (Radio Documentary) BBC Radio 4 1986

MITCHELL, D. BRITTEN (EDWARD) BENJAMIN, Baron Britten (1913–1976) The Dictionary of National Biography 1971–1980. Oxford, O.U.P., 1986

PALMER, B. 'Christmas at the Red House'. *European Gay Review* 1 (1986)

Whole issue *Opera Quarterly* 4 (Autumn 1986)

BEDFORD, S. 'Composer and conductor: annals of a collaboration'. *Opera Quarterly* 4 No. 3 (Autumn 1986)

ELLIOTT, G. 'The operas of Benjamin Britten: a spiritual view'. *Opera Quarterly* 4 No. 3 (Autumn 1986)

McDONALD, E. 'Women in Benjamin Britten's Operas'. *Opera Quarterly* 4 No. 3 (Autumn 1986)

SUTCLIFFE, J. H. 'A life for music: Benjamin Britten: a biographical sketch'. *Opera Quarterly* 4 No. 3 (Autumn 1986)

GLORIANA

'"Elizabeth and Essex": Mr Britten's plans' *Manchester Guardian* (May 30 1952)

'*Gloriana:* a great event in British music' *National and English Review* (1953)

COLEMAN, B. 'Problems and Solutions in the Production of *Gloriana*' *Tempo* 28 (Summer 1953)

'*Gloriana:* A synopsis' *Tempo* 28 (Summer 1953)

PLOMER, W. 'Notes on the libretto of *Gloriana*' *Tempo* 28 (Summer 1953)
'Coronation Opera Completed' *International Musical News* 45 (May–June 1953)
HOPE-WALLACE, P. '*Gloriana*: Royal Opera Gala at Covent Garden' *Manchester Guardian Weekly* (June 11 1953)
'*Gloriana* is born' *Picture Post* (June 13 1953)
SHAWE-TAYLOR, D. '*Gloriana*, Cheltenham, Glyndebourne.' *New Statesman* 45 (June 20 1953)
SHAWE-TAYLOR, D. 'Royal Operas' *New Statesman* 45 (June 13 1953)
WILLIAMS, S. 'Coronation Opera' *New York Times* 102 (June 14 1953)
'Opera and Concerts' *Monthly Musical Record* 83 (July–August 1953)
REDLICH, H. F. 'Uraufführung von Brittens Krönungsoper *Gloriana*' *Musikleben* 6 (July–August 1953)
SMITH, C. 'Elizabeth II Attends Premiere of Benjamin Britten's latest Opera' *Musical America* 73 (July 1953)
'*Gloriana*' *Musical Opinion* 76 (July 1953)
'A Pocket Guide to *Gloriana*' *Musical Opinion* 76 (July 1953)
'Sic Transit *Gloriana*?' *Musical Opinion* 76 (July 1953)
HEINITZ, T. 'The other side (Imported Recordings)' *Saturday Review* 36 (July 25 1953)
LITTLEFIELD, J. 'Britten's Coronation Opera' *Canon* 7 (August 1953)
MONTAGU, G. '*Gloriana* at Covent Garden' *London Music* 8 (August 1953)
PORTER, A. '*Gloriana*' *London Music* 8 (August 1953)
COTON, A. V. '*Gloriana* (review)' *Music Review* (August 1953)
KELLER, H. 'The half year's New Music' *Music Review* 14 (August 1953)
'Opera' *Music Review* 14 (August 1953)
NOTCUTT, A. 'London events range from *Gloriana* to Glyndebourne' *Musical Courier* 148 (August 1953)
BRADBURY, E. 'Opera in London' *Musical Times* 94 (August 1953)
BRADBURY, E. '*Gloriana*' *Musical Times* (August 1953)
MAYER, T., MANN, W., PORTER, A. and SMITH, C. 'Symposium' *Opera* 4 (August 1953)
KLEIN, J. W. 'Some Reflections on *Gloriana*' *Tempo* 29 (Autumn 1953)
'Notes of the Day (Publication of the Libretto)' *Monthly Musical Record* 83 (September 1953)
COOPER, M. '*Gloriana* and Benjamin Britten' *Score* 8 (September 1953)
GODDARD, S. 'London Letter' *Chesterian* 28 (October 1953)
PORTER, A. '*Gloriana*' *Music and Letters* 34 (October 1953)
BARKER, F. G. '*Gloriana*, the Coronation Opera (first performance)' *Opera News* 18 (October 1953)

KNYVETT, G. *'Gloriana' RCM Magazine* 49 (November 1953)
MITCHELL, D. 'Some Observations on *Gloriana*' *Monthly Musical Record* 83 (December 1953)
'*Gloriana* de Benjamin Britten' *Revista Musical Chilena* 9 (January 1954)
'Letters to Australia' *Canon* 7 (March 1954)
MANN, W. 'London Repetitions of Britten's *Gloriana* bring revised verdict on Opera' *Musical America* 74 (March 1954)
'*Gloriana*: Choral Dances for mixed choir' *Musical Letters* 35 (July 1954)
'The Second Lute Song' *Music and Letters* 36 (January 1955)
'The Half year's New Music' *Music Review* 16 (February 1955)
MITCHELL, D. 'Some First Performances' *Musical Times* 96 (February 1955)
'*Gloriana*: Symphonic Suite Op. 53a' *Music and Letters* 36 (July 1955)
MITCHELL, D. 'Some First Performances' *Musical Times* 96 (July 1955)
KELLER, H. 'The Half year's New Music' *Music Review* 16 (August 1955)
'*Gloriana*. Reduced for voice and piano by I. Holst' *Musical America* 75 (November 1955)
'Glorania; Opera in three acts' *Notes* 13 (March 1956)
TAUBMAN, H. 'May Festival (first American performance)' *New York Times* 105 (May 20 1956)
JONEN, L. J. 'Cincinnati' *Musical Courier* 153 (June 1956)
'*Gloriana*. Choral Dances; for SATB A Cappella' *Notes* 13 (June 1956)
'*Gloriana*. Symphonic Suite, Op. 53a' *Music Review* 17 (August 1956)
'The Courtly Dances from *Gloriana*' AFPB 1957
'First Recordings of Unfamiliar Britten' *American Record Guide* 28 (May 1962)
FAIRFAX, B. 'The Neglected Britten' *Music and Musicians* 12 (November 1963)
MITCHELL, D. 'A neglected masterpiece: Britten's *Gloriana*' *Listener* 70 (November 14 1963)
GOODWIN, N. '*Gloriana* Re-awakened' *Music and Musicians* 12 (January 1964)
COOPER, M. 'England: Slack Season' *Musical America* 84 (January 1964)
TRACEY, E. 'London Music' *Musical Times* 105 (January 1964)
'*Gloriana*; Royal Festival Hall' *Opera* 15 (January 1964)
HENDERSON, R. L. '*Budd* and *Gloriana* Reconsidered' *Tempo* 68 (Spring 1964)
PLOMER, W. 'The *Gloriana* libretto' *Sadler's Wells Magazine* (Autumn 1966)
KLEIN, J. W. 'Britten's Major Setback' *Musical Opinion* 90 (October 1966)
PORTER, A. '*Gloriana*' *Musical Times* 107 (October 1966)
MITCHELL, D. 'Public and Private Life in Britten's *Gloriana*' *Opera* 17 (October 1966)
KLEIN, J. W. 'Elizabeth and Essex' *Music and Musicians* 15 (November 1966)
EVANS, P. 'Britten in Merrie England' *Listener* 76 (November 3 1966)

GOODWIN, N. 'The Triumph of *Gloriana*' *Music and Musicians* 15 (December 1966)
BAKER, G. 'The Musical Scene' *Music Teacher and Piano Student* 45 (December 1966)
CHAPMAN, E. 'Britten's *Gloriana* revived' *Musical Events* 21 (December 1966)
'Sadler's Wells Opera' *Musical Opinion* 90 (December 1966)
DEAN, W. '*Gloriana* (Sadler's Wells)' *Musical Times* 107 (December 1966)
'*Gloriana*: Sadler's Wells' *Opera* 17 (December 1966)
KELLER, H. and WALSH, S. 'Two Interpretations of *Gloriana* as Music Drama' *Tempo* 79 (Winter 1966–67)
GREENFIELD, E. 'London Report' *Hi-Fi/Musical America* 17 (February 1967)
PAYNE, A. 'New Essex for *Gloriana*' *Music and Musicians* 15 (April 1967)
'*Gloriana*; Sadler's Wells' *Opera* 18 (April 1967)
GOODWIN, N. 'Festival from Philanthropy (Lisbon)' *Music and Musicians* 15 (July 1967)
'*Gloriana*; Sadler's Wells' *Opera* 18 (October 1967)
BLYTH, A. 'Elizabeth the Second' *Music and Musicians* 16 (November 1967)
NATAN, A. 'Götter und Könige; Premieren in Covent Garden und Sadler's Wells' *Opern Welt* 1 (January 1968)
SIMMONS, D. 'Concert Notes' *Strad* 78 (February 1968)
'Münster' *Neue Zeitschrift für Musik* 129 (July–August 1968)
'Münster' *Opera* 19 (August 1968)
WENDLAND, J. 'Ereignis und Rettung des Abends: Martha Moedl' *Opern Welt* 8 (August 1968)
'Münster' *Opera News* 33 (September 1968)
TUGGLE, R. A. 'London' *Opera News* 33 (September 1968)
GRIER, C. 'Less Immediate *Gloriana*' *Music and Musicians* 17 (April 1969)
CHAPMAN, E. '*Gloriana* at the Coliseum' *Musical Events* 24 (April 1969)
'London Opera Diary' *Opera* 20 (April 1969)
BRITTEN, B. 'Three scenes from *Gloriana*' AFPB 1970
KEMP, I. 'Aberdeen' *Musical Times* 112 (June 1971)
'Gastspiel der Sadler's Wells Opera London; *Gloriana*' *Oper und Konzert* 10 No. 10 (1972)
NORTHCOTT, B. '*Gloriana* (Sadler's Wells)' *Music and Musicians* 21 (October 1972)
SCHMIDT-GARRE, H. 'Sadler's Wells Opera spielt *Gloriana* in Adele-Sandrock-Look' *Neue Zeitschrift für Musik* 133 (October 1972)
ROSENTHAL, H. 'London Opera Diary' *Opera* 23 (October 1972)
ROSENTHAL, H. '*Gloriana*; English National Opera at the Coliseum' *Opera* 26 (May 1975)

SZMOLYAN, W. 'Brittens *Gloriana* in der Volksoper' *Oesterreiche Musikzeitung* 30 (July 1975)

MITCHELL, D. Sleeve note for Decca SXL 6788 (1976)

CROSS, J., PEARS, P. and EVANS, J. '*Peter Grimes and Gloriana*' PETER GRIMES/GLORIANA Benjamin Britten. London, John Calder, 1983 (English National Opera/The Royal Opera Guide 24)

HOLROYD, M. 'A daring experiment'. PETER GRIMES/GLORIANA Benjamin Britten. London, John Calder, 1983. (English National Opera/The Royal Opera Guide 24)

HART-DAVIS, R. 'The Librettist of *Gloriana*'. PETER GRIMES/GLORIANA Benjamin Britten. London, John Calder, 1983 (English National Opera/The Royal Opera Guide 24)

PALMER, C. 'The Music of *Gloriana*'. PETER GRIMES/GLORIANA Benjamin Britten, London, John Calder, 1983 (English National Opera/The Royal Opera Guide 24)

PETER GRIMES/GLORIANA Benjamin Britten. London, John Calder, 1983 (English National Opera/The Royal Opera Guide 24)

GOODWIN, N. '*Gloriana* (Proms)' *Music and Musicians* 22 (November 1983)

MITCHELL, D. 'Public and private in *Gloriana*' *The Britten Companion:* edited by Christopher Palmer, London, Faber (1984)

GOD SAVE THE QUEEN

'Whimper and Bang (arrangement of God Save the Queen)' *Music and Musicians* 10 (January 1962)

'Philharmonia Orchestra and Chorus (arrangement of God Save the Queen)' *Musical Opinion* 85 (January 1962)

REID, C. 'The Queen's Musick (arrangement of God Save the Queen) *Hi Fi* 12 (April 1962)

THE GOLDEN VANITY

BRITTEN, B. '*The Golden Vanity*' AFPB 1967

PORTER, A. 'Aldeburgh' *Musical Times* 108 (July 1967)

GOODWIN, N. 'Vaudeville for the Vienna Boys' *Music and Musicians* 15 (August 1967)

GREENFIELD, E. 'Britten and the Aldeburgh Miracle' Hi-Fi/Musical America 17 (September 1967)

WOCKER, K. H. 'Britische Musikfeste' *Neue Zeitschrift für Musik* 128 (September 1967)

WOCKER, K. H. 'Protest gegen die Routine' *Opern Welt* 9 (September 1967)

REYNOLDS, N. 'The Vanity Arrives' *Music and Musicians* 16 (February 1968)

BRITTEN, B. '*The Golden Vanity*' AFPB 1969

MITCHELL, D. Sleeve note for Decca SET 445 (1970)
JOSEPHSON, D. *The Golden Vanity*' AFPB 1974
'Britten: Az Arany Hiusag'. Magyarorszagi bemutato' *Muzsika* 13 (June 1970)
MITCHELL, D. 'Small victims: *The Golden Vanity* and *Children's Crusade*'
    The Britten Companion: edited by Christopher Palmer, London, Faber (1984)

HANKIN BOOBY
PORTER, A. 'Queen Elizabeth Hall' *Musical Times* 108 (April 1967)
DIXON, M. 'Elizabeth Hall: debut of a Hall' *Music and Musicians* 15 (May 1967)
WHITTALL, A. 'The Study of Britten: triadic harmony and tonal structure'
    Proceedings of the Royal Musical Association 106 (1979–80)

HARP SUITE
GOODWIN, N. 'Business as Usual' *Music and Musicians* 17 (August 1969)
BRITTEN, B. *'Suite in C for harp solo* Op. 83' AFPB 1969
LARNER, G. 'Aldeburgh' *Musical Times* 110 (August 1969)
MITCHELL, D. Sleeve note for Decca SXL 6788 (1976)

HOLIDAY DIARY
'Holiday Diary' *Tempo* 7 (O.S.) (June 1944)
STRODE, R. *'Holiday Diary,* Op. 5' AFPB 1980

THE HOLY SONNETS OF JOHN DONNE
'*Holy Sonnets of John Donne*' *Tempo* 13 (O.S.) (December 1945)
HARDY, E. 'Donne's Songs and Sonnets and his Holy Sonnets in Relation to
    Music' *R.C.M. Magazine* 42 No. 3 (1946)
REDLICH, H. F. 'Review of the *Holy Sonnets of John Donne*' *Music Review* 9 No. 2
    (May 1948)
'Britten's debt to Purcell' *Times* (June 6 1955)
'The Holy Sonnets of John Donne' AFPB 1956
HAMILTON, D. 'Britten's Unchanged Aesthetic (recording)' *Hi-Fi/Musical
    America* 19 (November 1969)
HERBERT, R. B. 'An Analysis of Nine *Holy Sonnets of John Donne* set to music by
    Benjamin Britten' *Ph.D The American University* 1974
MCNEFF, P. A. 'Vocal Registers: a Functional Analysis relating to the singing
    performances of selected songs from *The Holy Sonnets of John Donne* by
    Benjamin Britten' *M.A. California State University, Fullerton* (1980)
MATTHEWS, C. Sleeve note for EMI RLS 748 (1980)
EVANS, J. *'The Holy Sonnets of John Donne,* Op. 35' AFPB 1985

A HYMN OF SAINT COLUMBA
SACKVILLE-WEST, E. 'Report from Abroad' *Musical Times* 104 (July 1963)
JACOBSON, B. 'Schütz and Britten' *Music and Musicians* 12 (December 1963)

HYMN TO SAINT CECILIA
'Hymn to Saint Cecilia' *Tempo* 2 (American Series) No. 3 (September 1942)
'Hymn to Saint Cecilia' *Tempo* 6 (O.S.) (February 1944)
'First Recordings of Unfamiliar Britten' *American Record Guide* 28 (May 1962)
MATTHEWS, C. 'Hymn to Saint Cecilia, Op. 27' AFPB 1987

HYMN TO SAINT PETER
'Anthem by Britten' *Eastern Daily Press* (November 21 1955)
'Hymn to Saint Peter, for mixed choir with treble solo and organ' *Musical Opinion* 79 (February 1956)
'Hymn to Saint Peter, for mixed choir with treble solo and organ' *Chesterian* 30 (Spring 1956)
'Hymn to Saint Peter, for mixed choir with treble solo and organ' *Monthly Musical Record* 86 (March–April 1956)
'Hymn to Saint Peter, for mixed choir with treble solo and organ' *Music and Letters* 37 (July 1956)
'Hymn to Saint Peter for mixed choir with treble solo and organ' *Music Review* 17 (August 1956)

LES ILLUMINATIONS
'Les Illuminations' *Tempo* 4 (O.S.) (July 1939)
WESTRUP, J. 'Benjamin Britten and Arthur Bliss' *Daily Telegraph* (August 18 1939)
'Bliss and Britten' *Times* (August 18 1939)
'Les Illuminations' *Tempo* 1 (American series) No. 3 (September 1940)
EVANS, E. 'New Britten Scores' *Tempo* 5 (O.S.) (August 1941)
EVANS, E. 'Benjamin Britten's *Les Illuminations*' *Tempo* 2 (American series) No. 1 (October 1941)
'Les Illuminations' *Tempo* 2 (American series) No. 2 (February 1942)
'Les Illuminations, for soprano and string orchestra' *Los Angeles Philharmonic Symphony Magazine* (March 6 1952)
SACKVILLE-WEST, E. 'Les Illuminations' AFPB 1966
'Early Britten – by Britten and Pears (recording)' *Hi-Fi/Musical America* 18 (July 1968)
KONOLD, W. 'In Kiel erregt Donatoni Aufsehen' *Melos* 37 (July–August 1970)
'Les Illuminations, for soprano and string orchestra Op. 18' *Louisville Orchestra Programme Notes* (October 19–20 1973)

EVANS, J. Sleeve note for EMI EL 270654 1 (1987)

INSTRUMENTAL MUSIC
GODDARD, S. 'Britten as an Instrumental Composer' *Listener* (July 7 1949)
PAJA, T. 'Formy wariacyjne w tworzosci instrumentalnej Brittena' *Musyka* 22 (1977)

THE INSTRUMENTS OF THE ORCHESTRA
REED, P. 'Instruments of the Orchestra' AFPB 1983

INTRODUCTION AND RONDO ALLA BURLESCA
'Introduction and Rondo Alla Burlesca' *Tempo* 1 (American series No. 4 (January 1941)
'Introduction and Rondo Alla Burlesca' *Tempo* 5 (O.S.) (August 1941)
CHISSELL, J. 'Introduction and Rondo alla Burlesca Op. 23 No. 1' AFPB 1979

JOHNSON OVER JORDAN
'New Priestley play with ballet and music' *Observer* (January 29 1939)
MITCHELL, D. and BURROWS, J. Britten's Theatre Music AFPB 1980
CHESHIRE, D. F. 'J. B. Priestley's *Johnson Over Jordan* and the work of Edward Carrick' *Theatrefile* 1 No. 2 (March 1984)

JUBILATE
HARRIS, W. H. 'Britten's *Jubilate*' *Musical Times* 102 (September 1961)

LACHRYMAE
'New work for Aldeburgh Festival' *Times* (June 22 1950)
MANN, W. 'Britten's *Lachrymae*' *London Musical Events* 6 No. 12 (December 1951)
'*Lachrymae*, Op. 48, for viola and piano' *Musical Opinion* 75 (November 1951)
'*Lachrymae*, Op. 48, for viola and piano' *Strad* 62 (December 1951)
'*Lachrymae*, for viola and piano' *Music and Letters* 33 (January 1952)
'*Lachrymae*, for viola and piano' *Musical America* 72 (April 1952)
Lachrymae: Reflections on a Song of John Dowland Op. 48 AFPB 1952
ARONOWITZ, C. '*Lachrymae* Op. 48' AFPB 1970
STRODE, R. '*Lachrymae* Op. 48a' AFPB 1977
ELLIS, O. '*Lachrymae* Op. 48 arr. for viola and harp' AFPB 1979

LINE TO THE TSCHIERVA HUT
REED, P. 'Line to the Tschierva Hut' AFPB 1983

THE LITTLE SWEEP

CROZIER, E. 'Opera for young people: *Let's make an opera*' *Times Educational Supplement* 19 (March 1949)
CROZIER, E. *'Let's Make an Opera'* AFPB 1949
'Let's Make an Opera' Times (June 15 1949)
'Let's Make an Opera: First performance' *Musical Times* 90 (July 1949)
HEIMANN, H. *'Let's Make An Opera' Picture Post* (July 9 1949)
HOLST, I. 'The Aldeburgh Festival' *Ballet and Opera* 8 No. 2 (August 1949)
KELLER, H. 'Benjamin Britten and the Young' *Listener* (September 29 1949)
MITCHELL, D. 'Britten's *Let's Make an Opera* Op. 45' *Music Survey* 2 (Autumn 1949)
KELLER, H. 'Brittens Kinderoper' *Basler Nachrichten* 451 (October 22 1949)
'Benjamin Britten's New Children's Opera broadcast' *Strad* 60 (November 1949)
KELLER, H. 'First performances' *Music Review* 10 No. 4 (November 1949)
'Opera News' 14 (November 14 1949)
LOCKSPEISER, E. 'B.B.C. presents Britten Children's opera' *Musical America* 69 (December 1 1949)
'Let's make an opera' Music Parade 2 No. 2 (1950)
MITCHELL, D. *'Let's Make an Opera*: Britten's entertainment for young people' *Making Music* 12 (Spring 1950)
'A Children's Symposium on Britten's Children's opera' *Music Survey* 2 (Spring 1950)
SMITH, C. 'Educator's Conference hears Britten opera for children' *Musical America* 70 (April 1950)
HÜRLIMANN, B. 'Eine Kinderoper von Benjamin Britten' *Schweizerische Musikzeitung* (April 1950)
WHITE, E. W. *'Let's Make an Opera'* AFPB 1950
'Let's make an opera' Music Survey 3 (Summer 1950)
'Let's make an opera' Musical Opinion 73 (July 1950)
'The Little Sweep Op. 45' *Monthly Musical Record* 80 (October 1950)
'The Little Sweep' Music and Letters 31 (October 1950)
MITCHELL, D. 'Opera Notes: Aldeburgh' *Opera News* 15 (October 16 1950)
'Let's make an opera' House Beautiful 97 (December 1950)
HOLST, I. *'Let's Make an Opera' Tempo* 18 (Winter 1950–1951)
SMITH, C. *'Let's Make an Opera*, previewed in Boston' *Musical America* 79 (December 15 1950)
'Noble Experiment on Broadway' *Musical Courier* 143 (January 1951)
'Let's Make an Opera (Zürich)' *Opera* 2 (May 1951)
SKELTON, G. D. *'Let's make an Opera* in Germany' *Musical Opinion* 74 (April 1951)

PAAP, W. 'Een kinder-opera van Benjamin Britten' *Mens en Mel* 6 (July 1951)
MAYER, L. K. 'Lasst uns eine Oper machen' *Oberosterreichische Nachrichten* (February 8 1952)
HACKENBERG, K. 'Eine Schuloper' *Melos* 18 (March 1952)
'*Let's Make an Opera* given in Israel' *International Music News* 1 (November 1952)
LEWIS, J. '*Let's Make an Opera*' AFPB 1956
PARR, G. '*Let's Make an Opera*' AFPB 1965
MARI, P. 'Faisons un Opéra de Benjamin Britten: Création Française au Théâtre d'Avignon' *Journal de Musique Francais* 157 (May 1967)
WIENCKE, A. G. 'Schwerin – Benjamin Britten: *Wir Machen eine Oper*' *Musik und Gesellschaft* 18 (March 1968)
DINOV, I. 'Malkiybat kominochistach i negovite sputnitsi' *Bulgarska Muzika* 23 No. 5 (1972)
FORBES, E. 'Britten: *Let's Make an Opera*' *Opera* 32 (1981)
BABIC, K. 'Beograd' *Zvuk* 57 (1963)
HOLST, I. 'Entertaining the young' *The Britten Companion:* edited by Christopher Palmer, London, Faber (1984)

LOVE FROM A STRANGER
REED, P. 'Love from a Stranger' AFPB 1983

MAZURKA ELEGIACA
'*Mazurka Elegiaca*' *Tempo* 2 (American Series) No. 1 (October 1941)
CHISSELL, J. '*Mazurka Elegiaca*' AFPB 1979

MEN OF GOODWILL
EVANS, J. Sleeve note for EMI ASD 1436281 (1984)

MEN OF THE ALPS
REED, P. 'Men of the Alps' AFPB 1983

A MIDSUMMER NIGHT'S DREAM
WARRACK, J. Sleeve note for Decca SET 338–40 (1960)
JAKSIC, D. 'Opera na Holandskom festivalu 1960' *Zvulg Jugoslovenska Muzicka Revija* 41–42 (1960)
WINTERS, K. 'Report from the Festivals' *Canadian Music Journal* 5 No. 1 (1960)
ECKSTEIN, P. 'Nova Opera Benjamina Brittena' *Hudebni Rozhledy* 13 No. 16 (1960)
GODDARD, S. 'London Letter' *Chesterian* 35 No. 203 (1960)
'Amsterdam' *Rassegna Musicale* 30 No. 3 (1960)

EVANS, P. 'Britten's New Opera: a Preview' *Tempo* 53–54 (Spring–Summer 1960)
HOWARD, C. 'Britten's First New Opera for Six Years' *Music and Musicians* 8 (June 1960)
BRITTEN, B. 'A New Britten Opera' *Observer* (June 5 1960)
TAUBMAN, H. 'Britten's Dream' *New York Times* 109 (June 19 1960)
SENIOR, E. 'Is Britten's New Opera Really an Opera?' *Music and Musicians* 8 (July 1960)
NOBLE, J. 'Britten's Shakepeare Opera' *Canon* 14 (August 1960)
PAAP, W. 'Holland Festival 1960' *Mens en Mel* 15 (August 1960)
GOODWIN, N. 'New Opera by Britten sets Bard successfully' *Musical Courier* 162 (August 1960)
BOURKE, G. 'The Holland Festival' *Musical Opinion* 82 (August 1960)
GOODWIN, N. 'The Aldeburgh Festival' *Musical Times* 101 (August 1960)
MANN, W. 'Holland' *Opera* 11 (Autumn 1960)
ROSENTHAL, H. 'Aldeburgh' *Opera* 11 (Autumn 1960)
REID, C. 'Notes from Abroad' *Hi-Fi* 10 (September 1960)
van AMERINGEN, S. 'Holland – Festival' *Musica* 14 (September 1960)
HELM, E. 'Spread-out Festival' *Musical America* 80 (September 1960)
NOSKE-FRIEDLAENDER, L. 'Holland Festival Presents Badings and Britten Operas' *Musical Courier* 162 (September 1960)
HELM, E. 'Holland Festival' *Musical Times* 101 (September 1960)
THOMAS, E. 'Festival mit Mahler, Britten, Badings' *Neue Zeitschrift für Musik* 121 (September 1960)
DEGENS, R. N. 'Zwei neue Opern in Holland – Festival' *Melos* 27 (October 1960)
MINDSZENTHY, J. 'Refugees in Amsterdam' *Opera News* 25 (October 1960)
MITCHELL, D. 'In and Out of Britten's *Dream*' *Opera* 11 (December 1960)
WINTERS, K. 'Vancouver' *Canadian Music Journal* 6 No. 1 (1961)
KRAUSE, E. 'Berlinske *Sen Noci Svatojanske*' *Hudebni Rozhledy* 14 No. 16 (1961)
'Covent Garden' *Music Review* 22 No. 2 (1961)
STEVENS, D. 'England' *Musical Quarterly* 47 No. 2 (1961)
REDLICH, H. F. 'Britten's Idiom' *Music Review* 22 No. 3 (1961)
MORELLI-GALLET, W. 'Benjamin Brittens *Sommernachtstraum*: Hambürgische Staatsoper' *Schweizerische Musik* 101 No. 3 (1961)
PARMENTER, R. 'Performances of Britten's *Dream* may include a double US Premiere' *New York Times* 110 (January 8 1961)
PANTER-DOWNES, M. 'Letter from London' *New Yorker* 37 (February 25 1961)

SENIOR, E. 'The Dream at The Garden' Music and Musicians 9 (March 1961)
COOPER, M. 'Britten Triumphs' Musical America 81 (March 1961)
NOBLE, J. 'Britten's A Midsummer Night's Dream at Covent Garden' Musical Events 16 (March 1961)
'Covent Garden Opera' Musical Opinion 84 (March 1961)
'Covent Garden' Musical Times 102 (March 1961)
MEYERS, R. 'London's Premiere of Britten's new opera' Canon 14 (March–April 1961)
'Scenes from Performances at Hamburg, Covent Garden and Amsterdam' Tempo 57 (Spring 1961)
WAGNER, K. 'Liebermanns Woche des zeitgenössischen Musiktheaters' Melos 28 (April 1961)
BACHMANN, C. H. 'Wenn der Bann gebrochen ist . . .; Woche des zeitgenössischen Musiktheaters' Musica 15 (April 1961)
OTTAWAY, H. 'Radio Notes' Musical Opinion 84 (April 1961)
JOACHIM, H. 'Beispielhafter Woche des zeitgenössischen Musiktheaters' Neue Zeitschrift für Musik 122 (April 1961)
KOEGLER, H. 'Modern Hamburg' Opera News 25 (April 1961)
WALTER, F. 'Soltis erste Premiere in London: Britten Sommernachtstraum' Melos 28 (May 1961)
KORN, P. J. 'Munich' Musical Courier 163 (May 1961)
MORELLI-GALLET, W. 'Benjamin Brittens Sommernachtstraum an der Scala' Oesterreichische Musikzeitschrift 16 (May 1961)
JOACHIM, H. 'Modern Opera Week at Hamburg' Opera 12 (May 1961)
WEAVER, W. 'Reports from Abroad' Musical Times 102 (June 1961)
HOFFER, E. 'Britten's The Dream at La Scala' Music and Musicians 9 (July 1961)
KLEIN, J. W. 'Britten's Dream – and afterwards?' Musical Opinions 84 (July 1961)
KRAUSE, E. 'Panorama der neuen Oper (Hamburg)' Musik und Gesellschaft 11 (July 1961)
SARTORI, C. 'Sutherland and Britten at Milan' Opera 12 (July 1961)
UNGERER, I. D. 'Stagione lirica (Mailand)' Musica 15 (August 1961)
KOTSCHENREUTHER, H. 'Berlin' Musical Courier 3 (August 1961)
MORELLI-GALLET, W. 'Mailand' Musik und Gesellschaft 11 (August 1961)
BOLLERT, W. 'Vielseitige Opera (Berlin)' Musica 15 (September 1961)
KERENYI, K. 'Die Mythologie in Shakespeares Sommernachtstraum' Neue Zeitschrift für Musik 122 (September 1961)
STUCKENSCHMIDT, H. H. 'Felsenstein mounts Britten's Dream' Opera 12 (September 1961)

DOCHERTY, I. 'Jingling Cash Register (North American Premiere)' *Musical America* 81 (October 1961)
'Berlin' *Musik und Gesellschaft* 11 (October 1961)
'Vancouver's Midsummer (North American Premiere)' *Opera News* 26 (October 1961)
WALLACE, D. 'San Francisco: Britten in US' *Music Magazine* 163 (November 1961)
BLOOMFIELD, A. 'Britten Premiere (San Francisco)' *Musical America* 81 (December 1961)
GOTH, T. 'Felsenstein's Quandry' *Musical America* 81 (December 1961)
FRANKENSTEIN, A. 'San Francisco' *Opera* 12 (December 1961)
JACOBS, A. 'Düsseldorf, Munich, Vienna and Berlin' *Opera* 12 (December 1961)
'Zagreb' *Zvuk* 54 (1962)
MAREY, F. 'Sueno de una Noche de Verano' *Buenos Aires Musical* 17 No. 277 (1962)
MOKRI, K. 'Brittenov sen Noci Sevatojanskej prey raz new nas' *Hudebni Rozhledy* 15 No. 11 (1962)
POSPISIL, V. 'Brittenuv sen noci svatojanske-repertoarni Opera?' *Hudebni Rozhledy* 15 No. 15 (1962)
BERLING, B. 'Stryks saft paa ögonlock i sömn' *Musikrevy* 17 No. 13 (1962)
FRIED, A. 'Neue amerikanische Opern' *Melos* 29 (March 1962)
WEBSTER, E. M. 'Coventry – The Latter Glory' *Musical Opinion* 85 (July 1962)
ARNOSI, E. 'Buenos Aires' *Music and Musicians* 11 (September 1962)
WEISSSTEIN, C. B. 'Buenos Aires' *Opera* 13 (October 1962)
VALENTI FERRO, E. 'Argentina; *Pelléas, Pénélope* and *Dream*' *Musical America* 82 (November 1962)
KLEIN, R. 'Brittens *Sommernachstraum* in der Wiener Staatsoper' *Oesterreichische Musikzeitschrift* 17 (November 1962)
ECKSTEIN, P. 'Liberec' *Opera* 13 (November 1962)
WILLNAUER, F. 'Brittens *Sommernachstraum* in der Staatsoper' *Neue Zeitschrift für Musik* 123 (December 1962)
WECHSBERG, J. 'Vienna' *Opera* 13 (December 1962)
KNEPLER, G. 'Argentine Experiments (South American Premiere)' *Opera News* 27 (December 1962)
WECHSBERG, J. 'Vienna Nights' *Opera News* 27 (December 1962)
FIECHTNER, H. A. 'Oper-ballet-Mysterienspiel' *Musica* 17 No. 2 (1963)
SARGEANT, W. 'Musical Events' *New Yorker* 39 (May 1963)
KOLODIN, I. 'Music To My Ears' *Saturday Review* 42 (May 1963)
HELM, E. 'Editor's Choice' *Musical America* 83 (June 1963)

GOODWIN, N. 'Zagreb' *Music and Musicians* 11 (July 1963)
SABIN, R. 'New York' *Opera* 14 (July 1963)
ROSEBERRY, E. 'A Note on the Four Chords in Act II of *A Midsummer Night's Dream*' *Tempo* 66–67 (Autumn–Winter 1963)
SZENDREY, J. 'Debrecen: *The Dream* is staged' *Opera* 14 (October 1963)
SZENDREY, J. 'Debrecen: Brittens *Sommernachtstraum*' *Musik und Gesellschaft* 14 (March 1964)
ROZHDESTVENSKY, G. 'Son v Letnyuyu Noch" *Sovetskaya Muzyka* 28 (April 1964)
GOODWIN, N. 'Dream Dispelled' *Music and Musicians* 12 (June 1964)
'*A Midsummer Night's Dream*; Covent Garden' *Opera* 15 (June 1964)
GOLEA, A. 'La musique contemporaine à Strasbourg' *Musique* (Chaix) 139 (October 1965)
'Britten's Opera at the Bolshoi' *Musical Events* 20 (December 1965)
EGAN, J. 'Moscow' *Opera* 17 (January 1966)
KUZNETSOVA, I. 'Utverzhdenie pravdy' *Sovetskaya Musika* 30 (February 1966)
KELDYSH, Y. 'Novye puti' *Sovetskaya Muzika* 30 (March 1966)
GREENFIELD, E. 'London Report' *Hi-Fi/Musical America* 16 (April 1966)
TUBEUF, A. 'Strasbourg' *Opera* 17 (April 1966)
WEBER, H. 'Brittens *Sommernachstraum* in Düsseldorf' (reprinted from *Frankfurter Allgemeine Zeitung*, November 7 1966) *Orchester* 14 (December 1966)
'Twentieth Aldeburgh Festival' *About the House* 2 No. 7 (1967)
GOODWIN, N. 'Vaudeville for the Vienna Boys' *Music and Musicians* 15 (August 1967)
'*A Midsummer Night's Dream*; English Opera Group at Sadler's Wells' *Opera* 18 (September 1967)
WOCKER, K. H. 'Protest gegen die Routine' *Opern Welt* 9 (September 1967)
HAMILTON, D. 'Britten and the Bard – A New Midsummer Night (recording)' *Hi-Fi/Musical America* 17 (October 1967)
KRAUSE, E. 'Auffüllung des Spielplanes – Bemerkungen zu den Wiederaufnahmen der Komischen Oper' *Musik und Gesellschaft* 17 (October 1967)
GOODWIN, N. 'Tale of Two Festivals' *Music and Musicians* 16 (December 1967)
FLANAGAN, W. 'Benjamin Britten's *A Midsummer Night's Dream* (recording)' *Hi-Fi Review* 20 (January 1968)
DIETHER, J. '*A Midsummer Night's Dream* (London recording)' *American Record Guide* 34 (February 1968)

BALDWIN, O. and WILSON, T. 'Alfred Deller, John Freeman and Mr Pate' *Music and Letters* 50 (January 1969)

GREGOR, C. 'Dvakrat Fen Noci Svatojanske' *Hudebni Rozhledy* 23 No. 3 (1970)

BACH, J. M. 1. 'An analysis of Britten's *A Midsummer Night's Dream* 2. Spectra (original composition)' *D. Mus. University of Illinois at Urbana Champaign* (1971)

KERTESZ, I. 'Szentivaneji Alon – Benjamin Britten operajanak benutatoja (Budapest)' *Muzsika* 15 (March 1972)

SUTCLIFFE, T. 'Scottish Opera' *Music and Musicians* 21 (September 1972)

FAVRE, M. 'Bern: Brittens *Sommernachtstraum*' *Schweizerische Musikzeitung* 113 No. 6 (1973)

HODGSON, J. 'The English Opera Group' *Musical Events* 28 (January 1973)

SCHMIDT-GARRE, H. 'Die Schottische Oper spielt Brittens Shakespeare-Oper' *Neue Zeitschrift für Musik* 134 No. 3 (1974)

MULLNANN, B. 'Kassel: Der *Sommernachtstraum* findet in Saale statt' *Neue Zeitschrift für Musik* 135 No. 5 (1974)

'München' *Oper un Konzert* 12 No. 2 (1974)

'Cassel' *Oper und Konzert* 12 No. 9 (1974)

FORBES, E. 'British Isles' *Opera Canada* 15 No. 1 (1974)

DANLER, K. R. 'Die Schottische Oper in München' *Orchester* 22 (March 1974)

REYNOLDS, M. 'RNCM *Dream*' *Music and Musicians* 22 (February 1974)

MAYCOCK, R. 'Britten's *Dream* (Royal Opera)' *Music and Musicians* 22 (March 1974)

ROSENTHAL, H. 'London Opera Diary' *Opera* 25 (March 1974)

'Opera and Ballet in London' *Musical Opinion* 97 (April 1974)

ROTHON, T. 'Munich' *Opera* 25 (April 1974)

SUTCLIFFE, J. H. 'West Berlin/Kassel' *Opera News* 38 (May 1974)

SUTCLIFFE, J. H. 'Cassel' *Opera* 35 (August 1974)

FELDMAN, M. A. 'Central City' *Opera News* 39 (October 1974)

YOUNG, 'A. C. C. Opera *Midsummer Night's Dream*' *Hi-Fi/Musical America* 24 (November 1974)

REYNOLDS, M. 'Thoughts about the *Dream*' *Music and Musicians* 26 (January 1978)

RENSHAW, C. '*A Midsummer Night's Dream*' AFPB 1980

BLYTH, A. 'Britten: *A Midsummer Night's Dream*' *Opera* 32 (1981)

JACOBS, A. 'Britten: *A Midsummer Night's Dream*' *Opera* 32 (1981)

ROEWADE, S. 'Britten: *A Midsummer Night's Dream*' *Opera* 32 (1981)

BURRIDGE, C. J. 'Music such as charmeth sleep' *University of Toronto Quarterly* 51 (1981)

FELSENSTEIN, W. and ROTH, E. 'Briefwechsel mit Walter Felsenstein' *Sinn und Form* 33 No. 2 (March/April 1981)

BRITTEN, B. 'The composer's *Dream*' *The Britten Companion*: edited by Christopher Palmer. London, Faber (1984)
MELLER, W. 'The truth of the *Dream*' *The Britten Companion*: edited by Christopher Palmer. London, Faber (1984)
COOKE, M. 'Dramatic and musical cohesion in Britten's *A Midsummer Night's Dream*' B.A. *University of Cambridge* (1984)

MISSA BREVIS
'Missa Brevis' *Musical America* 80 (February 1960)
ROSEBERRY, E. 'A Note on Britten's *Missa Brevis*' *Tempo* 53–54 (Spring–Summer 1960)
'Missa Brevis' *Choral and Organ Guide* 13 (June–August 1960)
'Missa Brevis in D, Op. 63' *Caecilia* 88 No. 3 (1961)
HALL, M. V. 'Britten's *Missa Brevis*' *Musical Times* 103 (January 1962)
'Missa Brevis in D Op. 63' AFPB 1962
TORTOLANO, W. 'Melody in Twentieth Century Masses' *Diapason* 60 (April 1969)

MONT JUIC
ANDERSON, W. R. 'Wireless notes' *Musical Times* (February 1938)
'Mont Juic' *Tempo* 1 (American series) No. 3 (September 1940)
BERKELEY, L. 'Views from Mont Juic' *Tempo* 106 (September 1973)

MOTHER COMFORT
'Songs – Boosey and Hawkes' *Musical Times* (January 1938)

NIGHT COVERS UP THE RIGID LAND
EVANS, J. Sleeve note for EMI 27 0653 1 (1987)

NIGHT MAIL
'Realist Films' *Left Review* 7 (April 1936)
KELLER, H. 'Film Music: Britten' *Music Survey* 2 No. 4 (Spring 1950)
'Night Mail' AFPB 1961

NIGHT PIECE
WATERMAN, F. 'Britten's New Piano Piece' *Tempo* 66–67 (Autumn–Winter 1963)
CHISSELL, J. 'Leeds' *Musical Times* 104 (November 1963)
'Night Piece (Notturno) for piano' *Musical Times* 104 (December 1963)
THORPE, M. *Night Piece (Notturno)* for piano solo AFPB 1986

NOCTURNAL

'*Nocturnal* after John Dowland' AFPB 1964

GOODWIN, N. 'Commentary from Aldeburgh' *Music and Musicians* 12 (August 1964)

NOBLE, J. 'Britten's *Nocturnal*' *Musical Times* 105 (August 1964)

DIETHER, J. 'Two Recitals: on a Guitar and Lute – the Art of Julian Bream (recording)' *American Record Guide* 34 (July 1968)

NOCTURNE

BRADBURY, E. 'The Leeds Centenary Festival (First Performance)' *Musical Times* 99 (December 1958)

'*Nocturne*, Op. 60' AFPB 1959

HOLST, I. 'Britten's *Nocturne*' *Tempo* 50 (Winter 1959)

'Britten *Nocturne* Introduced by Little Orchestra' *Musical America* 80 (March 1960)

'The Little Orchestra Society' *Musical Courier* 161 (March 1960)

DIETHER, J. 'Britten's Nocturne (recording)' *American Record Guide* 27 (October 1960)

'Britten's New *Nocturne*: cycle of songs at Leeds Festival' *Times* (October 17 1958)

GOODWIN, N. 'Leeds and its new music' *Music and Musicians* (December 1958)

OTTAWAY, H. 'Radio Notes (First Performance)' *Musical Opinion* 82 (December 1958)

GOODWIN, N. 'London (First Performance)' *Musical Courier* 158 (December 1958)

'Leeds Festival 100 years old (First Performance)' *Musical America* 78 (December 1958)

'Festival Orchestra' *Musical America* 84 (December 1964)

EVANS, J. '*Nocturne* Op. 60' AFPB 1979

MITCHELL, D. 'Forms more real than living man': reflections on Britten's *Serenade* and *Nocturne*. Programme Book for Peter Pears Memorial Concert 3 April 1987

NOYE'S FLUDDE

GRAHAM, C. '*Noye's Fludde*' AFPB 1958

STEIN, E. 'Britten's New Opera for Children: *Noye's Fludde*' *Tempo* 48 (Summer 1958)

'Chester Miracle Play as Opera' *Times* (June 19 1958)

'By Ark and Rocket (First Performance)' *Time* 71 (June 30 1958)

JACOBS, A. '*Noye's Fludde* (First Performance)' *New York Times* 107 (July 6 1958)

AUSTEN, J. P. 'Aldeburgh and Ingestre (First Performance)' *Opera News* 23 (September 1958)
MYERS, R. H. 'Aldeburgh Festival (First Performance)' *Musical Times* 99 (August 1958)
'Aldeburgh (First Performance)' *Opera* 9 (August 1958)
ROSEBERRY, E. 'The Music of *Noye's Fludde*' *Tempo* 49 (Autumn 1958)
'Britten Kinderoper *Die Arche Noah*' *Neue Zeitschrift für Musik* 119 (October 1958)
JONES, S. H. 'London Letter' *Canon* 12 (January 1959)
'Southwark Cathedral' *Opera* 10 (January 1959)
MILBURN, F. '*Noye's Fludde* receives New York Premiere' *Musical America* 79 (April 1959)
HEYWORTH, P. '*Noye's Fludde*' *Canon* 12 (July 1959)
'Recitals and Concerts' *American Organ* 42 (August 1959)
'Trial by Jury' *Making Music* 41 (Autumn 1959)
GEORGE, G. 'Vancouver' *Canadian Music Journal* 5 No. 1 (1960)
'A Canadian Premiere' *Tempo* 55–56 (Autumn–Winter 1960)
DOCHERTY, I. 'Vancouver' *Opera* 11 (October 1960)
PAAP, W. '*Noye's Fludde* van Benjamin Britten' *Mens en Mel* 15 (November 1960)
'Britten at Aldeburgh' *Music Review* 22 No. 3 (1961)
USILL, H. 'Recording *Noye's Fludde*' *Gramophone* 39 (December 1961)
OSBORNE, C. L. 'Benjamin Britten's *Noye's Fludde* written for children but rewarding for all (recording)' *Hi Fi* 12 (August 1962)
'A Deluge of Floods (recordings)' *American Record Guide* 29 (September 1962)
ARDOIN, J. 'A flood and a Sonata (recording)' *Musical America* 82 (September 1962)
MELLERS, W. 'Music for Twentieth Century Children' *Musical Times* 105 (June 1964)
'St George's Church: *Noye's Fludde*' *Musical America* 84 (July 1964)
SPELDA, A. 'Brittenova potopa v Plzni' *Hudebni Rozhledy* 19 No. 9 (1966)
MATZNER, A. 'Ceskoslovenska premiera Brittenovej Potopy' *Slov Hud* 10 No. 6 (1966)
'Anstelveen: Noach op de Wateren van B. Britten' *Mens en Mel* 21 (May 1966)
WARBURTON, A. O. 'Set work for O Level, GCE' *Music Teacher and Piano Student* 47 (March 1968)
'*Noye's Fludde* (photographs)' *About the House* 3 No. 9 (1971)
CASANOVA, C. 'A la petite Scala: L'Arche de Noé de Britten' *Opéra* (France) 11 No. 96 (1971)
KESSLER, G. 'Mailand: Enttaüschungen und ein Fest' *Opern Welt* 5 (May 1971)

PIAMONTE, G. 'Da Milano' *Nuova Rivista Musicale Italiana* 5 (May–June 1971)
GRAHAM, C. *Noye's Fludde* AFPB 1971
PAAP, W. 'Noach en de Zondbloed' *Mens en Mel* 27 (May 1972)
REGITZ, H. 'Karlsruhe: Ein Mirakelspiel' *Opern Welt* 7 (July 1972)
ROBINSON, C. W. 'Part 1. The Departure: A Theatre-oriented theory of opera translation including an English version of *Die Abreise* by Eugen D'Albert. Part 2. Documentation of two opera productions: *Slow dusk* by Carlisle Floyde and *Noye's Fludde* by Benjamin Britten' *D.M.A. University of Washington* (1973)
REGITZ, H. 'Unterhaltsames Mysterium – Brittens *Arche Noah* in Ulm' *Opern Welt* 5 (May 1974)
SCHUTZ, A. 'Brittens *Arche Noah* in Lübeck' *Kirchmusiker* 26 No. 3 (1975)
'Brittens *Arche Noah* in Lübeck' *Musik und Kirche* 45 No. 4 (1975)
REED, P. 'Before the Fludde (film)' AFPB 1983
MELLERS, W. 'Through *Noye's Fludde*' *The Britten Companion*: edited by Christopher Palmer. London, Faber (1984)

OCCASIONAL OVERTURE
MITCHELL, D. Sleeve note for EMI EL2702 631 (1986)

ON THE FRONTIER
MITCHELL, D. and BURROWS, J. Britten's Theatre Music AFPB 1980

ON THIS ISLAND
'London Concerts – BBC Contemporary Concert' *Musical Times* (December 1937)
McDONALD, O. H. 'The Semantics of Music' *Music Survey* 1 No. 4 (September 1948)
'Now Thro' Night's Caressing Grip' *Music Survey* 1 No. 6 (1949)
MITCHELL, D. Sleeve note for BBC Artium REGL 417 (1981)

OUR HUNTING FATHERS
E. E. 'The Norwich Festival' *Musical Times* (October 1936)
E. E. 'London Concerts. BBC Contemporary music' *Musical Times* (June 1937)
LADERMAN, E. 'The BBC Symphony Orchestra' *Hi-Fi/Musical America* 15 (August 1965)
CHISSELL, J. 'The Proms' *Musical Times* 106 (October 1965)
STRODE, R. *'Our Hunting Fathers'* AFPB 1976
MITCHELL, D. Sleeve note for BBC Artium REGL 417 (1981)
MATTHEWS, C. Sleeve note for EMI ASD 4397 (1983)

OWEN WINGRAVE

'*Owen Wingrave* (photographs of the Television Production)' *About the House* 3 No. 9 (1971)
RAYNOR, H. 'Opera; *Owen Wingrave*' *Music Review* 32 No. 3 (1971)
HOMOLYA, I. 'A nagyvilag zeneje' *Muzsika* 14 (1971)
'Dokumentation' *Opern Welt Yearbook* (1971)
ORR, B. 'First Performances and Commissions' *Composer* 39 (Spring 1971)
'Britten's Television Opera' *Hi-Fi/Musical America* 21 (March 1971)
WHITE, E. W. '*Owen Wingrave*' *Music and Musicians* 19 (May 1971)
EVANS, P. 'Britten's television opera' *Musical Times* 112 (May 1971)
WARRACK, J. 'Britten's television opera' *Opera* 22 (May 1971)
KOLODIN, I. 'Music to my Ears' *Saturday Review* 54 (May 1971)
BENDER, W. 'Opera mundi' *Time* 97 (May 1971)
CULSHAW, J. 'The making of *Owen Wingrave*' *The Times* (May 8 1971)
MITCHELL, D. 'Donald Mitchell writes about Benjamin Britten's new opera *Owen Wingrave*' *Listener* 85 (May 13 1971)
GREENFIELD, E. 'A Benjamin Britten opera made for the "intimate subtleties" of TV' *Radio Times* (May 13 1971)
MANN, W. '*Owen Wingrave* BBC 2' *Times* (May 15 1971)
WARRACK, J. 'Box for the opera' *Sunday Telegraph* (May 16 1971)
COOPER, M. 'Powerful utterance of *Owen Wingrave*' *Daily Telegraph* (May 17 1971)
WHITE, E. W. '*Owen Wingrave*' *Music and Musicians* 19 (May 1971)
NOBLE, J. 'The Wrong Box?' *New Statesman* (May 21 1971)
HEYWORTH, P. 'Da Londra' *Nuova Rivista Musicale Italiana* 5 (May–June 1971)
'*Owen Wingrave*' *Opera News* 35 (June 1971)
LARGE, B. 'The making of *Wingrave*' *Records and Recording* 14 (June 1971)
WALSH, S. 'Last week's broadcast music' *Listener* (June 3 1971)
MITCHELL, D. Sleeve note for Decca SET 501–2 (1971)
'*Owen Wingrave*' *Music and Musicians* 19 (July 1971)
ROSEBERRY, E. 'Radio' *Music and Musicians* 19 (July 1971)
WEBSTER, E. N. 'Communication 2: the Ethos and the Ether' *Musical Opinion* 94 (July 1971)
SADIE, S. '*Owen Wingrave*' *Musical Times* 112 (July 1971)
ROSENTHAL, H. 'On Television: *Owen Wingrave*' *Opera* 22 (July 1971)
JUNGHEINRICH, H. K. and SCHNEIDERS, H. L. 'P. B. Shelley hat doch recht' *Opern Welt* 11 (July 1971)
SCHIFFER, B. 'Benjamin Brittens neue Fernsehoper' *Melos* 38 (July–August 1971)

GREENFIELD, E. 'Tippett's *Knot Garden*, Britten's *Owen Wingrave*' *Hi-Fi/Musical America* 21 (August 1971)
'*Owen Wingrave*' *Music Review* 32 (August 1971)
BRASCH, A. 'Musik für Zuschauer' *Neue Zeitschrift für Musik* 132 (September 1971)
'*Owen Wingrave*' *Contemporary Review* (November 1971)
MANN, W. '*Owen Wingrave* Royal Opera House' *The Times* (May 11 1973)
SHAWE-TAYLOR, D. 'Haunted House' *Sunday Times* (May 13 1973)
'The Saloon (correspondence between Henry James and George Bernard Shaw on the original dramatisation of story *Owen Wingrave*)' *About the House* 4 No. 2 (1973)
'*Owen Wingrave* (Covent Garden Production)' *About the House* 4 No. 3 (1973)
BAUCKE, L. 'Benjamin Britten's *Owen Wingrave* (Hanover)' *Musica* 27 No. 6 (1973)
EVANS, J. '*Owen Wingrave*: a case for pacifism' *The Britten Companion*: edited by Christopher Palmer: London, Faber (1984)
LIMMERT, E. 'Hannover: Ballade der Kriegsdienstverweigerung – deutsche Erstaufführung von Brittens *Owen Wingrave*' *Neue Zeitschrift für Musik* 134 No. 11 (1973)
'Hannover' *Oper und Konzert* 11 No. 11 (1973)
PURRINGTON, E. C. 'Santa Fe' *Opera Canada* 14 No. 4 (1973)
GOODWIN, N. '*Owen Wingrave* (Covent Garden)' *Music and Musicians* 21 (July 1973)
SLATER, C. '*Owen Wingrave* (Covent Garden)' *Musical Events* 28 (July 1973)
'Opera and Ballet in London' *Musical Opinion* 96 (July 1973)
DEAN, W. '*Owen Wingrave*' *Musical Times* 114 (July 1973)
ROSENTHAL, H. 'London Opera Diary' *Opera* 24 (July 1973)
BARKER, F. G. 'London' *Opera News* 38 (July 1973)
GREENFIELD, E. 'Britten's *Death in Venice*; *Owen Wingrave* staged' *Hi-Fi/Musical America* 23 (September 1973)
EATON, Q. 'What's New at Santa Fe?' *Music Journal* 31 (October 1973)
JENKINS, 'Santa Fe' *Opera News* 38 (October 1973)
OPPENS, K. and LIMMERT, E. 'Zweimal Brittens *Owen Wingrave* (Santa Fe und Hannover) *Opern Welt* 10 (October 1978)
DAMMENBERG, P. 'Der Tod eines Pazifisten – deutsche Erstaufführung von Brittens *Owen Wingrave*' *Neue Musikzeitung* 22 (October–November 1973)
PLEASANTS, H. 'A Plethora of Modern Opera (Covent Garden) stereo review' 31 (October 1973)
SAYLOR, B. 'Santa Fe: *Owen Wingrave* on Stage' *Hi-Fi/Musical America* 23 (November 1973)

WHITTALL, A. 'War and a Wedding: two modern British operas' *Music and Letters* 55 (July 1974)
BARKER, F. G. *'Owen Wingrave* (Covent Garden)' *Music and Musicians* 22 (July 1974)
'Opera and Ballet in London' *Musical Opinion* 97 (July 1974)
KASSOW, J. 'Ghent: Britten and Massenet' *Opera* 26 (February 1975)
'Opera School: *Owen Wingrave*' *RCM Magazine* 76 Nos 2 and 3 (1980)
GRAHAM, C. *Owen Wingrave* AFPB 1984

PAUL BUNYAN

'Paul Bunyan' *Tempo* 1 (American Series) No. 1 (March 1940)
KESTIN, D. 'Western Folklore in Modern American Opera' *Western Folklore* 16 (January 1957)
PEARS, P. 'Songs and ensembles from *Paul Bunyan*' AFPB 1974
JOSEPHSON, D. 'Three ballads from *Paul Bunyan*' AFPB 1974
GREENFIELD, E. *'Paul Bunyan' Guardian* (June 25 1974)
GREENFIELD, E. 'Aldeburgh' *Musical Times* 115 (August 1974)
OTTAWAY, H. 'Britten's *Paul Bunyan*' *Tempo* 110 (September 1974)
GOODWIN, N. 'Aldeburgh' *Music and Musicians* 23 (August 1975)
'How *Paul Bunyan* built America . . .' *Sunday Times* (January 25 1976)
BLYTH, A. *'Paul Bunyan* Radio 3 (tomorrow)' *Times* (January 31 1976)
CAIRNS, D. 'Review' *Sunday Times* (February 1 1976)
PORTER, P. 'Bunyan's Progress' *Times Literary Supplement* (February 20 1976)
COOPER, M. 'Britten's ingenuity matches Auden' *Daily Telegraph* (June 7 1976)
GREENFIELD, E. 'Pilgrim's progress' *Guardian* (June 7 1976)
MANN, W. *'Paul Bunyan*. Maltings, Snape' *Times* June 7 1976)
AUDEN, W. H. *Paul Bunyan* AFPB 1976
OTTAWAY, H. 'Britten's *Paul Bunyan*' *Tempo* 118 (September 1976)
DEAN, W. 'Review of English Music Theatre; *Paul Bunyan* at Sadler's Wells' *Musical Times* 117 (November 1976)
RAYNOR, H. *'Paul Bunyan' Music Review* 38 (May 1977)
NEWILL, H. *'Paul Bunyan*: critical study of an operetta by W. H. Auden and Benjamin Britten' *B.Mus. University of Sheffield* (June 1978)
PORTER, A. The first opera: *Paul Bunyan*. THE OPERAS OF BENJAMIN BRITTEN; edited by David Herbert, London, Hamish Hamilton 1979
MITCHELL, D. and BURROWS, J. Britten's Theatre Music AFPB 1980
MELLERS, W. *'Paul Bunyan*: the American Eden' *The Britten Companion*: edited by Christopher Palmer. London, Faber (1984)
FRAYNE, J. P. *Paul Bunyan's* Second Chances: Revisions and Revivals *American Music* 3 No. 1 (Spring 1985)

PEARS, PETER

PEARS, P. 'Neither a hero nor a villain' *Radio Times* (March 8 1946)
PEARS, P. 'Bach: *Cantatas* 156 and 161' AFPB 1949
PEARS, P. 'Bach and Purcell' AFPB 1949
PEARS, P. 'Handel: *Ode for Saint Cecilia's Day*' AFPB 1949
PEARS, P. 'A Recital of English Songs' AFPB 1949
'Peter Pears, Tenor' *Musical America* 69 (November 15 1949)
PEARS, P. 'The Counter Tenor' AFPB 1950
KELLER, H. 'Peter Pears' *Opera* 2 (May 1951)
PEARS, P. 'Monteverdi: *Il Combattimento di Tancredi e Clorinda*' AFPB 1951
PEARS, P. 'Purcell: *Dido and Aeneas*' AFPB 1951
PEARS, P. 'The Vocal Music' MITCHELL/KELLER 1952
PEARS, P. 'German Passion Music' AFPB 1954
MEADMORE, W. S. 'Peter Pears' *Gramophone* 32 (March 1955)
CRANBROOK, *Lady* Pears, P. and Britten, B. Forword to AFPB 1955
PEARS, P. 'Dietrich Buxtehude's "*The Last Judgement*"' AFPB 1957
PEARS, P. 'Fantasies, Galliards and Songs (Dowland)' AFPB 1958
PEARS, P. 'Homage to the British Orpheus: Henry Purcell 1659–1695' AFPB 1959
PEARS, P. 'Homage to the British Orpheus': Henry Purcell 1659–1695: essays on his music; edited by Imogen Holst London, O.U.P. 1959
PEARS, P. 'A Purcell Cabaret' AFPB 1959
PEARS, P. 'Form and performance'. BBC Third Programme (5 March 1960)
ROSENTHAL, H. 'Peter Pears' *Canon* 14 (September–October 1960)
PEARS, P. 'Some Notes on the Translation of Bach's Passions' TRIBUTE TO BENJAMIN BRITTEN ON HIS FFTIETH BIRTHDAY, ed. A. Gishford. London, Faber, 1963
PEARS, P. 'Francis Poulenc 1899–1963' AFPB 1964
PEARS, P. 'Sculpture by Georg Ehrlich' AFPB 1964
PEARS, P. Sleeve note for Argo ZRG 5418 (1964)
PEARS, P. 'Christian Rohlfs (1849–1938)' AFPB 1965
PEARS, P. 'The Madrigal: four hundred years on' AFPB 1965
'From Peter Pears, his third and best Britten *Serenade*' *American Record Guide* 31 (August 1965)
PEARS, P. 'Armenian Holiday: August 1965'. Privately published
PEARS, P. 'Armenian Holiday: Extracts from a diary, August 1965' AFPB 1966
PEARS, P. 'Tribute to Percy Grainger' AFPB 1966
PEARS, P. 'Elizabethan music' AFPB 1967
PEARS, P. 'Moscow Christmas: December 1966'. Privately published
PEARS, P. 'Russian New Year: extracts from a Diary, Winter 1966–67' AFPB 1967

PEARS, P. 'Schubert: Die schöne Müllerin' AFPB 1967
PEARS, P. 'Two Musical Families' AFPB 1967
PEARS, P. 'Antonio Vivaldi' AFPB 1968
PEARS, P. 'Elizabethan Music' AFPB 1968
PEARS, P. 'François Couperin Le Grand (1668–1733): II' AFPB 1968
PEARS, P. 'Heinrich Schütz (1585–1672)' AFPB 1968
PEARS, P. 'Musical Families I: The Wesleys' AFPB 1968
PEARS, P. 'Rejoice in the Lamb: Sidney Nolan – an exhibition of paintings for Aldeburgh 1968' AFPB 1968
PEARS, P. 'Satie: *Sports et Divertissements*; Debussy: *Suite: Estampes*; Poulenc: *Suite: Napoli*' AFPB 1968
PEARS, P. 'Up She Goes: Five centuries of Folk-Music' AFPB 1968
BLYTH, A. 'Peter Pears' *Gramophone* 46 (September 1968)
PEARS, P. 'Bach: *Cantata No. 55: Geist und Seele wird verwirret*' AFPB 1969
PEARS, P. and LEDGER, P. 'Claudio Monteverdi and Henry Purcell' AFPB 1969
PEARS, P. 'Composer's Choice: William Walton' AFPB 1969
PEARS, P. and HOLST, I. 'The Fairy Queen Henry Purcell (1659–95)' AFPB 1969
PEARS, P. 'John Dowland (1563–1626) Ayres, Dances and Fancies' AFPB 1969
PEARS, P. 'Julian Bream, guitar' (recital notes) AFPB 1969
PEARS, P. 'Mary Potter' AFPB 1969
PEARS, P. 'Musica Juventutis: The Teenagers' AFPB 1969
PEARS, P. 'Musica Senectutis: The Over-Seventies' AFPB 1969
PEARS, P. 'A Note on Percy Grainger' *Musical Times* 111 (March 1970)
PEARS, P. 'Schubert's last songs' AFPB 1970
PEARS, P. 'Up She Goes Again: Five Centuries of Folk-Music' AFPB 1970
PEARS, P. 'Mozart: *Concerto in C major* K314 for oboe' AFPB 1971
PEARS, P. 'Give-and-take in music' AFPB 1971
PEARS, P. 'Weber: *Konzertstück in F minor* Op. 79; Tchaikovsky: *Francesca da Rimini: Fantasy after Dante* Op. 32' AFPB 1971
PEARS, P. 'Music for York' AFPB 1971
PEARS, P. 'Originality & Influence: the problem of comprehensibility – a lecture by Hans Keller' AFPB 1971
PEARS, P. 'Schütz and Stravinsky' AFPB 1971
PEARS, P. 'Purcell: *Sonata in G minor* for violin and continuo' AFPB 1971
PEARS, P. 'Tchaikovsky & Rossini' AFPB 1971
PEARS, P. 'Three Poems of Michelangelo; Three Christmas Songs (Wolf)' AFPB 1971

PEARS, P. 'Turkish Delight or, The Lure of the East' AFPB 1971

PEARS, P. 'Violin and piano' (Mozart: *Sonata in A major* K526; Shostakovich: *Sonata* Op. 134) AFPB 1971

MITCHELL, D. 'Double Portrait: some personal reflections'. ALDEBURGH ANTHOLOGY; edited by Ronald Blythe. Aldeburgh, Snape Maltings Foundation in association with Faber Music Ltd, 1972

PEARS, P. 'Arne: *Rule Britannia*; Grainger: *Dollar and half a day*' AFPB 1972

PEARS, P. 'Duncan Grant at Charleston' AFPB 1972

PEARS, P. 'Elizabethan Music' AFPB 1972

PEARS, P. 'The Madrigal: Four hundred years on'. ALDEBURGH ANTHOLOGY: ed. Ronald Blythe. Aldeburgh, Snape Maltings Foundation in association with Faber Music Ltd, 1972

PEARS, P. 'Schubert Wine & Song' AFPB 1972

BRITTEN, B. and PEARS, P. 'Schumann: *Scenes from Goethe's "Faust"*' AFPB 1972

PEARS, P. Sleeve note for Decca 5BB 119–20 (1972)

PEARS, P. 'Britten: *Who are these children* Op. 84' AFPB 1972

PEARS, P. 'Percy Grainger' *Recorded Sound* 45–46 (January–April 1972)

TURNER, G. 'Singers' *Music and Musicians* 21 (January 1973)

PEARS, P. 'A Little Midsummer Madness' AFPB 1973

PEARS, P. 'Marriage at Ipswich 1296' AFPB 1973

PEARS, P. 'San Fortunato: From a diary' AFPB 1973

PEARS, P. 'Sterndale Bennett: *Concerto No. 4 in F minor* Op. 19 for piano and orchestra; Brahms: *Double concerto in A minor* for violin, cello and orchestra' AFPB 1973

PEARS, P. 'Venice – London 1590–1620' AFPB 1973

HEINITZ, T. 'The Art of Peter Pears' *Records and Recording* 16 No. 9 (June 1973)

McLACHLAN, D. 'Peter Pears Discography' *Records and Recording* 16 No. 9 (June 1973)

SOMMER, S. T. 'Weelkes by Pears: a Madrigal Classic (recording)' *Hi-Fi/ Musical America* 23 (November 1973)

PEARS, P. 'J. C. Bach: Concert Aria: *Io ti lascio, e questo addio*; Bridge: Two Songs for mezzo soprano and orchestra; Bridge: Three pieces for strings' AFPB 1974

PEARS, P. 'Black, White and Blue' AFPB 1974

PEARS, P. 'Delius: *On hearing the first cuckoo in spring*; Grieg: *Concerto in A minor* for piano and orchestra; Nordheim: *Zimbel*; Britten: *Suite from "The Prince of the Pagodas"*' AFPB 1974

BRITTEN, B., PEARS, P. and HOLST, I. 'Dido and Aeneas' AFPB 1974
PEARS, P. 'Fauré: *Cinq mélodies de Venise; Le Jardin Clos*' AFPB 1974
PEARS, P. 'Handel: Cantatas, Sonata, and Suite' AFPB 1974
PEARS, P. 'Music from Norway: Folk music played on the Hardanger fiddle; Grieg: *Slåtter*; Bibalo: *Sonata (1975)* for piano; Mortenson: *Fantasy and Fugue* Op. 13 for piano' AFPB 1974
PEARS, P. 'Saint Enoch: More pages from a Diary' AFPB 1974
PEARS, P. 'Schumann: *Minnespiel*' AFPB 1974
PEARS, P. 'Schumann: Piano Music and Songs (*Kreisleriana, Liederkreis* Op. 39, *Fantasiestücke, Fünf Lieder und Gesänge* Op. 127)' AFPB 1974
PEARS, P. 'Songs and ensembles from *Paul Bunyan*' AFPB 1974
PEARS, P. 'Wilbye: Madrigals; Byrd, Purcell, Boyce and others: Rounds, canons, catches and glees' AFPB 1974
GELLES, G. 'Peter Pears: the voice that inspired Britten' *New York Times* (November 2 1974)
JENKINS, S. 'Peter Pears bows at the Met.' *New York Post* (November 2 1974)
PEARS, P. 'From a Russian Diary' *Soundings* 4 (1974)
PEARS, P. 'Artist's Choice: Thea King' AFPB 1975
PEARS, P. 'The New York *Death in Venice*' AFPB 1975
PEARS, P. 'Purcell: *Since God so tender a regard*; Sterndale Bennett: *To Chloe in sickness*; Parry: *Through the Ivory Gate; Crabbed Youth and Age*' AFPB 1975
PEARS, P. '*Six Hölderlin Fragments*' AFPB 1975
PEARS, P. 'William Plomer: a celebration' AFPB 1975
PEARS, P. 'Handel's Favourite Tenor' AFPB 1976
PEARS, P. 'Nordheim: *Doria*' AFPB 1976
PEARS, P. and HOLST, I. 'Anniversaries' AFPB 1977
PEARS, P. 'Kilvert's Diary and Music' AFPB 1977
PEARS, P. 'Mozart: *Symphony No. 38 in D "The Prague"* (K.504)' AFPB 1977
PEARS, P. 'Sidney Nolan' AFPB 1977
PEARS, P. 'Tribute to Sylvia Townsend Warner' AFPB 1977
PEARS, P. 'Peter Pears talks about Benjamin Britten – as told to Louis Chalin' *Keynote* (April 1978)
PEARS, P. 'Haydn: *Six English Canzonets*' AFPB 1978
PEARS, P. 'John Piper' AFPB 1978
PEARS, P. 'Special I' AFPB 1978
PEARS, P. 'Birth of an opera' BBC Radio (28 September 1976)
PEARS, P. Preface to THE OPERAS OF BENJAMIN BRITTEN; edited by David Herbert. London, Hamish Hamilton 1979
PEARS, P. Sleeve note for RCA GL 42752 (1979)

PEARS, P. Foreword to *The Building of the House* AF-SMF Ltd, 1980
PEARS, P. 'Ein Leben für Britten' *Fono Forum* 16 (June 1980)
SWEETING, E. 'Happy birthday, Sir Peter Pears!' *Twenty Four Hours* 5 No. 5 (June 1980)
RICHARDS, D. 'Sir Peter Pears at 70' *Music and Musicians* (28 July 1980)
PEARS, P. Contribution to REMEMBERING BRITTEN: edited by Alan Blyth London, Hutchinson, 1981
PEARS, P. 'Special II: Alan Bush' AFPB 1981
PEARS, P. 'Special III: Malcolm Williamson' AFPB 1981
PEARS, P. 'Birthday Choice' AFPB 1982
PEARS, P. 'The Complete Songs of John Ireland' *RCM Magazine* 78 No. 2 (Summer 1982)
FLYNN, W. 'Britten the progressive' *Music Review* 44 (1983)
PEARS, P. 'J. C. Bach: *Aria: Non so d'onde viene*' AFPB 1983
PEARS, P. 'L. Berkeley: *Stabat Mater*' AFPB 1983
PEARS, P. '*Sechs Monologe aus "Jedermann"*' AFPB 1983
PEARS, P. 'Mozart: *Andante with Variations in G* (K.501)' AFPB 1983
PEARS, P. 'Mozart: *Recitative and Aria, Alcandro, lo confesso – Non so d'onde viene*' AFPB 1983
PEARS, P. 'A Personal Introduction to Percy Grainger' AFPB 1982
PEARS, P. 'Satie: *Avant-dernières pensées*' AFPB 1983
PEARS, P. 'Schubert: *Abschied von der Erde*' AFPB 1983
PEARS, P. '*Sonatina Romantica* (1940)' AFPB 1983
PEARS, P. 'Wagner: Three French Songs' AFPB 1983
PEARS, P. 'Wagner: Five Songs for mezzo, soprano and piano' AFPB 1983
CROSS, J. PEARS, P. and EVANS, J. '*Peter Grimes* and *Gloriana*' PETER GRIMES/GLORIANA Benjamin Britten. London, John Calder, 1983. (E.N.O./The R.O. Guide 24)
PEARS, P. 'Lute Songs and Solos' AFPB 1984
PEARS, P. A Tribute on His 75th Birthday; edited by Marion Thorpe. London, Faber Music in association with the Britten Estate, 1985 (A Britten–Pears Library Publication)
PEARS, P. 'For Nancy' AFPB 1985
PEARS, P. 'Sonnets and Songs' AFPB 1985
PEARS, P. 'Voices of War' AFPB 1985
WHO'S WHO 1986. 138th edition. London, Adam & Charles Black, 1986
Obituary *Daily Telegraph* (4 April 1986)
Obituary *Financial Times* (4 April 1986)
Obituary *Guardian* (4 April 1986)

Obituary *New York Times* (4 April 1986)
Obituary *Sunday Times* (4 April 1986)
Obituary *Times* (4 April 1986)
Obituary *Observer* (6 April 1986)
MITCHELL, D. 'Peter Pears (1910–1986)' *Aldeburgh Soundings* No. 5 (Spring 1986)
STRODE, R. 'Sir Peter Pears CBE (1910–1986)' *RCM Magazine* Vol. 82 No. 2 (1986)
CROZIER, E. 'Sir Peter Pears: an appreciation' *Opera Quarterly* 4 No. 3 (Autumn 1986)
PETER: A PERFORMER REMEMBERED. A Tribute to Peter Pears 1910–1986. Royal Opera House, Covent Garden 30 November 1987
PIPER, M. 'Peter Pears: The Collector' AFPB 1987

PETER GRIMES
FORSTER, E. M. 'George Crabbe the poet and the man' *Listener* (May 29 1941)
'*Peter Grimes*' *Tempo* 7 (O.S.) (June 1944)
SLATER, M. 'The plot of *Peter Grimes*' *Tempo* 9 (O.S.) (December 1944)
'*Peter Grimes*' *Tempo* 10 (O.S.) (March 1945)
'*Peter Grimes*' *Tempo* 11 (O.S.) (June 1945)
'Britten's Opera *Peter Grimes* re-opens Sadler's Wells Theatre' *New York Times* (June 8 1945)
'Sadler's Wells Opera – *Peter Grimes*' *Times* (June 8 1945)
SHAWE-TAYLOR, D. '*Peter Grimes*' *New Statesman* (June 9 and 16 1945)
NEWMAN, E. '*Peter Grimes*' *Sunday Times* (June 10, 17 and 24 1945)
HOPE-WALLACE, P. '*Peter Grimes*' *Time and Tide* (June 14 1945)
'*Peter Grimes* – second thoughts' *Times* (June 15 1945)
GLOCK, W. 'Music' *Observer* (June 24 1945)
ROTH, E. '*Peter Grimes*: a new British opera' *Picture Post* (June 30 1945)
McNAUGHT, W. '*Peter Grimes*' *Musical Times* (July 1945)
LAVAUDEN, T. '*Peter Grimes*, L'Oeuvre Géniale du Compositeur Anglais Benjamin Britten' *La Tribune de Genève* (July 11 1945)
BANNER, B. '*Peter Grimes*' *RCM Magazine* 41 No. 3 (1945)
WHITE, E. W. '*Peter Grimes*' *Penguin New Writing* 26 (Autumn 1945)
STEIN, E. 'Opera and *Peter Grimes*' *Tempo* 12 (O.S.) (September 1945)
FOSS, H. 'Britten and *Peter Grimes*' *Listener* (September 27 1945)
'Britten's dramatic music – *Peter Grimes*' *Times* (October 26 1945)
BLOM, E. '*Peter Grimes* reconsidered' *Birmingham Post* (October 29 1945)

BENJAMIN BRITTEN Peter Grimes; essays by Benjamin Britten and others. London, Governors of Sadler's Wells Foundation, 1946

SACKVILLE-WEST, E. 'The Musical and Dramatic Structure'. BENJAMIN BRITTEN Peter Grimes; essays by Benjamin Britten and others. London, Governors of Sadler's Wells Foundation, 1946

SLATER, M. 'The Story of the Opera'. BENJAMIN BRITTEN: Peter Grimes; essays by Benjamin Britten and others. London, Governors of Sadler's Wells Foundation, 1946

AVSHALAMOFF, J. 'Tanglewood in Retrospect' *Modern Music* 23 (1946)

JACOBS, R. L. 'The Significance of *Peter Grimes*' *Listener* (March 7 1946)

PEARS, P. 'Neither a Hero nor a Villain' *Radio Times* (March 8 1946)

HUSSEY, D. 'Broadcast Music – *Peter Grimes*' *Listener* (March 21 1946)

ATTERBERG, K. 'Britten's *Peter Grimes*' *Stockholms – Tidningen* (March 22 1945)

NEWMAN, E. '*Peter Grimes* and After – I' *Sunday Times* (March 24 1946)

NEWMAN, E. '*Peter Grimes* and After – II' *Listener* (March 31 1946)

GATTI, G. 'Un opera inglese: *Peter Grimes* di Britten' *La Nuova Stampa* (April 24 1946)

'*Peter Grimes*' *Tempo* 15 (O.S.) (June 1946)

DOWNES, O. 'Britten's *Grimes* unveiled at Lenox' *New York Times* (August 7 1946)

HAWKES, R. 'Festival at Tanglewood' *Tempo* 2 (December 1946)

ABBIATI, F. '*Peter Grimes:* guida musicale'. Milan, Instituto d'Alta Cultura (1947)

STUART, C. Peter Grimes. London, Royal Opera House, Covent Garden, 1947

WILSON, E. Account of *Peter Grimes* in 'London in Midsummer', in *Europe without Baedecker*. New York, 1947

HAWKES, R. '*Peter Grimes*' *Tempo* 3 (March 1947)

EINSIEDEL, W. von 'Benjamin Britten's *Peter Grimes*: Zur deutschen Erstaufführung' *Blick in die Welt* 8 (Spring 1947)

ESCHER, R. 'De Opera *Peter Grimes*' *De Groene* (June 1 1947)

CARDUS, N. '*Peter Grimes*' *Manchester Guardian* (November 12 1947)

KELLER, H. '*Peter Grimes* at Covent Garden' *Music Review* 9 (1948)

KING, W. G. 'New Opera in New York' *Cue* (February 7 1948)

THOMSON, V. 'Review' *New York Herald Tribune* (February 13 1948)

'Opera's new Face' *Time* 51 No. 7 (February 6 1948)

'The Baton Points at *Peter Grimes*' *Opera News* 12 No. 21 (March 8 1948)

FOERSTER, L. E. '*Grimes* Ahoy!' *Opera News* 12 No. 21 (March 8 1948)

'Metropolitan Grand Opera Season 1947–1948 (Programme)' *Opera News* 12 No. 21 (March 8 1948)

'The critics on *Peter Grimes*' *Opera News* (March 8 1948)

'Who was Who in *Peter Grimes*' *Opera News* 12 No. 21 (March 8 1948)

MICHEL, A. '*Albert Herring* et *Peter Grimes*' *Le Phare* (June 3 1948)

CROZIER, E. 'An Exhibition of Stage Models and Desgns for *Peter Grimes*' AFPB 1948

GOLDBECK, F. 'Un opéra anglais de 1945 nous tombe miraculeusement du ciel' *Le Figaro* (June 19 1948)

McNAUGHT, W. '*Peter Grimes*' *Musical Times* (July 1948)

KERMAN, J. '*Grimes* and *Lucretia*' *The Hudson Review* 2 (1949)

STEDMAN, J. W. '*Grimes* against The Borough' *Opera News* 13 (February 7 1949)

'The Costumes' *Opera News* 13 (February 7 1949)

'*Peter Grimes*' *Opera News* 13 (February 7 1949)

'The Settings' *Opera News* 13 (February 7 1949)

'What to read' *Opera News* 13 (February 7 1949)

KELLER, H. 'Britten: Thematic relations and the 'Mad' Interlude's 5th motif' *Music Survey* 4 No. 1 (1951)

KELLER, H. '*Peter Grimes*: II. The Story, the music not excluded'. MITCHELL/KELLER 1952

OLDHAM, A. '*Peter Grimes*: I. The Music, the story not excluded'. MITCHELL/KELLER 1952

STEIN, E. '*Peter Grimes*: III. Opera and Peter Grimes'. MITCHELL/KELLER 1952

TERRY, A. '*Peter Grimes* as Anti-British Propaganda' *Sunday Times* (January 6 1952)

'*Peter Grimes* revived at Covent Garden' *Tempo* 30 (Winter 1953–4)

'*Peter Grimes* revived' *Musical Opinion* 77 (February 1954)

HUSSEY, D. 'The Musician's Gramophone' *Musical Times* 35 (April 1954)

ROSENTHAL, H. 'New Operas and their Audiences' *London Music* 9 (October 1954)

'De Nederlandse Opera' *Mens en Mel* 10 (April 1955)

KLOPPENBURG, W. C. 'De oper *Peter Grimes* van Benjamin Britten' *Mens en Mel* 10 (March 1955)

NOSKE, F. 'Holland' *Musical Courier* 151 (June 1955)

SINCLAIR, J. 'Holland' *Opera* 6 (June 1955)

KELLER, H. 'The Fishing Englishman in Holland' *Musical Opinion* 79 (November 1955)

HAREWOOD, *Earl of* Sleeve note for Decca SXL 2150–2 (1959)

KREHN, W. '*Peter Grimes* Televised' *Canadian Music Journal* 3 (Spring 1959)

SMITH, E. '*Peter Grimes* in Stereo' *Gramophone* 37 (October 1959)
GARVIE, P. 'New Records' *Canadian Music Journal* 5 No. 1 (1960)
'*Peter Grimes* revived (recording)' *Music Review* 21 No. 3 (1960)
SHAWE-TAYLOR, D. 'The Gramophone and the Voice (recording)' *Gramophone* 37 (January 1960)
HALL, D. 'Britten's *Peter Grimes* (recording)' *Hi-Fi Review* 4 (February 1960)
DIETHER, J. '*Peter Grimes* (recording)' *American Record Guide* 26 (March 1960)
FRANKENSTEIN, A. '*Peter Grimes* recorded complete – with composer in command' *Hi Fi* 10 (March 1960)
SHNEYERSON, G. 'Bendshamin Britten i ego Opera' *Sovetskaya Muzyka* 24 (October 1960)
SCHMIDT, I. '*Peter Grimes* i stereoversion' *Musikrevy* 16 No. 5 (1961)
'Covent Garden' *Opera* 12 (January 1961)
SHNEYERSON, G. '*Peter Grimes* a Soviet view' *Opera* 12 (April 1961)
GLICKMAN, M. 'Rome' *Musical Courier* 163 (August 1961)
KRELLMANN, H. 'Brittens *Peter Grimes* wird in Wuppertal zum packenden Kleinstadtdrama' *Melos* 29 (July–August 1962)
BARKER, M. G. 'Gripping *Grimes*' *Music and Musicians* 11 (December 1962)
'Covent Garden' *Opera* 13 (December 1962)
GARBUTT, A. W. 'Music and Motive in *Peter Grimes*' *Music and Letters* 44 No. 4 (1963)
'The Sadler's Wells *Peter Grimes*' *Opera* 14 (June 1963)
PAYNE, A. 'Dramatic Use of Tonality in *Peter Grimes*' *Tempo* 66–67 (Autumn–Winter 1963)
GARBUTT, J. W. 'Music and motive in *Peter Grimes*' *Music and Letters* 44 (October 1963)
'*Peter Grimes*; Photographed by Houston Rogers' *Music and Musicians* 12 (November 1963)
GOODWIN, N. 'Maculated *Grimes*' *Music and Musicians* 12 (December 1963)
TRACEY, E. 'London Music' *Musical Times* 104 (December 1963)
'*Peter Grimes*; Sadler's Wells' *Opera* 14 (December 1963)
'Pismo iz Lenningrada' *Sovetskaya Muzyka* 28 (September 1964)
EGAN, J. 'Moscow: The Kirov's *Grimes*' *Opera* 16 (1965)
ROSENTHAL, H. '*Peter Grimes* and the rebirth of British opera' *Performing Right* No. 42 (May 1965)
CROZIER, E. '*Peter Grimes* an unpublished article of 1946' *Opera* 16 (June 1965)
MUSHKE, B. '*Pieter Graimes* (Riga)' *Sovetskaya Muzyka* 29 (July 1965)
BUCHT, B. K. 'Oslo' *Opera* 17 (January 1966)
LANDRY, R. J. 'Met. Echo after Eighteen Years Hints at Contemporary Example' *Variety* 245 (January 1967)

'Complete Issue of Opera News' *Opera News* 31 (February 1967)
KOLODIN, I. 'Music to my Ears' *Saturday Review* 15 (February 4 1967)
McDONALD, K. 'At Home with the Sea' *Opera News* 31 No. 16 (February 11 1967)
HAPKE, W. 'Brittens Oper *Peter Grimes*' *Die Volksbühne* 8 (March 1967)
LEINFRT, F. '*Peter Grimes* im Opernhaus' *Die Volksbühne* 8 (March 1967)
MAYER, M. 'The Met. New *Peter Grimes*' *Hi-Fi/Musical America* 17 (April 1967)
OPPENS, K. 'Ein Engländer in New York' *Opern Welt* 4 (April 1967)
HEINSHEIMER, H. 'New York: Eine denkwürdige Spielzeit' *Neue Zeitschrift für Musik* 128 (May 1967)
ROSENTHAL, H. '*Peter Grimes* and the Rebirth of British Opera' *Performing Right* 42 (May 1967)
SHAWE-TAYLOR, D. '*Peter Grimes* in Stockholm' *The Arts* (1968)
FARO, A. J. 'Rio de Janiero' *Opera* 19 (January 1968)
'*Peter Grimes*; Sadler's Wells' *Opera* 19 (July 1968)
HOWES, F. 'Sadler's Wells' *Musical Times* 109 (August 1968)
GUALERZI, G. 'Turin' *Opera* 19 (August 1968)
'Britten, Strauss and Wagner at Edinburgh' *Opera* 19 (Autumn 1968)
JENKINS, S. 'The Loners: *Peter Grimes* and *Wozzeck*, born over a century ago, are men for today' *Opera News* 33 No. 23 (April 5 1969)
'Metropolitan Opera Broadcast of the Week' *Opera News* 33 No. 23 (April 5 1969)
'Out of the Tempest: pictures of the broadcast opera' *Opera News* 33 No. 23 (April 5 1969)
WEINSTOCK, H. 'New York' *Opera* 20 (June 1969)
CHAPMAN, E. 'Brilliant *Grimes* Revival' *Music Events* 24 (July 1969)
DEAN, W. 'Edinburgh' *Musical Times* 109 (October 1968)
CULSHAW, J. '*Peter Grimes* for television' *Listener* 82 (October 16 1969)
HALL, B. '*Grimes* on Home Ground (television recording in The Maltings)' *Music and Musicians* 18 (November 1969)
ROSENTHAL, H. '*Peter Grimes* on T.V.' *Opera* 20 (December 1969)
SPENCE, K. 'Television' *Musical Times* 110 (December 1969)
MANN, W. '*Peter Grimes* (reprinted from *The Times* May 22 1969)' *About the House* 3 No. 3 (1969)
SLATER, C. 'England' *Opera Canada* 10 No. 3 (1969)
'*Peter Grimes*' *Variety* 254 (March 1969)
'Whole Issue devoted to *Peter Grimes*' *Opera News* 33 (April 1969)
MOVSHON, G. 'The Metropolitan Opera' *Hi-Fi/Musical America* 19 (June 1969)

McGIFFERT, G. W. 'The Musico-dramatic techniques of Benjamin Britten: a detailed study of *Peter Grimes*' Ph.D. *University of Denver* (1970)

DEAVEL, R. G. 'A study of two operas by Benjamin Britten: *Peter Grimes* and *The Turn of the Screw*' Ph.D. *University of Rochester, Eastman School of Music* (1970)

HEYWORTH, P. 'Da Londra (TV)' *Rivista Italiana di Musicologia* 4 (January–February 1970)

KOLODIN, I. 'Music to My Ears' *Saturday Review* 53 (June 1970)

MOVSCHON, G. '*Peter Grimes* on NET' *Hi-Fi/Musical America* 20 (August 1970)

'*Peter Grimes* (photographs of the Covent Garden Production)' *About the House* 3 No. 10 (1971)

TAURAGIS, A. 'B. Britten's opera *Peter Grimes*' *The Music History of Foreign Countries*, 1. Moscow: Muzyka, 1971 (Pitina, S. ed.)

DICKINSON, A. E. 'Renascence' *Music Review* 32 No. 4 (1971)

WARBURTON, A. O. 'Set work for O Level GCE' *Music Teacher and Piano Student* 50 (February 1971)

SLATER, C. '*Peter Grimes*' *Musical Events* 26 (August 1971)

SEIBER, M. 'England, Spring 1945 (2)' *Tempo* 100 (1972)

GARVIE, P. 'Plausible darkness: *Peter Grimes* after a quarter of a century' *Tempo* 100 (Spring 1972)

SACKVILLE-WEST, E. 'Four Sea Interludes and Passacaglia from *Peter Grimes*' AFPB 1972

SNYDER, L. 'Young Opera on Lincoln Center Stages' *Christian Science Monitor* 65 (March 1973)

'Whole Issue devoted to *Peter Grimes*' *Opera News* 37 (March 1973)

FITZGERALD, G. 'New York' *Opera News* 37 (April 1973)

MAYER, M. '*Peter Grimes*' *Hi-Fi/Musical America* 23 (June 1973)

'San Francisco' *Oper und Konzert* 12 No. 2 (1974)

STEDMAN, J. and McELROY, G. 'Chicago' *Opera News* 39 (December 1974)

'*Peter Grimes* (photographs of a new production of Benjamin Britten's opera)' *About the House* 4 No. 10 (1975)

JACOBI, P. 'Chicago' *Opera* 26 (January 1975)

GREENHALGH, J. '*Grimes* at the Garden' *Music and Musicians* 23 July 1975)

'*Peter Grimes*' *Music and Musicians* 24 September 1975)

TAYLOR, P. 'Opera and Ballet in London' *Musical Opinion* 98 (September 1975)

'*Peter Grimes*' *Musical Times* 116 (September 1975)

ROSENTHAL, H. '*Peter Grimes*, Royal Opera, Covent Garden' *Opera* 26 (September 1975)

GREENFIELD, E. 'Glyndebourne, Aldeburgh and Covent Garden' *Hi-Fi/ Musical America* 25 (October 1975)
GRANVILLE BARKER, F. 'London' *Opera News* 40 (November 1975)
'BIRTH OF AN OPERA' BBC Radio (28 September 1976)
SCHMIDGALL, G. 'Britten's opera and its inspiration' *Opera News* 42 No. 7 (1977)
CROSS, J. and AMIS, J. 'Recalling *Peter Grimes*' *Opera* 28 (February 1977)
BRETT, P. 'Britten and *Grimes*' *Musical Times* 118 (December 1977)
HEINSHEIMER, H. 'Born in exile: *Peter Grimes* was conceived in America' *Opera News* 42 No. 7 (1977)
SCHMIDGALL, G. 'Out of the Borough' *Opera News* 42 No. 7 (December 10 1977)
WHITE, E. W. Sleeve note for Philips 6769014 (1978)
HEINITZ, T. and DAVIS, C. 'Recording *Peter Grimes*' *Records and Recording* 21 (August 1978)
PORTER, A. 'What harbour shelters peace?' *New Yorker* (August 3 1978)
ROSENTHAL, H. 'Great recording of a great opera' *Opera* 30 (March 1979)
HEINITZ, T. 'A new Grimes' *Records and Recording* 22 (March 1979)
PORTER, A. 'Hero' *New Yorker* (July 21 1980)
'*Peter Grimes*' *L'Avant-Scene* (January/February 1981)
SCHUMACHER, G. 'The Kassel Music Festival, September 17–20 1981. Music in nature, nature in music' *Musica* 35 1981)
MILNES, R. 'Britten: *Peter Grimes*' *Opera* 32 (1981)
NORTHCOTT, B. 'The search for simplicity' *Times Literary Supplement* (February 15 1980)
BENJAMIN BRITTEN: Peter Grimes; compiled by Philip Brett. Cambridge C.U.P. 1983 (Cambridge Opera Handbook)
BRETT, P. 'Breaking the ice for British opera: *Peter Grimes* on stage'.
  BENJAMIN BRITTEN: Peter Grimes; compiled by Philip Brett. Cambridge, C.U.P. 1983
BRETT, P. 'Postscript'. BENJAMIN BRITTEN: Peter Grimes; compiled by Philip Brett. Cambridge, C.U.P. 1983
BRETT, P. '"Fiery Visions" (and revisions) *Peter Grimes* in progress'.
  BENJAMIN BRITTEN: Peter Grimes; compiled by Philip Brett. Cambridge, C.U.P. 1983
FORSTER, E. M. Two essays on Crabbe. BENJAMIN BRITTEN: Peter Grimes; compiled by Philip Brett. Cambridge, C.U.P. 1983
MATTHEWS, D. 'Act II Scene 1: an examination of the music'. BENJAMIN BRITTEN: Peter Grimes; compiled by Philip Brett. Cambridge, C.U.P. 1983
MITCHELL, D. 'Montagu Slater (1902–1956). Who was he?' BENJAMIN BRITTEN: Peter Grimes; compiled by Philip Brett. Cambridge, C.U.P. 1983

CROSS, J., PEARS, P. and EVANS, J. *'Peter Grimes* and *Gloriana'* PETER GRIMES/GLORIANA Benjamin Britten. London, John Calder, 1983. (English National Opera/The Royal Opera Guide 24)

PETER GRIMES/GLORIANA Benjamin Britten. London, John Calder, 1983. (English National Opera/The Royal Opera Guide 24)

WALSH, S. *'Peter Grimes*: a musical commentary'. PETER GRIMES/GLORIANA Benjamin Britten. London, John Calder, 1983. (English National Opera/The Royal Opera Guide 24)

EVANS, J. Sleeve note for *Four Sea Interludes* EMI ASD 143 6281 (1984)

PALMER, C. 'Chaos and cosmos in *Peter Grimes*' *The Britten Companion*: edited by Christopher Palmer. London, Faber (1984)

PEARS, P. 'On playing Peter Grimes' *The Britten Companion*: edited by Christopher Palmer. London, Faber (1984)

NORTHCOTT, B. 'Since *Grimes*: a concise survey of the British musical stage' *Musical Newsletter* 4 (Spring 1984)

PHAEDRA

BRITTEN, B. *'Phaedra* Op. 93' AFPB 1976

STADLEN, P. 'First performance of Britten's *Phaedra*' *Daily Telegraph* (June 17 1976)

LOPPERT, M. 'Britten's *Phaedra*' *Financial Times* (June 18 1976)

GREENFIELD, E. 'Britten premiere' *Guardian* (June 18 1976)

MANN, W. 'ECO/Bedford Snape Maltings' *Times* (June 18 1976)

LARNER, G. 'Britten's *Phaedra*' *Listener* 95 (June 24 1976)

STRODE, R. *'Phaedra'* AFPB 1977

LARNER, G. 'Britten's *Phaedra*: a kind of sample opera' *Listener* 98 (August 11 1977)

EVANS, J. Sleeve note for EMI EL 270654 1 (1987)

PHANTASY IN F MINOR

EVANS, J. *'Phantasy in F minor* (1932)' AFPB 1983

MITCHELL, D. and EVANS, J. Sleeve note for Unicorn-Kanchana DKP9020 (1983)

EVANS, J. Sleeve note for EMI EX 27 0502 5 (1986)

PHANTASY QUARTET

'The Music Society' *Daily Telegraph* (November 22 1933)

CAPELL, R. 'Markevitch and others: the twenty-year olds at the ISCM Festival' *Daily Telegraph* (April 14 1934)

EVANS, J. *'Phantasy* Opus 2' AFPB 1982

MITCHELL, D. and EVANS, J. Sleeve note for Unicorn-Kanchana DKP 9020 (1983)
EVANS, J. Sleeve note for EMI EX 27 0502 5 (1986)

PIANO CONCERTO
BRITTEN, B. Programme note on the *Piano Concerto*. Promenade Concert. (Thursday 18 August 1938)
'Review of first performance' *Times* (August 19 1938)
LAMBERT, C. 'Music: Britten's new concerto' *Listener* (August 25 1938)
McNAUGHT, W. 'The Promenade concerts' *Musical Times* (September 1938)
ANDERSON, W. R. 'Wireless notes' *Musical Times* (December 1938)
McPHEE, C. 'Scores and Records' *Modern Music* 17 (1939–40)
'New York Philharmonic Programme Notes' (November 27 1949)
HANSON, J. R. 'Macroform in selected Twentieth Century Piano Concertos' *Ph.D. Eastman School of Music University of Rochester* (1969)
BRITTEN, B. *Piano Concerto in D* Op. 13 AFPB 1971

THE POET'S ECHO
SMITH, P. J. 'Galina Vishnevskaya' *Hi-Fi/Musical America* 16 (March 1966)
CRICHTON, R. 'Festival Hall Recitals' *Musical Times* 107 (August 1966)
GREENFIELD, E. 'London Report: Festival in the Ancient City' *Hi-Fi/Musical America* 16 (October 1966)
LARNER, G. 'Song Cycles' *Records and Recording* 12 (May 1969)
RICHARDS, D. *'The Poet's Echo'* Music and Musicians 16 (April 1968)
THORPE, M. *'The Poet's Echo* Op. 76' AFPB 1968
The Poet's Echo Op. 76 AFPB 1975

PRAISE WE GREAT MEN
STIMPSON, M. 'Britten's *Praise We Great Men*' *Tempo* 155 (December 1985)
STRODE, R. *'Praise We Great Men'* Third Rostropovich Festival Programme Book 1985

PRELUDE AND FUGUE
'Prelude and Fugue for 18 part string orchestra' *Musical Opinion* 75 (October 1951)
STRODE, R. *'Prelude and Fugue'* AFPB 1977
STRODE, R. *'Prelude and Fugue* Op 29' AFPB 1985

PRELUDE AND FUGUE ON A THEME OF VITTORIA FOR ORGAN
'Prelude and Fugue on a Theme of Vittoria for Organ' *Musical Opinion* 76 (May 1953)
'Prelude and Fugue on a Theme of Vittoria for Organ' *Notes* 10 (September 1953)

'Prelude and Fugue on a Theme of Vittoria for Organ' *Music and Letters* 34 (October 1953)
'Prelude and Fugue on Theme of Vittoria for Organ' *Music Review* 16 (August 1955)
HARVERSON, A. 'Britten's *Prelude and Fugue*' *Musical Times* 102 (March 1961)
'Prelude and Fugue on a Theme of Vittoria' AFPB 1965
YOUNG, P. M. 'A Survey of Contemporary Organ Music; England' *Church Music* 2 (1967)

THE PRINCE OF THE PAGODAS

'The Prince of the Pagodas' *Tempo* 42 (Winter 1956–1957)
CRANKO, J. 'Making a Ballet' *Sunday Times* (January 13 1957)
'Heiress Presumptive (First Performance)' *Time* 69 (January 14 1957)
HALL, F. 'The New Britten – Cranko Ballet' *Saturday Review* 40 (January 26 1957)
KOEGLER, H. 'Brittens Ballett uraufgeführt' *Musica* 11 (February 1957)
ROSENTHAL, H. 'London witnesses Ballet Premiere' *Musical America* 77 (February 1957)
HASKELL, A. 'The Prince of the Pagodas' *London Music* 12 (February 1957)
DREW, D. 'London (First Performance)' *Musical Courier* 155 (February 1957)
'Sadler's Wells Ballet' *Musical Opinion* 80 (February 1957)
MITCHELL, D. 'Some First Performances' *Musical Times* 98 (February 1957)
PANTER-DOWNES, M. 'Letter from London' *New Yorker* 32 (February 19 1957)
GODDARD, S. 'London Letter (First Performance)' *Chesterian* 31 (Spring 1957)
WALTER, F. 'Das neue Britten – Ballett (First Performance)' *Melos* 24 (March 1957)
KOEGLER, H. 'Brittens *Prinz der Pagoden* in London' *Neue Zeitschrift für Musik* 118 (March 1957)
CLARKE, M. 'The Prince of the Pagodas' *Canon* 10 (April 1957)
DREW, D. 'London' *Musical Courier* 155 (April 1957)
SCHONBERG, H. C. 'Records' *New York Times* 106 (September 15 1957)
SARGEANT, W. 'Near Miss' *New Yorker* 33 (September 28 1957)
SABIN, R. 'Royal Ballet introduces six works new to New York' *Musical America* 77 (October 1957)
KOLODIN, I. 'The aspiring Cranko and the enduring Fonteyn' *Saturday Review* 40 (October 1957)
MARTIN, J. 'The Dance' *New York Yimes* 107 (October 6 1957)
EYSLOVZIL, J. 'Brittenuv *Princ ze zeme Pagod* poprve v CSR' *Hudebni Rozhledy* 12 No. 14 (1959)

EHINGER, H. *'Der Pagodenprinz'* Neue Zeitschrift für Musik 122 (March 1961)
ROSCHIETZ, K. 'Brittens Ballett der *Pagodenprinz* in der Staatsoper' Oesterreichische Musikzeitung 22 (June 1967)
MITCHELL, D. Sleeve note for Decca GOS 558–9 (1968)
PEARS, P. 'Suite from *The Prince of the Pagodas*' AFPB 1974
FABIAN, I. 'Britten-bemutato a Babszinhazban' *Muzsika* 13 (May 1970)
MITCHELL, D. 'Catching on to the technique in Pagoda-land' *Tempo* 146 (September 1983)
MITCHELL, D. 'An after word on Britten's *Pagodas*: the Balinese sources' *Tempo* 152 (March 1985)

THE PRODIGAL SON

'The Prodigal Son' *About the House* 2 No. 11 (1968)
KOCH MARTIN, N. 'El Festival de Flanders' *Buenos Aires Musicale* 23 No. 389 (1968)
MANN, W. 'Dve operni premiery v Aldeburghyu (translated from *The Times*)' *Hudebni Rozhledy* 21 No. 16 (1968)
WOCKER, K. H. 'Brittens Verlorener Sohn' *Musica* 22 No. 5 (1968)
'Britten's Church Operas and the Aldeburgh Festival' *Opera Journal* 1 No. 4 (1968)
KOEGLER, H. 'Zwischen Zirkus und Kirche' *Opern Welt Yearbook* (1968)
SIERPINSKI, Z. 'Holland Festival 1968' *Ruch Muzyczny* 12 No. 16 (1968)
HOLLANDER, H. 'Opernmotiven beim Aldeburgh Festival' *Schweizerische Musikzeitung* 108 No. 5 (1968)
SCHIFFER, B. 'Aldeburgh Festival' *World Music* 10 No. 4 (1968)
PLOMER, W. *'The Prodigal Son'* AFPB 1968
MANN, W. 'Britten's third church opera' *Times* (June 12 1968)
COOPER, M. 'Faultless setting for Britten' *Daily Telegraph* (June 13 1968)
SHAWE-TAYLOR, D. 'The Meeting of East and West' *Sunday Times* (June 16 1968)
MATTHEWS, D. 'Britten's *The Prodigal Son*' *Tempo* 85 (Summer 1968)
GOODWIN, N. 'Punch and *Prodigal*' *Music and Musicians* 16 (August 1968)
SIMMONS, D. 'London Music' *Musical Opinion* 91 (August 1968)
SADIE, S. 'Aldeburgh' *Musical Times* 109 (August 1968)
'Concert Notes' *Strad* 79 (August 1968)
GAL, Z. 'Aldeburgh es Bath – pillanatkepek ket Angliai fesztivalrol' *Musika* 11 (September 1968)
JACOBS, A. *'The Prodigal Son*; Orford Church' *Opera* 19 (Autumn 1968)
GREENFIELD, E. 'A Flowering of Festivals' *Hi-Fi/Musical America* 18 (September 1968)

CHAPMAN, E. 'City of London Festival' *Musical Events* 23 (September 1968)
KELLBERG, E. L. 'Holland: Festival ohne markante Höhepunkte' *Neue Zeitschrift fur Musik* 129 (September 1968)
TUGGLE, R. A. 'Bach, Aldeburgh' *Opera News* 33 (September 1968)
PLEASANTS, H. 'Festival of Britten' *Hi-Fi Review* (October 1968)
MITCHELL, D. Sleeve note for Decca SET 438 (1969)
KASTENDIECK, M. 'Premieres: *Elizabeth*, Britten's *Prodigal* (reprinted from *Christian Science Monitor* July 16 1969)' *Opera Journal* 2 No. 4 (1969)
CRICHTON, R. 'Canada' *Musical Times* 110 (July 1969)
SMITH, P. G. 'Caramoor' *Opera* 20 (Autumn 1969)
MOVSHON, G. 'Britten and Handel at Caramoor' *Hi-Fi/Musical America* 19 (September 1969)
'Katonah, N.Y.' *Opera News* 34 (September 1969)
WEINSTOCK, H. 'New York' *Opera* 21 (March 1970)
JACOBSON, R. 'Britten's Prodigal (recording)' *Saturday Review* 54 (May 1971)
CARSON, E. 'Choral Performances 1968–69: Canada' *American Choral Review* 11 No. 2 (1969)
DIETHER, J. 'A Second and Third One-Act Operas of Benjamin Britten (recordings)' *American Record Guide* 38 (September 1971)
EVANS, J. *'The Prodigal Son'* AFPB 1981
FORBES, E. 'Britten; *The Prodigal Son' Opera* 32 (1981)

PROLOGUE, SONG AND EPILOGUE
R.B. 'The Heart of the Matter' AFPB 1956
EVANS, J. Sleeve note for EMI 27 0653 1 (1987)

PSALM 150
ROSEBERRY, E. 'Britten's *Cantata Misericordium* and *Psalm 150*' *Tempo* 66–67 (Autumn–Winter 1963)
WARBURTON, A. O. 'Set Works for O Level, GCE' *Music Teacher and Piano Student* 49 (April 1970)

THE PUNCH REVUE
BARBER, J. 'The Gods Boo (and Harding growls at) that *Punch Revue' Daily Express* (September 29 1955)
'The Punch Revue' Times (September 29 1955)

PURCELL REALISATIONS
'Purcell Realisations' Tempo 12 (O.S.) (September 1945)
PEARS, P. *'Two Divine Hymns Job's Curse'* AFPB 1948

STEIN, E. *'The Golden Sonata for Two Violins, 'Cello and Figured Bass'* AFPB 1948
PEARS, P. 'Songs by Henry Purcell' AFPB 1949
HOLST, I. 'Purcell: *Sonata (Chacony) in G minor*' AFPB 1950
SWEETING, E. 'Recital of English Songs' AFPB 1951
'Purcell: *The Blessed Virgin's Expostulation*' AFPB 1952
'Purcell: *Cantata: O Lord, Rebuke me not*' AFPB 1952
MALCOLM, G. 'The Purcell Realizations' MITCHELL/KELLER 1952
PEARS, P. 'Homage to the British Orpheus: Henry Purcell 1659–1695' AFPB 1959
ROSEBERRY, E. 'Brittens *Purcell Realisations* and *Folksong Arrangements*' *Tempo* 57 (Spring 1961)
'Purcell: Secular Cantata: *When Night her Purple Veil had softly Spread*' AFPB 1965
WARRACK, J. *'When Night her Purple Veil'* Edinburgh Festival Programme (29 August 1968)
'Chacony in G Minor for Two Violins, Viola and Cello' AFPB 1969
HOLST, I. 'Purcell Made Practicable' *Music and Musicians* 17 (June 1969)
'The Fairy Queen. H. Purcell ed. by B. Britten and I. Holst. Version for Concert Performance by P. Pears' *Music Review* 32 No. 4 (1971)
NOBLE, J. 'Purcell's *Fairy Queen*' *Listener* 86 (September 2 1971)
MITCHELL, D. Sleeve note for Decca SXL 6608 (1972)
BRITTEN, B. *'Chacony in G minor'* AFPB 1973
ROSEBERRY, E. 'The Purcell Realisations' *The Britten Companion*: edited by Christopher Palmer. London, Faber (1984)
REED, P. *'If Music be the Food of love* (version 1); Mad Bess' AFPB 1987
EVANS, J. Sleeve note for EMI 27 0653 1 (1987)

QUARTETTINO
EVANS, J. Sleeve note for EMI EX 27 0502 5 (1986)

QUATRE CHANSONS FRANÇAISES
EVANS, J. *Quatre Chansons Françaises* AFPB 1980
MARK, C. 'Britten's *Quatre Chansons Françaises*' *Soundings* 10 (Summer 1983)
GREENFIELD, E. 'Young Britten' *Guardian* (June 12 1980)
WALSH, S. 'Abundant vitality' *Observer* (June 15 1980)
MITCHELL, D. Sleeve note for EMI ASD 4177 (1982)

THE RAPE OF LUCRETIA
'The Rape of Lucretia' *Tempo* 1 No. 13 (December 1945)

CROZIER, E. 'The Rape of Lucretia Benjamin Britten's Second Opera' The Arts (1946)
BRITTEN, B. 'Introduction to The Rape of Lucretia' in Duncan, R. The Rape of Lucretia (libretto), London, Boosey & Hawkes (1946)
DUNCAN, R. The Rape of Lucretia (libretto), London, Boosey & Hawkes (1946)
CROZIER, E. 'Benjamin Britten's Second Opera: The Rape of Lucretia' Tempo 1 No. 14 (March 1946)
'A new opera for Glyndebourne' Picture Post (July 13 1946)
BONAVIA, F. 'New Britten opera heard in England' New York Times (July 13 1946)
'Glyndebourne Opera – The Rape of Lucretia' Times (July 13 1946)
GRAY, C. 'New Britten Opera' Observer (July 14 1946)
BLOM, E. 'Benjamin Britten's Second Opera' Birmingham Post (July 15 1946)
SHAWE-TAYLOR, D. 'The Rape of Lucretia' New Statesman (July 20 1946)
NEWMAN, E. 'The Rape of Lucretia' Sunday Times (July 21 and 28 1946)
MENGELBERG, K. 'Brittens Nieuwe Opera' Nederland August 3 1946)
BOYS, H. 'Benjamin Britten and The Rape of Lucretia' Con Brio 1 No. 1 (1946)
KLEIN, J. W. 'The Rape of Lucretia. Benjamin Britten's new opera' Musical Opinion (September 1946)
HADDON-SQUIRE, W. H. 'The Aesthetic Hypothesis and The Rape of Lucretia' Tempo 1 (September 1946)
GLOCK, W. 'The Rape of Lucretia' Time and Tide (October 12 1946)
BLOM, E. 'Britten's Roman Opera' Listener (November 3 1946)
ANSERMET, E. 'Benjamin Brittens zweite Oper' Welt von Heute (December 4 1946)
KELLER, H. 'The Rape of Lucretia Albert Herring'. London, Boosey & Hawkes, 1947
COPLAND, A. 'The Rape of Lucretia (review of v.s.)' Notes (March 1947)
KELLER, H. 'Britten's New Opera in London' Reconstruction 12 No. 48 (1947)
WILLIAMS, S. 'Opera in London' Penguin Music Magazine 2 (May 1947)
THE RAPE OF LUCRETIA: A symposium by Benjamin Britten, Ronald Duncan, John Piper, Henry Boys, Eric Crozier, Angus McBean. London, Bodley Head, 1948
BOYS, H. 'Musico-dramatic Analysis in The Rape of Lucretia' The Rape of Lucretia: A Symposium, London, The Bodley Head (1948)
BRITTEN, B. 'Foreword' The Rape of Lucretia: A Symposium, London, The Bodley Head (1948)
CROZIER, E. 'Lucretia 1946' The Rape of Lucretia: A Symposium, London, The Bodley Head (1948)
DUNCAN, R. 'The Libretto: the Method of Work' The Rape of Lucretia: A Symposium, London, The Bodley Head (1948)

PIPER, J. 'The Design of Lucretia' *The Rape of Lucretia: A Symposium*, London, The Bodley Head (1948)

KELLER, H. 'Analytical note No. H. 619' *Excerpts from The Rape of Lucretia*, H.M.V. (March 1948)

EIMERT, H. 'Brittens *Raub der Lukrezia*' *Melos* (December 1948)

THOMPSON, V. 'The Theaters' *New York Herald Tribune* (December 30 1948)

DOWNES, O. '*The Rape of Lucretia*' *New York Times* (December 30 1948)

HAREWOOD, The Earl of 'Programme Notes' *Aldeburgh Festival Programme Book* (1949)

KERMAN, J. '*Grimes* and *Lucretia*' *The Hudson Review* 2 (1949)

'*The Rape of Lucretia* given first radio performance' *Musical America* 69 (January 1 1949)

DOWNES, O. 'Second Thoughts' *New York Times* (January 9 1949)

SMITH, C. '*The Rape of Lucretia* given first New York performance' *Musical America* 69 (January 15 1949)

'*The Rape of Lucretia*, in New York bow' *Musical Courier* 139 (January 15 1949)

'*The Rape of Lucretia*, New York production' *Musical News* 41 (February 1949)

FOERSTER, L. E. 'Obituary for *Lucretia*' *Opera News* 13 (February 7 1949)

Metronome 65 (March 1949)

HAREWOOD, Earl of '*The Rape of Lucretia*' AFPB 1949

PETERSEN, F. S. 'Benjamin Britten og *The Rape of Lucretia*' *Dansk Musiktidsschrift* No. 8 (August 24 1949)

PETERSEN, F. S. 'Omkring *The Rape of Lucretia* (review of THE RAPE OF LUCERTIA: a symposium by Benjamin Britten, Ronald Duncan, John Piper, Henry Boys and Eric Crozier, London, The Bodley Head, 1948)' *Dans Musiktidsschrift* No. 8 (August 24 1949)

BRITTEN, B. 'Programme note for Salzburg Festival' (1950)

KELLER, H. '*Der Raub* und *The Rape*' *Blätter der Salzburger Festspiele* No. 2 (1950)

KELLER, H. 'Zum *Raub der Lukrezia*' *Salzburger Nachrichten* (August 9 1950)

PLEASANTS, H. 'Three New operas at Salzburg Festival' *New York Times* 99 (September 3 1950)

BROECKX, J. L. 'De Festspiele 1950 te Salzburg' *Mens en Mel* 5 (October 1950)

PERL, E. 'Opera Notes; Salzburg, Austria' *Opera News* 15 (October 16 1950)

MITCHELL, D. 'A note on the *Flower aria* and *Passacaglia* in *Lucretia*' *Music Survey* 3 No. 4 (1951)

'*The Rape of Lucretia* (Mulhouse)' *Opera* 2 (May 1951)

DEL MAR, N. '*The Rape of Lucretia*' MITCHELL/KELLER 1952

'*The Rape of Lucretia*' AFPB 1954

SMITH, C. 'Festivals at Glyndebourne, Cheltenham and Aldeburgh' *Musical America* 74 (August 1954)

MITCHELL, D. 'Aldeburgh' *Opera* 5 (August 1954)

ERHARDT, O. 'Chamber Music on a big stage at the Teatro Colón, Buenos Aires' *Tempo* 38 (Winter 1955–56)

'The Royal Theatre' *Musical Denmark* No. 8 (January 1956)

SABISTON, C. 'Second Festival held in Stratford, Ontario (first North American performance)' *Musical America* 76 (August 1956)

'Gelsenkirchen nach 10 Jahren Brittens *Raub der Lukrezia*' *Melos* 25 (May 1958)

BOLLERT, W. 'Brittens *Lukrezia*' *Musica* 12 (June 1958)

'Britten's *The Rape of Lucretia* added to Repertoire' *Musical America* 78 (November 1958)

SARGEANT, W. 'Musical Events' *New Yorker* (November 1 1958)

GISHFORD, A. *'The Rape of Lucretia'* AFPB 1959

ANDREWES, J. *'The Rape of Lucretia'* AFPB 1960

KRENENLIEV, B.' *Los Angeles' Musical Courier* 163 (May 1961)

SADIE, S. *'The Rape of Lucretia*; St Pancras Town Hall' *Opera* 13 (July 1962)

'Edinburgh' *Opera* 14 (Autumn 1963)

'Brittenova Prvni Komorni Opera' *Hudebni Rozhledy* 19 No. 2 (1966)

'Amsterdam: *The Rape of Lucretia* van Benjamin Britten' *Mens en Mel* 22 (January 1967)

SARGEANT, W. 'Musical Events' *New Yorker* 42 (January 1967)

'New York' *Opera News* 31 (February 1967)

'Hamburg: Neues vom Nachwuchs' *Opern Welt* 4 (April 1967)

OPPENS, K. 'Ein Engländer in New York' *Opern Welt* 4 (April 1967)

CROZIER, E. *'The Rape of Lucretia* Benjamin Britten's second opera' *The Arts* (1968)

THOMAS, S. 'English Opera Group at Sadler's Wells Theatre' *Musical Events* 24 (November 1969)

DEAN, W. 'Music in London' *Musical Times* 11 (November 1969)

'London Opera Diary' *Opera* 20 (November 1969)

GRIER, C. *'Lucretia*, Twenty Years After' *Music and Musicians* 18 (December 1969)

SMITH, F. C. 'Baltimore' *Opera News* 34 (December 1969)

FRANZE, J. P. 'Una Opera de Britten en el alvear' *Buenos Aires Musicale* 25 No. 422 (1970)

RACKENANN, A. C. and F. 'Baltimore: Chamber Opera Society Young and Promising' *Hi-Fi/Musical America* 20 (January 1970)

GISHFORD, A. *'The Rape of Lucretia'* AFPB 1970

GREENFIELD, E. 'Aldeburgh: The Maltings Restored' *Opera* 21 (August 1970)
HARRIS, D. 'Britten's *The Rape of Lucretia* (recording)' *Hi-Fi/Musical America* 21 (October 1971)
NOTH, E. F. 'Urbana – Champaign (Illinois)' *Opera* 25 (August 1974)
PORTER, A. 'Music Events; Boris redivivus' *New Yorker* 50 (December 1974)
HAREWOOD, *Earl of* Sleeve note for 1G1 369 (1981)
WECHSLER, B. 'Britten: *The Rape of Lucretia*' *Music Journal* 39 (1981)
SHAWE-TAYLOR, D. 'Britten: *The Rape of Lucretia*' *Opera* 32 (1981)
HEADINGTON, C. '*The Rape of Lucretia*' *The Britten Companion*. Edited by Christopher Palmer. London, Faber (1984)
COLEMAN, B. '*The Rape of Lucretia*' AFPB 1987
COOKE, M. 'Lucretia: From the 1940's to the 1980's' AFPB 1987

REJOICE IN THE LAMB
Tempo 1 No. 8 (September 1944)
HOLST, I. '*Festival Cantata "Rejoice in the Lamb"* (orchestrated by Imogen Holst)' AFPB 1952
'Contemporary Chronicle' *Musical Opinion* 78 (December 1954)
'A Festival Cantata: "Rejoice in the Lamb"' AFPB 1963
WARBURTON, A. O. 'Set Works for O Level, GCE' *Music Teacher and Piano Student* 49 (April 1970)
HOLST, I. '*Rejoice in the Lamb*' AFPB 1972
LEPAGE, P. V. 'Benjamin Britten's *Rejoice in the Lamb*' *Music Review* 33 (May 1972)
ENGLAND, G. A. 'Critique: A Study to provide self-administering improvement in conducting specific rhythmic problems in two choral works of Benjamin Britten (University of Northern Colorado Ed.D.)' *Council for Research in Music Education Bulletin* 38 (Summer 1974)

THE RESCUE
Tempo 1 No. 14 (March 1946)

REVEILLE
EVANS, J. '*Reveille* (1937)' AFPB 1983

RHAPSODY (1929)
EVANS, J. Sleeve note for EMI EX 27 0502 5 (1986)
MATTHEWS, C. '*Rhapsody* (1929)' AFPB 1986

ROSSINI SUITE
REED, P. *Rossini Suite* (1935) AFPB 1987

RUSSIAN FUNERAL
EVANS, J. and MITCHELL, D. *Russian Funeral* (1936) AFPB 1984

SACRED AND PROFANE
WIDDICOMBE, G. *'Sacred and Profane' Financial Times* (September 16 1975)
STADLEN, P. 'Britten's artfulness in latest work' *Daily Telegraph* (September 17 1975)
MATTHEWS, C. *'Sacred and Profane,* Op. 91 AFPB 1987

SAINT NICOLAS
CROZIER, E. *'Saint Nicolas'* AFPB 1948
HOLST, I. 'Britten's *Saint Nicolas' Tempo* 10 (Winter 1948–1949)
KELLER, H. *'Saint Nicolas* (review of vocal score)' *Music Survey* 1 No. 6 (1949)
KELLER, H. 'New Music in the Old Year' *Music Parade* 1 No. 10 (1949)
Musical America 69 (January 1 1949)
Music and Letters 30 (April 1949)
CROZIER, E. *'Saint Nicolas'* AFPB 1949
Monthly Musical Record 79 (September 1949)
KELLER, H. 'First performances' *Music Review* 10 No. 4 (November 1949)
MITCHELL, D. 'A Note on *Saint Nicolas*: some points on Britten's style' *Music Survey* 2 (Spring 1950)
'Saint Nicolas, op. 42' *Music Survey* 2 (Winter 1950)
'Saint Nicolas and Bach *Magnificat* at Union Seminary' *Diapason* 42 (January 1951)
DERRY, W. R. *'Saint Nicolas* – a cantata' AFPB 1951
'Performance and Reviews' *Choral Guide* 5 (January 1953)
DIETZ, B. A. 'Britten Cantata staged in Dayton' *Musical America* 4 (January 1954)
GATHORNE-HARDY, E. *'Saint Nicolas'* AFPB 1955
'Hampstead Christmas Concert' *Strad* 32 (January 1962)
DERRY, W. *'St Nicolas'* AFPB 1963
CRANKSHAW, G. 'Direct Approach Wanted' *Music and Musicians* 14 (June 1966)
WARBURTON, A. O. 'Set works for O Level, GCE' *Music Teacher and Piano Student* 47 (April 1968)
CRICHTON, R. 'King's Lynn' *Musical Times* 110 (September 1969)
STRODE, R. *'Saint Nicolas,* Op. 42' AFPB 1985

SCHERZO
WINTERS, L. 'Playing Benjamin Britten's *Scherzo*' *The Recorder and Music Magazine* 1 No. 4 (February 1964)
NOBLE, R. 'The Recorder in Twentieth Century Music' *The Recorder and Music Magazine* 1 No. 4 (February 1964)

SCOTTISH BALLAD
Tempo 2 (American series) No. 1 (October 1941)
Tempo 2 (American series) No. 2 (February 1942)
Tempo 1 No. 6 (February 1944)
'*Scottish Ballad*, Op. 26, for two pianos and orchestra' *Cincinnati Symphony Programme Notes* (January 20 1956)
MITCHELL, D. Sleeve note for EMI ASD 4177 (1952)

SECHS HÖLDERLIN-FRAGMENTE
SHAWE-TAYLOR, D. 'Collaboration of genius' *Sunday Times* (February 7 1960)
WOOD, H. 'Britten's *Hölderlin Songs*' *Musical Times* 104 (November 1963)
DIETHER, J. 'Benjamin Britten: *Sechs Hölderlin-Fragmente* (recording)' *American Record Guide* 30 (January 1964)
PEARS, P. '*Six Hölderlin Fragments* Op. 61' AFPB 1975

SERENADE
Tempo 1 No. 7 (June 1944)
McDONALD, O. H. 'The Semantics of Music' *Music Survey* 1 No. 4 (September 1948)
Music Survey 1 No. 5 (1949)
BERGER, A. '*Serenade, Op. 31, for tenor, horn and string orchestra* (review of recording)' *Musical Quarterly* 40 (April 1954)
BRITTEN, B. Letter to the Editor regarding a review of the recording of *Serenade for tenor, horn and strings* Tempo 34 (Winter 1954–55)
ROSEBERRY, E. 'A Note on the Four Chords in Act II of *Midsummer Night's Dream*' *Tempo* 66–67 (Autumn–Winter 1963)
'From Peter Pears, third (and best) Britten *Serenade* recording' *American Record Guide* 31 (August 1965)
LICKEY, E. H. 'Part I: An Analysis of Samuel Barber's *Knoxville*, Summer of 1915 Part II: An Analysis of Benjamin Britten's *Serenade*, Op. 31' D.M. *Indiana University* (1969)
'*Serenade* Op. 31' AFPB 1969
GREENHALGH, J. 'Britten's *Serenade*' *Music and Musicians* 17 (August 1969)

WARBURTON, A. O. 'Set works for O Level GCE' *Music Teacher and Piano Student* 53 (February 1974)
MITCHELL, D. '"Forms more real than living man": reflections on Britten's *Serenade* and *Nocturne*'. Programme Book for Peter Pears' Memorial Concert 3 April 1987

SEVEN SONNETS OF MICHELANGELO

Tempo 1 (American series) No. 4 (January 1941)
STRODE, R. *'Seven Sonnets of Michelangelo'* AFPB 1978
MATTHEWS, C. Sleeve note for EMI RLS 748 (1980)
EVANS, J. Sleeve note for Hyperion A 66209 (1986)

A SHEPHERD'S CAROL

Tempo 1.No. 9 (December 1944)

SIMPLE SYMPHONY

ANDERSON, W. R. 'Wireless notes' *Musical Times* (February 1938)
Tempo 1 (American series) No. 4 (January 1941)
'Simple Symphony for String Orchestra' *Strad* 61 (August 1950)
BRITTEN, B. Sleeve note for Decca LW 5163 (1955)
SIMMONS, D. 'Concert Notes' *Strad* 78 (February 1968)

SINFONIA DA REQUIEM

Tempo 1 (American series) No. 3 (September 1940)
Tempo 1 (American series) No. 4 (January 1941)
Tempo 1 (American series) No. 5 (August 1941)
WESTRUP, J. 'The Virtuosity of Benjamin Britten' *Listener* (July 16 1942)
'Promenade Concerts – New work by English composer' *Financial Times* (July 23 1942)
BRITTEN, B. 'How a musical work originates' *Listener* (July 30 1942)
McNAUGHT, W. 'Broadcast music: mainly about Britten' *Listener* (July 30 1942)
'Chicago Symphony Programme Notes' (February 8 1949)
MASON, C. 'Britten's *Sinfonia da Requiem*' *Manchester Guardian* (May 17 1951)
GODDARD, S. 'Programme note for LCC concert' (September 26 1951)
'A modern programme' *Times* (September 27 1951)
MASON, C. 'Modern British Music' *Manchester Guardian* (September 28 1951)
MASON, C. 'Hallé Orchestra: *Sinfonia da Requiem*' *Manchester Guardian* (April 4 1952)
CHAPMAN, E. 'Musical Survey' *London Music* 13 (April 1958)

'BBC Symphony Concert' *Musical Times* 99 (April 1958)
'*Sinfonia da Requiem*, Op. 20' *San Francisco Programme Notes* (March 23 1963)
'*Sinfonia da Requiem*, Op. 20' *Chicago Symphony* (April 25 1963)
'1947–48 Copland – and Previn's Conducting Debut (recording)' *American Record Guide* 30 (August 1964)
'*Sinfonia da Requiem*' *San Francisco Symphony* (December 1964)
STRODE, R. '*Sinfonia da Requiem*' AFPB 1981
MITCHELL, D. Sleeve note for EMI EX 2702631 (1986)
MITCHELL, D. '*Sinfonia da Requiem*, Op. 20' AFPB 1987 and supplementary note 1987

SINFONIETTA

'Concerts and recitals. Patron's Fund Concert – Royal College of Music' *Morning Post* (January 21 1937)
Tempo 1 (American series) No. 3 (September 1940)
TRUSCOTT, H. '*Sinfonietta in D minor, Op. 1*' *Music Survey* 2 (Spring 1950)
STEIN, E. '*Sonfonietta*, Op. 1' AFPB 1952
STEVENS, H. '*Sinfonietta*, Op. 1 (recording)' *Musical Quarterly* 43 (October 1957)
GREENFIELD, E. '*Sonfonietta*, Op. 1' AFPB 1973

SIX METAMORPHOSES AFTER OVID

'Aldeburgh first performance: *Six Metamorphoses after Ovid*, Op. 49' *Times* (June 6 1952)
'*Six Metamorphoses after Ovid*, Op. 49, for oboe solo' *Musical Opinion* 75 (August 1952)
TRANCHELL, P. 'Review' *Music and Letters* 33 No. 4 (October 1952)
'*Six Metamorphoses after Ovid*, Op. 49, for Oboe Solo' *Notes* 10 (September 1953)
FUKAC, J. 'Metamorfozy Brnenskeho Balet' *Hudebni Rozhledy* 20 No. 3 (1967)

SOIRÉES MUSICALES

FRANK, A. 'New orchestral works' *Listener* (January 6 1937)
Tempo 1 (American series) No. 3 (September 1940)
Tempo 1 (American series) No. 4 (January 1941)
Tempo 2 (American series) No. 1 (October 1941)

SONATINA ROMANTICA

PEARS, P. '*Sonatina Romantica* (1940)' AFPB 1983

SONGS AND PROVERBS OF WILLIAM BLAKE

'*Songs and Proverbs of William Blake*' AFPB 1965

GOODWIN, N. 'Suffolk Constellation' *Music and Musicians* 13 (August 1965)
MANN, W. 'Aldeburgh' *Musical Times* 106 (August 1965)
WALSH, S. 'Three New Britten Works' *Tempo* 74 (Autumn 1965)
GREENFIELD, E. 'Bumper Britten Crop' *Hi-Fi/Musical America* 15 (September 1965)
BARKER, F. G. 'Blake by Britten' *Music and Musicians* 14 (February 1966)
'New Works' *Music Journal* 25 (March 1967)
'*Songs and Proverbs of William Blake*' AFPB 1968
WARRACK, J. '*Songs and Proverbs of William Blake*' Edinburgh Festival Programme (29 August 1968)
EVANS, P. Sleeve note for Decca 5XL 6391 (1969)
HAMILTON, D. 'Britten's Unchanged Aesthetic (recording)' *Hi-Fi/Musical America* 19 (November 1969)

SONGS FROM THE CHINESE
AMIS, J. 'Aldeburgh Festival (First Performance)' *Musical Times* 99 (August 1958)
NOBLE, J. 'Britten's *Songs from the Chinese*' *Tempo* 52 (Autumn 1959)

SPRING SYMPHONY
'Spring, Britten's new symphony' *Boston Symphony Concert Bulletin* 20 (March 25 1949)
'*Spring Symphony*' *Times* (July 22 1949)
SHAWE-TAYLOR, D. '*Spring Symphony*' *New Statesman* (July 23 1949)
'*Spring Symphony* to have its world premiere' *Etude* 67 (August 1949)
'*Spring Symphony*' *Musical America* 69 (September 1949)
GOLDBECK, F. 'The Holland Festival and Britten's *Spring Symphony*' *Chesterian* 24 (October 1949)
KELLER, H. 'First performances' *Music Review* 10 No. 4 (November 1949)
HILL, R. 'First performances' *Music* (1950)
BRITTEN, B. A note on the *Spring Symphony*. Music Survey 2 (Spring 1950)
'So they said; First performance' *Music Survey* 2 (Spring 1950)
STEIN, E. 'Britten's *Spring Symphony*' *Tempo* 15 (Spring 1950)
BRITTEN, B. 'A Note on the *Spring Symphony*' *Music Survey* 2 (Spring 1950)
BARKER, G. 'Britten and his *Spring Symphony*' *Philharmonic Post* 5 No. 4 (March–April 1950)
CAPELL, R. 'Britten's new Symphony' *Daily Telegraph* (March 10 1950)
'The *Spring Symphony* – Britten's new work' *Times* (March 10 1950)
SHAWE-TAYLOR, D. 'Britten's *Spring Symphony*' *New Statesman* (March 18 1950)

COOPER, M. 'Music' *Spectator* (March 18 1950)
CARNER, M. 'New Music' *Time and Tide* (March 18 1950)
'*Spring Symphony*: first London performance' *Times* (March 10 1950)
GRAY-FISKE, C. 'London Philharmonic Orchestra (review of 1st English performance)' *Musical Opinion* (April 1950)
'*Spring Symphony*' *Musical Times* 91 (April 1950)
'*Spring Symphony*' *Strad* 60 (April 1950)
'In the Concert Room' *Monthly Musical Record* 80 (May 1950)
'First Performances – their pre – and reviews' *Music Review* 11 (May 1950)
'*Spring Symphony*' *Music Survey* 3 (Summer 1950)
BERKELEY, L. 'Britten's *Spring Symphony*' *Music and Letters* (July 1950)
OTTAWAY, H. 'The *6th Symphony* of Serge Prokofiev and the *Spring Symphony* of Benjamin Britten' *Musical Opinion* 73 (July 1950)
'*Spring Symphony*' *Monthly Musical Record* 80 (September 1950)
KELLER, H. 'Review of *Spring Symphony*' *Music Review* 11 No. 4 (November 1950)
'*Spring Symphony*' *Music Teacher* 29 (November 1950)
'*Spring Symphony*, Op. 44' *Musical Opinion* 74 (March 1951)
BERKELEY, L. 'Benjamin Britten's *Spring Symphony*' *Philharmonic Post* 5 No. 10 (April–May 1951)
MASON, C. 'Britten's *Spring Symphony*' *Manchester Guardian* (May 26 1951)
MASON, C. 'Britten's *Spring Symphony*' *Manchester Guardian* (July 23 1951)
'*Spring Symphony*, Op. 44' *Musical Times* 92 (August 1951)
BLOM, E. 'Vernal Anthology' *Observer* (December 2 1951)
CROZIER, E. 'Symphony of an English Spring' *Radio Times* (May 23 1952)
'*Spring Symphony*' *Musical Times* 94 (July 1953)
KOLODIN, I. 'Music to my Ears' *Saturday Review* 46 (May 1963)
BOLEK, J. 'Vecer teri Premier' *Hudebni Rozhledy* 17 No. 3 (1964)
'*Spring Symphony*' *Cleveland Orchestra* (March 23 1967)
HENDERSON, R. 'Bridge and Britten' *Musical Times* 108 (June 1967)
WERKER, T. '*Spring Symphony* van Benjamin Britten' *Mens en Mel* 23 (April 1968)
GOODWIN, N. '*Spring Symphony*, Op. 44' Edinburgh Festival Programme (18 August 1968)
BRITTEN, B. '*Spring Symphony*, Op. 44' AFPB 1986

STRING QUARTET IN D MAJOR (1931)
STADLEN, P. 'Quartet by Britten at 19 has premiere' *Daily Telegraph* (June 9 1975)

GREENFIELD, E. 'Britten premiere' *Guardian* (June 9 1975)
WIDDICOMBE, G. 'Britten's Quartet' *Financial Times* (June 10 1975)
BRITTEN, B. *'String Quartet in D major'* AFPB 1975
MANN, W. 'Britten's prehistory – Aldeburgh Festival' *Times* (June 10 1975)
ORR, B. *'Quartet for Strings, No. 1, D major.* First performances and commissions of British music' *Composer* 55 (Summer 1975)
GOODWIN, N. 'Aldeburgh' *Music and Musicians* 23 (August 1975)
GREENFIELD, E. 'Glyndebourne, Aldeburgh, Covent Garden 'Hi-Fi/Musical America 25 (October 1975)
EVANS, J. Sleeve note for EMI EX 27 0502 5 (1986)

STRING QUARTET No. 1

Tempo 2 (American series) No. 1 (October 1941)
McPHEE, C. 'Scores and Records' *Modern Music* 20 (1942–43)
'New Chamber Music – Boosey and Hawkes concert' *Times* (April 29 1943)
BERKELEY, L. 'Britten and his String Quartet' *Listener* (May 27 1943)
'Temporada de Musica de Camara' *Revista Musical Chilena* 9 (July 1954)
McCABE, N. 'Bournemouth' *Musical Times* 108 (May 1967)
WHITE, E. W. Sleeve note for Decca SXL 6564 (1972)
EVANS, J. *'String Quartet No. 1 in D major* Op. 25' AFPB 1981
EVANS, J. Sleeve note for EMI EX 27 0502 5 (1986)

STRING QUARTET No. 2

BERKELEY, L. 'Britten and his String Quartet' *Listener* (May 27 1943)
McNAUGHT, W. 'Broadcast music: potentialities' *Listener* (October 14 1943)
Tempo 1 No. 13 (December 1945)
KELLER, H. 'Benjamin Britten *Second Quartet*' *Tempo* 3 (March 1947)
KELLER, H. 'Britten *Second String Quartet*' *Musical Times* (June 1948)
ATKINS, J. 'Chamber Music: an Impression' *Penguin Music Magazine* 6 (June 1948)
STEIN, E. *'String Quartet No. 2 in C* Opus 36' AFPB 1953
DIETHER, J. 'Fine Arts String Quartet' *Musical America* 80 (December 1960)
TRUMPFF, G. A. 'Neue englische Musik (Schallplatten)' *Neue Zeitschrift für Musik* 125 No. 6 (1964)
WARRACK, J. *Quartet No. 2 in C* Op. 36 Edinburgh Festival Programme (29 August 1968)
WHITE, E. W. Sleeve note for Decca SXL 6564 (1972)
POPLE, R. Sleeve note for CRD 1095 (1981)
EVANS, J. Sleeve note for EMI EX 27 0502 5 (1986)

STRING QUARTET No. 3
WIDDICOMBE, G. 'Britten's Op. 94' *Financial Times* (December 20 1976)
COLE, H. 'Britten premiere Maltings, Snape' *Guardian* (December 20 1976)
HEYWORTH, P. 'Midwinter memorial' *Observer* (January 2 1977)
STADLEN, P. 'Leith Hall, Edinburgh, Amadeus Quartet' *Daily Telegraph* (September 12 1977)
MATTHEWS, D. 'Britten's *Third Quartet*' *Tempo* 125 (1978)
MATTHEWS, C. *'String Quarter No. 3*, Op. 94' AFPB 1978
KELLER, H. 'Britten's last masterpiece' *Spectator* (June 2 1979)
POPLE, R. Sleeve note for CRD 1095 (1981)
EVANS, J. Sleeve note for EMI EX 27 0502 5 (1986)
MATTHEWS, D. *'Death in Venice* and *Third String Quartet'*. BENJAMIN BRITTEN: Death in Venice; compiled and edited by Donald Mitchell. Cambridge, C.U.P. 1987

SUITE Op. 6
'New Music – Violin' *Musical Times* (March 1936)
'Notes on the Week's Programmes' *Listener* (March 1936)
'London Concerts – Concerts of Modern music' *Musical Times* (July 1938)

SUITE ON ENGLISH FOLK TUNES
BRITTEN, B. *'Suite on English Folk Tunes "A time there was"'* AFPB 1975
BARRELL, B. 'Regional Report: East Anglia' *Composer* 55 inside back cover (Summer 1975)
ORR, B. 'First Performances and Commissions of British Music' *Composer* 55 (Summer 1975)
GREENFIELD, E. 'Britten premiere' *Guardian* (June 14 1975)
CHISSELL, J. 'Aldeburgh Festival – *Death in Venice* and Patron's Choice' *Times* (June 14 1975)
SHAWE-TAYLOR, D. 'On Britten's home ground' *Sunday Times* (June 22 1975)
GOODWIN, N. 'Aldeburgh' *Music and Musicians* 23 (August 1975)
LOPPERT, M. 'Aldeburgh' *Musical Times* 116 (August 1975)
GREENFIELD, E. 'Glyndebourne, Aldeburgh and Covent Garden' *Hi-Fi/Musical America* 25 (October 1975)
'Suite on English Folk Tunes: "A time there was"' AFPB 1978
MITCHELL, D. Sleeve note for EMI EX 27 02631 (1986)

THE SWORD IN THE STONE
STRODE, R. 'Incidental music from "The Sword in the Stone"' AFPB 1983

THE SYCAMORE TREE
'The Sycamore Tree' AFPB 1968

TE DEUM
POOLER, M. 'Part 1: Analyses of choral settings of the *Te Deum* by the contemporary composers Benjamin Britten, Leo Sowerby, Halsey Stevens and Vincent Persichetti' *M.A. California State University, Fullerton* (1971)

TEMA...SACHER
STRODE, R. '*Tema... Sacher* for solo cello' AFPB 1985

TEMPORAL VARIATIONS
MITCHELL, D. and EVANS, J. Sleeve note for Unicorn-Kanchana DKP 9020 (1983)
MATTHEWS, C. '*Temporal Variations*' AFPB 1980

THIS WAY TO THE TOMB
AMIS, J. 'Composers in the Theatre' *Tempo* 1 No. 13 (December 1945)

THREE DIVERTIMENTI
EVANS, E. 'Brilliant playing by Horowitz' *Daily Mail* (February 26 1936)
'New English music' *Daily Telegraph* (February 26 1936)
EVANS, J. '*Three Divertimenti* (1936)' AFPB 1982
MITCHELL, D. and EVANS, J. Sleeve note for Unicorn-Kanchana DKP 9020 (1983)
EVANS, J. Sleeve note for EMI EX 27 0502 5 (1986)

THREE EARLY SONGS
EVANS, J. Sleeve note for EMI 27 0653 1 (1987)

TIT FOR TAT
BRITTEN, B. '*Tit for Tat*' AFPB 1969
LARNER, G. 'Aldeburgh' *Musical Times* 110 (August 1969)
DEVINE, G. F. '*Tit for Tat*, Five settings from Boyhood of Poems by Walter de la Mare (Review)' *Notes* 27 (September 1970)
MITCHELL, D. Sleeve note for Decca SXL 6608 (1972)
BRITTEN, B. '*Tit for Tat* (1928–31, rev. 1968)' AFPB 1983

TO LIE FLAT ON THE BACK
EVANS, J. Sleeve note for EMI 27 0653 1 (1987)

THE TOCHER
REED, P. The Tocher AFPB 1983

THE TURN OF THE SCREW
Review of first performance *Manchester Guardian* (15 September 1954)
Review of first performance *Times* (15 and 16 September 1954)
MASON, C. 'Britten's New Opera at Venice Festival' *Manchester Guardian Weekly* (September 23 1954)
'Song, Dance, Music' *Newsweek* 44 (September 27 1954)
JOLLY, C. 'Britten Opera' *New York Times* 104 (October 3 1954)
NEWMAN, E. '*The Turn of the Screw*' *Sunday Times* (October 10 1954)
MONTAGU, G. '*The Turn of the Screw*' *London Music* 9 (November 1954)
STEINECKE, W. 'Benjamin Brittens *Sündige Engel* in Venedig' *Melos* 21 (November 1954)
UNGER, M. '*The Turn of the Screw*; First Performance' *Musica* 8 (November 1954)
THORESBY, C. 'Britten Premiere' *Musical America* 74 (November 1954)
NOTCUTT, A. 'London' *Musical Courier* 150 (November 1954)
'The English Opera Group' *Musical Opinion* 38 (November 1954)
'Return of the Screw' *Musical Times* 95 (November 1954)
STEVENS, D. 'Radio Notes' *Musical Times* 95 (November 1954)
'Britten in Venice' *Time* 64 (September 27 1954)
JOLLY, C. 'Venice Turns the Screw' *Opera News* 19 (October 1954)
MILA, M. 'Lettera da Venezia' *Rassegna Musicale* 24 (October–December 1954)
'*The Turn of the Screw*' *Opera* 5 (November 1954)
THORESBY, C. 'Venice Festival' *Strad* 65 (November 1954)
HAMBURGER, P. '*The Turn of the Screw*' *Musikleben* 7 (December 1954)
MILA, M. '*The Turn of the Screw*' *Score* 10 (December 1954)
STEIN, E. '*The Turn of the Screw* and its musical idiom' *Tempo* 34 (Winter 1954–5)
GODDARD, F. S. 'London Letter' *Chesterian* 29 (January 1955)
WEISSMANN, J. S. 'Current Chronicle: Italy' *Musical Quarterly* 41 (January 1955)
'*The Turn of the Screw*' *Musical Opinion* 78 (January and February 1955)
'The Half year's New Music' *Music Review* 16 (February 1955)
REDLICH, H. F. 'New British Operas' *Chesterian* 29 (April 1955)
GLOCK, W. 'Lettera da Londra' *Rassegna Musicale* 25 (April–June 1955)
MITCHELL, D. '*The Turn of the Screw*: A note on its thematic organisation' *Monthly Musical Record* 85 (May 1955)

PIPER, M. *'The Turn of the Screw'* AFPB 1955
NOTCUTT, A. 'Four New British Operas' *Musical Courier* 151 (June 1955)
'Gespenster gehen im Schlosstheater um – Britten dirigiert in Schwetzingen' *Melos* 22 (July–August 1955)
'The Turn of the Screw (Review of Recording)' *Gramophone* 33 (August 1955)
SCHOUTE, R. *'The Turn of the Screw' Mens en Mel* 10 (August 1955)
BRINDLE, R. S. 'The Florence Maggio Musicale' *Musical Times* 96 (August 1955)
BRIGGS, J. 'Records: Britten Opera' *New York Times* 105 (October 2 1955)
'Scala Theatre, English Opera Group' *Opera* 6 (November 1955)
'Britten's Eighth, Walton's First' *Saturday Review* 38 (November 1955)
'The Turn of the Screw. Vocal score by I. Holst' *Musical Opinion* 79 (March 1956)
'The Turn of the Screw. Vocal score by I. Holst' *Music and Letters* 37 (July 1956)
'The Turn of the Screw. Vocal score by I. Holst' *Music Review* 17 (August 1956)
ROSTAND, C. 'Paris hat ein neues Musikfest' *Melos* 23 (October 1956)
Whole issue *Das Neue Forum* 7 (1957/8)
KREHM, W. 'Stratford Gleanings' *Canadian Music Journal* 2 (Autumn 1957)
MILBURN, F. 'Stratford Festival introduces Britten Opera' *Musical America* 77 (September 1957)
'Cheers for Premiere' *Newsweek* 50 (September 2 1957)
THOMAS, E. 'Modernes Darmstadt' *Neue Zeitschrift für Musik* 119 (February 1958)
SARGEANT, W. 'A Glimpse Ahead' *New Yorker* 34 (March 29 1958)
'Of Ghosts and Soap' *Time* 71 (March 31 1958)
'New York News (First US Performance)' *Opera News* 22 (April 1958)
'The Turn of the Screw' Canadian Music Journal 2 (Summer 1958)
'The Turn of the Screw' Musical Courier 157 (May 1958)
MITCHELL, D. 'Television' *Opera* 11 (February 1960)
SWEETING, E. *'The Turn of the Screw'* AFPB 1961
DUNN, R. W. 'Boston' *Musical Courier* 163 (August 1961)
STORREY, W. A. *'The Turn of the Screw* in Boston' *Opera* 12 (October 1961)
BOCCIA, B. *'The Turn of the Screw* di Benjamin Britten' *Rassegna Musicale* 32 Nos 2–4 (1962)
KOLODIN, I. 'Music to my Ears' *Saturday Review* 45 (April 7 1962)
HELM, E. *'The Turn of the Screw' Musical America* 82 (May 1962)
REPASS, R. 'Five Homegrown Operas' *Opera* 13 (July 1962)
'The Turn of the Screw; Sadler's Wells *Opera* 13 (December 1962)
PIPER, M. 'Some thoughts on the Libretto of *The Turn of the Screw*' TRIBUTE TO BENJAMIN BRITTEN ON HIS FIFTIETH BIRTHDAY; edited by Anthony Gishford. London, Faber, 1963

MITCHELL, D. 'Britten's Revisionary Practice: Practical and Creative' *Tempo* 66–67 (Autumn–Winter 1963)
GOLEA, A. 'Les Surprises de l'Opéra de Marseille' *Musique (Chaix)* 132 (March 1965)
GOODWIN, N. 'Campus Opera' *Music and Musicians* 14 (April 1966)
BLYTH, A. '*The Turn of the Screw*. Morley College' *Opera* 17 (April 1966)
DANNENBERG, P. 'Gemütliches und beklemmendes' *Opern Welt* 3 (March 1977)
'Gelsenkirchen: Ohne Uberzeugungskraft' *Opern Welt* 5 (May 1967)
ROEWADE, S. A. 'Copenhagen' *Opera* 18 (June 1967)
KOEGLER, H. 'Gelsenkirchen' *Opera* 18 (July 1967)
'*The Turn of the Screw*' *Opera* 19 (Autumn 1968)
GOLEA, A. 'Le Tour D'Ecrou de Britten à Tours' *Journal de Musique Français* 177 (February 1969)
'Helsinki' *Opera* 20 (May 1969)
CRICHTON, R. 'Music in London' *Musical Times* 110 (October 1969)
LOWENS, I. and HUME, E. 'Britten in Washington' *American Music Digest* 1 (December 1969)
DEAVEL, R. G. 'A study of two operas by Benjamin Britten: *Peter Grimes* and *The Turn of the Screw*' Ph.D. *University of Rochester, Eastman School of Music* (1970)
'Washington, D.C.' *Opera News* 34 (January 1970)
'Washington, D.C.' *Opera* 21 (March 1970)
MARTIN, G. 'Another Turn' *Opera News* 34 (March 1970)
'Washington, D.C.' *Musical Times* 111 (April 1970)
'New York' *Opera News* 34 (April 1970)
SMITH, P. J. 'New York City Opera' *Hi-Fi/Musical America* 20 (May 1970)
GOODWIN, N. 'Two New Scottish Productions' *Music and Musicians* 18 (June 1970)
'New York' *Opera* 21 (June 1970)
KRAUSE, J. 'Resumme einer Spielzeit' *Opern Welt* 8 (August 1970)
WILSON, C. 'Scottish Opera Post Script' *Opera* 21 (September 1970)
BONISCONTI, A. M. 'Da Roma' *Nuova Revista Musicale Italiana* 4 (November–December 1970)
OPPENS, K. 'New York: Crime and Sex' *Opern Welt* 6 (June 1971)
GREENHALGH, J. 'English Opera' *Music and Musicians* 20 (November 1971)
HOWARD, P. 'Music in London' *Musical Times* 112 (November 1971)
LOPPERT, M. 'Italy' *Music and Musicians* 20 (April 1972)
MITCHELL, D. '*The Turn of the Screw*' AFPB 1972

INGLIS, R. 'Scotland' *Opera Canada* 14 No. 2 (1973)
REYNOLDS, M. '*The Turn of the Screw* (English Opera Group)' *Music and Musicians* 22 (December 1973)
HOWARD, P. '*The Turn of the Screw* (English Opera Group)' *Musical Times* 114 (December 1973)
'Le Tour d'Ecrou de Britten' *Schweizerische Musikzeitung* 114 No. 1 (1974)
GIFFIN, G. 'The Colorado Opera Festival: Good News from the Rockies' *Hi-Fi/Musical America* 25 (October 1975)
ECKERT, T. 'Soprano faces supreme test in Met. debut' *Christian Science Monitor* 67 (November 1975)
SCHOLL-PEDERSEN, K. 'Benjamin Britten: *The Turn of the Screw*: an exemplification of Britten's operatic ideas' *M.A. University of Copenhagen* (1976)
CORSE, S. 'From Narrative to Music: Benjamin Britten *The Turn of the Screw*' *University of Toronto Quarterly* 51 (1981)
BAKER, N. 'Britten's musical and dramatic *Screw*' *Washington Opera Magazine* (Winter 1982/3)
PIPER, M. *'The Turn of the Screw'* AFPB 1983
MITCHELL, D. *'The Turn of the Screw'* AFPB 1983
KENNEDY, M. Sleeve note for Philips 410 426–1 (1983)
GOWERS, J. M. 'What has she written?' *M.Mus. University of Surrey* (1983/4)
MELLERS, W. 'Turning the Screw' *The Britten Companion*: edited by Christopher Palmer. London, Faber (1984)
BENJAMIN BRITTEN: The Turn of the Screw; edited by Patricia Howard. Cambridge, C.U.P., 1985 (Cambridge Opera Handbook)
EVANS, J. 'The Sketches: chronology and analysis'. BENJAMIN BRITTEN: The Turn of the Screw; edited by Patricia Howard. Cambridge, C.U.P., 1985 (Cambridge Opera Handbook)
JONES, V. 'Henry James's *The Turn of the Screw*'. BENJAMIN BRITTEN: The Turn of the Screw; edited by Patricia Howard. Cambridge, C.U.P., 1985 (Cambridge Opera Handbook)
HOWARD, P. 'Myfanwy Piper's *The Turn of the Screw*: libretto and synopsis'. BENJAMIN BRITTEN: The Turn of the Screw; edited by Patricia Howard. Cambridge, C.U.P., 1985 (Cambridge Opera Handbook)
HOWARD, P. 'Structure: an overall view'. BENJAMIN BRITTEN: The Turn of the Screw; edited by Patricia Howard. Cambridge, C.U.P., 1985 (Cambridge Opera Handbook)
HOWARD, P. *'The Turn of the Screw*: in the theatre'. BENJAMIN BRITTEN: The Turn of the Screw; edited by Patricia Howard. Cambridge, C.U.P., 1985 (Cambridge Opera Handbook)
PALMER, C. 'The colour of the music'. BENJAMIN BRITTEN: The Turn of the Screw; edited by Patricia Howard. Cambridge, C.U.P., 1985 (Cambridge Opera Handbook)

STIMPSON, M. *Drama and meaning* in *The Turn of the Screw Opera Quarterly* 4 No. 3 (Autumn 1986)

TWELVE VARIATIONS (1931)
MATTHEWS, C. '*Twelve Variations* (1931) for piano solo' AFPB 1986

TWO INSECT PIECES
MATTHEWS, C. '*Two Insect Pieces*' AFPB 1980
MITCHELL, D. and EVANS, J. Sleeve note for Unicorn-Kanchana DKP 9020 (1983)

UNDERNEATH THE ABJECT WILLOW
'Songs – Boosey and Hawkes' *Musical Times* (January 1938)

VARIATIONS ON A THEME OF FRANK BRIDGE
'London Concerts – String Orchestra' *Musical Times* (November 1937)
RUBBRA, E. 'Review of Full Score of *Variations on a Theme of Frank Bridge*' *Music and Letters* 19 (July 1938)
Tempo 1 No. 1 (January 1939)
Tempo 1 (American series) No. 4 (January 1941)
'*Variations for String Orchestra on a Theme of Frank Bridge*, Op. 10' *Boston Symphony Concert Bulletin* 14 (February 3 1950)
'*Variations on a Theme of Frank Bridge* for string orchestra, Op. 10' *Musical Opinion* 74 (September 1951)
'*Variations on a Theme of Frank Bridge*, Op. 10 for String Orchestra' *Music and Letters* 33 (January 1952)
HASKELL, A. L. 'John Cranko's New Ballet' *London Music* 9 (August 1954)
LEWINSKI, W. E. von 'Hindemith and Britten – zweimal Thema mit Variationen' *Musik und Szene* 8 No. 5 (1963–64)
'Early Britten – by Britten and Pears (recording)' *Hi-Fi/Musical America* 18 (July 1968)
'Night Moves' AFPB 1982
STRODE, R. '*Variations on a theme of Frank Bridge*' AFPB 1983

VARIATIONS ON AN ELIZABETHAN THEME (SELLENGER'S ROUND)
'*Variations on Sellenger's Round* For String Orchestra' AFPB 1953
STRODE, R. '*Variations on an Elizabethan Theme (Sellenger's Round)*' AFPB 1980

VIOLIN CONCERTO
'Benjamin Britten's *Violin Concerto*' *Tempo* 1 (American series) No. 2 (April 1940)
DOWNES, O. 'Britten concerto in premiere here' *New York Times* (March 29 1940)
BRENNECKE, W. 'Strauss, Britten, Sibelius' *Musica* 11 (December 1957)
BROWN, P. 'Fugal Flop' *Music and Musicians* 15 (June 1967)

GOODWIN, N. *'Concerto for Violin and Orchestra* Op. 15' Edinburgh Festival Programme Book (18 August 1968)
CRICHTON, R. 'Music in London' *Musical Times* 110 (April 1969)
ORGA, A. 'Fresh New World' *Music and Musicians* 17 (May 1969)
BOWEN, M. 'Lubotsky's Devastating Skill' *Music and Musicians* 19 (September 1970)
BRITTEN, B. *'Violin Concerto* Op. 15' AFPB 1971
CROSSE, A. 'Birmingham' *Musical Times* 115 (February 1974)

VOCAL MUSIC
BREWSTER, R. G. 'The relationship between poetry and music in the original solo vocal works of Benjamin Britten through 1965' *Ph.D Washington University* (1967)

VOICES FOR TODAY
'Voices for Today' *New York Philharmonic* (October 25 1965)
'Eloquent Britten work speaks to U.N.' *Times* (October 25 1965)
COLE, H. 'Britten's *Voices for Today*' *Tempo* 75 (Winter 1965/66)
PORTER, A. 'Occasional Britten' *Musical Times* 106 (December 1965)
THANT, U. 'United Nations 20th Anniversary Concert Message' *Pan Pipes* 58 No. 3 (1966)
'Voices for Today' *Pan Pipes* 58 No. 3 (1966)
NOBLE, J. 'Aldeburgh Festival' *Musical Times* 107 (August 1966)
GOODWIN, N. *'Voices for Today* Op. 75' Edinburgh Festival Programme (18 August 1968)
EVANS, J. *'Voices for Today,* Op. 75' AFPB 1985

WAR REQUIEM
EVANS, P. 'Britten's *War Requiem*' *Tempo* 61-2 (1962)
RAYMENT, M. 'Brittenovo Rekievien v Coventry a Sostakovicovy Symfonie e Londyne' *Hudebni Rozhledy* 15 Nos 23-4 (1962)
'Das Weltmusikfest in London' *Schweizerische Musikzeitung* 102 No. 4 (1962)
HOLST, I. 'Britten's *War Requiem*' *Musical Events* 17 (May 1962)
ROBERTSON, A. 'Britten's *War Requiem*' *Musical Times* 103 (May 1962)
'Britten's masterpiece denounces war' *Times* (May 25 1962)
PANTER-DOWNES, M. 'Letter from Coventry' *New Yorker* 38 (June 1962)
HEYWORTH, P. 'The Two Worlds of Modernism' *Observer* (June 3 1962)
SHAFFER, P. 'The pity war distilled: *War Requiem*' *Time and Tide* 43 (June 7 1962)

HEYWORTH, P. 'New Music to Consecrate a New Cathedral' *New York Times* 111 (June 17 1962)
WARRACK, J. 'Britten and Tippett at Coventry' *Canon* 15 (July 1962)
GOODWIN, N. 'Coventry Phoenix' *Music and Musicians* 10 (July 1962)
COOPER, M. 'Britten, Tippett, Bliss' *Musical America* 82 (July 1962)
MASON, C. 'Two New Choral Works' *Musical Events* 17 (July 1962)
WEBSTER, E. M. 'Coventry – The Latter Glory' *Musical Opinion* 85 (July 1962)
PORTER, A. 'The Coventry Festival' *Musical Times* 103 (July 1962)
GOODWIN, N. 'London; Festivals on the Outskirts' *Music Magazine* 164 (August 1962)
CAIRNS, D. 'Sublime compassion: *War Requiem*' *Spectator* (December 21 1962)
PLOMER, W. Sleeve note for Decca SET 252–3 (1963)
'Grabacion Monumental de una obra memorable *War Requiem* de Benjamin Britten' *Buenos Aires Musical* 18 No. 296 (1963)
HOLZKNECHT, V. '*Requiem* Britten o valce' *Hudebni Rozhledy* 16 No. 14 (1963)
MITCHELL, D. 'Britten a jeho rekviem o valce' *Hudebni Rozhledy* 16 No. 20 (1963)
'*War Requiem*' *Music and Letters* 44 No. 2 (1963)
BOLLERT, W. 'Henze, Britten, Kaminski, Janacek' *Musica* 17 No. 2 (1963)
'Lenox, Masachusetts' *Musical Quarterly* 49 No. 4 (1963)
KONDRACHI, M. 'List z USA' *Ruch Muzyczny* 7 No. 19 (1963)
OEHLMANN, W. 'Das Requiem von Coventry' *Neue Zeitschrift für Musik* 124 No. 1 (1963)
ERHARDT, L. 'Benjamin Britten, kompozytor Tradycyjny' *Ruch Muzyczny* 7 No. 23 (1963)
JAKSIC, D. 'Ratni Rekvijem Benjamina Brittena' *Zvuk* 60 (1963)
STUCKENSCHMIDT, H. H. 'Karajan auch in Schoenbergs Orchestervariationen vorbildlich' *Melos* 30 (January 1963)
'*War Requiem*' *Music and Musicians* 11 (January 1963)
NOBLE, J. 'War and the Pity of War' *Music and Musicians* 11 (January 1963)
'*War Requiem*' *Musical Opinion* 86 (January 1963)
'Emotion and technique in Britten's *War Requiem*' *Times* (January 11 1963)
MASON, C. 'Benjamin Britten's Monumental *War Requiem*' *Canon* 16 (February 1963)
'The Missing Page (Campaign for Nuclear Disarmament Advertisement)' *Music and Musicians* 11 (February 1963)
NOBLE, A. 'Applauded *Requiem*' *Music and Musicians* 11 (February 1963)
WARRACK, J. 'A New Look at Gustav Holst' *Musical Times* 104 (February 1963)

HEINITZ, T. 'The Other Side' *Saturday Review* 46 (February 23 1963)
MASON, E. 'Music in Concert; Britten's *War Requiem*' *Choir* 54 (March 1963)
GOODWIN, N. 'Solemn Hush (reaction of the Church)' *Music and Musicians* 11 (March 1963)
TRACEY, E. 'London Music' *Musical Times* 104 (March 1963)
JOUBERT, J. 'Birmingham: Britten's *War Requiem*' *Musical Times* 104 (April 1963)
GOODWIN, N. 'Britten's *War Requiem*' *Records and Recording* 6 No. 8 (May 1963)
KOLODIN, I. 'Britten's *War Requiem*' *Saturday Review* 46 (May 25 1963)
BARKER, F. G. 'And Bugles Answer'd (recording)' *Music and Musicians* 11 (June 1963)
ERICSON, R. 'Records: Britten's *War Requiem*' *New York Times* 112 (June 16 1963)
WESTBROOK, F. B. 'Britten's *War Requiem*, a Remarkable Achievement' *Choir* 54 (July 1963)
'New Gramophone Records' *Musical Opinion* 86 (July 1963)
DIETHER, J. 'From London, Britten's Overpowering *War Requiem* (recording)' *American Record Guide* 29 (August 1963)
WHITTALL, A. 'Tonal instability in Britten's *War Requiem*' *Music Review* 24 No. 3 (August 1963)
ARDOIN, J. 'A Warning for Our Time (recording)' *Musical America* 83 (August 1963)
KRAUSE, E. 'Otto Reinhold und Benjamin Britten' *Musik und Gesellschaft* 13 (August 1963)
KOLODIN, I. 'Music to my Ears' *Saturday Review* 46 (August and November 1963)
MACGOWEN, W. 'Recitals and Concerts' *American Organ* 46 (September 1963)
KENYON, N. 'New Recordings: Britten's *War Requiem*' *Choir* 54 (September 1963)
WERKER, G. 'Het *War Requiem* van Benjamin Britten' *Mens en Mel* 18 (September 1963)
REYNOLDS, M. 'Muted *Requiem*' *Music and Musicians* 12 (September 1963)
CHAPIN, L. 'Massachusetts' *Musical America* 83 (September 1963)
HARRISON, J. S. 'The New York Music Scene' *Musical America* 83 (November 1963)
SARGEANT, W. 'Musical Events' *New Yorker* 39 (November 1963)
GROSS, C. 'Britten's Masterpiece?' *Listen* 1 (December 1963)
WEBSTER, E. M. 'Lines of Communication' *Musical Opinion* 87 (December 1963)

'Discos' *Arte Musicale* 29 Nos. 20–22 (1963–64)

PICKER, M. 'Benjamin Britten's *War Requiem*' *American Choral Review* 6 No. 2 (1964)

UNGERER, I. D. 'Britten's *War Requiem*' *Musica* 18 No. 2 (1964)

'*Requiem Wojenne*' *Ruch Muzyczny* 8 No. 9 (1964)

BARKER, F. G. 'Britten Conducts' *Music and Musicians* 12 (February 1964)

ROBIN, H. 'California/Reverberation Time' *Musical America* 84 (July 1964)

'Eindhoven' *Mens en Mel* 19 (December 1964)

JURIK, M. 'Valecne Rekviem v Bratislave' *Hudebni Rozhledy* 18 No. 22 (1965)

RIMMER, F. 'Sequence and Symmetry in Twentieth Century Melody' *Music Review* 26 No. 1 (1965)

FIECHTNER, H. A. 'Ravel und Britten' *Musica* 19 No. 1 (1965)

PAYNE, A. 'Golden *Requiem*' *Music and Musicians* 13 (January 1965)

POP'BALENI, V. '*Recviem de Razboi* de Benjamin Britten' *Muzica* 15 (January 1965)

ZHITONIRSKY, D. 'Voennyy Rekvien Brittena' *Sovetskaya Muzyka* 29 (May 1965)

HARRIS, J. 'On Performing the *War Requiem*' *Making Music* 58 (Summer 1965)

'Mahnung und Verpflichtung; Brittens *War Requiem* in Dresden' *Musik und Gesellschaft* 15 (June 1965)

PAYNE, A. 'Blurred Britten' *Music and Musicians* 13 (July 1965)

'*War Requiem* Opus 66' *Notes* 22 No. 2 (1965–66)

'*Requiem de Guerra* de Britten' *Buenos Aires Musicale* 21 No. 353 (1966)

VOLEK, J. 'Brittenuv pomnik obeten valky' *Hudebni Rozhledy* 19 No. 4 (1966)

HURD, M. 'Britten's *War Requiem*' *Music in Education* 30 No. 318 (1966)

GREENFIELD, E. 'London Report' *Hi-Fi/Musical America* 16 (April 1966)

SKUL'SKY, A. 'Moskovskie prem'ery: Voennyy Reqviem Brittena' *Sovetskaya Muzyka* 30 (September 1966)

ORLOV, G. 'Britten's *War Requiem*' *Questions of Theory and Aesthetics of Music*; Part V. Leningrad, Muzyka (1967) (Tjulin, J. N. ed.)

LEMMONDS, W. W. 'Benjamin Britten's *War Requiem* (reprinted from *Emory University Quarterly*, Winter 1965)' *Choral Journal* 8 No. 1 (1967)

STOCKL, R. 'Nürnberg' *Neue Zeitschrift für Musik* 128 (February 1967)

SARGEANT, W. 'Musical Events' *New Yorker* 43 (April 1967)

STEVENSON, R. 'Britten's *War Requiem*' *Listener* 78 (November 2 1967)

JACOBSON, B. 'Chicago' *American Choral Review* 10 No. 4 (1968)

'Edinburgh Festival 1968' *Music* (SMA) 2 No. 4 (1968)

SCHWINGER, E. 'Britten und Pears: Berlin' *Musica* 22 No. 2 (1968)

'Concert Notes' *Strad* 79 (August 1968)

GOODWIN, N. *'War Requiem'* Edinburgh Festival Programme (1 September 1968)
BOYD, M. 'Britten, Verdi and the Requiem' *Tempo* 86 (Autumn 1968)
TSCHULIK, N. 'Aus den Wiener Konzertsaalen' *Oestereichische Musikzeitung* 23 (December 1968)
CRANKSHAW, G. 'Double Command' *Music and Musicians* 17 (January 1969)
SCHAEFER, H. 'Schallplatten Mosaik' *Musik und Gesellschaft* 19 (May 1969)
HALL, W. D. 'A Requiem Mass: a study of performance practices from the Baroque era to the present day as related to four requiem settings by Gilles, Mozart, Verdi and Britten' *D.M.A. University of Southern California* (1970)
COX, R. 'Student Concern Fires War Requiem Venture' *Choral Journal* 11 No. 1 (1970)
FIERZ, G. 'Brittens *War Requiem*' *Schweizerische Musikzeitung* 110 No. 2 (1970)
CRICHTON, R. 'Music in London (Tenth Anniversary)' *Musical Times* 113 (March 1972)
LAWRENCE, R. 'Orchestral' *Music and Musicians* 20 (April 1972)
'War Requiem Brittena na Slasku' *Ruch Muzyczny* 18 No. 4 (1974)
JIRKO, I. 'Brittenovo Valecne Rekviem' *Hudebni Rozhledy* 28 No. 3 (1975)
JOHNSON, L. B. 'Milwaukee: *War Requiem*' *Hi-Fi/Musical America* 25 (May 1975)
JUUL-HANSEN, A. 'Benjamin Britten's *War Requiem* and Wilfred Owen's text' *Musikforskning* 3 (1977)
WEBER, H. 'The 1981 Frankfurt-Feste' *Musica* 35 (1981)
SCHMITT, F. P. 'The Workhouse' *Sacred Music* 108 (1981)
OTTAWAY, H. Sleeve note for EMI SLS 1077573 (1983)
'War Requiem The First Performances' A Tribute to Peter Pears 1910–1986. Royal Opera House, Covent Garden 30 November 1986

A WEALDEN TRIO
'A Wealden Trio' AFPB 1968

A WEDDING ANTHEM
'A Musical Occasion (Harewood Wedding)' *Times* (September 30 1949)
'A Wedding Anthem' AFPB 1950
'A Wedding Anthem' *Music Review* 13 (May 1952)
MITCHELL, D. 'The Poetic Image; a Note on Britten's *Wedding Anthem*' *Tempo* 25 (Autumn 1952)

WELCOME ODE
HENDERSON, R. 'Ipswich Corn Exchange: *Welcome Ode*' *Daily Telegraph* (July 12 1977)

'Britten and the writing of *Welcome Ode*' (K. Shaw) BBC R3 1977

WHO ARE THESE CHILDREN?
WALSH, S. 'A chilly chamber' *Observer* (March 14 1971)
'Cardiff' *Musical Times* 112 (May 1971)
'Cardiff' *Music and Musicians* 19 (June 1971)
GREENFIELD, E. 'The Proms, Aldeburgh, Glyndebourne' *Hi-Fi/Musical America* 21 (December 1971)
PEARS, P. *'Who are these children?* Op. 84' AFPB 1972
MITCHELL, D. Sleeve note for Decca SXL 6608 (1972)
MANN, W. 'Britten/Pears. Maltings, Snape' *Times* (June 5 1972)
MANN, W. 'Britten, Pears and Soutar in childhood's lyrics, rhymes and riddles' *Times* (June 6 1972)
GOODWIN, N. 'Aldeburgh' *Music and Musicians* 21 (September 1972)
ROGERS, J. S. 'A study of the relationship between poetry and music in Benjamin Britten's song cycle *Who are these children?* Op. 84' M.Mus. University of Southern Illinois at Carbondale (May 1977)
EVANS, P. Sleeve note for *Dawtie's Devotion, Tradition, The Gully* EMI 27 06531 (1987)

WINTER WORDS
'Leeds Triennial Festival' *Manchester Guardian Weekly* (October 15 1963)
'Britten and Marschner' *Musical Opinion* 77 (January 1954)
KELLER, H. 'The Half Year's New Music' *Music Review* 15 (February 1954)
MITCHELL, D. 'Songs' *Musical Times* 95 (March 1954)
'*Winter Words* (T. Hardy), for high voice and piano' *Musical Opinion* 78 (December 1954)
'*Winter Words* (T. Hardy)' *Musical Courier* 151 (January 1955)
'*Winter Words* (T. Hardy)' *Musical Times* 96 (April 1955)
'*Winter Words* (T. Hardy)' *London Music* 10 (May 1955)
'*Winter Words* (T. Hardy)' *Music and Letters* 36 (July 1955)
'*Winter Words* (T. Hardy)' *Musical America* 75 (December 1955)
'*Winter Words*; for high voice and piano' *Music Review* 17 (August 1956)
WILLIAMS, P. '*Winter Words* Op. 52' Edinburgh Festival Programme (3 September 1968)
EVANS, J. Sleeve note for Hyperion A66209 (1986)
EVANS, J. Sleeve note for *The Children and Sir Nameless* and *If it's ever spring again* for EMI 27 0653 1 (1987)

YOUNG APOLLO
STRODE, R. *'Young Apollo'* AFPB 1979
MITCHELL, D. 'Sleeve note for *Young Apollo*' EMI ASD 4177 (1982)
YOUNG APOLLO (TV Documentary) BBC TV 1985

THE YOUNG PERSON'S GUIDE TO THE ORCHESTRA
KELLER, H. 'A Film Analysis of the Orchestra' *Sight and Sound* 16 No. 61 (Spring 1947)
SHAWE-TAYLOR, D. *'Instruments of the orchestra' New Statesman* (February 1 1947)
CAMERON, K. and KELLER, H. 'Correspondence on *Instruments of the Orchestra*' *Sight and Sound* 16 No. 62 (Summer 1947)
GERMAIN, J. *'Variations et fugue sur un thème de Purcell' Disques* 3 Nos 23–4 (1950)
LONCHAMPT, J. *'Les Variations sur un thème de Purcell* de Benjamin Britten' *Journal des Jeunesses Musicales de France* 3e année No. 3 (November 21 1950)
'Young Person's Guide to the Orchestra' *Music Teacher and Piano Student* (September 1947)
'Variations and Fugue on a Theme of Purcell' *Philharmonia Orchestra Programme Notes* (January 28 1955)
'Variations and Fugue on a Theme by Purcell Op. 34' *San Francisco Symphony Programme Notes* (February 14 1957)
'Variations and Fugue on a Theme of Purcell Op. 34' *National Symphony Programme Notes* (February 6 1962)
SCHUBERT, L. 'Benjamin Brittens *The Young Person's Guide to the Orchestra* und seine Behandlung in Musikunterricht' *Musik in Schule* 18 No. 7–8 (1967)
BOOKSPAN, M. 'The Basic Repertoire (recordings)' *Stereo Review* 26 (March 1971)
REED, P. 'Instruments of the Orchestra' AFPB 1983
EVANS, J. Sleeve note for EMI ASD 143 6281 (1984)

INDEX OF BRITTEN'S WORKS

A.M.D.G. (Hopkins) for mixed chorus 42, 184
Adagio ma non Troppo – Allegro quasi Presto 8
Advance Democracy (film) 143
Advance Democracy (motet) 41, 143
The Agamemnon 33, 146
Ah fly not, pleasure, pleasant-hearted pleasure (Wilfred S. Blunt), for two voices and piano 17
Albert Herring Op.39 62, 64, 65, 68, 76, 84, 98, 100, 169, 184–7
Alla Marcia, for string quartet 23, 188
Alla Quartetto Serioso 'Go Play, Boy, Play' 23, 25, 30, 189
   Alla Valse, arranged for flute, oboe and piano 25
   Alla Romanza, arranged for flute, oboe and piano (incomplete) 25
Allegro (1925), for orchestra (incomplete) 5
Allegro (1926), for orchestra (incomplete) 8
Allegro con Spirito, for piano 5
Allegro Maestoso, for piano and orchestra 8
Allegro Moderato, orchestra 12
Allegro Molto e con Brio (incomplete), for orchestra 5
Alleluia! For Alec's 80th Birthday 117
Alpine Suite 81, 189
Am Stram Gram 79, 153, 153 n. 32
An American in England No. 1: London by Clipper 51, 159
An American in England No. 2: London to Dover 51, 159–60
An American in England No. 3: Ration Island 51, 160
An American in England No. 4: Women of Britain 53, 161
An American in England No. 5: The Yanks are here 53, 161
An American in England No. 6: The Anglo-American Angle 53, 161
An American Overture 47
And seeing the multitudes, for soprano and piano (recitative) 3
Antiphon Op.56b 83, 189
Appointment 51, 159
Around the Village Green 33, 139–40

The Ascent of F6 35, 40, 134–5, 135 n.5, 146–7
Aube (Rimbaud), for soprano and string orchestra 43
Autumn (de la Mare), for voice and string quartet 19

Bagatelle, for piano trio 14, 15
Ballad of Heroes Op.14 41, 154, 189
The Ballad of Little Musgrave and Lady Barnard 57, 189
Ballet on a Basque scenario, for orchestra (incomplete) 21
Banking for 1,000,000s 137
The Beggar's Opera Op.43 66, 67, 68, 69, 189–91
Beware (Longfellow) 3
Billy Budd Op.50 68, 72, 75, 76, 77, 90, 91, 169, 191–6
The Birds (Belloc), for soprano and strings 14, 17, 24, 30
A Birthday Hansel Op.92 122, 123, 125, 196
Blessed are they that mourn, for soprano and piano (aria, incomplete) 3
Book Bargain 142
Bourées, for piano 5
A Boy was Born Op.3 22, 24, 25, 27, 80, 84, 86, 92, 169, 196–7
Britain to America, Series I No. 9: Britain through American Eyes 53, 162
Britain to America, Series II No. 4: Where Do I Come In? 53, 162
Britain to America, Series II No. 13: Where Do We Go From Here? 53, 162–3
The Brook, for voice and violin 7
The Building of the House Op.79 106, 107, 202
The Burning Fiery Furnace Op.77 102, 104, 106, 116, 169, 202–3

C.T.O. – The Story of the Central Telegraph Office 29, 134
Cabaret Songs 35, 39, 146–7, 147 n.23, 153
   Calypso 43
   Tell me the truth about love 153

Cadenzas to Haydn's Cello Concerto in C (Hoboken VII b.i) 203
Calendar of the Year 33, 134
Canadian Carnival Op.19   43, 45, 204
Cantata Academica Op.62 89, 91, 92, 204
Cantata Misericordium Op.69   97, 98, 99, 169, 204–5
Canticle I Op.40   65, 66, 92, 174, 205
Canticle II Op.51   75, 92, 174, 182, 205–6
Canticle III Op.55   81, 83, 92, 174, 206
Canticle IV Op.86   115, 117, 118, 174, 206
Canticle V Op.89   121, 123, 206–7
Cavatina in A, for string quartet 9
Cello Sonata in C Op.65   90, 92, 93, 94, 95, 175, 207
Cello Suite No. 1 Op.72   100, 101, 103, 207–8
Cello Suite No. 2 Op.80   107, 109, 208
Cello Suite No. 3 Op.87   114, 115, 123, 208
Cello Symphony Op.68   97, 99, 100, 171, 208–9
A Ceremony of Carols Op.28   48, 51, 53, 57, 78, 170, 209
Chamber Music V (Joyce), for soprano (or tenor) and piano 17
Chaos and Cosmos: Symphonic Poem in E, for orchestra 9
A Charm of Lullabies Op.41   67, 69, 174, 209–10
The Chartists' March 39, 156
The Children and Sir Nameless (Hardy), for high voice and piano 79
Children of Love (Munro), for SSA 15
Children's Crusade Op.82   109, 111, 112, 170, 210
Choral Music 210–1
Chorale (after an old French Carol), for SATB 57, 164, 211
Christmas Sequence 125
Church Music 211
Church Parables 146, 211
Clarinet Concerto 51
Coal Abstract 134
Coal Face 29, 132–3, 138, 211
Come Little Babe (Nicholas Breton), for mezzo-soprano and piano 67
The Company of Heaven 37, 154–5, 156
Concerto in B minor, for violin, viola and orchestra 21
Conquering Space – The Story of Modern Communications 29, 136

Corpus Christi Carol 92, 93, 174
Cradle Song (Blake), for two voices and piano 39
Curlew River Op.71   98, 99, 101, 102, 106, 170, 212–3

Dans Les Bois, for orchestra 11
Dans Les Bois (Nerval), for voice (soprano) and piano 11
The Dark Tower 61, 164–5, 213
The Dark Valley 45, 158
Dawtie's Devotion (Soutar), for tenor and piano 113
Death in Venice Op.88   114, 116, 118, 119, 120, 121, 122, 213–20
Deus in adjutorium meum, for SATB 151, 220
Diaphenia (Constable), for tenor and piano 15
Dinner Hour 29, 135, 136
Diversions Op.21   45, 49, 78, 170, 220
Divertimento (Ballet) 47
The Duchess of Malfi 63, 152
The Dynasts 45, 158

The Eagle Has Two Heads 63, 151–2
Easter 1916   31, 145, 145 n.19
Eight Rounds (sacred), for voices 9
Einladung zur Martinsgans, eight-part canon for voices and piano 87
Elegy, for string orchestra 11
Elegy, for viola 17, 220
Elizabeth Variations, for piano 13
Epilogue: Perchance he for whom the bell tolls be so ill (Donne), for high voice and piano 59
Etude, for viola 13
Evening Hymn, for SATB 15
Everyone Sang (Sassoon), for tenor and small orchestra 15

Fancie 93
A Fanfare for D.W. (David Webster) 113, 115
Fanfare for SS Oriana 91
Fanfare for St Edmundsbury 89, 221
Fantasia in A, for piano 7
Fantasias, for piano 5
Farfield 81, 221
Felixtown, for piano (incomplete) 5
Festival Te Deum Op.32   57, 59, 221

INDEX OF BRITTEN'S WORKS

Film Music 131–44, 221–2
First Loss, for viola and piano 7
Fish in the Unruffled Lakes (Auden) 37
Five Flower Songs Op.47   73, 75, 222
Five Walztes 110, 111
For a Song 222
Four Barriers 33, 140 n.9, 141
Four Etudes Symphoniques, for piano 5
The Four Freedoms No. 1: Pericles 55, 163
Four Nursery Rhymes (anon), for voice and piano 9
Friday Afternoons Op.7   22, 29, 104, 115, 170, 175
Funeral Blues (Stop all the clocks) 147

Gas Abstract 29, 134
Gemini Variations Op.73   100, 101, 103, 222
Gloriana Op.53   77, 98, 104, 170, 244–8
   Courtly Dances 84, 85
   Morris Dance 76
   Symphonic Suite Op.53a   79
God Save the Queen 248
God, who created me (H. C. Beeching), for mixed chorus and organ (School anthem) 49
God's Chillun 29, 134–5
Going down hill on a bicycle (after H. C. Beeching), for violin and piano 21
The Golden Vanity Op.78   105, 107, 112, 175, 248–9
GPO Title Music 1 and 2   29, 138–39
The Gully (Soutar), for tenor and piano 113

H.P.O., or 6d. Telegram 133
Hadrian's Wall 37, 155
Hankin Booby 105, 107, 249
Harp Suite Op.83   111, 249
Here we go up in a flung festoon (Kipling), for voice and piano 3
Holiday Diary Op.5   27, 249
The Holly and the Ivy 85
The Holy Sonnets of John Donne Op.35   58, 59, 61, 64, 106, 175, 249
How the Dial Works 29, 136
Humoreske in C, for orchestra 11
A Hymn of St Columba 97, 250
Hymn to St Cecilia Op.27   48, 51, 53, 250
Hymn to St Peter Op.56a   81, 250
A Hymn to the Virgin 17, 19, 24

I Saw Three Ships see The Sycamore Tree
I Saw Three Witches (de la Mare), for soprano, contralto and piano 19
If It's ever spring again (Hardy), for high voice and piano 79
If Thou Wilt Ease Thine Heart (Beddoes), for voice and piano 51
Les Illuminations Op.18   41, 43, 45, 60, 86, 104, 148, 170, 250–1
   Being Beauteous 41, 43
   Marine 41, 43
The Instruments of the Orchestra 61, 63, 143–4, 251
Introduction, for string orchestra 5
Introduction and Allegro, for piano trio 23
Introduction and Allegro, for viola and strings 15
Introduction and Rondo Alla Burlesca Op.23 No. 1   45, 55, 56, 175, 251

Jam Tart (Auden), for voice and piano 35
Johnson over Jordan 41, 150–1, 251
   The Spider and the Fly 151
Jubilate Deo 93, 95, 251
Jubilate Deo in E flat, for choir and organ 27

King Arthur 35, 154
King Herod and the Cock 103
The King's Stamp 29, 131–2, 140, 142, 143
Kyrie in B minor, for chorus and orchestra 9

Lachrymae Op.48   73, 251
   orchestrated for viola and string orchestra Op.48a   124, 125, 251
Lento con Introduzion [sic] – Allegro ma non troppo, for piano (incomplete) 5
Lilian (Tennyson), for voice and piano 13
Line to the Tschierva Hut 33, 140, 140 n.9, 251
Lines on the Map 37, 155–6
A Little Idyll, for piano 15
The Little Sweep Op.45   68, 71, 72, 80, 170, 252–3
Love from a Stranger 33, 141–2, 253
Love Me Not For Comely Grace (anon), for SSAT 19

Lullaby for a Retired Colonel, for two pianos 31
Lumberjacks of America 51, 160–1

Malayan National Anthem 83
The Man Born to be King No. 10: The Princes of this World 51, 53, 160
The Man Born to be King No. 11: The King of Sorrows 51, 53, 162
Mony a Pickle 37, 132, 143
Mass, for four voices 18, 19
Mass in E minor, for soloists, chorus and orchestra 4, 6, 7
Matinées Musicales Op.24 47, 133
May (anon) 27
May in the Greenwood (anon), for two voices and piano 17
Mazurka Elegiaca Op.23 No. 2 47, 49, 55, 56, 175, 253
Mazurka in F sharp minor, for piano 7
Men Behind the Meters 29, 135, 136
Men of Goodwill 67, 165, 165 n.49, 253
Men of the Alps 33, 132, 134, 140, 140 n.9, 253
Menuetto, for piano 11
Message from Geneva 33, 140, 140 n.9
Methods of Communication 136
A Midsummer Night's Dream Op.64 88, 91, 165, 170, 253–9
Miniature Suite, for string quartet 13
Missa Brevis in D Op.63 89, 259
Modern Post Office Methods 136
Mon Rêve Familier (Verlaine), for soprano and orchestra 12
Mont Juic Op.12 37, 259
The Moon (after Shelley), for violin and piano 21
The Moth (de la Mare), for bass and piano 19
Mother Comfort (Slater) 33, 259

Negroes 134, 135 n.4
The New Operator 29, 137
A New Year Carol (anon) 115
Night covers up the rigid land (Auden), for high voice and piano 37, 259
Night Mail 28, 31, 138, 139, 259
Night Piece (Notturno) 97, 259
Nocturnal after John Dowland Op.70 99, 100, 260
Nocturne Op.60 87, 88, 170, 260
Novelette, for string orchestra 13
Noye's Fludde Op.59 84, 85, 87, 260–2
The Nurse's Song (Blake), for soprano, contralto and piano 17

O Lord, forsake me not, motet for double chorus 19
O What is that sound? (Auden), for voice and piano 49
Occasional Overture 63, 262
Octett in D, for strings 5
Of A' The Airts (Burns), for voice and piano 13
Oh, That I'd ne'er been married (Burns), for voice and piano 3, 127
Oh Why did e'er my thoughts aspire (Sackville), for voice and piano 13
Old friends are best (Plomer), for voice and piano 153
On the Frontier 39, 149–50, 262
On this Island Op.11 34, 37, 148, 175, 262
Out of the Picture 37, 148, 149
Ouverture ('Never Unprepared'), for orchestra 7
Overture No. 1 in C, for orchestra 7
Our Hunting Fathers Op.8 30, 31, 33, 148, 170, 262
Owen Wingrave Op.85 108, 110, 112, 114, 115, 117, 121, 170, 263–5
The Owl (Tennyson), for voice and piano 15
The Oxen 107

Pageant of Empire 35, 147–8
Partita, for chamber orchestra 51
Passacaglia, for organ 17
Paul Bunyan Op.17 42, 45, 47, 121, 122, 125, 265
Peace of Britain 31, 139
Pericles see The Four Freedoms No. 1
Peter Grimes Op.33 48, 50, 52, 56, 57, 58, 59, 60, 61, 64, 78, 88, 92, 98, 110, 112, 122, 145, 170, 271–8
Four Sea Interludes Op.33a 59, 86
Passacaglia Op.33b 86
Phaedra Op.93 123, 125, 278
Phantasy in F minor, for string quintet 21, 22, 23, 278
Phantasy Quartet Op.2 22, 23, 25, 26, 278–9
Philip's Breeches (Charles and Mary Lamb), for mixed voices 33
Piano Concerto Op.13 38, 39, 40, 45, 56, 61, 114, 170, 279
Impromptu 154
Piece, for piano 11
Piece in A, for violin, cello and double bass 3

INDEX OF BRITTEN'S WORKS

Piece in C (incomplete), for piano and string quartet 5
Piece in D flat, for violin and piano 3
Piece in F minor 8
Piece in G (incomplete), for strings 5
Plymouth Town (after Violet Alford), ballet for small orchestra 21
A Poem of Hate, for piano 15
Poème No. 1 in D, for orchestra 7
Poème No. 2 in B minor, for small orchestra 9
Poème No. 3 in E, for orchestra 8, 9
Poème No. 4 in B flat, for small orhestra 9
Poème No. 5 in F sharp minor, for small orchestra 9
A Poet's Christmas 57, 164
The Poet's Echo Op.76   103, 279
A Poison Tree (Blake), for baritone and piano 29
Praise we great men (E. Sitwell) (incomplete), for soloists, chorus and orchestra 124, 126, 279
Prelude and Fugue Op.29   54, 55, 171, 279
Prelude and Fugue on a Theme of Vittoria 63, 279–80
Presto, for orchestra 12
Presto con molto fuoco, for orchestra 5
The Prince of the Pagodas Op.57   82, 83, 84, 171, 280–1
The Prodigal Son Op.81   106, 109, 110, 171, 281–2
Prologue, Song and Epilogue (E. Sitwell), for tenor, horn and piano 83, 282
Prometheus Unbound in B flat, for chorus, strings and piano 9
Psalm 130, for chorus and orchestra 20, 21
Psalm 150, for chorus and orchestra 20, 21, 282
Psalm 150 Op.67   95, 97, 104, 171, 282
The Punch Revue 81, 153, 282

The Quartette (de la Mare), for SATB quartet 13
Quartettino, for string quartet 15, 283
Quatre Chansons Françaises (Hugo and Verlaine) 12, 13, 283

Radio Music 154–65
The Rape of Lucretia Op.37   60, 61, 62, 63, 64, 74, 94, 100, 112, 114, 144, 151, 171, 182, 283–7

Rejoice in the Lamb Op.30   55, 84, 118, 171, 287
Requiem in B minor, for chorus and orchestra 9
The Rescue 57, 163, 287
Reveille, concert study for violin and piano 35, 287
Rhapsodie, for piano 11
Rhapsody, for string quartet 13, 287
Rhapsody, for violin, viola and piano 15
The Rocking-Horse Winner 47, 158–9
Rondo in C sharp minor, for piano 7
Rondo in D, for piano 7
Rondo Capriccio, for piano 7
Rossini Suite 133, 139, 140, 287
Russian Funeral 31, 288

Sacred and Profane Op.91   122, 123, 288
Saint Nicolas Op.42   68, 69, 70, 80, 171, 288
The Saving of Bill Blewitt 33, 141
The Savings Bank 29, 137
A Sea Symphony 124
Scherzo 81, 289
Scherzos, for piano 5
Scottish Ballad Op.26   49, 55, 289
Sechs Hölderlin-Fragmente Op.61   87, 88, 94, 175, 289
Serenade Op.31   55, 57, 96, 152, 171, 289–90
 Dirge 152
Seven Sonnets of Michelangelo Op.22   44, 45, 52, 53, 56, 62, 78, 92, 175, 290
Sextet, for flute, oboe, clarinet, bass clarinet, horn and bassoon 17
A Shepherd's Carol 57, 164, 290
The Ship of Rio 96, 97
Silver (de la Mare), for voice and piano 11
Simple Symphony Op.4   24, 25, 27, 108, 171, 290
Sinfonia da Requiem Op.20   43, 47, 48, 51, 78, 100, 171, 290–1
Sinfonietta Op.1   22, 23, 34, 291
Six Metamorphoses after Ovid Op.49   73, 75, 291
Six Songs, for voice and piano 9
Sketch No. 1 'D. Layton', for string orchestra 17
Sketch No. 2 'EBB', for viola and strings 17

Sleep My Darling (MacNeice), for voice and piano (Cradle Song) 51
Soirées Musicales Op.9 31, 40, 47, 133, 291
Somnus the humble god that dwells in cottages and smokey cells (Denham), for mezzo-soprano and piano 67
Sonata in A, for cello and piano 7
Sonata in C minor, for viola and piano 7
Sonata in C sharp minor, for piano 7
Sonata in D, for violin and piano 5
Sonata in F sharp minor, for violin and viola with cello (ad lib) 7
Sonata in G minor, for violin and piano 7
Sonata (Grand) No. 8 in C minor, for piano 7
Sonata No. 10 in B flat, for piano 11
Sonata No. 11 in B, for piano 10, 11
Sonate pour orgue ou pédale-pianoforte 7
Sonatina, for viola and piano 11
Sonatina, for piano 13
Sonatina Romantica, for piano 45, 291
A Song of Enchantment (de la Mare), for voice and piano 13
Songs and Proverbs of William Blake Op.74 101, 102, 103, 175, 291–2
Songs from the Chinese Op.58 85, 87, 292
Sorting Office 29, 137
Spain 39, 148–9
Sport (W. H. Davies), for bass and piano 19
Spring Symphony Op.44 68, 70, 71, 72, 73, 86, 90, 171, 292–3
Stay Down Miner 31, 145
Stratton 71, 152–3
String Quartet in A minor 9
String Quartet in B flat (incomplete) 8
String Quartet in D major (1931) 21, 120, 121, 123, 293–4
String Quartet in F 11
String Quartet in G 9
String Quartet in G minor 9
String Quartet No. 1 in D Op.25 47, 55, 294
String Quartet No. 2 in C Op.36 61, 294
String Quartet No. 3 Op.94 124, 125, 126, 127, 295
Suite Fantastique in A minor, for large orchestra and piano obbligato 7
Suite No. 5 in F, for piano 5

Suite Op.6, for violin and piano 26, 27, 29, 30, 31, 38, 295
Suite on English Folk Tunes Op.90 122, 123, 295
Suites, for piano 5
The sun shines down (Auden), for high voice and piano 37
Sweet was the Song the Virgin Sung 19, 104, 105
Swiss Telephone 140 n.9
The Sword in the Stone 41, 295
The Sycamore Tree 17, 19, 24, 106, 107, 109, 296
Symphony in C (incomplete) 3
Symphony in D minor, for orchestra 9 arranged for piano duet (incomplete) 9
Symphony in F major/minor 3

Te Deum (incomplete), for choir and organ 93
Te Deum in C major 27, 29, 296
Telegrams 29, 133
Tema – 'Sacher', for cello solo 125, 296
Temporal Variations 33, 296
Theatre Music 144–53
'Theme' for one of four improvised movements for a symphony, for organ 33
They Walk Alone 41, 150
This Way to the Tomb 61, 151, 296
Three Canons, for two violas and piano 7
Three Divertimenti, for string quartet 30, 31, 296
Three Early Songs 296
Three Fugues, for piano 21
Three Pieces, for piano 19
Three Poems, for string quartet 11
Three Small Songs (Samuel Daniel, John Fletcher), for soprano and small orchestra 21
Three Toccatas, for piano 5
Three Two-Part Songs (de la Mare), for high voice and piano 21, 23, 96
Thy King's Birthday (Southwell and The Bible): Christmas Suite, for soprano, contralto and mixed chorus 19
  New Prince, New Pomp 81
Timber 161
Timon of Athens 29, 144
Timpani Piece for Jimmy 81
Tit for Tat (de la Mare) 11, 12, 13, 108, 109, 111, 118, 175, 296
Title Music III 29, 136

INDEX OF BRITTEN'S WORKS 315

To Electra: I Dare Not Ask a Kisse (Herrick), for voice and piano 17
To lie flat on the back (Auden), for high voice and piano 37, 296
To the Willow-Tree, for SATB 19
The Tocher 29, 133–4, 133 n.3, 139, 140, 297
Tradition (Soutar), for tenor and piano 113
Trio in Fantastic Form in E minor, for violin, viola and piano 7
Trio in G minor, for violin, viola and piano 11
The Turn of the Screw Op.54   78, 79, 80, 82, 84, 100, 172, 297–301
Twelve Variations on a Theme, for piano 21, 301
Two Insect Pieces 29, 301
Two Part-Songs, 23, 25
Two Pieces, for violin, viola and piano 15
Two Songs (Fletcher), for SATB quartet 15

Underneath the Abject Willow (Auden) 33, 301
   version for voice and piano 49
Up the Garden Path 33, 35

Variations (incomplete) for piano 102
Variations on a French Carol (Carol of the Deanery of Saint-Ménéhould), for women's voices, violin, viola and piano 21
Variations on a Theme of Frank Bridge Op.10   35, 37, 104, 172, 301
Variations on an Elizabethan Theme (Sellenger's Round) 76, 77, 301
Variations on Dyke's 'How Bright These Glorious Spirits Shine', for chorus, string quintet, organ and piano 5
Venite Exultemus Domino, for choir and organ 93
Vigil (de la Mare), for bass (or contralto) and piano 18, 19
Village Organist's Piece (incomplete) 51
Violin Concerto Op.15   43, 45, 47, 86, 114, 172, 301–2
Vocal Music 302
Voices for Today Op.75   103, 104, 302
Voluntary (Chorale prelude in D minor), for organ 51

Waltzes, for piano 5
The Waning Moon (Shelley), for voice and piano 11

War Requiem Op.66   92, 94, 95, 96, 98, 100, 108, 172, 302–6
The Way to the Sea 33, 142
A Wealden Trio: The Song of the Women (Ford Madox Ford), for women's voices 14, 17, 106, 107, 109, 306
A Wedding Anthem (Amo ergo sum) Op.46   70, 71, 306
Welcome Ode Op.95   125, 306–7
What's on your mind? (Auden), for voice and piano 49
Who are these children? (Soutar) Op.84   111, 113, 115, 117, 118, 175, 307
A Widow Bird Sate Mourning For Her Love (Shelley), for voice and piano 19
Wild Time (de la Mare), for soprano and strings 15
Wild with Passion (Beddoes), for voice and piano 51
Winter Words (Hardy) Op.52   78, 79, 118, 175, 307
Witches' Song (Jonson), for voice and piano 13
The World of the Spirit 39, 156–7

Young Apollo 43, 308
The Young Person's Guide to the Orchestra Op.34   63, 92, 96, 143, 172, 308

ARRANGEMENTS, EDITIONS, REALIZATIONS

Bach, Johann Sebastian ed. Britten
   Five Spiritual Songs (Geistliche Lieder) 110, 111
Bridge, Frank arr. Britten
   The Sea: Moonlight 26
Chopin, Frédéric arr. Britten
   Les Sylphides 43
Dibdin, Charles arr. Britten
   Tom Bowling 175
Folksongs arr. Britten 55, 56, 58, 64, 78, 88, 90, 93, 94, 95, 222
Folksongs arr. Britten Eight Folksong Arrangements 127
Folksongs arr. Britten French Folksongs 54, 65
Folksong arr. Britten The Ash Grove 175–6
Folksong arr. Britten Avenging and bright 175
Folksong arr. Britten La Belle est au jardin d'amour 176

Folksong arr. Britten The Bonny Earl O'Moray 176
Folksong arr. Britten The Brisk Young Widow 176
Folksong arr. Britten Ca' the yowes 176
Folksong arr. Britten Come you not from Newcastle? 176
Folksong arr. Britten Early one morning 176
Folksong arr. Britten The Foggy, foggy dew 176
Folksong arr. Britten Heigh-ho! Heigh-hi! 176
Folksong arr. Britten How sweet the answer 176
Folksong arr. Britten The Last Rose of Summer 177
Folksong arr. Britten Little Sir William 177
Folksong arr. Britten The Lincolnshire poacher 177
Folksong arr. Britten The Miller of Dee 177
Folksong arr. Britten The Minstrel Boy 177
Folksong arr. Britten O Waly, Waly 177
Folksong arr. Britten Oft in the stilly night 177
Folksong arr. Britten Oliver Cromwell 177
Folksong arr. Britten Le Roi s'en va-t'en chasse 177
Folksong arr. Britten Sally in our Alley 177
Folksong arr. Britten The Salley Gardens 177
Folksong arr. Britten Sweet Polly Oliver 178
Folksong arr. Britten There's none to soothe 178
Folksongs arr. Britten The Twelve Apostles 97
Haydn, Joseph
  Cello Concerto in C. Cadenzas by Britten 101

Mahler, Gustav
  What the wild flowers tell me 49
Mozart, Wolfgang Amadeus
  Piano Concerto in E flat K.482. Cadenzas by Britten 105
The National Anthem arr. Britten
  1946 setting 63
  1961 setting 94, 95, 173, 248
  1971 setting 117, 173
Purcell, Henry
  Chacony in G minor Z.730 ed. Britten 101, 173, 282–3
  Dido and Aeneas ed. Britten and I. Holst 72, 73, 94, 220, 282–3
  Fairest Isle real. Britten and Pears 282
  The Fairy Queen ed. Britten and I. Holst 104, 105, 107, 114, 116, 173, 221, 282–3
  Job's Curse real. Britten and Pears 73, 282–3
  The Knotting Song real. Britten and Pears 51
  Orpheus Britannicus real. Britten and Pears
    Five Songs 91, 282–3
    Seven Songs 65, 282–3
    Six Duets 93, 282–3
    Six Songs 69, 282–3
    Suite of Songs 83, 282–3
  The Queen's Epicedium real. Britten and Pears 61, 64, 65, 179, 282–3
  Sweeter than roses real. Britten and Pears 179, 282–3
  Three Divine Hymns real. Britten and Pears 67, 282–3
  Two Divine Hymns and Alleluia real. Briten and Pears 91, 282–3
  When Night her Purple Veil real. Britten and Pears 102, 103, 282–3
Shield, William arr. Britten
  The Ploughboy 180–1
Who is this in Garments Gory? (Hymn. Tune: Ebenezer) arr. Britten 49

GENERAL INDEX

Adeney, Richard 169, 170, 171
Aeolian Hall, London 45
Aeschylus 146
Aitken, D. F. 155
Aix-en-Provence, France 76
Albert Hall, Nottingham 75
Albery Theatre, London 150 n.28
Aldeburgh 64, 68, 74, 76, 96, 126
Aldeburgh Festival 64, 66, 68, 70, 72, 74, 76, 78, 80, 82, 84, 86, 88, 90, 92, 96, 100, 104, 106, 108, 110, 112, 114, 116, 118, 120, 122, 124, 187–8
  Club 88
  Exhibition Gallery 88
Aldeburgh Festival Chamber Orchestra 69
Aldeburgh Festival Choir 69
Aldeburgh Festival Chorus 80, 171
Aldeburgh Festival Orchestra 80, 82, 171, 173, 174
Aldeburgh Festival Singers 174
Aldeburgh Festival – Snape Maltings Foundation 112
Aldeburgh Parish Church 68, 69, 73, 77, 81, 83, 97, 105, 109, 126
Alford, Violet 21
All Saints, Margaret Street, Choir, London 169
Alleyn's School Choir, London 170
Alston, Audrey 2, 10
Alway, E. J. 155
Amadeus String Quartet 126, 127
Amalgamated Engineering Union 145
Ambrosian Opera Chorus 169, 173
Ambrosian Singers 109, 172
American Academy of Arts and Letters, New York, USA 84
American Ballet Company 47
Amit, Sheila 169
Amityville, Long Island, USA 42, 46, 48
Amsterdam 71
Anderson, Hedli 39, 146
Anderson, Max 134
Ansermet, Ernest 63, 99
Anstey, Edgar 135
Anthony, Trevor 170
Arlen, Albert 145
Armenia, USSR 102
Aronowitz, Cecil 169, 170, 171
Arts Theatre, Cambridge 39, 69, 149

Argentina 106
The Artist and his Medium (BBC programme) 62
Aspen Award 100
Associated Board of the Royal Schools of Music 4
Astle, Ethel 2
Auden, Wystan Hugh 28, 33, 34, 35, 37, 38, 39, 41, 42, 43, 44, 45, 49, 51, 132, 134, 138, 139, 142, 146–7, 149, 152, 153, 155, 158, 164, 276
  For the Time Being 164
  The Line Waits 142
  O lurcher-loving collier 132
  Roman Wall Blues 155
  This is the night mail crossing the border 138
Ausonia (ship) 40
Australia 112
Austria 74, 104
Axel Johnson (ship) 48
Aylmer, Felix 154, 156
Azavia, Victor 153

Bach, Johann Sebastian 42, 110, 112
  Brandenburg concertos 1–6, 108, 169
  St John Passion 116, 169
  St Matthew Passion 147
Bach Choir 172
Bainbridge, Elizabeth 171
Baker, Dame Janet 94, 112, 121, 125, 170, 171
Baker, Marilyn 170
Balanchine 47
Balfe, Michael
  The Bohemian Girl ('I dreamt that I dwelt in Marble Halls') 135, 136
Balinese Ceremonial Music 46
Ballet Club (Mercury) Theatre, London 23, 25, 27
Ballets Russes 144 n.16
Bannerman, Betty 33
Barbirolli, Sir John 45, 47
Barcelona 30
Barcombe Mills, Sussex 120, 122
Barrymore Theater, New York 63
Bartlett, Ethel 45, 46, 49
Basel, Switzerland 92
  University 91
Basel University Chorus 91

Basler Kammerorchester 91
Bavaria 88
BBC 25, 30, 31, 34, 35, 40, 41, 52, 53, 54,
  56, 58, 60, 62, 63, 64, 66, 67, 68,
  72, 87, 90, 91, 92, 98, 106, 110,
  112, 114, 117, 125, 156 n.37
  BBC Bristol 45
  BBC London 140, 154, 155, 156, 157,
    159, 160, 161, 162, 163, 164, 165
  BBC Newcastle upon Tyne 155
  BBC New York 160
  BBC Northern Region 62
BBC Chorus 35, 39, 154
BBC Concert Hall 64
BBC Men's Chorus 39, 156
BBC Midlands Chorus 75
BBC North American Service 162
BBC Northern Singers 125
BBC Northern Symphony Orchestra 125
BBC Orchestra 154, 156, 157
BBC Singers 53, 57, 156, 157, 164
BBC Sound Archive 160 n.43
BBC Symphony Orchestra 39, 41, 43,
  57, 63, 87, 163
BBC Third Programme 62
BBC Wireless Singers (A) 25
Bebb, Emlyn 39, 156
Beddoes, Thomas Lovell 51
Bedford, Steuart 118, 120, 121, 123,
  125, 157
Beeching, H. C. 21
Beethoven, Ludwig van
  Quintet in E flat Op.16   174
  Symphony No. 6 *Pastoral*   157
Beinecke Library, Yale University 144
Belgium 60, 70, 74, 80
Belgrade, Yugoslavia 80
Belloc, Hilaire 17
Benjamin, Arthur 18
Bennett, Harry 152
Berg, Alban
  Wozzeck 26
Bergen, Norway 124
Bergner, Elisabeth 152
Berkeley, Lennox 149
  How love came in 174
  There was neither grass nor corn 164
  Stabat Mater 64, 68
  Variations on an Elizabethan Theme 174
Berlin 82, 84
Bernstein, Leonard 62
The Bible 19
Binyon, Helen 148

Binyon, Margaret 148
Binyon Puppets 39, 148
Birmingham, England 68, 79
Birmingham Philharmonic String Orchestra 41
Blackburn, Harold 170
Blackstone Theater, Illinois, USA 45
Blades, James 81, 169, 170, 171
Blake, William 17, 29, 39
Blunt, Wilfred S. 17
Blythburgh Parish Church 101, 110, 111
Bond, Ralph 143
Bonn 74
Boosey & Hawkes Music Publishers Limited 30, 100
Boston (Mass.) 48, 112
Boston Symphony Orchestra 48
Boughton, Joy 75
Boult, Sir Adrian 26, 40, 63
Bowman, David 169
Bowman, James 117, 173, 174, 179
Bowman, Robert 169
Boyce, Bruce 73
Boyd Neel Orchestra 35, 37, 45, 54, 55, 171
Brahms, Johannes 151
  Piano Trio in E flat Op.40   14
Brain, Dennis 57, 81, 83, 171
Brander Matthews Hall, Columbia University, New York 47
Brannigan, Owen 169, 170, 171, 173
Bray, Eric 25
Brazil 106
Bream, Julian 87, 101
Brecht, Bertolt 152
Brenner, Roger 169
Breton, Nicholas 67
Brett, Charles 173
Bridge, Frank 12, 22, 34, 44, 66, 98, 108, 197
  Cello Sonata 108, 174
  Enter Spring 10
  Go not, happy day 174
  Goldenhair 174
  Journey's End 174
  Love Went a-riding 174
  The Sea 4
  Sir Roger de Coverley 169
  So perverse 174
  'Tis but a week 174
  When you are old 174
Bridson, D. Geoffrey 154
Britisch-Deutsche Musiktage 88, 110
British Commercial Gas Association 134, 135, 136

GENERAL INDEX

British Council 64, 66, 96
British Library 138, 146, 164
Britten, Barbara 2
Britten, Benjamin *passim*
Britten, Beth 2
Britten, Edith Rhoda (née Hockey) 2, 26
Britten, Robert 2, 22
Britten, Robert Victor 2
Britten Festival, Yerevan, USSR, 1965 102
Britten–Pears Library 126, 130, 144 n.15, 150 n.29, 155, 157 n.39
Britten–Pears School for Advanced Musical Studies 118, 202
Broadcasting House, Concert Hall, London 72
Brontë, Emily
  A thousand gleaming fires (A Day Dream) 155
Brooklyn Heights, New York 44
Brosa, Antonio 30, 31, 35, 45
Browne, E. Martin 151
Browning, Robert 165
Bryn-Jones, Delme 169
Budapest 98
Burgess, Russell 111, 170, 175
Burns, Robert 13, 123
Burrell, John 163
Burrowes, Norma 173
Bury St Edmunds, Suffolk 89
Bush, Alan 31
Bush, Henry 169
Butterworth, George
  A Shropshire Lad: Is my team ploughing? 175

Caine, Natalie 33
California 46
Cambridge, England 55
  University 88
Cambridge Festival 68
Cambridge University Musical Society 104
Camden Theatre, London 68
Cameron, Basil 47, 51, 55
Canada 40, 48, 70, 84, 92, 106
Canadian Broadcasting Corporation 43
Canal holiday (1975) 122
Cantelo, April 169, 170
Cardiff, University College 115, 125
Carlyle Singers 23
Carnegie Hall, New York 45, 47, 48
Carrick, Edward 150
Catto, Max 150

Cavalcanti, Alberto 132, 133, 138, 139, 140, 141, 143
Cavelti, Elsa 91
CBS, New York 45, 159, 160, 161
  Columbia Workshop 45, 47, 158, 159
Cecil Sharp House, London 58
CEMA (Council for the Encouragement of Music and the Arts) 50
Central Hall, London 65, 72
Ceylon *see* Sri Lanka
Chapel House, Horham, Suffolk 112
Charlottenburger Schloss, Berlin 82, 84
Cheatle, John 157
Cheltenham, England 74
Cheltenham Festival 61
Chester Miracle Plays 84
Chile 106
China 38
Christie, Dame Agatha
  Philomel Cottage 141
Christie's 92
Chuhaldin, Alexander 43
Cincinnati Symphony Orchestra 49
Cioppa, Guy della 158
City of Birmingham Symphony Orchestra 79, 95, 97
Clive House (school), Prestatyn, N. Wales 22
Cobbett Prize 22
Cocteau, Jean 151
Coldstream, Sir William 131, 134
Coleby, Geoffrey 169
Coleman, Basil 98
Coleman, C. J. R. 26
Collins' Music Hall, London 147
Colorado 100
Columbia University Theater Workshop, New York 47
Colwall, Herefordshire 28
Comedy Theatre, London 150
Company of Four 151
Conservatoire of Music, Moscow 103
Companionage of Honour 76
Conscientious Objection 50, 54
Coolidge String Quartet 47
Copenhagen 76, 108
Copenhagen Boys' Choir 170
Copland, Aaron
  The Second hurricane 38
  Folksong arrangements:
    Old American Songs 72
    The Boatmen's dance 176
    The Dodger 176
    I bought me a cat 176
    Long time ago 177
    Simple gifts 178

Cornford, Frances 164
Corwin, Norman 159, 160, 161
Cottrell, Leonard 165
Covent Garden Wind Ensemble 86
Coventry 94, 97
Coventry Festival Chorus 95
Crabbe, George 46
　The Borough 48
Crag House, Aldeburgh 64, 76, 84
Cranko, John 83
Cross, Joan 58, 59, 64, 73, 171, 172
Crown Film Unit 63, 143
Crozier, Eric 62, 64, 68, 69, 71, 72, 75, 143 n.14
Curzon, Clifford 55, 56, 173, 175

Daniel, Samuel 21
Danish Symphony Orchestra 171
Darmstadt 89
Davies, Meredith 87, 97
Davies, W. H. 19
De la Mare, Walter 11, 12, 13, 15, 18, 19, 21, 108, 109, 111, 113, 118, 175, 296
Dean, Basil 150
Dean, Stafford 169
Deanery of Saint Ménéhould 21
Debussy, Claude 60
　Cello sonata 94, 175
Decca Record Company Limited 56, 58, 60, 64, 78, 80, 84, 88, 90, 92, 94, 96, 98, 100, 102, 104, 108, 110, 112, 114, 116, 118, 150
Del Mar, Norman 71, 153
Delius, Frederick 108
　On hearing the first cuckoo in spring 157
　Two Aquarelles 172
Deller, Alfred 91
Dempsey, Gregory 169
Denham, Sir John 67
Denmark, 78, 108
Dennis Brain Wind Quintet 174
Diaghilev, Serge 144 n.16
Dickinson, Meriel 174
Dillon, Francis 157
Donegal (County), Northern Ireland 97
Donlevy, Edmund 171
Doone, Rupert 144, 144 n.16, 146, 148, 149
Douglas, Nigel 170
Dowland, John 56, 82, 98, 101
The Downs School, Colwall, Herefordshire 28

Downside School Choir (Purley) 104, 170, 171
Drake, Bryan 169, 170, 171
Drottningholm Court Theatre, Sweden 94
Dublin 145
Dubrovnik 88, 94
Dufay Colour 131 n.1
Duke of York's Theatre, London 153
Duncan, Ronald 50, 61, 71, 151, 152–3, 153
Düsseldorf 92
Dutch Radio Chorus 71
Dyer, Olive 172

Easdale, Brian 133, 146, 148, 149
East Anglian Choirs 107, 173
Edinburgh, Prince Philip, Duke of 106, 112
Edinburgh Festival 86, 108
Elgar, Sir Edward 108
　The Dream of Gerontius 116, 172
　Introduction and Allegro 172
Eliot, Thomas Stearns 115, 121
Elizabeth, Queen Mother 114, 122
Elizabeth II, *Queen* 76, 106, 112, 122
Ellis, Osian 111, 123, 125, 169, 170, 171
Elmau, Schloss, West Germany 88, 110, 118, 123
Elms, Lauris 170
Elton, Arthur 135
Elton, Ralph 136
Empire Marketing Board Film Unit 137, 137 n.6
Empire Theatre, Leicester Square, London 63, 144
EMPO 131, 131 n.1, 132
English Chamber Orchestra 85, 100, 101, 104, 107, 112, 114, 117, 121, 123, 125, 169, 170, 171, 172, 173, 174
English Music Theatre Company 125
The English Opera Group 64, 65, 68, 69, 71, 73, 74, 75, 76, 79, 80, 82, 84, 90, 91, 94, 98, 100, 101, 102, 104, 106, 107, 109, 110, 112, 114, 116, 117, 121, 221
　Boys' Voices 169
　Orchestra 71, 153, 170, 171
Ernest Farrar Prize for Composition (1931) 20, (1933) 24
Escondido, California 46
Ethel Barrymore Theater, New York 152
Eton Boating Song 157

Euripides
  Trojan Women 158 n.40
Evans, Edgar 159
Evans, Sir Geraint 170
Evans, Nancy 67, 69, 73
Expo '67, Montreal 106

Faber and Faber Limited 98
Faber Music Limited 100
Fairhurst, Robin 170
Fauré, Gabriel 60
Felling Male Voice Choir 37, 155
La Fenice, Teatro, Venice 79
Fernald, John 152
Ferrier, Kathleen 71, 72, 75, 78, 171, 182
Festival of Britain Exhibition, London, 1951 70, 74
Festival of British Music, USSR, 1963 96
Finland 102
Fischer-Dieskau, Dietrich 95, 98, 99, 102, 103, 169, 172, 174, 175
Fisher, Sylvia 169, 170
Fleet Street Choir 53
Fletcher, John 15, 21
Florence 26
Folksong 140
Forces' Networks 159
Ford, Ford Madox 17
Forster, Edward Morgan 46, 68, 72, 75
Forty Years On 157
Foulds, John 141, 143
France 68, 98, 114
Francke, Donald 171
Frankfurt 98
Freedom of the Borough of Aldeburgh 96
Freemason's Hall, Edinburgh 86
Freenat Films (League of Nations Film Unit) 139
Friedmann, Barnett 131
Friston, Sussex 10, 22

Gabrieli String Quartet 123
Garrett, Eric 169
Garton, Co. Donegal, Northern Ireland 97
Gas Light and Coke Co. 134
Gay, John 66, 67
Gendron, Maurice 60
Geneva 92, 140
Genn, Leo 154, 156
Geraldo's Orchestra 151
German South-west Radio Symphony Orchestra 171

Germany 57, 58, 76, 82, 84, 88, 92, 98, 110, 118, 122, 123
Giebel, Agnes 91
Gielgud, Val 154, 160, 162
Gillian, Lawrence 162, 165
Giulini, Carlo Maria 108, 110
Globe Theatre, London 149
Glossop, Peter 169
Glyndebourne Festival Opera 62, 63, 65, 151
God rest ye merry, Gentlemen 165
Goehr, Walter 57, 61, 67, 157, 164, 165
Goldberg, Albert 45
Goodall, Reginald 59, 64, 78
Goodman, Benny 51
Goossens, Leon 25, 49
Gould, Graham 157
GPO Film Unit 28, 30, 131, 132, 133, 134, 136, 137, 138, 139, 140, 141, 142, 143
Graham Colin 105, 110
Grainger, Percy 72, 108, 118
  Folksong arrangements: Bold William Taylor 172
  The 'Duke of Marlborough' Fanfare 172
  I'm seventeen come Sunday 172
  The jolly sailor song 176
  Let's dance gay in green meadow 177
  Lisbon 172
  Lord Maxwell's Goodnight 172
  The Lost Lady Found 172
  My Robin is to the Green Wood Gone 172
  The pretty maid milkin' her cow 177
  Shallow Brown 172
  Shepherd's Hey 172
  Six dukes went a-fishin' 178
  The Sprig of thyme 178
  There was a pig went out to dig 172
  Willow Willow 172
Graves, Robert 23
Great Glemham House 87
Greece 90, 96
Green, Phil 142
Gresham's School, Holt, Norfolk 12, 14, 16
Grieg, Edvard
  Peer Gynt Suite No. 1: In the Hall of the Mountain King 142
Grierson, John 131 n.1, 132, 137, 137 n.6, 138, 140, 141
Grierson, Marion 139
Griller String Quartet 55

Grinke, Frederick 38
The Group Theatre 28, 29, 33, 35, 37, 39, 144, 146, 148, 149
Gysegham, André van 145
The Hague 69
Haffenden, Elizabeth 150
Hahessy, John 92, 174
Hales, Gordon 134
Halifax, Nova Scotia, Canada 48
Hallis, Adolph 33
Hamburg 92
Hammersmith, London 39, 63, 73
Handel, George Frideric 151
  Messiah 68, 182
  Ode for St Cecilia's Day 173
Hanover 92
Hanser, Frank 150
Harding, Ann 141
Harding, Victor 39, 156
Hardy, Thomas 78, 79, 118, 158, 175, 307
Harewood, Earl of 71, 74
Harewood House 79
Harper, Heather 95, 121, 169, 170
Hartnett, Michael 169, 171
Harvey, Trevor 39, 154, 156
Harwood, Elizabeth 174
Hawkes, Ralph 28, 30
Haydn, Joseph 82, 84
  Canzonets 94, 178
  Cello Concerto in C 100, 101, 173
  Symphony No. 45 'Farewell' 173
  Symphony No. 55 'Schoolmaster' 173
Hays, H. R. 152
Heart Surgery 118
Heath-Stubbs, John 164
Helsinki 102
Helweg, Marianne 157
Hemmings, David 170, 171, 172
Herrick, Robert 17
Herrmann, Bernard 158
Herrey, Herman 150
Hesse and the Rhine
  Prince Ludwig 74, 80, 82, 84, 86, 88, 96, 98, 100
  Princess Margaret 74, 80, 82, 84, 86, 88, 96, 98, 100, 114, 118
Hesse Student Scheme 86, 88
Highgate School Choir 172
Hill, Jenny 171
Hilversum 37
His Master's Voice 52, 72
Hock, Johann C. 41
Hockey, Edith Rhoda 2
Hockey, Sarah Fanny (Aunt Queenie) 2

Hodgson, Alfreda 169, 173, 174
Holland, 37, 60, 68, 74
Holland Festival 64, 71, 82
Holmes, John B. 142
Holst, Gustav
  Humbert Wolfe Songs 106, 178
  Persephone 178
  The Wandering Scholar ed. Britten and I. Holst 74
Holst, Imogen 74, 76, 81, 82, 86, 94, 100, 105
Holy Trinity Church, Leamington 95
Holy Trinity Church, London 164 n.45
Holy Trinity Church, Stratford upon Avon 95
Homer
  Odyssey 163
Hong Kong 80
Hope, Vida 153
Hopkins, Gerard Manley 42
Horham, Suffolk 112, 120
Howell, Gwynne 169
Hughes, John
  Cwm Rhondda 145
Hugo, Victor 12, 13, 283
Humby, Betty 27
Humperdink, Engelbert 151
Hunting 12

Iceland 114
Illinois 45
Illinois Symphony Orchestra 45
India 80, 100
Ingram, Michael 170
International Society of Contemporary Music
  Barcelona Festival 1936 30
  Florence Festival 1934 26
  London Festival 1938 38
The International String Quartet 25
The Internationale 143
Ipswich 97
Ireland, John 18, 98
  Friendship in misfortune 178
  I have twelve oxen 178
  The land of lost content 178
  Love and friendship 178
  The one hope 178
Irving, Ernest 150–1
Isherwood, Christopher 38, 39, 134, 146, 149
Islington Town Hall, London 31, 145
Istanbul 80
Italy 64, 66, 70, 84, 98, 106, 124

GENERAL INDEX

James, Henry 78, 108
Japan 80
Jeney, Gabriel 98, 100, 103
Jeney, Zoltán 98, 100, 103
Johnson over Jordan 150
Jones, Philip 171
Jonson, Ben 13
Joyce, James 17
Jubilee Hall, Aldeburgh 66, 71, 85, 88, 95, 97, 101, 103, 111

Kahn, Charles 145, 147
Karachi 80
Karlsruhe 92
Katchen, Julius 78, 170
Keats, John 133
Kells, Iris 170
Kelly, David 169, 170
Kennard, Frank 148
Kennedy, John F. 98
King's College Choir, Cambridge 172
Knussen, Stuart 170
Korchinska, Maria 57
Koussevitzky, Natalie 48
Koussevitzky, Serge 48, 62
Koussevitzky Music Foundation 48
Kirov Theatre 98
Kraus, Otakar 171

Lamb, Charles 33
Lamb, Mary 33
Lambert, Constant 41
Lancing College 68, 69
Langdon, Michael 169
Lanigan, John 170
Lawrence, David Herbert 158
Lawrence, T. B. 53
Layton, D. 17
League of Nations Film Unit (Freenat Films) 139
Ledger, Philip 108, 112, 169, 170, 171
Lee, Laurie 164
Lee, Rowland V. 141
Leeds 95
Leeds Festival 79, 86, 87
Leeds International Piano Competition 102
Leeds Parish Church 95
Leeds Town Hall 87
Leeming, Peter 169
Left Review 148
Left Theatre 28, 31, 35, 145, 147
Legg, Stuart 134, 136, 137
Lehmann, Liza
  Bird Songs 157

Leigh, Walter 140
Lemare, Iris 23, 27
Leningrad 98, 116
Leslie Russell Quartet 37, 155
Lewis, Cecil Day 164
Library of Congress Medal 46
Life Peerage 124
The Listener 46
Liszt, Franz 151
Little Theatre, London 146
Liverpool 74
Liverpool Philharmonic Orchestra 63
Lloyd, Peter 174
London Ballet 40
London Boy Singers 97
London City Council 70
London Co-operative Societies 143
London Labour Choral Union 150
London Philharmonic Choir 73
London Philharmonic Orchestra 33, 47, 51, 59, 73
London Symphony Chorus 169, 172, 173
London Symphony Orchestra 35, 53, 67, 88, 94, 96, 98, 144, 154, 162, 165, 169, 170, 172, 173
London Symphony Orchestra Chorus 94
London Telephone Directory 142
Long Island, USA 42, 46
Los Angeles 47
Lowestoft 2, 26
  Freedom of the Borough 74
Lowestoft Choral Society 2, 19
Lubotsky, Mark 114, 172
Lumsden, Norman 169
Lush, Ernest 67
Luxon, Benjamin 169, 170
Lyric Theatre, Hammersmith 63, 73, 151

Macau 80
MacDonald, Murray 151
MacDougall, Ranald 160
McLaren, Norman 142
MacNaughten-Lemare Concerts 23, 25, 27
MacNeice, Louis 51, 146, 148, 162, 163, 164, 164 n.47
McPhee, Colin 46, 178
  transcription: The Music of Bali 178
Mahler, Gustav 30, 66
Maida Vale Studios 34
Maine, USA 44
Malcolm, George 89, 171

The Maltings Concert Hall, Snape 106, 107, 109, 110, 112, 114, 116, 117, 118, 120, 121, 123, 125, 127
Manchester 68
Mangeot, André 25
Mann, Thomas 116
Marjoram, Keith 169, 171
Margis, Alfred
    Valse Bleue 151
Maribor 80
Marion, Frances 141
Marion E. Wade Collection, Illinois 160 n.42
Mark, Geoffrey W. 148
Marrakesh 104
Mary, Queen 70
Mason, Gwendolen 53
Massingham, Richard 143
Matthews, Thomas 47
Mathieson, Muir 53, 143, 162
Maupassant, Guy de 62
Mayer, Elizabeth 42, 46
Mayer, Dr William 42, 46
Medley, Robert 144, 146, 148, 149
Melos Ensemble 97, 172
Menuhin, Sir Yehudi 58
Mercury Theatre, London 23, 25, 27, 35, 39, 61, 146, 151
Metropolitan Theater, Providence, Rhode Island 152
Mexico 106
Mewton-Wood, Noel 61
Middagh Street, Brooklyn Heights, New York 44
Miller, J. H. 156
Miller, James 155
Ministry of Education 144
Minton, Yvonne 172
Mitchell, Donald 120, 122
Mitchell, Kathleen 120, 122
Moeran, E. J.
    In Youth is Pleasure 178
Monck, Nugent 144
Montreal 106
Morgan, Brewster 158
Morley, Thomas 82
Morrison, Rona 134, 136
Morriston Boys' Choir 57
Moscow, USSR 103, 116
Moscow Philharmonic Orchestra 99
Le Motet de Genève 99
Mousehole, Cornwall 141
Mozart, Wolfgang Amadeus 54, 82, 112, 116, 151
    Idomeneo 110, 112
    Piano Concerto in A K.414 173
    Piano Concerto in D Minor K.466 173
    Piano Concerto in E flat K.482 105
    Piano Concerto in B flat K.595 173
    Piano Sonata in C K.521 178
    Serenade in B flat K.361 86
    Serenata Notturna K.239 108, 173
    Symphony No. 25 in G minor K.183 173
    Symphony No. 29 in A K.201 114, 173
    Symphony No. 38 in D 'Prague' K.504 114, 173
    Symphony No. 39 in E flat K.549 26
    Symphony No. 40 in G minor K.550 108, 173
    Trio in E flat for piano, clarinet and viola K.498 14
Mozarteum 37
Murrill, Herbert 144
Murrow, Edward R. 159, 160, 161
Music for the People Festival, Queen's Hall, London 41
Music Magazine (BBC programme) 58
Musicians' Union 112

National Arts Foundation, USA 74
National Gallery, London 52
    Concerts in Second World War 53
National Gallery of Scotland 117
National Heart Hospital 118
National Institute of Arts and Letters, USA 84
National Portrait Gallery, London 2
NBC, New York 77, 162
Neel, Boyd 34, 35, 37, 45, 141
Nelson, Havelock 97
Nerval, Gérard de 11
Nettleship, Ursula 50
New Philharmonia Orchestra 100, 171
New Theatre, London 41, 150
New York 42, 44, 45, 46, 48, 103, 106, 112
    Town Hall 49
New York Philharmonic Orchestra 45, 47
New York Schola Cantorum 47
New Zealand 112
Newby, James 169
Nieman, Alfred 146
Nilsson, Raymond 170
Nobel, Felix de 69
Noble, John 169

GENERAL INDEX

Norfolk and Norwich Triennial Festival (1924) 4, (1927) 10, (1936) 33
North America 40
Northern Ireland 97
Northgate (Ipswich) School Choir and Orchestra 97
Northwestern University, Illinois 154 n.34
Norway 124
Norwich 2, 27, 53
Norwich String Orchestra 27
Nottingham 75
Nova Scotia 48

Obey, André 60
Occidental College, Los Angeles 47
O'Donnell, Rudolf P. 51, 53, 159, 160, 161
Oflag VIIb Camp, Germany 57
The Old Mill, Snape 34, 36, 38, 50
The Old Vic, London 146
Oldham, Arthur 151
   Three Chinese Lyrics 178
   Variations on an Elizabethan Theme 174
Ontario 84
L'Orchestre de la Suisse Romande 99
Order of Merit 100
Orford 87
Orford Parish Church 101, 105, 109
Ormandy, Eugene 49
Osborn, James 92
Owl's Head, Maine, USA 44
Oxfordshire 122

Pacifism 12
Pageant of Magna Carta 89
Pageant of Dream Children 2
Palmer, Felicity 174
Paris 56, 103
Paul Sacher Foundation, Basel 92
Partridge, Ian 173
Pashley, Anne 169
Pears, Sir Peter 34, 36, 38, 40, 41, 42, 44, 46, 48, 50, 52, 53, 54, 56, 57, 58, 59, 60, 61, 62, 64, 65, 66, 67, 69, 70, 71, 72, 73, 74, 75, 78, 79, 80, 81, 82, 83, 84, 86, 87, 88, 89, 91, 92, 93, 94, 95, 96, 97, 98, 99, 100, 102, 104, 106, 108, 109, 110, 111, 112, 114, 115, 116, 117, 118, 120, 121, 122, 123, 124, 125, 127, 149, 154, 155, 169, 170, 171, 172, 173, 174, 175, 176, 177, 178, 179, 180, 181, 182, 266–71

Pease, James 170
Peasenhall, Suffolk 36
Peerage 124
Pemberton, Reece 152
Pepusch, Johann Christoph 66, 67
Perkin, Helen 25
Peru 106
Peters, Johanna 169
Philadelphia Orchestra 49
Pilgrim Players 61, 151
Piper, John 64, 84, 114, 116
Piper, Myfanwy 78, 79, 84, 108, 114, 115, 116
Plomer, William 76, 77, 81, 98, 99, 105, 109, 153
Pollak, Anna 171
Pontresina, Switzerland 140
Pope, Alexander 133
Portsmouth 142
Potter, Mary 80
Potter, Stephen 155
Preston, Simon 172
Priestley, J. B. 150
Primrose, William 73
Pritchard, John 95
Pro Telephon, Zürich 140, 140 n.9, 141
Procter, Norma 86, 171
Promenade Concerts 116
Pudney, John 155, 156
Purcell, Henry 42, 56, 58, 60, 66, 86, 108, 118
   King Arthur: Fairest Isle 155
   Fantasia upon one note Z.745 181
The Purcell Singers 81, 84, 105, 169, 171
Pushkin, Alexander 103

"Q" Theatre, London 41, 150
Quarles, Francis 65
Quebec 40
Queen Elizabeth Hall, London 107, 112
Queen's Hall, London 38, 39, 41, 43, 47

RAF Orchestra 51, 53, 159, 160, 161
Raikes, Raymond 150
Rathbone, Basil 141
Ravel Prize 122
Raybould, Clarence 35, 45, 57, 154, 163
Read, David 169
Realist Film Unit 143
The Red Flag 143
The Red House, Aldeburgh 84, 126
Reed, Henry 164
Rehfuss, Heinz 9
Reiniger, Lotte 133
Reizenstein, Franz 35

Rex, Sheila 169
Rhine (river) 74
Richter, Sviatoslav 105, 114, 170, 173, 178, 179, 180
Ridler, Ann 164
Rimbaud, Arthur 41, 43
Ritchie, Margaret 171
Riverhead, New York 42
Roberts, R. Ellis 154, 156
Robertson, Alec 117
Robertson, Rae 45, 46, 49
Rogers, Nigel 169
Ronald Duncan Literary Foundation 153
Ross, Hugh 47
Rossini, Gioachino 31, 46, 133, 140
   Guglielmo Tell: 'Passo a Sei' 133–4
Rostropovich, Mstislav 90, 99, 100, 101, 102, 103, 104, 108, 109, 123, 125, 171, 173, 174, 175, 179, 180
Rotha, Paul 139, 142
Roumania 98
Roussin, André 153
Royal Albert Hall, London 51, 55, 60, 73, 100, 110, 116
Royal Ballet 83
Royal College of Music 18, 20, 22, 23, 24, 146
The Royal Festival Hall 70, 90, 98, 112
Royal Liverpool Philharmonic Orchestra 95
Royal Opera House, Covent Garden 64, 78, 83, 90, 92, 114, 120, 121, 122
Royal Opera House Chorus 75, 170
Royal Opera House Orchestra 75, 83, 84, 170, 171
Royal Philharmonic Society Gold Medal 100
Russia *see* USSR
Rylands, George 152

Sacher, Paul 91, 92
Sackville, Charles 13
Sackville-West, Edward 163, 164
Sackville-West, Vita 164
Sadler's Wells Opera Company 58, 59, 104
Sadler's Wells Theatre, London 58, 59, 98, 104, 112
St Andrew's Church, Holborn, London 110
St John's Church, Lowestoft 2, 19, 26
St John's Church, Red Lion Square, London 33
St John's Institute, London 25
St Jovite, Quebec 40
St Mark's, North Audley Street, London 25, 71
St Mark's Church, Swindon, Wilts. 59
St Matthew's Church, Northampton 55, 63
St Michael's Cathedral, Coventry 94, 97
St Michael's Singers, St Michael Cornhill, London 29
St Paul's Cathedral, London 111
St Peter Mancroft, Norwich 81
Salzburg, Austria 76
Salzburg Festival 33, 37
Samuel, Harold 12
Sanders, Neil 169, 170, 171
Sargent, Sir Malcolm 63, 144
Sassoon, Siegfried 15
Saville Theatre, London 150
Sayers, Dorothy L. 160, 162
La Scala, Milan 84
Schach, Max 141
Schenk Jnr, Charles A. 160
School Certificate 16
Schubert, Franz 59, 62, 72, 82, 84, 86, 88, 108, 112, 116, 118, 151
   Abendbilder 179
   Abendstern 179
   Am See 179
   An die Entfernte 179
   An die Laute 179
   Andantino Varié in B minor D.823/2 179
   Arpeggione sonata 108, 179
   Atys 179
   Auf dem Wasser zu singen 179
   Auf der Bruck 179
   Auflösung 179
   Der blinde Knabe 179
   Das war ich 179
   Du bist die Ruh 179
   Eight Variations on an Original Theme in A flat D.813 179
   Der Einsame 179
   Fantasie in F minor D.940 179
   Geheimes 179
   Der Geistertanz 179
   Gesang des Harfners 180
   Die Götter Griechenlands 180
   Grand Duo in C major D.812 180
   Ihr Grab 180
   Im Frühling 180
   Lachen und Weinen 180
   Das Lied im Grünen 180
   Der Musensohn 180
   Nacht und Träume 180

GENERAL INDEX

Nachtstück 180
Die schöne Müllerin 72, 88, 92, 180
Schwanengesang: Das Fischermädchen 180
Schwanengesang: Die Stadt 180
Schwanengesang: Die Taubenpost 180
Sprache der Liebe 180
Symphony No. 8 'Unfinished' 173
Der Winterabend 180
Die Winterreise 98, 114, 118, 180
Schumann, Robert 58, 86
   Cello Concerto 173
   Dichterliebe 52, 98, 180
   Fünf Stücke im Volkston 94, 180
   Scenes from Goethe's 'Faust' 118, 174
   Sechs Gedichte 118
Schwarz, Rudolf 79, 87
Searle, Humphrey
   Variations on an Elizabethan Theme 174
Second World War 42
Shaftesbury Theatre, London 150
Shakespeare, William 88, 144
Shakespeare Festival, Stratford, Ontario 84
Shaw, Alexander 143
Sheffield 56
Shelley, Percy Bysshe 9, 11, 19, 21, 133
Shetland Islands 118
Shield, William
   The Ploughboy 149
Shirley-Quirk, John 111, 117, 121, 169, 170, 171, 172, 173, 174, 175
Shostakovich, Dimitri 90
   Symphony No. 14 112
Silver Jubilee of Queen Elizabeth II 125
Singapore 80
Sino-Japanese War 38
Sitwell, Dame Edith 81, 83, 124, 126, 164
Les Six 52
Slater, Montagu 33, 50, 57, 132, 143, 145, 147–8, 148–9
   Seven Ages of Man 149
   The Station Master 149
Snape, Suffolk 36, 50
Sonning Prize 108
Soskin, Gabriel 170
South Lodge Preparatory School, Lowestoft 2, 8, 10, 12
Southern Railways 142
Southolme (school), Lowestoft 2
Southwark Cathedral, London 69, 112
Southwell, Robert 19
Spanish Civil War 30
Sparrow's Nest Theatre, Lowestoft 2

Speaight, Robert 154, 156
Spice, Evelyn 139
Sri Lanka 80, 100
Steele, Jonathan 171
Stein, Erwin 26
Stein, Marion *see* Thorpe, Marion
Stevens, Pauline 174
Stokes, Leslie 155
The Story of Music (Britten and I. Holst) 86
Strand Films 139, 142
Strasbourg 98
Strasfogel, Ignatz 152
Stratford, Ontario 84
Stratton Quartet 31
Strauss, Richard
   Le bourgeois gentilhomme 157
Strode, Rosamund 81, 100
Stuart Hall, Norwich 27
Studholme, Marion 170
Suffolk (England) 125
Suffolk County, Long Island, USA 46
Suffolk Friends of Music Orchestra 46
Sweden 94
Swingler, Randall 41, 143
Switzerland 64, 80, 91, 92, 99, 125

Tanglewood Festival 62
Tarasp, Schloss, Switzerland 82, 96
Tear, Robert 169, 171
Temianka, Henri 27
Tennyson, Alfred Lord 13, 15
Terry, Stephen 169
Thames Television 127
Théâtre des Champs-Elysées, Paris 76
Theatre Royal, Brighton 71, 152
Thailand 80
Thomas, Nancy 170
Thomson, Rita 120
Thorpe, Marion (née Stein) 71, 74
Tippett, Sir Michael
   Boyhood's End 54
   The Heart's Assurance 74
   Songs for Ariel 100
   The Weeping Babe 164
   Variations on an Elizabethan Theme 174
Todd, Philip 171
Toronto 43
Toynbee Hall Theatre, London 79, 153
Travel and Industrial Development Association 139
Trafalgar Films 141
Trevelyan, Julian 39
Tuckwell, Barry 92, 96, 171, 174

Tudor, Anthony 40, 150
Tunnard, Viola 104, 169, 170, 171, 177

Ulster Singers 97
Union of Soviet Socialist Republics 96, 98, 100, 102, 103, 104, 112, 116
United Nations 103
United States of America 42, 44, 70, 100
Uppman, Theodor 75, 77
Uruguay 106
Usher Hall, Edinburgh 86

Van Beinum, Eduard 71, 73
Variations on an Elizabethan Theme 'Sellenger's Round' 174
Vaughan, Lyn 170
Vaughan Williams, Ralph
  On Wenlock Edge 58, 181
Veni Creator Spiritus 157
Venice 68, 79, 88, 98, 106, 124
Verlaine, Paul 12, 13
Vickers, Jon 122
Vienna 26, 56, 74
Vienna Boys' Choir 107
Viertel, Bertold 150
Vignoles, Roger 127
Vincent, Jo 71
Vishnevskaya, Galina 102, 103, 104, 108, 172
Vosper, Frank 141
Vyvyan, Jennifer 79, 91, 170, 171, 172, 173, 174

Wagner, Richard
  Siegfried 157
Wales 120
Walter, Wilfred 145
Walton, William
  Variations on an Elizabethan Theme 174
Wandsworth School Boys' Choir 111, 112, 169, 170, 174, 175
Wandsworth School Orchestra 111
Ward, Joseph 169
Warlock, Peter
  Yarmouth Fair 181
Watson, Clare 170
Watson, Jean 170
Watt, Harry 137, 138, 140, 141
Watts, Helen 174
Webb, Bruce 170
Webster, David 113, 115
Webster, John 152
Wells, Mary 173
Westminster Cathedral, London 89

Westminster Theatre, London 29, 31, 33, 37, 144, 145, 146, 148
White, Miles 152
White, T. H. 157
Whitty, Dame May 45, 158
Whitworth, Robin 154, 156
Wiesbaden 74
Wigmore Hall, London 27, 31, 33, 35, 37, 52, 53, 55, 57, 58, 60, 61, 74, 81, 92
Wihuri Sibelius Prize 102
Wilbye Consort 123
Williams, Grace 146
Wilson, Catherine 169
Withers, George 23
Wittgenstein, Paul 49
Wolf, Hugo 72, 84
  An einer Aeolsharfe 181
  Beherzigung 181
  Bein einer Trauung 181
  Denk'es, o Seele! 181
  Die den Gott gebarst 181
  Frühling übers Jahr 181
  Führ'mich, Kind 181
  Ganymed 181
  Der Gärtner 181
  Heimweh 181
  Im Frühling 181
  Jägerlied 181
  Lied eines Verliebten 181
  Sankt Nepomuks Vorabend 181
  Schlafendes Jesuskind 181
  Der Scholar 181
  Spottlied 182
  Wenn ich dein gedenke 182
  Wie sollt' ich heiter bleiben? 182
Wolfsgarten, Schloss, West Germany 74, 89, 118, 122
Wood, Anne 39, 73, 156
Wood, Sir Henry 39, 43, 57
Woodgate, Leslie 25, 41, 53, 57, 69, 157, 164
Wormwood Scrubs (prison) 54
Wright, Basil 138
Wyss, Sophie 30, 33, 37, 39, 41, 43, 45, 52, 54, 148, 154, 156, 176, 177

Yates, Victor 143
Yale University 92
Yerevan, Armenia, USSR 102
Yugoslavia 80, 88, 94

Zagreb 80
Zorian String Quartet 58, 61, 66, 181, 182